Disability as Diversity

Lisa M. Meeks ⓘ • Leslie Neal-Boylan
Editors

Disability as Diversity

A Guidebook for Inclusion in Medicine,
Nursing, and the Health Professions

Editors
Lisa M. Meeks (iD)
Department of Family Medicine
The University of Michigan Medical School
Ann Arbor, MI
USA

Leslie Neal-Boylan
Solomont School of Nursing
University of Massachusetts Lowell
Lowell, MA
USA

ISBN 978-3-030-46186-7   ISBN 978-3-030-46187-4 (eBook)
https://doi.org/10.1007/978-3-030-46187-4

This Springer imprint is published by the registered company Springer Nature Switzerland AG
The registered company address is: Gewerbestrasse 11, 6330 Cham, Switzerland

To the many nurses and nursing students with disabilities who inspire us all with their strength, fortitude and dedication to nursing despite the barriers they frequently encounter.

Also, to my very great friend Dr. Sharron Guillett and her daughter Alexis Guillett both of whom first opened my eyes about disability and instilled in me the passion to get involved.

Leslie Neal-Boylan

This work would not have been possible without the collective efforts of the greats that came before us—the faculty, researchers and trailblazers that have been championing inclusion for several decades.

This book is dedicated to the disability resource and student affairs professionals who work to ensure access in programs across the nation; to Michigan Medicine and the Department of Family Medicine for supporting the work; to the non-profits and associations championing the work; and most importantly to the students who have boldly challenged the 'status quo' to claim their rightful place as health science professionals.

To the authors—the squad—you have my deepest respect and profound gratitude.
—Go Blue!

Lisa Meeks

Foreword

Disability as Diversity: A Guidebook for Inclusion in Medicine, Nursing, and the Health Professions. Disability and inclusion. These two words in the title of this book are powerful. The implications, when institutions embrace these ideals, are enormous.

I was born in the last millennium, long before the Americans with Disabilities Act was a concept, and even before the less potent federal Rehabilitation Act of 1973 was the law of the land. In my early days, people with disabilities of any type were relegated to the background. Everyone born with or acquiring a disability at a young age quickly found that there was little opportunity for success in life-and there was no concept of equal access. People with disabilities were shunted to unskilled jobs and were disregarded by society. This foreordained pathway to unskilled labor perpetuated the concept that people with disabilities, as a whole, were incapable of engaging in a full life. I was an exception. This was only because my parents refused to limit my potential. They were progressive in their insistence that I be given an equal opportunity to acquire a quality education.

In the last 50 years we have witnessed a slow, but steady, increase in equal access to health professions' education and practice, but we have a long way to go. Just like the landmark Civil Rights Act of the 1960s, the 1990 Americans with Disabilities Act (ADA) and the 2008 ADA Amendment Act provide a strong legal framework for equal access and opportunity for people with disabilities. I believe that these laws, coupled with technological advancements, success in the courts, and an increasing focus on the value of a diverse health-care workforce, explain the increasing number of clinicians with disabilities.

However, the letter of the law is not enough. It is one thing to pass a law, and another to truly embrace its spirit. In 2020, people with disabilities still fight for equal access and many leaders within health-care and academic institutions still do not fully understand or embrace the benefit, or the moral imperative, for disability inclusion. For these reasons, this book is a critical equalizer. It provides sorely needed practical information for such leaders, faculty, and administrators in the health professions. Moreover, the book justifies the need in society to have such clinicians and offers practical ways to educate and launch people with disabilities into health professions careers.

We've come a long way from the last millennium, when I was a young child, a time when people with disabilities were almost never given opportunities to succeed, to a world where the value of disability is increasingly celebrated and people with disabilities have greater opportunities. "Disability Inclusion." It is indeed a powerful concept. When we truly embrace clinicians and students with disabilities, we improve understanding of disability, and that in turn has the potential to improve patient care. This book will help us move even closer to the ideal state. Read it. Understand it. Use it. And embrace it so that everyone wins.

Philip Zazove, MD
Professor and Chair of Family Medicine at
The University of Michigan Medical School
Ann Anbor, MI, USA

Contents

Contributors

Nicole D. Agaronnik, BS Mongan Institute Health Policy Research Center, Massachusetts General Hospital, Boston, MA, USA

Sarah Ailey, PhD, PHNA-BC, CDDN, RN Professor, Department of Community, Systems and Mental Health Nursing, College of Nursing, Rush University Medical Center, Chicago, IL, USA

Samuel Bagenstos, JD Professor, University of Michigan Law School, Ann Arbor, MI, USA

Steve Ciesielski, MA Assistant Dean for Student Success, MGH Institute of Health Professions, Boston, MA, USA

Grace C. Clifford, MAEd Cleveland State University, Department of Student Affairs, Cleveland, OH, USA

James Cooke, MD Executive Director, Clinical Simulation Center, Associate Professor, Department of Family Medicine, University of Michigan Medical School, Ann Arbor, MI, USA

Raymond H. Curry, MD Professor of Medicine and Medical Education, Senior Associate Dean for Educational Affairs, University of Illinois College of Medicine, Chicago, IL, USA

William Eidtson, EdD Geisel School of Medicine at Dartmouth, Hanover, NH, USA

Maureen Fausone, MD, MA University of Michigan Medical School, Ann Arbor, MI, USA

Steven Gay, MD Assistant Dean for Admissions, Associate Professor of Internal Medicine, The University of Michigan Medical School, Ann Arbor, MI, USA

Sharron Guillett, PhD, RN Eleanor Wade Custer School of Nursing, Shenandoah University, Winchester, VA, USA

Maureen Hillier, DNP, RN, CCRN, CHSE School of Nursing, MGH Institute of Health Professions, Boston, MA, USA

Lisa I. Iezzoni, MD, MSc Professor of Medicine Harvard Medical School, Mongan Institute Health Policy Research Center, Massachusetts General Hospital, Boston, MA, USA

Department of Medicine, Harvard Medical School, Boston, MA, USA

Neera R. Jain, MS, CRC School of Curriculum and Pedagogy, University of Auckland, Faculty of Education and Social Work, Auckland, New Zealand

Wei Wei Lee, MD, MPH Assistant Dean of Students, Director, Wellness Programs, Assistant Professor Department of Medicine University of Chicago Pritzker School of Medicine, Chicago, IL, USA

Marie Lusk, MBA, MSW, LSW Director, Student Accessibility Services for Rush University, Chicago, IL, USA

Patricia Lussier-Duynstee, PhD, RN Assistant Professor Emerita, School of Nursing, MGH Institute of Health Professions, Boston, MA, USA

Christopher McCulloh, MD Department of Pediatric Surgery, Nationwide Children's Hospital, Columbus, OH, USA

Michael M. McKee, MD, MPH Department of Family Medicine, The University of Michigan Medical School, Ann Arbor, MI, USA

Lisa M. Meeks, PhD, MA Assistant Professor, Department of Family Medicine, Director of MDisability Education, The University of Michigan Medical School, Ann Arbor, MI, USA

Lina Mehta, MD Associate Dean for Admissions, Professor of Radiology, Case Western Reserve School of Medicine, Cleveland, OH, USA

Michelle Miller, JD, MPH, RN Chair, Department of Legal Studies, College of Arts and Sciences, Quinnipiac University, Hamden, CT, USA

Christopher J. Moreland, MD, MPH Associate Professor, Department of Medicine, Associate Director Internal Medicine Residency, Dell Medical School at the University of Texas at Austin, Austin, TX, USA

Joseph F. Murray, MD Associate Professor Department of Psychiatry, Former Associate Dean of Student Affairs, Weill Cornell Medical College, New York, NY, USA

Leslie Neal-Boylan, PhD, RN, CRRN, APRN, FAAN Dean and Professor, Solomont School of Nursing, University of Massachusetts Lowell, Lowell, MA, USA

Vice Dean, Zuckerberg College of Health Sciences, University of Massachusetts Lowell, Lowell, MA, USA

Charlotte O'Connor, MEd Office of Medical Student Education, University of Michigan School of Medicine, Ann Arbor, MI, USA

Rahul Patwari, MD Associate Dean, Curriculum Rush Medical College, Associate Professor, Department of Emergency Medicine, Chicago, IL, USA

Kristina H. Petersen, PhD Assistant Professor, Department of Biochemistry & Molecular Biology, Director of Academic Support Programs, New York Medical College, Valhalla, NY, USA

Neal Rosenburg, PhD, RN Professor, College of Health Professions, University of Detroit Mercy, Detroit, MI, USA

Erene Stergiopoulos, MD, MA University of Toronto Faculty of Medicine, Toronto, ON, Canada

Bonnielin K. Swenor, PhD, MPH Associate Professor, Ophthalmology at the Wilmer Eye Institute at Johns Hopkins and Epidemiology at the Johns Hopkins Bloomberg School of Public Health, Baltimore, MD, USA

Nichole L. Taylor, DO Assistant Dean of Student Affairs; Associate Professor Department of Anesthesiology, Wake Forest School of Medicine, Winston-Salem, NC, USA

Introduction: The Shift Towards Disability Inclusion in Health Science Education

How Do We Change from Within When Transformation Is Needed?

Fundamentally this is not just an academic or organizational exercise. It is true that change involves both of these dimensions. But change is also a deeply personal journey, challenging how we feel. In this pioneering textbook, the first of its kind, the authors challenge us intellectually and emotionally.

Change is difficult. Niccolò Machiavelli captured this essence in his book, *The Prince*, when he stated that "there is nothing more difficult to carry out, nor more doubtful of success…than to initiate a new order of things; for the reformer has enemies in *all those who profit by the old order,* and only lukewarm defenders in all those who would profit by the new order…arising partly from the incredulity of (person) kind who does not truly believe in anything new *until they actually have experience of it.*"[1]

In this book, the authors offer us a roadmap to embrace a new lens of the philosophical possibility of inclusion. They offer dynamic definitions of disability within the learning context and entreat us to understand our learners' *full* social context and intersectional identities. The first few chapters of this text present a new framing to help us understand the scale of the issue, *why* we must transform our practices, and *how* to consider the issues we confront as we strive to advocate for the education of individuals with disabilities in health sciences education.

If we truly want to contemplate what it will take to transform our approach to disability inclusion, we should pay attention to what Machiavelli noted. First, those of us involved in health professions education must confront the reality that "*we profit from the old order.*" We look at new work and difficult discussions with trepidation, even though we may believe in the new order. Second, we must challenge our deeply held assumptions that inform our approach to our work, our view of education, and how it must "be." To be more precise, most of us have not "*had the experience of it,*" as Machiavelli notes, and thus we find ourselves instinctively lukewarm defenders of the future state. We *must* counter that instinct by listening to new

---

[1] Machiavelli, Niccolò, 1469–1527. The Prince. Harmondsworth, Eng.; New York, N.Y.: Penguin Books, 1981.

voices and authentically considering new ideas. And it begins with embracing this book.

Authentically engaging with the content in this book requires an emotional AND intellectual "reset." As you begin your journey through the chapters I offer some advice:

1. Understand and acknowledge your own abilities and ways in which your experience may color your understanding and acceptance of the principles explained by the authors.
2. Be ready to challenge long held assumptions. The first chapter advocates for a "restless reflexive" stance when considering these issues. Indeed, while this approach is intended for an organization, it also pertains directly to us as individual readers of this book.
3. Think carefully about the voices that are missing at your institutions or programs as decisions about change and transformation loom. If individuals with disabilities have not been included in our profession how can they be included in how our profession changes?

Overall, the authors challenge us to consider the lived, *full* experience of our students with disabilities. In all of health sciences education, we teach our students to serve others. Etienne Wenger's work presents education in a social context; a set of activities that must embrace "legitimate peripheral participation."[2] Restrictions on participation thereby prevent learning. Bias and stereotypes about the identities of our students may serve as barriers to inclusion. Thus, the intersectionality of student identities must be considered holistically to promote the optimal engagement of students, while we also consider their whole, lived experience.

As we begin Part I, we become aware of the exclusionary practices that educational structures present that inhibit participation of students with disabilities. Many are rooted in risk aversion, framed by legal requirements, albeit with well-intentioned actions to push the boundaries of compliance. However, even the most liberal of approaches built upon legal frameworks attempt to retrofit the environment within the existing structures, resulting in "accommodations." Even the word accommodation conveys a "less than" feeling.

The authors ask us to think "what if?" What if universal design was deployed in all educational environments, supporting all students? Indeed, these learning settings would continuously evolve as they are informed by each student and their diverse needs. In this approach the student could demonstrate proficiency in the ways that align with *their* abilities; Yet, a risk-averse, structured approach is how we have been professionalized in education throughout all phases of our own learning programs. So how do we challenge ourselves to think differently? As we continue in Part I, we discover the heterogeneity in the definitions, and the prevalence of different manifestations of disabilities among students. Each expression is unified

---

[2] Lave, Jean; Wenger, Etienne (1991), *Situated Learning: Legitimate Peripheral Participation*, Cambridge University Press

by their interference with students' participation in the educational program, either through impacts on health or through structural impediments in the learning environment based on a legal framework of interpretation.

The authors further state that this attitude of skepticism towards patients with disabilities by the health-care industry may also influence how students and providers with disabilities encounter their work, resulting in concealment of issues and "pushing through" for fear of reprisal. Part I continues in a broader, holistic direction, focusing on intersectionality and how social and structural barriers affect learners from many different backgrounds. The intersectional diversity is emphasized as a strength, rather than a hindrance, bringing *expertise* and *excellence*, both to other learners and the patients they ultimately will serve. As this part concludes, the book begins to turn from a statement of "Why" and the conceptual lenses through which to engage the rest of the book to a description of "How" programs can take steps to capture intersectionality of identities and amplify the voice of those who are structurally excluded from our profession.

As the reader moves on to Part II, the authors take us into the relationships between well-being and learning in an environment that is inclusive, supportive, and forward-thinking. While the lens of inclusivity and diversity is a useful framework to push our traditional thinking, the "How" is further articulated as we consider the challenges health science professions face in terms of well-being. Transitions, imposter syndromes, and work that is focused on transactional aspects of health care rather than the building of interpersonal relationships all strain the learner and practitioner and their sense of meaning at work. These are challenged further for students with disabilities. Part II also deepens the focus on how learning occurs in the current environment, presenting a description of the barriers derived from faculty perceptions, curricular structure and how the concept of universal design challenges us all to approach the environment in a manner that embraces different styles of learning, from students with different abilities.

Part III moves us towards the "What," in addition to the "How," as leaders, educators, and administrators strive to make learning environments inclusive. The chapters acknowledge the legal framework as a bare minimum for schools' creation of policies as well as the technical implications of failing to adhere to them, including an important description of the procedures that are invoked for appeals where students have newly identified disabilities or have not disclosed a disability. As this part concludes, we return to an overview of the approach to technical standards as both policy and a communication vehicle for students and the specific steps that can be taken in a self-study to resolve the gaps to promote alignment with a more institutional-specific philosophy.

As the reader continues through the text into Part IV, more detailed descriptions of how physical and attitudinal barriers in the clinical setting, and in the simulated, practice, and high-stakes testing environments, are addressed with specific recommendations for the myriad assessments that our students face. Importantly, like all students, those with disabilities may fall short of competence targets; therefore, remediation strategies for these learners are also described.

Finally, the case book companion for *Disability as Diversity* brings all of the issues described in the book to life through the use of vivid cases depicting the variety of disability categories including sensory, physical, learning, psychological, and chronic health, each within both the medical and nursing contexts, with an accompanying description of "best practices."

At the end of the book, it is worth stepping back and reflecting on any discomfort we may feel. It may be rooted in our own lived experience, "raised" in the family of medicine, nursing, and science that has not witnessed an enriched educational environment that is inclusive of students with disabilities. Are we capable of identifying the barriers our students experience? Or are we just focused on our own experiences, ignorant to those of *all* our learners?

We must recognize that this movement is not merely about opportunity; it is about understanding our own emotions and promoting *feelings* of inclusion that will bolster learning. But we must also realize that as educators, administrators, and leaders, we have direct responsibility for the policies and environment that our students experience. *We* need to come together to lead the change that will enable the necessary inclusive practices and culture, so that all our students can thrive.

"It's not about them needing us, it is about us needing us," as a colleague of mine once said. We know this to be true. Let's make it true.

In partnership, Raj

Rajesh S. Mangrulkar, MD
Professor of Medical Education and Associate Dean for Medical Student
Education University of Michigan Medical School
Ann Arbor, MI, USA

Frameworks for Inclusion: Toward a Transformative Approach

Neera R. Jain

Introduction

The category of "disability" encompasses heterogeneous experiences. Conceptualizing disability is an ongoing and contested project that represents various personal and political perspectives [3]. The dominant ways to understand disability, often referred to as the *medical, tragedy, or charity* models of disability, suggest that it is an individual problem caused by biomedical factors [3]. In this conception, the solution is to provide treatment that ideally cures the individual or normalizes their social and vocational functioning [4, 5]. Furthermore, any efforts toward societal inclusion of persons with disabilities constitute benevolent acts as such persons are considered "abnormal" and therefore justifiably excluded from society [5, 6]. Alternative ways of knowing disability emerged from disability rights movements and scholarship primarily authored by disabled people [4, 5]. To varying degrees, these alternate conceptions (e.g., the *social, cultural, ecological, bio-psycho-social-environmental*, and *rights/minority group models*) suggest that social arrangements informed by the medical model, in a complex interplay with individual impairment, create disability (see also Chap. 2, for further discussion of disability conceptualization) [3, 4, 7]. In these conceptions of disability, attending to the ways social institutions exclude people is more important than finding remedies that operate at the individual level. While these alternate conceptions of disability have gained recognition through hard-fought activism and rights movements, they remain

---

In this chapter I move, intentionally, between person-first (e.g., "person with a disability") and identity-first language (e.g., "disabled person"). This recognizes the contested nature of preferred language among persons with disabilities [1, 2].

N. R. Jain (✉)
School of Curriculum and Pedagogy, University of Auckland, Faculty of Education
and Social Work, Auckland, New Zealand
e-mail: neera.jain@auckland.ac.nz

© Springer Nature Switzerland AG 2020
L. M. Meeks, L. Neal-Boylan (eds.), *Disability as Diversity*,
https://doi.org/10.1007/978-3-030-46187-4_1

subjugated knowledges insofar as ableism remains a deeply entrenched structuring force in society [8, 9].

At the heart of educational inclusion movements is the recognition that disabled peoples' embodiments have been used as grounds for exclusion. Societies have used constructs of normality to deny disabled peoples' essential humanity and engineer educational environments that exclude [4, 10–12]. Against this societal prejudice, inclusion movements posit that disabled people, like all people, have beneficial capabilities that ought to be enabled through equal access to social structures such as education [11, 13]. This way of thinking positions disabled peoples' modes of functioning as *different*, rather than *lesser* [5]. These movements have successfully won legislation to assert disabled peoples' human rights in many parts of the world.

Most countries have passed legislation that, at least nominally, prevents educational programs from discriminating against persons with disabilities. Regulations, enforcement, and case law may explicate expectations further (for further discussion, see Chap. 7) [14], but the degree of guidance available varies internationally. In the United States, disability rights legislation has codified equal access to higher educational settings since 1973, with Section 504 of the Rehabilitation Act [15]. This landmark legislation prevented exclusion of "otherwise qualified" persons with disabilities from programs (public or private) receiving federal funding, that is, essentially most higher education settings. The Americans with Disabilities Act, 1990 [16], and the subsequent 2008 Amendments Act [17], further mandated that public and private colleges and universities include students with disabilities. Under these laws, programs must ensure program accessibility to "otherwise qualified" students with disabilities and provide reasonable adjustments and auxiliary aids to assist in this process. The 2008 Amendments Act, furthermore, clarified that disability encompasses a broad range of impairment groups including physical, sensory, chronic health conditions, learning disabilities, and attention deficit-hyperactivity disorder (AD/HD) [17]. The ADA is discussed throughout this book as it pertains to various aspects of the academic experience.

Given the broad language of legislation, multiple interpretations of nondiscriminatory action and what constitutes sufficient inclusion exist. Although a baseline of adherence to legal requirements outlined through legislation, case law, and other regulatory measures is expected, enforcement is largely responsive, reliant on individuals contesting institutional practices through litigation and complaint procedures. The law also does not necessarily limit what programs may do in service of inclusion. Under US law, for example, programs are not required to fundamentally alter their standards in order to include learners with disabilities. Some programs, however, do choose to establish less restrictive standards with the understanding that professional opportunities are vast and that persons who may not fit traditional notions of embodiment can meaningfully contribute to the profession [18]. Indeed, the federal regulations do not prohibit provision of "benefits, services, or advantages to individuals with disabilities" beyond that which the law requires [19]. Health science programs, thus, may take various approaches to including learners with disabilities [20].

Health science programs may differ in their recognition of social privilege and willingness to challenge professional norms when faced with the question of disability inclusion. While some may recognize a duty to include learners with disabilities to the extent that they can fit existing training environments with "reasonable" adjustments, others may recognize a broader duty to facilitate learner belonging in line with missions to increase diversity and address healthcare disparities [21]. Decisions about how to approach inclusion are multifaceted. They reflect, for example, historical, material, political, philosophical, and social conditions at multiple levels. Factors at the level of the program, school, institution, clinical training sites, and field of study, nationally, and even internationally may influence a program's approach to disability inclusion. Nonetheless, the chosen approach enacts programmatic culture, affecting disabled-learner possibilities in training and practice [22–24].

Titchkosky suggests a "restless reflexive" stance when considering the question of access, a constant questioning that unearths the roots of current action and disrupts certainty to evoke a "politics of wonder" about new possibilities for disability and access [6]. In this chapter, I adopt this stance to consider three approaches to inclusion: the "strict compliance" approach, the "spirit of the law" approach, and the transformative approach. I conceive of these models as ideal types, heuristic devices for analytic purposes rather than exact descriptors of existing realities [25]. The central features and major implications of each approach are summarized in Table 1.1 and will be explored in greater detail below.

Table 1.1 Approaches to inclusion, defining features, and implications

	Defining features	Implications
Compliance	Strict legal interpretation Risk orientation Disability is an individual, medical problem	Accommodations to address individual barriers Focus on lawsuit prevention Learners with disabilities challenge academic integrity and practice standards; accommodations are closely guarded Rigid interpretation of technical and academic standards
Spirit of the law	Liberal legal interpretation Opportunity orientation Disability is individual and social in nature	Accommodations as one tool to address barriers Changes to "level the playing field"; implement universal design where opportunities arise Scope for innovative accommodations to support the mission of diversifying the health profession field Scope to interpret what is essential to technical and academic standards
Transformative	Social justice as guiding principle Intentional inclusion orientation Disability is normal human variation, a valued social identity	Learning environment intentionally designed to include diverse learners, with built-in flexibility Change is ongoing and iterative to improve inclusion for all learners Diverse learners with disabilities add value to the professions Programs assume differentiated graduates, thus allowing learners to demonstrate proficiency in variable ways (technical standards obsolete)

Programs may wish to critically examine their current approach to determine whether it aligns with their aspirations for disability inclusion and, if not, consider ways to realign their practices with their values. To aid readers in envisioning these approaches, Table 1.2 offers an illustration of the student experience under each.

Table 1.2 Illustrative examples of each approach

Introduction

Ava is an entering medical student recently diagnosed with Ehlers-Danlos syndrome. Although she used accommodations as an undergraduate (note-taking services and extended time for exams), she is uncertain what barriers she will encounter at medical school and how to address them. She did not disclose her disability in the course of admissions.

"Strict compliance" approach

Ava receives her medical school acceptance letter. A copy of the school's technical standards is included for students to sign. The standards state, "The candidate must be able to execute motor movements reasonably required to provide general and emergency medical care such as suturing of wounds. . . Such actions require coordination of both gross and fine muscular movements. . ." Ava is uncertain that she can meet these requirements. When she searches for information about disability resources at the school, information is oriented around legal compliance, stating that "As required by the ADA and Section 504 of the Rehabilitation Act, the school provides only those accommodations deemed reasonable, that do not alter essential requirements, cause undue administrative or financial burden, or compromise patient, staff, or fellow trainee safety." Ava worries that disclosing her disability might cause the school to rescind her admission. When she reaches the school's identified contact person for students with disabilities, they inform her that she will need to undergo a thorough assessment of her fine and gross motor capabilities to determine what can be done. The contact person states there are no guarantees anything is possible and that if Ava cannot meet the technical standards, she is subject to dismissal.

"Spirit of the law" approach

Ava receives her medical school acceptance letter. The admissions materials provide clear information about how students request accommodations, along with a smiling photo of the school's disability resource professional (DRP). The materials state that the school "has a history of graduating medical students with all types of disabilities and we pride ourselves in developing innovative accommodation approaches." They include disability as one category of diversity recognized and valued by the school. The technical standards note that, "We understand there may be multiple ways to achieve these standards, including using a trained intermediary. Our Disability Resources Professional is here to work with you and the faculty to identify possible accommodation solutions." Ava sees this information as a positive opening and reaches out to the DRP. They organize a meeting to talk about what she might need, including early sessions with a faculty member and an occupational therapist in the simulation center to explore possible accommodations. The DRP introduces Ava to a few other medical students with disabilities who had similar questions and are thriving in their clerkships.

Transformative approach

Ava receives her medical school acceptance letter. The admissions materials describe the features of their universally designed curriculum and learning spaces. They explain that the mission of the school is to graduate students uniquely positioned to address the most pressing health equity concerns in society. As such, they recognize that due to factors such as disabilities, family care, and cultural responsibilities, students may, for example, not take a standard number of courses each semester. They emphasize that flexibility and creativity is central in the design of the program and provide examples of the unique paths students have taken to illustrate this. Each student has an advisory team that works alongside them to understand the flexible features of the curriculum, plan how they will engage with the educational program, and resolve any unanticipated barriers. The team members may adapt over time as they (re)consider what expertise might benefit the student's experience. As part of the pre-matriculation process for all students, Ava meets with her primary advisor to begin discussing her plan for medical school and building her advisory team. She joins a student society focused on disability justice in medicine.

The "Strict Compliance" Approach

The strict compliance approach to inclusion comprises three core features. First, a strict interpretation of legal requirements to include persons with disabilities in educational environments; the law provides a ceiling for disability inclusion. Second, the approach invites a risk orientation to inclusive action: the goal is to minimize possible institutional risks rather than ensure accessibility. Third, disability is understood as an individual, medical problem, not a social one. This approach to inclusion may be the most common among health science programs, given its dominance more generally in academic settings[22] and the tendency to adhere to prescriptive (organic) technical standards in the field [26, 27]. At least four implications follow from this approach, which are outlined below.

Implications

The first implication of this approach is that programs achieve inclusion primarily through individual accommodations. This follows from a strict reading of legal standards that name accommodations and auxiliary aids as the key mechanisms to remove barriers for "otherwise qualified" learners [28, 29]. While this technique may appear to bring flexibility into inaccessible educational spaces insofar as it allows learners to achieve tasks in different ways, this configuration centers the individual with a disability as the source of barriers. With this lens, programs manage access on an individual basis, with "special" services offered to facilitate this [30]. The extent of needed accommodations and associated costs to retrofit environments for access reflect individual need, rather than situational inaccessibility [31]. This engenders passivity in programs, as learners are tasked with identifying and requesting accommodations. Programs then respond to such requests rather than proactively removing barriers. This also obscures exclusionary forces in the environment and positions learners with disabilities as "needy," a condition antithetical to traditional notions of health professionals. The risk of being perceived as "needy," or perhaps incapable, may encourage students to downplay access barriers.

The second implication of this approach is a focus on lawsuit prevention. Where legal requirements are the impetus for inclusion and lawsuits the primary enforcement measure, programs adopt a defensive posture to avoid legal action. Though this might encourage programs to advance beyond legally required action to ensure compliance, programs will more likely operate within minimum requirements. This protectionist stance provokes the question, "do we have to?" in response to individual requests for change, stifling innovation. Legal standards provide the limit to what programs must allow for inclusion. As such, legal language citing the law as the motivating factor and outlining limits to inclusive action dominates policies, which may alienate learners with disabilities [32]. This sets up an adversarial relationship with learners, encouraging legal action (or threats thereof) as a method to drive change, regardless of any original intention to sue. Anticipating legal action positions learners as foes rather than valued partners in inclusion.

The third implication is that programs see learners with disabilities as challenging academic integrity and practice standards; accommodations are closely guarded. This follows from understanding disability as an individual problem, associated with inability. Legal provisions to include "unable" students pose a threat to professional standards and thus must be implemented conservatively to ensure programs do not lose control.

Finally, but closely linked to this third implication, the compliance model adheres to a rigid interpretation of academic and technical standards. Under legal frameworks, academic programs can set non-negotiable standards for learners to meet, with or without accommodations. Under a compliance approach, these standards tend to be centered on dominant, normative ways of completing clinical tasks (e.g., organic technical standards) [33]. Because there is little impetus to evolve practices for accommodation in the absence of legal challenges, the compliance approach will tend to uphold standards as written.

The compliance approach operates within the bounds of lawful practice. As such, program administrators may find it a suitable option to protect the institution from liability. In resource-strapped environments, a program may perceive that doing the minimum required is the only option available. Certainly, a strict compliance approach to inclusion is better than excluding students with disabilities outright. In this approach, however, learners with disabilities are only included to the extent that they can overcome deficit-oriented assumptions and fit into existing environments with minor adjustments [34]. Under the law, programs are not required to address cultural frameworks in which disability figures as a stigmatized identity. Thus, in the strict compliance approach, focusing on the broader environment and whether it allows students to flourish is unlikely. Experience shows this approach pays lip service to inclusion rather than considering what it actually requires to include disabled people, meaningfully, in the professions. This amounts to a missed opportunity to realize the full potential of learners with disabilities.

The "Spirit of the Law" Approach

In "spirit of the law" approaches, programs attempt to move away from the rigid nature of compliance by prioritizing the substantive spirit or intention that animates disability rights legislation. The approach entails three core features. The first is that programs interpret legal requirements liberally; the law provides a baseline from which inclusive practice begins. Second, learners with disabilities present opportunities for programs to evolve practices or environments. Finally, disability is understood as a product of individual impairment in interaction with the social environment.

Implications

The first implication of the "spirit of the law" approach is that accommodations are seen as one among several tools to address barriers. Legal parameters suggest that accommodations are necessary and central to inclusion. This approach, however, recognizes the potentially stigmatizing effects of this individualizing approach and takes measures to counter this when conceptualizing accommodation policies and procedures. Inclusion policies do not center compliance, but rather a goal of equal access. Programs promote these policies and practices to all students, signaling that learners with disabilities are expected community members [35]. Recognizing that the qualitative experience of accessing accommodations can impact their effectiveness [23], procedures to request and implement accommodations are streamlined. In an effort to share power with learners, accommodations are determined as part of a genuine collaboration between the program, faculty members, a disability resource professional, and the learner.

The second implication is that programs make inclusive changes to "level the playing field" for learners with disabilities. In line with equity-oriented practice, programs let go of strict understandings of fairness and offer differentiated treatment in recognition that learners start with different strengths and abilities. This acknowledges that aspects of social privilege affect how learners with disabilities understand their rights and the support they may need. Programs may take action such as consciously unpacking the hidden curriculum of accessing accommodations, offering additional support services, fostering disabled student community-building, or coaching students to develop their self-advocacy skills. Furthermore, recognizing that features of the environment can produce disability, programs look for opportunities to implement universal design in curriculum, procurement, and physical spaces. Universal design, as originally conceived, is "the design of products and environments to be usable by all people, to the greatest extent possible, without the need for adaption or specialized design." [36] The concept has its origins in architecture but has been extended to other areas, including educational contexts (evident, e.g., in theories of Universal Design for Learning) [30, 37]. In the ways described here, in the "spirit of the law" approach, inclusion is not just responsive to individual requests for accommodations but also engineered through policy and practice.

In the "spirit" approach, the third implication is that including students with disabilities supports a program's diversity mission. This provides scope to innovate accommodations and inclusive practice beyond legal parameters. Programs avoid rigid defenses of program standards and invite creative thinking to foster inclusion. Because learners with disabilities have the potential to benefit patients, peers, teachers, and professional practice, it is in a program's best interest to invest in their success beyond the minimum legally required. This mindset may inspire greater investment in inclusion, for example, hiring a disability resource professional experienced in facilitating inclusion in clinical environments to lead program efforts, or engagement in proactive redesign of spaces, curriculum, or policy for inclusion. Seeing disability as a valuable form of diversity also offers a new lens for holistic admissions decisions and opens the possibility to include disability in existing diversity programming. Acknowledging disability as a form of diversity motivates greater investment and broader action than a solely compliance mindset permits.

The final implication of this approach is that there is scope to interpret what is essential in implementing technical and academic standards. Standards are written more inclusively (e.g., "functional" rather than "organic" technical standards) [26,

33]. With a "spirit of the law" approach, programs also seek alternate ways for learners with disabilities to meet these standards. This may mean offering students the option to articulate the cognitive subroutine of a procedure, directing an intermediary to perform it, or performing the procedure on a simulated rather than a live patient. Programs may also offer students exceptions in how they complete required rotations depending on the specialty they plan to pursue. In other words, programs interpret academic and technical standards case by case, with a flexible approach, looking for creative ways to include learners with disabilities.

The "spirit of the law" approach, like the "strict compliance" approach, operates within legal requirements for access. This approach, however, takes into consideration that actions beyond individual accommodations may be required to facilitate equity, due to social forces such as stigma. A possible downside of this approach, from some perspectives, is that it will require additional financial and human resources to individually assess student needs and devise creative solutions. Furthermore, it will push the boundaries of professions as we currently know them, requiring consideration of alternate ways to conduct tasks, which traditionalists may find threatening.

The Transformative Approach: A Philosophical Ideal

"Compliance" and "spirit" approaches are institutionally embedded practices that center inclusive action upon disability rights legislation. In other words, legislation provides the fundamental framework for current practices. While both approaches seek to include learners with disabilities, they primarily rely on retrofits to largely inaccessible environments that can only result in incremental change. The "transformative" approach is a philosophical possibility that, if translated into practice, would move us beyond both the spirit of the law and compliance approaches. It can be summarized according to three key tenets. First, social justice is the guiding principle for educating health professionals. Second, this approach imagines a social world in which the realities of disability and other forms of human difference are assumed and honored, and institutions are built accordingly. Third, the educational system ought to ensure that health professionals are reflective of the totality of societal variation. This approach attempts to dismantle ableist conceptions of "standard" learners by embracing the actual complexity of human abilities and ways of being in the world.

Implications

The first implication of this approach is that the learning environment is flexible and intentionally designed to include diverse learners. This distinguishes the transformative approach from other modes of inclusion in that the *environment* is the key site of change, rather than individualized, incremental change. Furthermore, all institutional agents would hold responsibility for inclusion, rather than delegating responsibility to agents of compliance. Embodying the principles of universal design, all aspects of educational programs would be conceived with all types of learners in mind [30], rather than centering a "normative" student. Through this approach, disabled learners do not pose a "problem" in the educational environment; rather, their ways of learning and doing inform how the program works. This manner of design would have multifaceted benefits across all types of learners, especially those from socially marginalized groups (e.g., due to race/ethnicity, low socioeconomic status, caregivers, those with cultural and familial responsibilities, first generation to college, and so on). The transformative approach resists siloed inclusion by offering flexible options to approach education differently for all learners, not just those with disabilities. Following a social justice ethos, designing for inclusion would aim to dismantle institutional arrangements that privilege dominant ways of being, thereby allowing learners to embody their rich complexity throughout training and into practice [38, 39].

The second implication of this approach is that change is ongoing and iterative. Although the educational program is conceived with the intent of broad inclusion, this does not end the inclusive project [31, 37]. Human variation is vast and complex. As such, the unanticipated will inevitably arise [40]. The transformative approach would include mechanisms for ongoing feedback and evaluation to consider further inclusion and learning outcomes. In this way, achieving inclusion is a *point on the horizon* rather than a *destination*, which forces programs to remain alert, always looking for ways to improve and evolve.

The third implication is that diverse learners with disabilities add value to the professions. This approach would accept the principle that health professionals should reflect the diversity of patient populations and ensure that program development and learner populations are representative of this diversity [21, 41–46]. Recognizing that disability is an intersectional category, this approach considers ways to design for students that experience disability differently, for example, due to their gender, race, sexuality, and/or citizenship status [47, 48].

The final implication of the transformative approach is that programs would assume differentiated graduates, thus allowing learners to demonstrate proficiency in variable ways. This would render technical standards obsolete. Recognizing that all health professionals either specialize by dint of the training structure (e.g., during residency and fellowship for medicine), or through self-selection in employment and self-regulated practice, the necessity to prepare pluripotent graduates can be dispensed with. In this way, rather than offering exceptions to standards for some students, programs consider diverse ways to move through educational programs and meet academic standards as a starting point. This would allow for early specialization options or alternative participation in some clinical spaces to all students. This new way of educating would require strong, creative, solution-focused support for all learners to consider their strengths, interests, and possibilities to engage in various professional environments, consistent with the inclusive starting point of this approach.

The transformative approach signals a possibility that reimagines health science education entirely, building from a starting point of inclusion through universal design. This approach would likely create initial discomfort, as principles of fairness tend to assume sameness rather than differentiation in practice. Furthermore, a total reimagination of program structures may feel challenging, given outside pressures that privilege adherence to conformity. There are also risks that this approach may devolve into a situation where inclusion is left to the whim of individual faculty members or that as everyone's responsibility, no one is keeping watch. To counter this possibility, a genuine institutional commitment with checks and balances to review effectiveness and build the necessary skills to work in new ways would be needed. The potential of a transformative approach hinges on a new ethos, one that fosters cooperation, interdependence, and collective benefit rather than individual success, assumptions of independence, and competition as driving principles. A radically new image of health education and practice, one that centers justice while ensuring high standards of patient care, is necessary.

Conclusion

This chapter has outlined three approaches to inclusion in health science education and the implications that follow. The purpose of doing so is to prompt reflection among faculty and administrators concerning what philosophical positions drive their work, how their approach to inclusion is currently structured, and the possibilities for inclusion that follow.

While these may seem to be three distinct approaches, it is perhaps more accurate to think of them as existing along a continuum. Programs may find themselves taking a transformative approach in some respects while holding a compliance stance in others. Some programs likely exist in a "pre-compliance" state. Nursing programs still rarely admit students with obvious physical disabilities, despite strong arguments that inclusion is possible [49–51]. A recent study of disabled-learner prevalence in US medical schools found that some responding programs had no registered students with disabilities [52]. These findings raise serious questions about the inclusion practices in these programs. Although it is conceivable that the medical programs were universally designed, so students had no need for accommodations, it is probably safe to assume this is not the case. Instead, a "pre-compliance" or "strict compliance" state is more likely, wherein programs screened out students with disabilities or discouraged them from seeking formal accommodations through policy and practice (or lack thereof). Attention to your program's current positioning and related institutional arrangements that uphold the approach is the first step in self-reflection.

Wherever your program sits on the spectrum, considering our work in a constant state of "becoming inclusive" is valuable. This stance allows for critical examination of our current state as agentic, with possibilities for change always available. The current state of inclusion in health science education is complicated by wider tensions in the cultures of programs, clinical environments, licensing bodies, and healthcare systems. The demands by healthcare environments and neoliberal universities (in which education is increasingly treated as a commodity) further constrain possibilities [53, 54]. Furthermore, under neoliberal logics, institutions tend to find ways to appropriate the gloss of inclusion while leaving the roots of exclusion intact [55]. Nonetheless, imagining new futures for disability inclusion in health science requires us to question the naturalness and inevitability of the barriers that learners currently experience [56]. Employing a "politics of wonder" [6] and a "restless reflexive" [6] stance allows us to question the known and familiar ways of working to imagine how new approaches to inclusion might be possible with our work ever in progress.

References

1. Zola IK. Self, identity and the naming question: reflections on the language of disability. Soc Sci Med. 1993;36(2):167–73.
2. Dunn DS, Andrews EE. Person-first and identity-first language: developing psychologists' cultural competence using disability language. Am Psychol. 2015;70(3):255–64.
3. Goodley D. Disability studies: an interdisciplinary introduction. 2nd ed. London: Sage; 2017.
4. Linton S. Claiming disability: knowledge and identity. New York: NYU Press; 1998.
5. Longmore PK. The second phase: from disability rights to disability culture. In: Longmore PK, editor. Why I burned my book and other essays on disability. Philadelphia: Temple University Press; 2003.
6. Titchkosky T. The question of access: disability, space, meaning. Toronto: University of Toronto Press; 2011.
7. World Health Organization. Towards a common language for functioning, disability, and health: the international classification of functioning, disability, and health (ICF). Geneva: World Health Organization; 2002.
8. Campbell FK. Contours of ableism: the production of disability and abledness. Hampshire: Palgrave Macmillan; 2009.
9. Foucault M. Two lectures. In: Gordon C, editor. Power/knowledge: selected interviews and other writings, 1972–1977. New York: Pantheon; 1980.
10. Davis LJ. Introduction: disability, normality, and power. In: Davis LJ, editor. The disability studies reader. 4th ed. New York: Routledge; 2013.
11. Oliver M. Understanding disability: from theory to practice. New York: St. Martin's Press; 1996.
12. Skidmore D. A theoretical model of pedagogical discourse. Disabil Cult Educ. 2002;1(2):119–31.
13. Scotch RK. From good will to civil rights: transforming federal disability policy. 2nd ed. Philadelphia: Temple University Press; 2001.
14. Bagenstos SR. Technical standards and lawsuits involving accommodations for health professions students. AMA J Ethics. 2016;18(10):1010–6.
15. Rehabilitation Act of 1973, P.L. No. 93–122, § 87 Stat. 394.
16. Americans with Disabilities Act of 1990, P.L. No.101–336, §104 Stat. 328.
17. ADA Amendments Act of 2008, P.L. No. 110–325, § 110 Stat. 3406.
18. McCulley v. The University of Kansas School of Medicine, Case No. 13–3299 (10th Cir. 2014).
19. General prohibitions against discrimination, 28 C.F.R. § 35.130 (2016).
20. Meeks LM, Jain NR. Accessibility, inclusion, and action in medical education: lived experiences of learners and physicians with disabilities. Washington (DC): AAMC; 2018.
21. DeLisa JA, Lindenthal JJ. Reflections on diversity and inclusion in medical education. Acad Med. 2012;87(11):1461–3.
22. Guzman A, Balcazar FE. Disability services' standards and the worldviews guiding their implementation. J Postsecondary Educ Disabil. 2010;23(1):48–62.

23. Kurth N, Mellard D. Student perceptions of the accommodation process in postsecondary education. J Postsecondary Educ Disabil. 2009;19(1):71–84.

24. Shrewsbury D, Mogensen L, Hu W. Problematizing medical students with disabilities: a critical policy analysis. MedEdPublish. 2018;7(1):1–15.

25. Weber M. Objectivity in social science and social policy. In: Shils EA, Finch HA, editors. The methodology of the social sciences. Glencoe: Free Press; 1949. p. 49–112.

26. Kezar LB, Kirschner KL, Clinchot DM, Laird-Metke E, Zazove P, Curry RH. Leading practices and future directions for technical standards in medical education. Acad Med. 2019;94(4):520–7.

27. Zazove P, Case B, Moreland C, Plegue MA, Hoekstra A, Ouellette A, et al. U.S. medical schools' compliance with the Americans with disabilities act: findings from a national study. Acad Med. 2016;91(7):979–86.

28. Modifications in policies, practices, or procedures, 28 C.F.R. § 36.302 (2016).

29. Auxiliary aids and services, 28 C.F.R. § 36.303 (2016).

30. Burgstahler S, Cory R. Moving in from the margins: from accommodations to universal design. In: Gabel SL, Danforth S, editors. Disability and the politics of education. New York: Peter Lang; 2008. p. 561–81.

31. Dolmage JT. Academic ableism: disability and higher education. Ann Arbor: University of Michigan Press; 2017.

32. Lester JN, Dostal H, Gabriel R. Policing neurodiversity in higher education: a discourse analysis of the talk surrounding accommodations for university students. In: Herrera CD, Perry A, editors. Ethics and Neurodiversity. Newcastle upon Tyne: Cambridge Scholars Publisher; 2013. p. 52–66.

33. McKee M, Case B, Fausone M, Zazove P, Ouellette A, Fetters MD. Medical schools' willingness to accommodate medical students with sensory and physical disabilities: ethical foundations of a functional challenge to 'organic' technical standards. AMA J Ethics. 2016;18(10):993–1002.

34. Jain NR. Risking capability for access: disabled students negotiating the capability imperative in medical education. Paper presented at the American Educational Research Association Annual Meeting; Toronto; 5–9 April 2019.

35. Meeks LM, Jain NR. The guide to assisting students with disabilities: equal access to health science and professional education. New York: Springer Publishing; 2015.

36. Center for Universal Design. The principles of universal design [Internet]. Raleigh: NC State; 1997. [cited 2018 July 28]. Available from: https://projects.ncsu.edu/www/ncsu/design/sod5/cud/about_ud/udprinciplestext.htm.

37. Dolmage JT. Disability studies pedagogy, usability and universal design. Disabil Stud Q. 2005;25(4). https://dsq-sds.org/article/view/627/804.

38. Tsai J. Diversity and inclusion in medical schools: the reality. Scientific American [internet magazine]. 2018 July 12 [cited 2019 June 2]. Available from: https://blogs.scientificamerican.com/voices/diversity-and-inclusion-in-medical-schools-the-reality/.

39. Fergus KB, Teale B, Sivapragasam M, Mesina O, Stergiopoulos E. Medical students are not blank slates: positionality and curriculum interact to develop professional identity. Perspect Med Educ. 2018;7(1):5–7.

40. Knoll KR. Feminist disability studies pedagogy. Fem Teach. 2009;19(2):122–33.

41. Iezzoni LI. Why increasing numbers of physicians with disability could improve care for patients with disability. AMA J Ethics. 2016;18(10):1041–9.

42. McKee MM, Smith S, Barnett S, Pearson TA. Commentary: what are the benefits of training deaf and hard-of-hearing doctors? Acad Med. 2013;88(2):158–61.

43. Nivet MA. Commentary: diversity 3.0: a necessary systems upgrade. Acad Med. 2011;86(12):1487–9.

44. Nivet MA. A diversity 3.0 update. Acad Med. 2015;90(12):1591–3.

45. Marks B. Cultural competence revisited: nursing students with disabilities. J Nurs Educ. 2007;42(2):70–4.

46. Mogensen L, Hu W. "A doctor who really knows ...": a survey of community perspectives on medical students and practitioners with disability. BMC Med Educ. 2019;19:1–10.

47. Hirschmann NJ. Disability, feminism, and intersectionality: a critical approach. Radic Philos Rev. 2013;16(2):649–62.
48. Annamma SA, Connor D, Ferri B. Dis/ability critical race studies (DisCrit): theorizing at the intersections of race and dis/ability. Race Ethn Educ. 2013;16(1):1–31.
49. Neal-Boylan L, Smith D. Nursing students with physical disabilities: dispelling myths and correcting misconceptions. Nurse Educ. 2016;41(1):13–8.
50. Carroll SM. Inclusion of people with physical disabilities in nursing education. J Nurs Educ. 2004;43(5):207–12.
51. Evans BC. Nursing education for students with disabilities: our students, our teachers. In: Oermann MH, Heinrich KT, editors. Annual review of nursing education. New York: Springer Publishing Company; 2005. p. 3–22.
52. Meeks LM, Herzer KR. Prevalence of self-disclosed disability among medical students in US allopathic medical schools. JAMA. 2016;316(21):2271–2.
53. Ward SC. Neoliberalism and the global restructuring of knowledge and education. New York: Routledge; 2012.
54. Nishida A. Neoliberal academia and a critique from disability studies. In: Block P, Kasnitz D, Nishida A, Pollard N, editors. Occupying disability: critical approaches to community, justice, and decolonizing disability. Dordrecht: Springer; 2016. p. 145–57.
55. Mitchell DT. Disability, diversity, and diversion: normalization and avoidance in higher education. In: Bolt D, Penketh C, editors. Disability, avoidance and the academy: challenging resistance. Oxon: Routlege; 2016. p. 9–20.
56. Kafer A. Feminist, queer, crip. Bloomington: Indiana University Press; 2013.

Healthcare Disparities for Individuals with Disability: Informing the Practice

2

Lisa I. Iezzoni and Nicole D. Agaronnik

According to developers of the World Health Organization's *International Classification of Functioning, Disability, and Health* (ICF) [1], disability is "a continuum, relevant to the lives of all people to different degrees and at different times in their lives," virtually a "universal phenomenon" and "natural feature of the human condition [2]." A report on the future of disability in America noted that, considering all the persons who now have disability and those who will develop disability in coming years, "disability affects today or will affect tomorrow the lives of most Americans. Clearly, disability is not a minority issue [3]." Furthermore, anyone can become disabled in an instant, with sudden trauma or a catastrophic health event. Nonetheless, despite this near universality, persons with disability often remain marginalized and stigmatized in the USA today, including in health care.

This chapter describes the diversity and prevalence of Americans with disability. We then briefly examine evidence of disparities experienced by many individuals with disability in the US health care system. We next flip our lens to look at the persons who are providing this care. How widely are individuals with disability represented among the ranks of physicians, nurses, and other health care professionals? We begin below by defining disability.

L. I. Iezzoni (✉)
Professor of Medicine Harvard Medical School, Mongan Institute Health Policy Research Center, Massachusetts General Hospital, Boston, MA, USA

Department of Medicine, Harvard Medical School, Boston, MA, USA
e-mail: liezzoni@mgh.harvard.edu

N. D. Agaronnik
Mongan Institute Health Policy Research Center, Massachusetts General Hospital, Boston, MA, USA

© Springer Nature Switzerland AG 2020
L. M. Meeks, L. Neal-Boylan (eds.), *Disability as Diversity*,
https://doi.org/10.1007/978-3-030-46187-4_2

Definitions of Disability

No single consensus definition of disability exists that suits all governmental, regu-latory, societal, and individual purposes. Defining disability – specifically, identify-ing characteristics that qualify as disability – became important many centuries ago, as human communities coalesced and began helping members who could not sub-sist without that aid. Supporting small children, orphans, widows, and older people seemed obvious societal responsibilities, as did helping persons with severe disabil-ity. But here problems arose: as early as the Renaissance, European authorities dis-missed some of their citizenry as lazy, angling to avoid work or malingering by faking disability [4]. Differentiating meritorious persons with disability from unde-serving slackers proved challenging until the nineteenth century, with the invention of new diagnostic tools. Through these putatively objective assessments, using new technologies such as stethoscopes, ophthalmoscopes, spirometers, and radiographs, health care providers could distinguish persons with "real" disabling conditions from those feigning disability [4]. The medical model of disability arose from this emerging medical authority, viewing "disability as a problem of the person, directly caused by disease, trauma or other health condition, which requires medical care ... Management of the disability is aimed at cure or the individual's adjustment and behaviour change [1]." Obtaining medical care became the primary imperative, with people adapting on their own to loss and limitations.

By the mid-twentieth century, attitudes about disability began shifting. Harbingers of these changing attitudes had been accumulating [5]. During World War II, previ-ously unemployed persons with disability were hired and labored on the home front alongside women, while able-bodied men fought abroad [6]. Employers laid off these workers with disability and women when the veterans returned home, but World War II veterans with disability received accommodations to obtain college degrees and jobs [7]. These precedents sometimes extended to non-veterans with disability. Over the ensuing 20 to 30 years, other forces propelled broader social change, including the independent living movement, increasing interest in self-help rather than professional direction, large-scale deinstitutionalization of persons with various disabilities, and nationwide campaigns for civil rights and equal opportunity for racial minorities and women. These attitudes propelled the "social" model of disability, which treats disability "mainly as a socially created problem, and basi-cally as a matter of the full integration of individuals into society. Disability is not an attribute of an individual, but rather a complex collection of conditions, many of which are created by the social environment [1]." The social model posits disability as a human rights issue.

In defining disability for ICF, the World Health Organization developers recog-nized that this binary distinction – medical versus social model – was too simplistic to support the full range of societal needs for disability definitions, which differ by context (e.g., qualifying for legal protections, income support eligibility, compensa-tion for workplace injuries). ICF therefore considers three interrelated concepts: impairments of body functions or structures; activities, the execution of tasks or actions; and participation in daily life situations, which includes social and community interactions. Using these concepts, ICF defines disability as an "umbrella term for impairments, activity limitations or participation restrictions," conceiving "a person's functioning and disability ... as a dynamic interaction between health conditions ...and contextual factors," including the physical, social, and societal environments, as well as individuals' personal attributes [1].

Table 2.1 shows definitions of disability used for different purposes, each of which emphasizes its own specific aspect of ICF's model. Definitions have

Table 2.1 Definitions of disability

Source	Definition
Civil rights law	
Americans with Disabilities Act (ADA), 1990	"The term 'disability' means, with respect to an individual — (A) a physical or mental impairment that substantially limits one or more of the life activities of such individual; (B) a record of such an impairment; or (C) being regarded as having such an impairment [82]." "Major life activities include, but are not limited to, caring for oneself, performing manual tasks, seeing, hearing, eating, sleeping, walking, standing, lifting, bending, speaking, breathing, learning, reading, concentrating, thinking, communicating, and working [82]." *Major life activities* also entail "the operation of a major bodily function, including but not limited to, functions of the immune system, normal cell growth, digestive, bowel, bladder, neurological, brain, respiratory, circulatory, endocrine, and reproductive functions [82]."
ADA Title V (Miscellaneous)	This title identifies a list of conditions not considered disabilities, including: "transvestism, transsexualism, pedophilia, exhibitionism, voyeurism, gender identity disorders not resulting from physical impairments, other sexual behavior disorders, compulsive gambling, kleptomania, pyromania, and psychoactive substance use disorders resulting from current illegal use of drugs. Homosexuality and bisexuality, since they are not impairments, can not be considered disabilities under the ADA [83, 84]."
ADA Amendments Act, 2008	The ADAA clarifies that the definition of disability should be construed more broadly "in order to effectuate Congress's intent to restore the broad scope of the ADA by making it easier for an individual to establish that he or she has a disability [85]." The ADAA expands the definition of *major life activities* by providing a non-exhaustive list of such activities, which include major bodily functions. Furthermore, it clarifies that the term "substantially limits" should be "construed broadly in favor of maximum coverage [85]." It clarifies that "ameliorative effects of mitigating measures other than 'ordinary eyeglasses or contact lenses' shall not be considered in assessing whether an individual has a 'disability [85].'" Most importantly, the ADAA emphasizes that the interpretation of the law should be focused on whether "an entity covered under the ADA has complied with its obligations and whether discrimination has occurred, not the extent to which the individual's impairment substantially limits a major life activity [85]."

(continued)

Table 2.1 (continued)

Source	Definition
Income support and other programs	
Social Security Administration	*Disability* is the "inability to do any substantial gainful activity by reason of any medically determinable physical or mental impairment which can be expected to result in death or which has lasted or can be expected to last for a continuous period of not less than 12 months [86]."
AMA Guide 6th Edition	*Disability* is an "activity limitation and/or participation restriction in an individual with a health condition, disorder or disease [87]." *Impairment* is "a significant deviation, loss or loss of use, of any body structure or body function in an individual with a health condition, disorder or disease [87]." *Impairment rating* is "a consensus-derived percentage estimate of loss of activity, which reflects severity of impairment for a given health condition, and the degree of associated limitations in terms of activities of daily living (ADLs) [87]."
Vocational Rehabilitation	*Disability* is "a physical or mental impairment (which must include legal blindness) that results in a substantial impediment to employment; and who can benefit in terms of an employment outcome from vocational rehabilitation services [88]."
Models of disability	
Medical model	*Disability* is a "feature of the person, directly caused by disease, trauma or other health condition, which requires medical care provided in the form of individual treatment by professionals. Disability, on this model, calls for medical or other treatment or intervention, to 'correct' the problem with the individual [89]."
Social model	*Disability* is a "socially created problem and not at all an attribute of an individual. On the social model, disability demands a political response, since the problem is created by an unaccommodating physical environment brought about by attitudes and other features of the social environment [89]."
Bio-psycho-social-environmental model (World Health Organization International Classification of Functioning, Disability, and Health)	*Disability* is an "umbrella term for impairments, activity limitations and participation restrictions [89]" while *functioning* "refers to all body functions, activities and participation [89]." This model elaborates that *disability* is the "interaction between features of the person and features of the overall context in which the person lives, but some aspects of disability are almost entirely internal to the person, while another aspect is almost entirely external. In other words, both medical and social responses are appropriate to the problems associated with disability; we cannot wholly reject either kind of intervention [89]."

important implications, depending on the context. In health care settings, the medical model, which views "disability as an individual deficit to be cured [8]," frequently serves as a heuristic for understanding and evaluating the experiences of patients with disability. In contrast, the social model identifies disability as a "culturally and historically specific phenomenon [8]." The social model suggests a unique cultural experience, which unifies the diverse disability community, rather than a list of common clinical symptoms. Reconciling these two models can prove especially challenging for students with disability pursuing health professions if they feel that their disability is perceived by peers and colleagues through the medical model lens. Meanwhile, efforts to facilitate access for students with disability and concerns about potential legal liability have caused health profession schools to primarily focus on using the 1990 Americans with Disabilities Act [9] definition of disability to identify students qualifying for accommodations. However, meeting legal obligations to accommodate students with disability generally is insufficient to create a supportive inclusive environment, which may also require celebrating disability as an identity that enhances diversity in health profession schools.

Diversity of Disability and Implications for Accommodations

Disabilities are heterogenous, so much so that grouping all disabling conditions together is almost meaningless. Some disabling conditions are present at birth and last a lifetime, such as cerebral palsy, spina bifida, and certain conditions related to chromosomal factors; the extent of impairments caused by these congenital conditions varies widely. Others occur suddenly, such as with serious injury or acute illness, and may resolve over time or persist until death. Yet other functional impairments progress gradually – perhaps with sporadic exacerbations – over years. Some conditions have stable or constant functional deficits across time, such as congenital blindness or deafness, and do not necessarily require medical intervention but would require communication accommodation. In contrast, other congenital conditions, such as intellectual disability and some developmental disabilities, may benefit from rehabilitation therapy, assistive technology, and other supportive services and have functional impairments that can progress over time.

Of special relevance in educational settings, learning disabilities encompass a diverse range of experiences and accommodation needs. Some individuals experience difficulties with learning basic skills, such as reading, writing, or arithmetic, while others have challenges with higher functions, such as organization, time planning, short-term memory, or attention [10]. Learning disabilities are among the most common disability type among health science students, with one estimate suggesting that 21.5% of students with disability in medical school have a learning disability and 33.7% of students with disability have attention deficit hyperactivity disorder [11]. Given the heterogenous nature of learning disabilities, the individual experiences of health science students often are not captured by the implied precision of the *Diagnostic and Statistical Manual of Mental Disorders* [12]. Students may become frustrated by broad categorizations and erroneous assumptions about their abilities in an academic setting [13].

Other disabilities arise from chronic diseases, such as diabetes, cardiovascular diseases, chronic obstructive pulmonary disease, neurodegenerative disorders, some cancers, musculoskeletal conditions, organic brain syndromes, and serious mental illness. Sometimes medical treatments can significantly palliate these conditions, allowing persons to function without obvious impairments. The need for medical treatments and disability accommodations for persons with some chronic conditions can fluctuate over time, with periodic exacerbations of disease, or may increase over time with progressive functional impairment.

Secondary disabilities can also pose substantial limitations. These conditions arise as consequences of an underlying disability and can compound functional impairments or need for accommodations. Examples of secondary disability include pressure injuries (also known as pressure ulcers or sores), recurrent urinary tract infections, falls with injuries, and depression. Depending on the type, timing, and trajectory of disability and the presence of secondary disability, accommodation and support needs can arise suddenly, remain roughly stable for many years, steadily increase, or rise and fall over time.

Prevalence of Disability

No comprehensive data source exists about disability prevalence in the USA. The Social Security Administration tracks the numbers of persons who qualify as disabled under their criteria, which relate to the ability to pursue substantial gainful employment and the presence of long-term, documented medical conditions (Table 2.1). To be eligible for Social Security disability benefits, individuals must demonstrate that they are unable to engage in "substantial gainful activity," currently designated as being able to earn at least $2040 for statutorily blind individuals and at least $1220 for all other individuals with disability [14]. Among persons qualifying for Social Security Disability Insurance, 32.7% have a musculoskeletal system or connective tissue condition, representing the most common cause for disability determination [15]. The diagnostic category of "all other mental disorders" closely follows at 26% of recipients [15]. However, Social Security disability numbers represent only a select subgroup of Americans with disability – those who choose to apply for this benefit and who meet the specific criteria defining disability (i.e., an employment-based definition).

Most data on disability prevalence in the USA comes from population-based surveys. Survey data represent the views of participants about their functional abilities without confirmation by some outside source; cultural norms and social desirability and other biases can affect willingness to report disability. Over many decades, numerous federal surveys have collected information about disability but using different questions; not surprisingly, estimated population prevalence of disability therefore varied depending on the survey source [16]. Section 4302 of the Patient Protection and Affordable Care Act of 2010 required the federal government to create standard questions for identifying disability that would be implemented uniformly across federal surveys to improve consistency and comparability of data from different surveys. In 2018, the Office of Minority Health in the US Department of Health and Human Services published its data collection standards for disability, which included six questions [17]. Table 2.2 presents estimates of disability prevalence from data obtained by the Behavioral Risk Factor Surveillance System (BRFSS) Survey [18], which implemented the six federally required disability questions starting in 2016 [19].

Table 2.2 Disability prevalence in 2016 and 2017

Disability type	Population prevalence (%) by year in the USA and territories					
	2016			2017		
	Ages 18–44	Ages 45–64	Ages 65+	Ages 18–44	Ages 45–64	Ages 65+
Cognitive	10.5%	11.9%	9.5%	11.4%	12.3%	9.7%
Hearing	2.0	5.8	14.7	2.3	6.1	15.1
Mobility	4.8	18.1	26.9	5.1	18.6	27.2
Vision	2.8	6.2	6.8	3.0	6.3	6.9
Self-care	1.7	5.5	5.5	1.9	6.0	6.0
Independent living	4.5	8.2	9.9	5.1	8.7	9.7
Demographic Variable	Population prevalence (%) by year in USA and territories for ages 18+					
	2016		2017			
	Any disability	No disability	Any disability	No disability		
Sex						
Male	23.3%	76.7%	24.1%	75.9%		
Female	25.8	74.2	27.0	73.0		
Race/ethnicity						
White, non-Hispanic	23.3	76.7	24.4	75.6		
Black, non-Hispanic	28.2	71.8	29.2	70.8		
Asian, non-Hispanic	14.3	85.7	15.7	84.3		
Native Hawaiian or Other Pacific Islander, non-Hispanic	25.4	74.6	28.7	71.3		
American Indian or Alaska Native, non-Hispanic	38.7	61.3	40.8	59.2		
Other/multi-race, non-Hispanic	35.0	65.0	34.2	65.8		
Hispanic	29.3	70.7	29.3	70.8		

[a]Data source: Behavioral Risk Factor Surveillance System (BRFSS) Survey, which used the standard disability questions mandated by Section 4302 of the 2010 Patient Protection and Affordable Care Act Centers for Disease Control and Prevention, National Center on Birth Defects and Developmental Disabilities, Division of Human Development and Disability. Disability and Health Data System (DHDS) Data [online]. [accessed Jul 26, 2019]. URL: https://dhds.cdc.gov

Health Care Disparities and People with Disability

About 40 years ago, the federal government started producing decennial reports about public health priorities for the coming decade, identifying subgroups of Americans with particular health concerns. The third installment of these reports, *Healthy People 2010*, was released in 2000 and identified public health priorities for the first decade of the twenty-first century. *Healthy People 2010* was the first of these reports to identify Americans with disability as experiencing health care disparities, cautioning that "as a potentially underserved group, people with disability would be expected to experience disadvantages in health and well-being compared with the general population." [20] Of note, *Healthy People 2010* indicated that common misconceptions about persons with disability may contribute to their health care disparities, including lower rates of screening tests, disease prevention, and health promotion services. Five years later, on July 26, 2005, the 15th anniversary of the signing of the Americans with Disabilities Act, US Surgeon General Richard Carmona issued a *Call to Action* echoing this concern that persons with disability may lack equal access to health care [21, 22]. Observing that "every life has value and every person has promise," Carmona urged recognition that people with disability can lead long, healthy, and productive lives; health care providers should screen, diagnose, and treat people with disability with dignity as whole persons; and health care services should become fully accessible to maximize the independence of people with disability [21, 22].

Healthy People 2010 and the 2005 Surgeon General's *Call to Action* initiated a period of intensified research into health care disparities experienced by persons with disability. Data limitations have impeded assessments of health care disparities for persons with disability across a full range of health care services and settings [23]. Research has focused on some subgroups of individuals with disability more than others; importantly, the nature and extent of disparities can vary by type of disability. Examples of either disparities or outright substandard quality of care for persons with disability include the following:

- National Health Interview Survey (NHIS) data from 1994–1995 suggested that women with major mobility difficulty experienced 40% lower rates of Papanicolaou testing than other women [24]. Based on NHIS data between 1998 and 2010, rates of Pap testing for all women have not changed over time, remaining at around 84–87%, but women with severe mobility disability continued to have significantly lower Pap test rates than other women (in 2010, an adjusted odds ratio of 0.35) [25].
- Disparities in mammography screening between women with and without disability have grown over time, with NHIS data from 1998–2010 suggesting that some subgroups of women with movement disability experience an approximately 50% lower screening rate [26]. A systematic review indicated that mammography screening tends to decrease as disability level increases [27]. Women with disability living in rural areas were 30% less likely than women without disability in urban areas to have access to timely breast and cervical cancer screening [28]. Inaccessible medical equipment, including mammography machines and examination tables, may contribute to these disparities [29].
- Medical Expenditure Panel Survey data from 2002 to 2008 suggested that women with complex or severe disability were less likely to be up to date with breast or cervical cancer screening, although all women regardless fell short of *Healthy People 2020* recommendations [30].
- Women with breast cancer who receive Social Security Disability Insurance and Medicare coverage were significantly less likely to receive breast-conserving surgery than other women; importantly, if they did have lumpectomy, women

with disability were significantly less likely than other women to receive the radiotherapy required to maximize disease-free survival. Women with disability also experienced significantly higher all-cause mortality rates (adjusted hazard ratio = 2.02) and breast-cancer specific mortality (adjusted hazard ratio = 1.31) compared to other women [31].

- Disparities in colorectal cancer screening for people with disability appeared to decrease according to NHIS data from 1998 to 2010 [32]. However, findings of disability disparities in colorectal cancer screening have been inconsistent across studies. An analysis of 2013 NHIS data suggested that increasing disability severity was associated with decreasing odds of screening after adjusting for covariates including age and comorbidities [33].

- Among Medicare beneficiaries, people with disability who were diagnosed with non-small cell lung cancer experienced higher cancer-specific mortality rates (adjusted hazard ratio = 1.37) than people without disability, with persisting effects after adjustment for demographic and tumor characteristics [34]. People with disability were less likely to undergo surgery for their lung cancer [34].

- A national survey of maternity care for women with physical disability found that 40.3% of women reported that their prenatal care provider lacked knowledge about how physical disability affects their pregnancy [35]. Women with disability who reported that their providers lacked knowledge were more likely to indicate unmet needs in maternity care [35]. Interviews with health care practitioners providing maternity care to women with physical disability suggested unwillingness to provide care, inaccessible medical equipment, time limitations, insufficient reimbursement, and paucity of disability-specific clinical data [36].

- Evidence primarily drawing upon in-depth interviews with women with physical disability suggests accessibility barriers to obtaining routine prenatal care, including lack of height-adjustable exam tables and accessible weight scales. This results in substandard care, including examination of women while seated in their wheelchairs and lack of routine weight measurement during prenatal visits [37].

- In-depth interviews with physicians suggests that lack of accessible medical diagnostic equipment contributes to substandard care, including avoidance of transferring patients with physical disability onto exam tables, evaluation of patients while seated in their wheelchairs, and skipped routine weighing [38]. One study suggested that 70–87% of patients who use wheelchairs were examined in their wheelchairs [39]. Other studies suggest that people with disability are often asked to self-report weight during clinical exams [37], for purposes including prenatal assessments and estimation of medicine dosages [29, 40].

The *2013 National Disparities Report* from the Agency for Healthcare Research and Quality (AHRQ), which looked at overall quality of care, included a special focus on persons with disability [41]. AHRQ examined the proportion of quality measures that had improved over time, and persons with disability had worse outcomes than all other groups studied. In 2013, the percent of quality measures that showed improvement by population subgroup were as follows: 59.5% for all persons; 58.3% for Hispanics; 57.1% for Blacks; 56.9% for Asians; 53.7% for poor persons; 42.0% for American Indians and Alaskan Natives; but only 36.0% for persons with "basic action limitations" (difficulties walking, seeing/hearing, cognition, and mental health) and 20.8% for persons with "complex action limitations" (difficulties with activities of daily living, social roles, or work).

Reasons for Health Care Disparities for Persons with Disability

Many factors likely contribute to the disparities and substandard quality of care experienced by persons with disability, including patients' preferences, physical access barriers, communication barriers, inadequate efforts to accommodate patients' needs, and stigmatized or discriminatory attitudes among health care providers [36, 38, 42–44]. Societal attitudes toward persons with disability – including both explicit and implicit bias – are often negative, although the nature of stigmatization likely varies by disability type (e.g., often persons with intellectual disability generate the most negative perceptions) [45–47]. Health care professionals, as members of society, may share these explicit or implicit biases toward persons with disability, affecting the care and interpersonal interactions they have with patients with disability.

Research involving physicians has demonstrated that they share broader societal prejudices concerning persons with disability [48–53]. Studies have found that attitudes of physicians toward persons with disability can vary by disability type; physicians' own sociodemographic characteristics; prior experiences with individuals with disability; and the clinical context [48–53]. In 1994, a seminal study reported the attitudes of 233 physicians, nurses, and emergency medical technicians from three Level I trauma centers about treating persons with spinal cord injury (SCI) [54]. The researchers compared clinicians' responses with those from a previous survey of individuals with SCI. Among clinicians, 22% reported they would not want life-sustaining treatment if they had a SCI; only 18% imagined being glad to be alive after SCI. In contrast, 92% of respondents with SCI said they were glad to be alive. Furthermore, 41% of clinicians felt that staff in their emergency departments tried "too hard to resuscitate or save" persons with new SCIs [54]. A more recent report suggests that negative attitudes can be changed over time, such as by having clinicians interact with people who use wheelchairs and contradict societal stereotypes [53].

In one study, Iezzoni interviewed 22 practicing physicians about caring for persons with progressive walking difficulties [55]. Many interviewees admitted having no training on addressing mobility disability. As one general internist said, "Addressing walking is outside of those things that you view as doing doctoring. ... [Its] social worker-type stuff. It's useful, but it's not really internal medicine." Another general internist observed:

> [Disability] doesn't fit the paradigm of the people who run medical schools: the job is cure. If you find out what's happening on the most molecular level, you can figure out how to fix it. ... Just put in some new DNA, and all the problems of society go away. That simplistic, reductionist view is, I think, the fantasy of why people went to medical school. To cure, to be the hero [55].

Sometimes relationships between patients and physicians become polarized around whether walking problems are "legitimate" – in physicians' minds, whether patients are "malingering" or indeed have provable physical disorders [55]. Most physicians interviewed by Iezzoni did not practice in settings with automatically adjustable examination tables. Even those who did admitted to being unsure how to use the equipment. In addition, in a busy practice, scheduling specific patients for a particular room is often logistically complex. One internist said she disliked the adjustable table: it rose and lowered too slowly for her practice style. Because physicians protested, the clinic considered removing the automatic tables but kept them because of patients' needs [55].

One study about access to outpatient medical practices for patients with mobility disability used a "secret shopper"-type telephone survey [56]. With Institutional Review Board approval, research staff telephoned subspecialty offices purportedly to make an appointment for a fictional patient with hemiparesis who was obese, used a wheelchair, and could not self-transfer onto an examination table. They spoke with 256 endocrinology, gynecology, orthopedic surgery, rheumatology, urology, ophthalmology, otolaryngology, and psychiatry practices in four US cities. Fifty-six (22%) said that they could not accommodate the patient; 9 (4%) reported an inaccessible building; and 47 (18%) said they could not transfer the patient onto an examination table [56]. Only 22 (9%) offices reported using either a height-adjustable examination table or a lift for transfer. Gynecology had the highest rate of inaccessible practices (44%) [56]. The researchers found that respondents at inaccessible practices freely explained their reasons for refusing the patient, suggesting they did not realize their refusal to schedule the patient was likely illegal.

Health Care Professionals with Disability

The stigmatized or discriminatory attitudes about disability among health care professionals described above are troubling, although as noted they largely reflect societal views. Nonetheless, given the ethical imperatives governing health care, these negative attitudes raise important questions, including: How many health care professionals themselves have disability? What accommodations do these professionals need to practice within their clinical field? Would increasing the number of health care professionals with disability begin to improve equity of care for patients with disability? Little information is available to answer these questions [57]. Historically, health care professionals have been afraid to reveal disability for fear of being forced to leave practice or undergo withering scrutiny [58]. Therefore, little is known about this largely invisible group of health care professionals.

Nurses with disability often try to hide their disability, pursue graduate school to obtain employment in less physically demanding nursing jobs, or leave the profession because of concerns about patient safety [59–61]. Nurses who ask for accommodations frequently do not receive them or are viewed as slackers. Similarly, nurses who require breaks to accommodate fatigue or dietary needs related to their disability are perceived as not pulling their weight [59, 62]. A study comparing the work life experiences of nurses and physicians with disability found that they had similar experiences. Colleagues generally were not receptive to attempts to safely compensate if tasks could not be performed in the usual way, and peers were typically not supportive [63].

Many racial and ethnic minorities experience health care disparities, and studies relating to physicians suggest that racial and ethnic concordance between patients and physicians can significantly improve communication, patients' participation in clinical decision-making, patients' willingness to adhere to clinicians' recommendations, and overall satisfaction with care [64, 65]. Recommendations for increasing racial and ethnic diversity within the physician workforce aim explicitly, in part, to improve care and reduce care inequities [66, 67]. Whether concordance on disability status between patients and their health care professionals would similarly enhance equitable care remains unknown.

Answering this question will be challenging. As some have argued, increasing the presence of individuals with disability within the health care professional workforce must recognize the absolute priority of ensuring patient safety [68, 69]. Little information is available about the prevalence of disability among clinical practitioners and trainees. Most likely, the prevalence of disability is bimodal for age: there may be a small peak at younger ages, as students with ADA-mandated accommodations enter training, and prevalence may rise steadily with aging, as health care professionals develop aging-related chronic, disabling conditions. As shown in Table 2.2, disability rates are higher for older compared with younger individuals, and that is likely also true among health care professionals. Health care professionals, with the exception of licensed practical nurses, are less likely than the general public to smoke [70] and less likely to be overweight or obese [71], which might reduce likelihood of disability related to these chronic conditions or risk factors compared with the general population.

Accommodating Health Care Professionals with Disability

Given the multifaceted demands of health professions, it is unrealistic to expect that persons with certain forms of disability – such as significant intellectual or cognitive disability, certain types of serious mental illness, or major communication disorders – can work in these fields. Nonetheless, reasonable accommodations are now available to support students with significant disability in becoming proficient and productive practitioners. However, an unanswered question is the extent to which training programs meet their legal obligations to make reasonable accommodations for students with disability.

At medical schools, being required to demonstrate proficiency on specified technical standards may prevent otherwise qualified persons from graduating [72–74]. Nursing programs frequently list technical standards that confuse the essential functions of nursing work with academic standards. Technical standards may also vary across different health profession schools [74], even though the "essential functions of the job with or without reasonable accommodation [75]," as required by Title I of the Americans with Disabilities Act, may not differ dramatically across different care settings (given the consistent, fundamental aspects of providing good-quality patient care). Recent publications have suggested that health profession schools are not complying with some ADA requirements.

Increased efforts to meet legal requirements and avoid liability may outpace initiatives to foster inclusive communities that are welcoming for students with disability within health profession schools. Furthermore, this emphasis may also deter students with disability from applying. For example, some secondary applications to medical schools require that students read and electronically sign a statement relating to performing technical standards before being permitted to pay the fee and submit their application. Nursing schools often require students to read and sign technical standards shortly after admission. A welcoming alternative would invite applicants to communicate with a disability service provider or other representative of the school about whether they can pursue the academic program and fulfill the technical standards with their specific accommodation needs.

Accommodating health care professionals who develop disability in mid- or late-career raises complex issues. As noted above, individuals may hesitate to reveal disability or be "in denial" about whether they can safely continue working [69]. Physicians can "appear reluctant to identify themselves as disabled or use available accommodations, in part out of fear of reprisal [76]." Nurses with disability try to hide their disability whenever possible because they fear they will not be hired or retained in their jobs [59, 60, 62]. Decisions about whether physicians can practice safely are generally made by state licensing boards, which do not always fully follow ADA requirements [77]. Nursing faculty are given the responsibility of ensuring that new nurse graduates can practice safely.

Health care professionals educated after 1990 (post-ADA) who have explicitly needed to invoke their legal rights to receive accommodations during training may imbue a "disability identity" [6] that informs their professional practice. These young professionals may thus be "disability culturally competent [78–81]," with an empathic understanding of the lived experience of disability. In contrast, health care professionals aging with chronic disabling conditions may deny their limitations and eschew a disability identity. It is unclear whether denying disability in themselves might affect how they view or treat patients with disability [57]. It is also unclear whether these health care professionals would become more knowledgeable about their legal obligations to accommodate patients and improve equity of care when they themselves become disabled.

Concluding Thoughts

Facilitating access and inclusion for students with disability pursuing education as health care professionals requires a thorough understanding of perceptions concerning disability across society. Although meeting legal requirements may be of primary concern to many institutions, addressing factors beyond the law will ultimately be key to creating inclusive educational and practice settings. Building a professional health care workforce that mirrors the diversity of the patient population will require a comprehensive effort, including addressing barriers posed by technical standards that may not be relevant to the ultimate practice plans of students.

References

1. World Health Organization. International classification of functioning, disability, and health. Geneva: World Health Organization; 2001.
2. Ustun TB, Chatterji S, Kostansjek N, Bickenbach J. WHO's ICF and functional status information in health records. Health Care Financ Rev. 2003;24(3):77–88.
3. Institute of Medicine Committee on Disability in America Board on Health Sciences Policy. In: Field M, Jette A, editors. The future of disability in America. Washington, DC: National Academies Press; 2007.
4. Stone D. The disabled state. Philadelphia: Temple University Press; 1984.
5. Iezzoni LI, O'Day BL. More than ramps. A guide to improving healthcare quality and access for people with disabilities. New York: Oxford University Press; 2006.
6. Linton S. Claiming disability. Knowledge and identity. New York: New York University Press; 1998.
7. Litvak S, Enders A. Support systems. The interface between individuals and environments. In: Handbook of disability studies. Thousand Oaks: Sage Publications; 2001. p. 711–33.
8. Shakespeare T. The social model of disability. In: Davis LJ, editor. The disability studies reader. 5th ed. New York: Routledge; 2017.
9. 110th Congress. An act: to restore the intent and protections of the Americans with Disabilities Act of 1990. 3553 U.S.; 2008.
10. National Institute for Learning Development. What are the types of learning disabilities? http://nild.org/learning-disabilities/dyslexia-dysgraphia-dyscalculia/. Accessed April 16, 2020.
11. Meeks LM, Herzer KR. Prevalence of self-disclosed disability among medical students in US allopathic medical schools. JAMA. 2016;316(21):2271–2.
12. American Psychiatric Association. Diagnostic and statistical manual of mental disorders. 5th ed. Arlington, VA: American Psychiatric Association; 2013.
13. Takakuwa KM. Coping with a learning disability in medical school. JAMA. 1998; 279(1):81.
14. Social Security Administration. Substantial gainful activity. https://www.ssa.gov/oact/cola/sga.html. Accessed April 16, 2020.
15. Social Security Administration. Annual statistical report on the social security disability insurance program, 2017. Washington, DC: Social Security Administration; 2018.
16. Freedman V, Crimmins E, Schoeni R, et al. Resolving inconsistencies in trends in old-age disability: report from a technical working group. Demography. 2004;41(3):417–41.
17. Office of Minority Health, US Department of Health and Human Services. Data collection standards for race, ethnicity, sex, primary language, and disability status. https://minorityhealth.hhs.gov/omh/browse.aspx?lvl=2&lvlid=23. Accessed April 16, 2020.
18. Centers for Disease Control and Prevention. About Behavioral Risk Factor Surveillance System. https://www.cdc.gov/brfss/about/index.htm. Accessed April 16, 2020.
19. Centers for Disease Control and Prevention. Disability datasets. Population surveys that include the standard disability questions. https://www.cdc.gov/ncbddd/disabilityandhealth/datasets.html. Accessed April 16, 2020.
20. US Department of Health and Human Services. Health people 2010. Understanding and improving health. Washington, DC: Department of Health and Human Services; 2000.
21. Office of the Surgeon General, US Department of Health and Human Services. The surgeon general's call to action to improve the health and wellness of persons with disabilities. Washington, DC: Department of Health and Human Services; 2005.

22. Carmona RH, Cabe J. Improving the health and wellness of persons with disabilities: a call to action. Am J Public Health. 2005;95(11):1883.
23. Iezzoni LI. Using administrative data to study persons with disabilities. Milbank Q. 2002;80(2):347–79.
24. Iezzoni LI, McCarthy EP, Davis RB, Siebens H. Mobility impairments and use of screening and preventive services. Am J Public Health. 2000;90(6):955–61.
25. Iezzoni LI, Kurtz SG, Rao SR. Trends in Pap testing over time for women with and without chronic disability. Am J Prev Med. 2016;50(2):210–9.
26. Iezzoni LI, Kurtz SG, Rao SR. Trends in mammography over time for women with and without chronic disability. J Womens Health (Larchmt). 2015;24(7):593–601.
27. Andresen EM, Peterson-Besse JJ, Krahn GL, Walsh ES, Horner-Johnson W, Iezzoni LI. Pap, mammography, and clinical breast examination screening among women with disabilities: a systematic review. Womens Health Issues. 2013;23(4):e205–14.
28. Horner-Johnson W, Dobbertin K, Iezzoni LI. Disparities in receipt of breast and cervical cancer screening for rural women age 18 to 64 with disabilities. Womens Health Issues. 2015;25(3):246–53.
29. Iezzoni LI, Kilbridge K, Park ER. Physical access barriers to care for diagnosis and treatment of breast cancer among women with mobility impairments. Oncol Nurs Forum. 2010;37(6):711–7.
30. Horner-Johnson W, Dobbertin K, Andresen EM, Iezzoni LI. Breast and cervical cancer screening disparities associated with disability severity. Womens Health Issues. 2014;24(1):e147–53.
31. McCarthy EP, Ngo LH, Roetzheim RG, et al. Disparities in breast cancer treatment and survival for women with disabilities. Ann Intern Med. 2006;145(9):637–45.
32. Iezzoni LI, Kurtz SG, Rao SR. Trends in colorectal cancer screening over time for persons with and without chronic disability. Disabil Health J. 2016;9(3):498–509.
33. Gofine M, Mielenz TJ, Vasan S, Lebwohl B. Use of colorectal cancer screening among people with mobility disability. J Clin Gastroenterol. 2018;52(9):789–95.
34. Iezzoni LI, Ngo LH, Li D, Roetzheim RG, Drews RE, McCarthy EP. Treatment disparities for disabled medicare beneficiaries with stage I non-small cell lung cancer. Arch Phys Med Rehabil. 2008;89(4):595–601.
35. Mitra M, Akobirshoev I, Moring NS, et al. Access to and satisfaction with prenatal care among pregnant women with physical disabilities: findings from a national survey. J Womens Health (Larchmt). 2017;26(12):1356–63.
36. Mitra M, Smith LD, Smeltzer SC, Long-Bellil LM, Sammet Moring N, Iezzoni LI. Barriers to providing maternity care to women with physical disabilities: perspectives from health care practitioners. Disabil Health J. 2017;10(3):445–50.
37. Iezzoni LI, Wint AJ, Smeltzer SC, Ecker JL. Physical accessibility of routine prenatal care for women with mobility disability. J Womens Health (Larchmt). 2015;24(12):1006–12.
38. Agaronnik N, Campbell EG, Ressalam J, Iezzoni LI. Accessibility of medical diagnostic equipment for patients with disability: observations from physicians. Arch Phys Med Rehabil. 2019;100(11):2032–8.
39. Frost KL, Bertocci G, Stillman MD, Smalley C, Williams S. Accessibility of outpatient healthcare providers for wheelchair users: pilot study. J Rehabil Res Dev. 2015;52(6):653–62.
40. Story MF, Schwier E, Kailes JI. Perspectives of patients with disabilities on the accessibility of medical equipment: examination tables, imaging equipment, medical chairs, and weight scales. Disabil Health J. 2009;2(4):169–179.e1.
41. Agency for Healthcare Research and Quality. 2013 National healthcare disparities report. Rockville, MD: Agency for Healthcare Research and Quality; 2014.
42. Agaronnik N, Campbell EG, Ressalam J, Iezzoni LI. Communicating with patients with disability: perspectives of practicing physicians. J Gen Intern Med. 2019;34(7):1139–45.
43. Agaronnik N, Campbell EG, Ressalam J, Iezzoni LI. Exploring issues relating to disability cultural competence among practicing physicians. Disabil Health J. 2019;12(3):403–10.
44. Agaronnik ND, Pendo E, Campbell EG, Ressalam J, Iezzoni LI. Knowledge of practicing physicians about their legal obligations when caring for patients with disability. Health Aff (Millwood). 2019;38(4):545–53.

45. Wilson MC, Scior K. Attitudes towards individuals with disabilities as measured by the implicit association test: a literature review. Res Dev Disabil. 2014;35(2):294–321.
46. Wilson MC, Scior K. Implicit attitudes towards people with intellectual disabilities: their relationship with explicit attitudes, social distance, emotions and contact. PLoS One. 2015;10(9):e0137902.
47. Kerins G, Petrovic K, Gianesini J, Keilty B, Bruder MB. Physician attitudes and practices on providing care to individuals with intellectual disabilities: an exploratory study. Conn Med. 2004;68(8):485–90.
48. Antonak RF, Livneh H. Measurement of attitudes towards persons with disabilities. Disabil Rehabil. 2000;22(5):211–24.
49. Satchidanand N, Gunukula SK, Lam WY, et al. Attitudes of healthcare students and professionals toward patients with physical disability: a systematic review. Am J Phys Med Rehabil. 2012;91(6):533–45.
50. Paris M. Attitudes of medical students and health care professionals toward people with disabilities. Arch Phys Med Rehabil. 1993;74(August):818–25.
51. Tervo RC, Azuma S, Palmer G, Redinius P. Medical students' attitudes toward persons with disability: a comparative study. Arch Phys Med Rehabil. 2002;83(11):1537–42.
52. Tervo RC, Palmer G, Redinius P. Health professional student attitudes towards people with disability. Clin Rehabil. 2004;18(8):908–15.
53. Galli G, Lenggenhager B, Scivoletto G, Molinari M, Pazzaglia M. Don't look at my wheelchair! The plasticity of longlasting prejudice. Med Educ. 2015;49(12):1239–47.
54. Gerhart KA, Koziol-McLain J, Lowenstein SR, Whiteneck GG. Quality of life following spinal cord injury: knowledge and attitudes of emergency care providers. Ann Emerg Med. 1994;23(4):807–12.
55. Iezzoni LI. When walking fails. JAMA. 1996;276(19):1609–13.
56. Lagu T, Hannon NS, Rothberg MB, et al. Access to subspecialty care for patients with mobility impairment: a survey. Ann Intern Med. 2013;158(6):441–6.
57. Iezzoni LI. Why increasing numbers of physicians with disability could improve care for patients with disability. AMA J Ethics. 2016;18(10):1041–9.
58. Steinberg AG, Iezzoni LI, Conill A, Stineman M. Reasonable accommodations for medical faculty with disabilities. JAMA. 2002;288(24):3147–54.
59. Neal-Boylan L. An exploration and comparison of the worklife experiences of registered nurses and physicians with permanent physical and/or sensory disabilities. Rehabil Nurs. 2012;37(1):3–10.
60. Neal-Boylan L. Nurses with disabilities: their job descriptions and work expectations. Rehabil Nurs. 2014;39(4):169–77.
61. Neal-Boylan L, Miller M. Treat me like everyone else: the experience of nurses who had disabilities while in school. Nurse Educ. 2017;42(4):176–80.
62. Neal-Boylan LJ. The nurse with a profound disability: a case study. Workplace Health Saf. 2019;67(9):445–51.
63. Neal-Boylan L, Hopkins A, Skeete R, Hartmann SB, Iezzoni LI, Nunez-Smith M. The career trajectories of health care professionals practicing with permanent disabilities. Acad Med. 2012;87(2):172–8.
64. Cooper-Patrick L, Gallo JJ, Gonzales JJ, et al. Race, gender, and partnership in the patient-physician relationship. JAMA. 1999;282(6):583–9.
65. Street RLJ, O'Malley KJ, Cooper LA, Haidet P. Understanding concordance in patient-physician relationships: personal and ethnic dimensions of shared identity. Ann Fam Med. 2008;6(3):198–205.
66. Cohen JJ, Gabriel BA, Terrell C. The case for diversity in the health care workforce. Health Aff (Millwood). 2002;21(5):90–102.
67. Silver JK, Bean AC, Slocum C, et al. Physician workforce disparities and patient care: a narrative review. Heal Equity. 2019;3(1):360–77.
68. Melnick DE. Commentary: balancing responsibility to patients and responsibility to aspiring physicians with disabilities. Acad Med. 2011;86(6):674–6.

69. Altchuler SI. Commentary: granting medical licensure, honoring the Americans with disabilities act, and protecting the public: can we do all three? Acad Med. 2009;84(6):689–91.
70. Sarna L, Bialous SA, Nandy K, Antonio ALM, Yang Q. Changes in smoking prevalences among health care professionals from 2003 to 2010–2011. JAMA. 2014;311(2):197–9.
71. Barnett KG. Physician obesity: the tipping point. Glob Adv Heal Med. 2014;3(6):8–10.
72. DeLisa J, Silverstein R, Thomas P. Commentary: more implications of the 2008 amendments to the Americans with Disabilities Act: influencing institutional policies, practices, and procedures. Acad Med. 2011;86(6):677–9.
73. Eickmeyer SM, Do KD, Kirschner KL, Curry RH. North American medical schools' experience with and approaches to the needs of students with physical and sensory disabilities. Acad Med. 2012;87(5):567–73.
74. Zazove P, Case B, Moreland C, et al. U.S. Medical Schools' compliance with the Americans with Disabilities Act: findings from a national study. Acad Med. 2016;91(7):979–86.
75. U.S. Equal Employment Opportunity Commission. The ADA: Your responsibilities as an employer. https://www.eeoc.gov/facts/ada17.html. Accessed April 16, 2020.
76. Churgay CA, Smith MA, Woodard L, Wallace LS. A survey of family medicine department chairs about faculty with disabilities: a CERA study. Fam Med. 2015;47(10):776–81.
77. Schroeder R, Brazeau CMLR, Zackin F, et al. Do state medical board applications violate the americans with disabilities act? Acad Med. 2009;84(6):776–81.
78. Eddey GE, Robey KL. Considering the culture of disability in cultural competence education. Acad Med. 2005;80(7):706–12.
79. Kirschner KL, Curry RH. Educating health care professionals to care for patients with disabilities. JAMA. 2009;302(12):1334–5.
80. Minihan PM, Robey KL, Long-Bellil LM, et al. Desired educational outcomes of disability-related training for the generalist physician: knowledge, attitudes, and skills. Acad Med. 2011;86(9):1171–8.
81. Iezzoni LI, Long-Bellil LM. Training physicians about caring for persons with disabilities: "nothing about us without us!". Disabil Health J. 2012;5(3):136–9.
82. 110th Congress. An act: to restore the intent and protections of the Americans with Disabilities Act of 1990. 3553 U.S.; 2008.
83. Mid-Atlantic ADA Center. More on Title V. https://www.adainfo.org/content/more-title-v.
84. The Public Health and Welfare, 42 U.S.C. § 12201—12213 (2008).
85. Civil Rights Division. Final rule implementing the ADA Amendments Act of 2008.
86. Basic Definition of Disability, 20 C.F.R. § 404.1505 (2012).
87. Rondinelli R. AMA guides to the evaluation of permanent impairment. In: Genovese E, Katz R, Mayer T, Mueller K, Ranavaya M, editors. Sixth. American Medical Association; 2007.
88. New York State Office of Children and Family Services. Determination of eligibility-overview. https://ocfs.ny.gov/main/cb/vocrehab_manual/04_Eligibility.htm. Accessed April 16, 2020.
89. Towards a common language for functioning, disability, and health: the international classification of functioning, disability, and health (ICF). Geneva: World Health Organization; 2002.

Intersectional Identities

3

Erene Stergiopoulos and Neal Rosenburg

Introduction

Health science programs across the globe are working to bring greater socioeconomic, racial, geographic, and gender diversity to their student populations through fine-tuned admission processes, pipeline programs, post-baccalaureate programs, and bridging courses [1, 2]. These strategies have improved recruitment rates to health science programs, allowing students from underrepresented backgrounds "in the door" [1, 3]. Yet once in the door, these students can face unique barriers and unintended roadblocks to their education and training, ranging from social isolation and stigma to a lack of mentorship and financial support [4, 5].

According to Davidson and colleagues, for students with varying abilities, four significant barriers exist for providing accommodations in health professions education/training [6]. These include the heterogeneity of practice settings; stereotypical views about the capabilities required to deliver safe care; clinician and patient expectations; and a professional environment in which providing accommodations can be challenging [6]. Addressing these barriers requires us to understand how different forms of marginalization interact with one another. In other words, *an intersectional approach is essential*. When we consider supports for students with disabilities, how might other forms of discrimination based on identities including but not limited to race, religion, sexuality, or socioeconomic disadvantage compound the barriers they face? Intersectionality as a framework allows us to shine light on these unique barriers and provides concrete opportunities for action for ensuring meaningful inclusion.

E. Stergiopoulos (✉)
University of Toronto Faculty of Medicine, Toronto, ON, Canada
e-mail: erene.stergiopoulos@mail.utoronto.ca

N. Rosenburg
Professor, College of Health Professions, University of Detroit Mercy, Detroit, MI, USA
e-mail: rosenbns@udmercy.edu

© Springer Nature Switzerland AG 2020
L. M. Meeks, L. Neal-Boylan (eds.), *Disability as Diversity*,
https://doi.org/10.1007/978-3-030-46187-4_3

In this chapter, we aim to define intersectionality in the context of broadly supporting and working with students with varying abilities. In doing so, we explore the social and structural barriers that students from diverse backgrounds face in health science education. We also illustrate how their life experiences provide resilience, grit, tenacity, and clear benefits for themselves as professionals and for their patients. We then consider how disability layers onto other aspects of identity and the impacts of these intersections on students' access to support mechanisms. This also involves understanding the "hidden curriculum" surrounding wellness and diversity and how institutions may unintentionally send mixed messages around student well-being and accessibility through policy, institutional jargon, systemic biases, and program structure and timelines. Finally, this chapter provides practice points for supporting diverse students with disabilities, using the concept of cultural safety. As Kellett and Fitton explain, "cultural safety presents a framework that moves beyond a reduction of complex individual experience to a list of assumed qualities, and the need to understand a group is replaced with acceptance" [7]. Cultural safety, in other words, can inform curricular and structural interventions for educators and programs to support and include students meaningfully and in a student-centered way.

Understanding Intersectionality

Najja is 2 months into his third year of nursing school. He is a first-generation college student, and his parents emigrated from Uganda before he was born. Both his parents worked full time, and as the eldest of four siblings, Najja helped to raise his brothers and sister. He received tuition remission as part of his father's employment benefits at the local state college, where he studied engineering, played varsity basketball, and was president of his student body.

Najja was diagnosed with ADHD before starting nursing school, when he noticed symptoms of inattention while trying to study for the ACT. He passed the first 2 years, remediated two courses, and required extensive support (including a learning specialist, disability accommodations, wellness visits, and a life coach). He is not currently being treated for ADHD. He is registered with disability services and receives time and one half on his exams in a reduced distraction location. He is taking out the full loan amount to cover his tuition and living expenses. He also works 15 hours each weekend at a local gym.

On his first medical-surgical nursing clinical rotation, Najja's clinical preceptor notes that he is "fuzzy" with details and misses too much information. During a meeting of clinical nursing directors, one nursing director expresses concern about the student, doubt that the student will be successful, and concern for patient safety.

Case adapted from Meeks, L. (2018) AAMC.

Intersectionality is an analytical framework that identifies how an individual's identity markers (such as race, class, religion, gender, sexuality, and disability) overlap in unique ways to shape that person's experience of marginalization [8, 9]. An intersectional approach emphasizes the fact that subjective experience is not merely the sum of different identity categories [9, 10]. Instead, our subjectivities emerge from the unique overlapping of different identities that might each result in

> **Box 3.1 Origins of Intersectionality**
> The term intersectionality was coined by black feminist scholar Kimberlé Crenshaw to articulate the unique forms of oppression experienced by black women [9]. Crenshaw found that while existing frameworks like critical race theory centered black men, and feminist theory centered white women, these lenses proved inadequate for understanding black women's experiences. That is, the experiences of being black, and of being a woman, were not merely additive, but intersected in unique ways.

different forms of discrimination and oppression [11, 12] (see Box 3.1). According to Jackson-Best and Edwards (2018), the overlap of different types of disease stigma and the rootedness of stigma in larger systems of inequality and webs of power have pushed researchers to consider different ways to investigate and analyze it [13].

An intersectional approach therefore allows us to ask complex and often difficult questions. It recognizes that by treating students with disabilities (SWDs) as a homogeneous category, we may unintentionally assume that *all* SWDs regardless of race, class, gender, sexuality, socioeconomic status, and religion share the same experiences and priorities [10]. In making these assumptions, whose voices might we ignore in the process? And, who is at risk of being excluded? As intersectionality scholar Ange-Marie Hancock Alfaro explains, "The primary pursuit of this focus is inclusion — incorporating previously ignored and excluded populations into preexisting [sic] frameworks to broaden our knowledge base" [11].

Applying an intersectional lens allows us to critically examine how overarching policies and interventions affect diverse SWDs and how these policies may unintentionally exclude some students. Indeed, criticism of contemporary disability rights activism has argued that the movement often centers the experiences of white, middle-class disabled Americans, which further marginalizes the subjectivities of disabled people of color [14]. Working from a framework of intersectionality, institutions can attend to the unique barriers facing all SWDs and work toward universal design for meaningful inclusion.

Barriers and the Effects of Marginalization

Much like students with disabilities, students from a variety of underrepresented backgrounds face barriers to success in health science education. These barriers often occur at both individual and structural levels [4, 15]. For example, at an individual level, students often lack emotional support and experience social isolation and discrimination. At a structural level, they face roadblocks to accessing financial support, academic advising, mentorship, and professional socialization [4, 15]. While the experiences of students from different underrepresented backgrounds are clearly unique, the parallels across their experiences form an entry point for improving systems and achieving greater inclusion. Most notably, they highlight the need for an intersectional understanding of the student.

Social Isolation

Social isolation appears as an overwhelmingly common experience among students from underrepresented backgrounds. Literature on health science students from racialized, LGBTQ+, economically disadvantaged, and international student communities reveals that these students often feel they don't "fit in" among their peers. This takes an important toll on students' mental health and feelings of belonging in the profession [16].

The literature on the experiences of underrepresented minority (URM) nursing students highlights the ways in which social isolation takes place through a lack of collegiality and lack of support and understanding of cultural differences from peers and educators [17–19]. In studies of African American nursing students in predominantly white programs, students disclosed feelings of alienation and feeling left out in a predominantly white environment [20–22]. In these settings, students described being chosen last as lab partners and being unable to form study groups with other classmates [22].

Similarly, URM medical students found that a lack of social support from peers and administrators was a barrier to success in their programs. They noted that ethnic majority classmates often lacked an appreciation for their diversity experiences and made URM students feel unable to form cross-racial study groups [23]. URM students also felt pressure to represent their entire ethnic or racial community in the classroom or in clinical spaces. This created a self-imposed pressure to do well and perform perfectly [5].

While the literature is scant on the experiences of international students in health science education, existing research reveals similar themes of isolation. In a study of international nursing students from Nigeria, all participants reported experiencing some form of social isolation and lack of relationships with classmates [24]. They also noted that they had been forewarned of the many challenges they would face as nursing students, which they perceived a signal that they do not belong [24].

LGBTQ+ students also face unique forms of isolation, notably from the contrasts between their personal experience and the content of their health science training. As Carabez and colleagues have pointed out, in many North American nursing programs, gender diversity and trans identities are neglected topics [25]. When these topics do appear in curricula, they are often presented in the context of discussing how non-binary status is a risk factor for other stigmatized conditions, including sexually transmitted infections, and mental health conditions [25]. For trans students, this is an incredibly isolating experience; the community they identify with is either not recognized or becomes pathologized in the medical model.

Students from economically disadvantaged backgrounds similarly face social isolation, along with experiences of identity conflict. A study of working-class medical students found that these students experience a conflict between their background of origin and their new professional identities. On the one hand, participants felt they had deviated from the educational expectations of their upbringing, but on the other, they continued to feel they did not belong in their new profession [1]. One student reflecting on her experience growing up in poverty noted the isolation she experienced in her medical class: "Placed at a school attended by mostly middle-class students, this underprivileged experience became part of my identity, and to be different was incredibly isolating" [26].

Discrimination and Microaggressions

Alongside experiences of isolation among students from underrepresented backgrounds, students may also face instances of overt discrimination. In a survey of medical, physiotherapy, and physician assistant students, participants reported witnessing other students, residents, or faculty displaying disparaging or offensive behaviors toward minority groups (including people with strong religious beliefs, non-English speakers, women, and people from URM, LGBTQ+, and economically disadvantaged communities) [27]. Indeed, URM students in nursing and medicine report experiencing microaggressions, everyday racism, and cultural insensitivity from peers on a regular basis [17, 18, 27–30]. This constant reality has a hugely detrimental impact on these students' well-being [16].

Social Capital

Social capital is a sociological concept that refers to the "cause and effect of engaging in social groups" [31]. In other words, it describes the social connections that spark and maintain an individual's belonging to a specific group, such as the health professions. For example, having a parent in healthcare grants the student insider knowledge of the profession, along with access to mentors, research positions, and placement opportunities that may enhance a student's career. Notably, URM students often lack access to social capital that implicitly drives success in health science programs [31]. Meanwhile, non-minority students tend to group together and share study resources through learning communities and informal study groups. This leaves URM students cut off from social and academic communities that facilitate career advancement and learning [31]. Of significant concern, URM students report the further lack of social capital through fewer opportunities for professional socialization and program mentorship [15].

Access to Services and Resources

While health science programs may offer academic and support services, students from underrepresented backgrounds may be aware that these services are available to them [30]. Moreover, this problem is often long-standing, dating from before the student entered health science education. For example, participants in one study of URM nursing students reported that they had lacked appropriate advising since high school and early college years about GPA and prerequisite course requirements [18].

Faculty Role Models and Student Groups

URM students identified the lack of minority faculty to serve as mentors and role models as a challenge for their learning and professional development [19]. Students felt that having professional mentors from the communities they identified with would provide them with necessary role models. Moreover, students reported that a lack of minority student groups (or lack of knowledge about them or lack of time to attend meetings) was an additional barrier [30]. When these groups did exist, students reported them to be very helpful to members by providing motivational support and information about classes and strategies to improve academic performance [30].

Stigma and the Pressure to Remain Invisible

LGBTQ+ health science students frequently face stigma and hostility because of their sexuality or gender identity or lack of understanding by peers or educators. Nearly 30% of LGBTQ+ medical students conceal their sexual identity in medical school [32]. In nursing, LGBTQ+ students and practitioners often choose to remain invisible, when possible, in the workforce [33]. Moreover, these issues are frequently not discussed in professional, institutional settings or in the academic nursing literature [33]. Giddings and Smith explored the experiences of lesbian nurses, who frequently concealed their sexual orientation, isolated themselves, and experienced discrimination, self-loathing, and shame [34].

The pressure to remain invisible resonates strongly with students with less apparent disabilities, who often choose not to disclose due to fear of stigma, and fear of being perceived as weak or inappropriate for health science education [35–37].

Moreover, while LGBTQ+ students can experience overt stigma and discrimination, they also point out the challenges of trying to move their professional cultures in more positive directions, from acceptance to meaningful inclusion. A survey of 261 nurses from the Gay and Lesbian Medical Association found that while 70% of nurses reported working in an LGBTQ+-friendly work environment, participants noted that this did not necessarily make their workplaces welcoming or inclusive. As one participant explained, "I guess it's not that it's friendly, so much as not hostile" [38].

Lack of Personal Resources

Students from underrepresented backgrounds, including URM and socioeconomically disadvantaged students, frequently face a lack of time to focus on their studies due to family responsibilities or a need to work to support themselves [4, 15]. This introduces barriers to academic success, when students must divide their time between their studies, employment, and family responsibilities. The added pressure of loans creates additional challenges, when students seeking leave time from their programs must face the burden of repayment while they are not studying.

Najja is struggling in his first months of his medical-surgical nursing clinical rotation. He feels he can't keep up with studying after long days on the units and preparing for didactics the following day. The nursing clinical instructor and the nursing preceptor on the unit frequently remind him to come to clinical fully prepared by thoroughly reviewing the assigned patient, history, and nursing care plan, but he feels this is impossible given how little time he has at the end of the day to cook, clean, and prepare for the next day. The clinical nursing preceptor speaks to him privately one day to ask if there is something wrong because he is missing important details around patient assignments and doesn't always follow through on tasks discussed at team nursing rounds. He discloses that he has a diagnosis of ADHD, and while the nursing clinical instructor is concerned, she is not sure how she can help. On the units, Najja faces an elderly patient who insists she wants to see "the real nurse" each time he arrives to assess her. The patient is appeased when the white female nursing student in the nursing student cohort takes Najja's place.

Najja feels alone. The other nursing students on the rotation seem to be managing the new workload of patient assignments well and have time to study outside of the hospital. Many of the students drive to the hospital, while Najja commutes by bus nearly an hour each way from his apartment to the hospital and back. A group of classmates in his rotation have created a study group that meets in the evenings, but because he does not have close friends in the group, he is hesitant to join. He feels so behind on the material that he feels he would not be able to participate anyway.

Najja continues to work at the gym 15 hours every weekend. He has maximized his loan and focuses on cooking cheap meals that last several days. He notes that his classmates often buy lunch and sometimes dinner at the cafeteria to save time for studying. His parents voice concerns that he is not calling home as much and they worry he is working too hard.

At the end of his medical-surgical clinical rotation, Najja is exhausted, anxious, and overwhelmed. At his final post medical-surgical clinical check-offs, he manages a "borderline satisfactory." He meets with the clinical nursing instructor to discuss areas to improve before proceeding to his next medical-surgical clinical rotation; Najja discloses that he has been struggling to stay afloat. The clinical nursing instructor recommends that Najja meet with his disability resource professional.

Strengths, Supports, and Sources of Resilience

For health science students from underrepresented backgrounds, flexibility and positive institutional supports can become enablers of success. In a study of African-born international nursing students in the USA, several factors including flexible curricular designs and helpful campus resources supported students' educational experiences [39]. Similarly, a series of focus groups with URM students found that enablers of success included financial support from scholarships, professional exposure programs, and social supports during undergraduate education and medical school (including family, friends, colleagues, religion, and school administration members such as advisors, mentors, and deans) [23]. Moreover, URM students noted that their own identities as minority health professionals facilitated success in their interactions with minority patients that provided an important confidence boost for students who saw the direct impact of their care on patients.

These findings point toward overarching principles for designing universally accessible and inclusive curricula for all students. To do so, programs must make practical commitments to diversity, including policies to ensure safe spaces for all (e.g., zero-tolerance policies for discrimination), as well as supports for students (access to mentors, flexible curricular design, and financial support). Finally, curricular content must similarly demonstrate a commitment to diversity, by teaching about the health needs of diverse communities and encouraging students to reflect on their own social positions in their future work as healthcare providers.

What is likely to occur during a positive and productive meeting between Najja and his disability resource professional? Are additional programmatic supports available to Najja? It is important to recognize the barriers students face are not just about their disability. For Najja, the barriers he faces occur on multiple levels, given his identity as a first-generation African American student with limited financial resources and a recently diagnosed disability. These identities intersect in unique ways and highlight both barriers and sources of resilience for Najja that in turn can inform how his program can support him as he continues his education and training.

Consider the following issues that might come up when Najja meets with his disability resource professional:

- *Support for ADHD.* Najja was recently diagnosed with ADHD. This means he does not have a history of understanding his disability, accommodating his disability, or building compensatory skills. He is currently not receiving treatment for ADHD. Does he have insurance? Is there a wellness team he can tap into at the school?

- *Optimizing learning.* Najja was a successful athlete and leader; he likely learns by *doing* and retains more when studying with groups rather than individually. It may be that practice, for Najja, is the key. Can you open the simulation lab for Najja and a group of students to practice patient interactions, presenting patient cases, and reporting back in a safe environment? Making this educational opportunity available to all students would also provide an opportunity for universal design, whereby all students can benefit from improved access based on their learning needs and goals. Najja might also benefit from clinical skills remediation, additional observation on the unit, a mentor that provides feedback in vivo, or working with 4th year nursing student directly.

- *Mentorship.* As a first-generation college student, Najja may not be as experienced with nursing and the team structure model in training environments. Additionally, he may not have the support system his classmates have or the family lineage of medicine. He has been incredibly resilient so far in managing the novelty of the clinical environment. To support him further, could he benefit from a peer nursing student mentor? Could he be paired with a minority advisor or faculty mentor to help him successfully navigate the landscape and provide a safe exchange of frustrations and concerns that may be culturally specific or informed?
- *Financial support.* Najja continues to work 15 hours every weekend, possibly late into the evening. He may be having financial difficulties. Financial stress and burden might be contributing to lack of sleep, anxiety, and exacerbating symptoms such as inattention. These may also be impacting his ability to study and prepare patient nursing plans. Could he benefit from a review of finances and financial need? He may indeed benefit from access to needs-based scholarships or reduced-cost housing.
- *Curricular flexibility and universal design.* Institutions can enhance access to their curriculum through the use of universally designed curricula and building some flexibility into their programs. For example, incorporating some white space each week where students who require appointments to maintain their health are able to do this without the added burden of missing class or having to disclose a need and get a "doctor's note." Moreover, creating support systems for all students, including advisors and academic support counselors, can help to support students with a wide variety of learning needs.

(Case and recommendations adapted from Meeks L (2018) AAMC)

Health science students do not enter their education and training as "blank slates" [40]. Instead, they draw from diverse life experiences to develop a nuanced professional identity and a sense of accountability for the patient populations they serve. Zhou describes a kind of "empathic privilege" she retains when she has encountered patients from a similarly socioeconomically disadvantaged background to the one she grew up in [26]. She writes, "To come from [poverty] grants a different, more subtle form of privilege beyond that of wealth and social networks. I call it an 'empathic privilege' that allows one to be more cognizant of the social determinants of health that patients often leave unspoken when seeking medical care" [26]. This empathic privilege resonates strongly with authors who advocate for the inclusion of people with disabilities in health science training, arguing that these providers deliver "more holistic and empathic [sic] care" to their patients [6, 41, 42].

There are clear educational benefits to increased diversity within health science education. As Rumala and Cason (2007) outline, diversity enhances professionalism, educational experiences for all students, and cultural sensitivity via cross-cultural exchange [43]. These benefits also extend to the population level. From the perspective of social justice, diverse students represent the populations they serve, which works toward creating a more equitable society and directly benefits patients [44]. Moreover, diverse students have the ability to provide culturally competent care and to enhance overall cultural competence across the healthcare workforce [45]. Minority providers are more likely to provide care to minority, underserved, disadvantaged, and low-income populations [43], while diversity in the healthcare workforce is linked with improved healthcare quality and access for minority patients [46].

Disability as an Added Layer of Stigma: Effects on Disclosure and Accommodations

When we consider the intersectional identities of diverse students with disabilities, we must consider how students might experience the compounded effects stigma and discrimination from both their disability and other intersecting identities. Commonly, students from underrepresented backgrounds face a lack of understanding of their unique identities from peers and faculty. They face ignorance, misconceptions, and myths and often find themselves alone in having to dispel them while educating those around them. In Najja's case, he might feel compelled to explain his disability to a concerned supervisor and to educate them on how this affects his performance. African American nursing students in predominantly white programs found that nursing curricula did not always include cultural differences and were not inclusive, ultimately finding themselves having to take on the role of teacher to correct misconceptions [47]. Similarly, Indigenous nursing students struggle with stereotypes and racist attitudes, isolation, and assumptions about cultural identity [29].

In addition to the existing stigma of being different from one's classmates, adding a layer of disability carries implications about competence, technical standards, and patient safety [36, 48–50]. Students from underrepresented backgrounds often face personal expectations to persist in the face of multiple roadblocks, often leading them to avoid seeking support because they do not want to be seen as different [17, 24, 36].

There are also specific financial and social barriers that may influence a student's access to accommodations. Without appropriate mentors and professional supports, students from underrepresented backgrounds may not feel able to advocate for themselves and may wish to avoid standing out and feeling like a burden. From a financial perspective, students require medical documentation to receive approved accommodations; yet if the student does not have a primary care provider and does not have insurance, they face additional barriers. In Najja's case, he has not undergone a complete psychoeducational assessment to assess his learning needs and potential targets for learning strategies. If an assessment is not available through his school, how will he access this given his limited finances?

Given these unique and layered barriers, how can programs best support diverse SWDs? Health science programs offer complex systems of support to students – including disability, financial, academic, and career support. Yet students often lack knowledge about available supports and may not know where to find the necessary information to access them. As a result, transparency, knowledge, and communication among these services are essential for navigating the multiple barriers a student may face. In Najja's case, he requires a series of coordinated referrals and cross-training by the professionals managing these services to best support him. For example, his disability resource professional could better help him to succeed by recognizing how his financial situation has compounded his academic difficulties and connecting him with financial services at his school for housing and scholarship support. Najja might also benefit from connecting with organized social initiatives at his school, including existing URM student groups and faculty mentorship programs. Knowledge of these services and coordination among them is essential for ensuring that students receive support that is tailored to their unique needs and identities.

The Hidden Curriculum

To understand the barriers affecting diverse students, we must also understand the mixed messages they receive throughout their training. The hidden curriculum is a concept that refers to the commonly held understandings and assumptions that exist within health science education that are shaped by policies, practices, resource allocation, and institutional slang [51]. The hidden curriculum often contrasts with the formal curriculum – which consists of didactic and experiential learning that students are explicitly taught during their training.

The hidden curriculum is a useful concept for uncovering mixed messages that students may encounter in their education. That is, while health science curricula may *formally* promote accessibility, equity, diversity, and inclusion, students often in fact receive conflicting messages about the "appropriateness" of coming from a diverse background in the healthcare milieu [52]. For example, mixed messages around wellness in resident education reveal that while programs promote wellness and self-care, residents face a reality in which they are rewarded for self-sacrifice and over-work [53]. Similarly, a survey of physician assistant, physiotherapy, and medical student perspectives showed that while students believed their school was committed to diversity, they also reported that discriminatory experiences were still highly prevalent in individual interactions with fellow students and faculty members [27].

Understanding these mixed messages demands understanding the culture of an organization and recognizing the attitudinal barriers that may limit students from diverse backgrounds from seeking support for a disability. It clarifies the barriers that diverse students continue to face, even when schools already officially promote diversity and inclusion in their missions. This understanding also helps us uncover new areas for curricular, faculty, and administrative development to achieve meaningful inclusion.

Conclusion: Practice Points for Supporting Diverse Students with Disabilities

As health science programs continue their missions to promote equity, diversity, and inclusion, they must pay close attention to the effects of layered stigma and mixed messages that may present unintended barriers for diverse students to access support. As Neal-Boylan suggests, the programmatic and institutional changes needed to achieve meaningful inclusion of students with disabilities must occur on four fronts: within policy, education, stakeholder attitudes, and practice [45].

To this end, we propose a cultural safety model to support all aspects of students' identities in their education, extending across institutional policy, educational curricula, stakeholders, and clinical practice. The following practice points are suggested for ensuring cultural safety for diverse students, to honor their intersectional identities, resilience, and the strengths they bring to their chosen health professions.

Information systems:

Programs should pay attention to the language they use in curricular content and websites for student support. This can combat the assumption that many students face that they must remain invisible. For example, they may ask:

- Is there a statement about inclusivity student support services websites?
- Is information about accommodations for disabilities transparent and easily accessible on the program's website?
- Do application and demographic forms allow for more than a two-gender option? Do they allow students to enter their preferred name and/or pronouns?

Creating safe spaces:

- Does the program have specific zero-tolerance policies around racism, homophobia, and transphobia?
- Are there student-led interest groups organized around underrepresented identities such as African American, underrepresented minority, LGBTQ+, or disabled students?
- Are there gender-neutral and accessible bathrooms available to students?

Designing inclusive curricula:

- Does the curriculum include education about caring for underrepresented groups in healthcare? Does it include concepts of cultural safety?
- Does teaching around the health effects of marginalization include voices and perspectives from people from those marginalized communities (i.e., lived experience panels, co-taught sessions by patients)?
- Does the curriculum include opportunities for students to self-reflect on their own intersectional identities and the ways in which their life experiences influence their professional identities and career trajectories?

Creating mentorship opportunities:

- In the admissions process, are their opportunities for applicants from underrepresented backgrounds to connect with students or faculty for support in their application?
- For current students, are there opportunities for students from underrepresented backgrounds to connect with faculty or senior student mentors for advice, guidance, and support?

Advocating for diversity:

- Are there advocacy initiatives in place at the school that promote diversity?
- Are there opportunities for students to become involved in diversity advocacy initiatives?
- Are there clinical practicum opportunities available to students who wish to develop specific competencies in caring for diverse patients?

Adapted from Kellet and Fitton (2017) Framework on supporting trans nursing students [7]

For Najja, a cultural safety framework would allow him to thrive in his program where his unique life experiences are seen as sources of resilience and expertise for training in healthcare. This means designing inclusive curricula that represent the healthcare needs of diverse populations and the social determinants that affect them in unique ways. It also means ensuring access to student support services (disability, academic, financial) that are transparent and coordinated to support him as a whole person. Finally, this means creating safe spaces and mentorship opportunities to ensure rich social networks of support where Najja can thrive and build on his strengths as a leader and team player.

References

1. Mathers J, Parry J. Why are there so few working-class applicants to medical schools? Learning from the success stories. Med Educ. 2009;43(3):219–28.
2. Frenk J, Chen L, Bhutta ZA, Cohen J, Crisp N, Evans T, et al. Health professionals for a new century: transforming education to strengthen health systems in an interdependent world. Lancet. 2010;376(9756):1923–58.
3. Young K. Working towards widening participation in nurse education. Br J Nurs. 2016;25(2):112–6.
4. White BJ, Fulton JS. Common experiences of African American nursing students: an integrative review. Nurs Educ Perspect. 2015;36:150417122026003.
5. Orom H, Semalulu T, Underwood WI. The social and learning environments experienced by underrepresented minority medical students: a narrative review. Acad Med. 2013;88(11):1765.
6. Davidson PM, Rushton CH, Dotzenrod J, Godack CA, Baker D, Nolan MN. Just and realistic expectations for persons with disabilities practicing nursing. AMA J Ethics. 2016;18(10):1034–40.
7. Kellett P, Fitton C. Supporting transvisibility and gender diversity in nursing practice and education: embracing cultural safety. Nurs Inq. 2017;24(1):e12146.
8. Hancock A-M. Intersectionality: an intellectual history. Oxford, New York: Oxford University Press; 2016. 272 p.
9. Crenshaw K. Mapping the margins: Intersectionality, identity politics and violence against women of colour. In: Crenshaw K, Gotanda N, Peller G, Thomas K, editors. Critical race theory: the key writings that informed the movement. New York: New York Press; 1995. p. 357–83.
10. Hankivsky O, Reid C, Cormier R, Varcoe C, Clark N, Benoit C, et al. Exploring the promises of intersectionality for advancing women's health research. Int J Equity Health. 2010;9(1):5.
11. Hancock A-M. Intersectionality as a normative and empirical paradigm. Polit Gend. 2007;3(2):248–54.
12. Simien EM. Doing Intersectionality research: from conceptual issues to practical examples. Polit Gend. 2007;3(2):264–71.
13. Jackson-Best F, Edwards N. Stigma and intersectionality: a systematic review of systematic reviews across HIV/AIDS, mental illness, and physical disability. BMC Public Health. 2018;18(1):919.
14. Frederick A, Shifrer D. Race and disability: from analogy to intersectionality. Soc Race Ethnicity. 2019;5(2):200–14.
15. Loftin C, Newman SD, Dumas BP, Gilden G, Bond ML. Perceived barriers to success for minority nursing students: an integrative review. ISRN Nurs [Internet]. 2012 May 30 [cited 2019 Jul 7]; 2012. Available from: https://www.ncbi.nlm.nih.gov/pmc/articles/PMC3369480/.
16. Perry SP, Hardeman R, Burke SE, Cunningham B, Burgess DJ, van Ryn M. The impact of everyday discrimination and racial identity centrality on African American Medical Student well-being: a report from the Medical Student CHANGE Study. J Racial Ethn Health Disparities. 2016;3(3):519–26.
17. France N, Fields A, Garth K. "You're just shoved to the corner:" The lived experience of black nursing students being isolated and discounted. A pilot study. Visions J Rogerian Nurs Sci. 2004;12(1):28–36.
18. Gardner J. Barriers influencing the success of racial and ethnic minority students in nursing programs. J Transcult Nurs. 2005;16(2):155–62.
19. Mills-Wisneski S. Minority students perceptions concerning the presence of minority faculty: inquiry and discussion. J Multicult Nurs Health. 2005;11:49–55.
20. White BJ. African American nurses describe pre-licensure education experiences: a qualitative study. J Prof Nurs. 2018;34(5):346–51.
21. Murray TA. Factors that promote and impede the academic success of African American students in prelicensure nursing education: an integrative review. J Nurs Educ. 2015;54(9):S74–81.

22. Coleman LD. Experiences of African American students in a predominantly White, Two-Year Nursing Program. ABNF J. 2008;19(1):8–13.
23. Odom KL, Roberts LM, Johnson RL, Cooper LA. Exploring obstacles to and opportunities for professional success among ethnic minority medical students. Acad Med. 2007;82(2):146.
24. Sanner S, Wilson AH, Samson LF. The experiences of international nursing students in a baccalaureate nursing program. J Prof Nurs. 2002;18(4):206–13.
25. Carabez R, Pellegrini M, Mankovitz A, Eliason M, Ciano M, Scott M. "Never in all my years…": nurses' education about LGBT health. J Prof Nurs. 2015;31(4):323–9.
26. Zhou SY. Underprivilege as privilege. JAMA. 2017;318(8):705–6.
27. Dhaliwal JS, Crane LA, Valley MA, Lowenstein SR. Student perspectives on the diversity climate at a U.S. medical school: the need for a broader definition of diversity. BMC Res Notes. 2013;6:154.
28. Beagan BL. "Is this worth getting into a big fuss over?" everyday racism in medical school. Med Educ. 2003;37(10):852–60.
29. Weaver HN. Indigenous nurses and professional education: friends or foes? J Nurs Educ. 2001;40(6):252–8.
30. Amaro DJ, Abriam-Yago K, Yoder M. Perceived barriers for ethnically diverse students in nursing programs. J Nurs Educ. 2006;45(7):247–54.
31. Vaughan S, Sanders T, Crossley N, O'Neill P, Wass V. Bridging the gap: the roles of social capital and ethnicity in medical student achievement. Med Educ. 2015;49(1):114–23.
32. Mansh M, White W, Gee-Tong L, Lunn MR, Obedin-Maliver J, Stewart L, et al. Sexual and gender minority identity disclosure during undergraduate medical education: "in the closet" in medical school. Acad Med. 2015;90(5):634–44.
33. Levesque P. Meeting the needs of the transgender nursing student. Nurse Educ. 2015;40(5):244–8.
34. Giddings LS, Smith MC. Stories of lesbian in/visibility in nursing. Nurs Outlook. 2001;49(1):14–9.
35. Meeks LM, Jain NR. Learners and physicians with disabilities: accessibility, action, and inclusion in medical education. Washington, DC: Association of American Medical Colleges; 2018.
36. Neal-Boylan L, Miller M. Treat me like everyone Else: the experience of nurses who had disabilities while in school. Nurse Educ. 2017;42(4):176–80.
37. Chew-Graham CA, Rogers A, Yassin N. "I wouldn't want it on my CV or their records": medical students' experiences of help-seeking for mental health problems. Med Educ. 2003;37(10):873–80.
38. Eliason MJ, DeJoseph J, Dibble S, Deevey S, Chinn P. Lesbian, gay, bisexual, transgender, and queer/questioning nurses' experiences in the workplace. J Prof Nurs. 2011;27(4):237–44.
39. Ezeonwu M. Baccalaureate nursing education experiences of African-Born Nurses in the United States. J Nurs Educ. 2019;58(5):281–9.
40. Fergus KB, Teale B, Sivapragasam M, Mesina O, Stergiopoulos E. Medical students are not blank slates: positionality and curriculum interact to develop professional identity. Perspect Med Educ. 2018;7(1):5–7.
41. Mogensen L, Hu W. "A doctor who really knows …": a survey of community perspectives on medical students and practitioners with disability. BMC Med Educ. 2019;19(1):1–10.
42. Shrewsbury D. Disability and participation in the professions: examples from higher and medical education. Disabil Soc. 2015;30(1):87–100.
43. Rumala BB, Cason FD. Recruitment of underrepresented minority students to medical school: minority medical student organizations, an untapped resource. J Natl Med Assoc. 2007;99(9):1000–9.
44. Easterbrook A, Bulk L, Ghanouni P, Lee M, Opini B, Roberts E, et al. The legitimization process of students with disabilities in health and human service educational programs in Canada. Disabil Soc. 2015;30(10):1505–20.
45. Neal-Boylan L, Marks B, McCulloh KJ. Supporting nurses and nursing students with disabilities: AJN. Am J Nurs. 2015;115(10):11.

46. Powe NR, Cooper LA. Diversifying the racial and ethnic composition of the physician workforce. Ann Intern Med. 2004;141(3):223.
47. Jordan JD. Rethinking race and attrition in nursing programs: a hermeneutic inquiry. J Prof Nurs. 1996;12(6):382–90.
48. Neal-Boylan L, Smith D. Nursing students with physical disabilities: dispelling myths and correcting misconceptions. Nurse Educ. 2016;41(1):13–8.
49. Neal-Boylan L, Hopkins A, Skeete R, Hartmann SB, Iezzoni LI, Nunez-Smith M. The career trajectories of health care professionals practicing with permanent disabilities. Acad Med. 2012;87(2):172–8.
50. Ashcroft TJ, Lutfiyya ZM. Nursing educators' perspectives of students with disabilities: a grounded theory study. Nurse Educ Today. 2013;33(11):1316–21.
51. Hafferty FW. Beyond curriculum reform: confronting medicine's hidden curriculum. Acad Med. 1998;73(4):403–7.
52. Stergiopoulos E, Fernando O, Martimianakis MA. "Being on both sides": Canadian medical students' experiences with disability, the hidden curriculum, and professional identity construction. Acad Med. 2018;93(10):1550–9.
53. Meeks LM, Ramsey J, Lyons M, Spencer AL, Lee WW. Wellness and work: mixed messages in residency training. J Gen Intern Med. 2019;34(7):1352–5.

Creating a Program Within a Culture of Inclusion

4

Lina Mehta, Lisa M. Meeks, Marie Lusk,
Bonnielin K. Swenor, and Nichole L. Taylor

A Commitment to Equal Access: An Overview

Per federal law [1, 2], institutions are responsible for engaging students with disabilities in an interactive process to determine reasonable accommodations (Fig. 4.1). Having an informed, transparent, and deliberate process within a structured office is an efficient way of meeting these requirements and displays a commitment to equal access for qualified students with disabilities. A structured and transparent approach also ensures standardization of process across the institution. In addition, students who require access to accommodations may be more inclined to request accommodations at institutions where a formalized and transparent process is in place.

The original version of this chapter is revised and updated. The correction to this chapter can be found at https://doi.org/10.1007/978-3-030-46187-4_14

L. Mehta (✉)
Associate Dean for Admissions, Professor of Radiology, Case Western Reserve School of Medicine, Cleveland, OH, USA
e-mail: lxm12@case.edu

L. M. Meeks
Assistant Professor, Department of Family Medicine, Director of MDisability Education, The University of Michigan Medical School, Ann Arbor, MI, USA

M. Lusk
Director, Student Accessibility Services for Rush University, Chicago, IL, USA

B. K. Swenor
Associate Professor, Ophthalmology at the Wilmer Eye Institute at Johns Hopkins and Epidemiology at the Johns Hopkins Bloomberg School of Public Health, Baltimore, MD, USA

N. L. Taylor
Assistant Dean of Student Affairs; Associate Professor Department of Anesthesiology, Wake Forest School of Medicine, Winston-Salem, NC, USA

© Springer Nature Switzerland AG 2020
L. M. Meeks, L. Neal-Boylan (eds.), *Disability as Diversity*,
https://doi.org/10.1007/978-3-030-46187-4_4

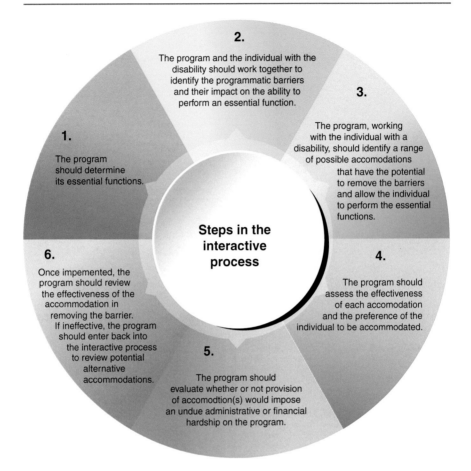

Fig. 4.1 Steps in the interactive process. (Adapted with permission from the Association of American Medical Colleges [3])

Improving Outcomes and Accessibility

Developing a program that is committed to equal access for students with disabilities may improve student performance and retention. When students engage with the disabilities office and barriers are removed, they benefit from full access to the curriculum and are better able display their knowledge. Equal access must also be delivered via a high-efficiency and specialized accommodative process. Health science education programs are fast-paced with high-stakes; the rigor and speed of these generally demanding curricula require expedited responses to barriers so that students do not lag behind. Transparency of the process is beneficial for students, faculty, and staff and helps to expedite the process by ensuring every stakeholder is aware of the steps for requesting accommodations. For students, transparency can

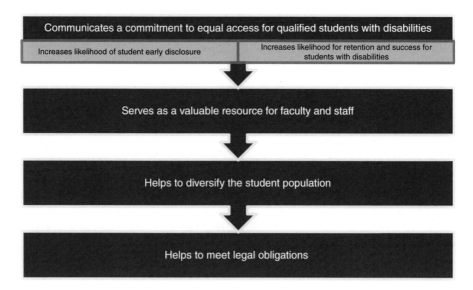

Fig. 4.2 Benefits of a comprehensive program

also help remove some of the stigma and fear that can be associated with accommodation requests, while transparency for faculty and staff will lead to greater understanding and ease of referral for students who disclose a disability.

Programs that seek to diversify their student bodies by including students with disabilities will also be well served by a formalized and transparent process that communicates the institution's commitment to disability inclusion. Finally, a comprehensive program (Fig. 4.2) will serve as a resource for all stakeholders, including students, faculty, staff, and administration, and will help to ensure that the institution is meeting its legal and philosophical commitments to qualified students with disabilities.

Developing an Accessible Application and Admissions Process

As noted, it is against federal law to discriminate against persons with disabilities, and this should be amplified throughout the program, beginning with the admissions process. Rather than serving as a point of entry for students with disabilities, admissions processes can often function as a roadblock, with stereotypes and stigma presenting some of the largest barriers for students with disabilities in the health professions [3–5].

There are a number of stereotypes regarding disability that may lead to preconceived ideas or assumptions about students and their abilities, further leading to dangerous assumptions about the inability of a person with a disability to complete a health science program. Not all disabilities present in the same way, and admissions decisions that are grounded in assumptions about an applicant's functional abilities or that are based on limited information about the student's abilities introduce the potential for bias in the process. Without a full understanding of a student's experiences and abilities, assumptions may be made, which can lead to discriminatory outcomes.

Admissions decision-makers, including application screeners, interviewers, and admissions committee members, should be trained to evaluate a candidate's qualifications and candidacy based on criteria set by the program. It is not the role of these decision-makers to assess whether or not an applicant can meet the technical standards of the program, as this will be determined through an interactive process with an informed disability services professional. Instead, decision-makers must objectively assess a candidate's qualifications [6].

Stigma, in this case, a negative association made by others in association with a particular disability, often prevents students from disclosing a disability for fear that they will be seen as less qualified than their nondisabled peers or that the disclosure will impact their prospects for admission. When students do not disclose their disability at the appropriate time, they also neglect to request accommodations that may be critical to their success. For this reason, it is important for admissions teams to promote a culture of inclusion by including disability in all diversity narratives and by using welcoming language in all communications. A welcoming vision/mission statement can help to set the tone for applicants (see Box 4.1).

Admissions teams and health science education programs can remove many of the barriers faced by students with disabilities and work to actively recruit this population through educating admissions stakeholders and through subtle yet impactful changes to their language and processes.

First, admissions teams should be familiar with the Americans with Disabilities Act Amendment Act (ADAAA) (2008) [1]. This law governs equal access and ensures protection against discrimination for applicants and students with disabilities. Training admissions teams to recognize and manage unconscious biases about persons with disabilities is also beneficial. The greatest education can often result from sharing stories of current practicing healthcare providers who have

---

Box 4.1 Case Western Reserve University Vision/Mission Statement
"Case Western Reserve University aspires to be an inclusive environment, believing the creative energy and variety of insights that result from diversity are a vital component of the intellectual rigor and social fabric of the university. As a scholarly community, CWRU is inclusive of all people of all racial, ethnic, cultural, socioeconomic, national and international backgrounds, welcoming diversity of thought, pedagogy, religion, sexual orientation, gender identity/expression, political affiliation, and disability….."

disabilities. Campaigns like the #DocsWithDisabilities [7] and #NursesWithDisabilities hashtag campaigns on Twitter [7] and podcasts about providers with disabilities [8, 9] serve as inexpensive, easily accessible resources for training admissions teams. Through these stories, teams can challenge their perceptions of what it means to be a provider with a disability.

Point of Contact

Individuals who serve in an evaluative capacity in the admissions process should not serve as points of contact for accommodations. Ideally, a neutral third-party expert, such as a disabilities resources professional (DRP), would serve in this capacity instead. By introducing a neutral party, applicants are permitted to engage in an exploratory conversation with an unbiased expert who can address many of their questions and potentially alleviate reservations, clarify technical standards, and/or provide additional information about procedural competencies and requirements of the program.

Communicating Policy and Procedure to Applicants with Disabilities

Policies and procedures related to requesting accommodations should be clearly posted in multiple sites, relevant websites, and in relevant admissions materials (see Boxes 4.2 and 4.3). Prominent posting of this information helps students to better understand when and how to best disclose a disability.

Box 4.2 Sample Interview Invitation Language
"If you require accommodations to access the interview day, please contact our disability services office at xxx-555-5555, or at contact@x.edu."

Box 4.3 Sample Acceptance Letter Wording
"Case Western Reserve School of Medicine welcomes qualified students with disabilities who meet the technical standards of the program, with or without accommodations. Our technical standards are listed below. If you are a student with a disability who needs reasonable accommodations to fully participate in the School of Medicine and its associated programs, please contact disability resources at contact@x.edu or xxx-555-5555. To ensure equitable access, students are encouraged to register with Disability Resources far in advance of the start of the program."

Making Space for Dialogue About Disability

Some applicants, particularly those interested in the health sciences, may disclose their disability in their application, as many applicants were first motivated to enter into the field based on their own experiences. As such, admissions team members should receive training on how to approach disability topics with sensitivity and how to create a safe space for any related discussion. An admissions team member may be hesitant to center discussion around a disclosed disability, for fear of appearing biased or discriminatory. However, silence around a disclosed disability may be perceived as disingenuous for the applicant and may leave the applicant feeling like disability is a taboo topic [3, 10]. Methods of opening up a safe space for dialogue may include such questions such as:

1. *What challenges do you think you may face as a student?*
2. *Tell me about a challenge you have faced during your life and how it has shaped who you are today.*
3. *How have your past experiences shaped your attitudes toward healthcare?*

Admissions committees should consider incorporating these questions into all applicant interviews in a standardized fashion, such that they are applicable to all interviewees. This avoids singling out those with disabilities yet allows an applicant the freedom to discuss their disability should they wish. Even if an applicant has a visible disability, no assumptions should be made regarding potential need for accommodations or level of functional limitation. Admissions decisions should remain grounded in holistic candidacy evaluation, not on supposition.

Admissions committees must ensure that their program's technical standards are not discriminatory and that the technical standards focus on the attributes needed *prior* to admission, not the essential functions of eventual employment or the skills that will be learned *after* matriculation. (For a full discussion of technical standards, see Chap. 9.) For example, the ability to insert an IV is not an appropriate technical standard, as this is a skill taught after matriculation. Finally, information regarding the availability of reasonable accommodations should be infused into the technical standards language [6].

The admissions team's responsibility is to accept the best applicants for the program, to maintain an equitable and fair process, and to ensure a diverse student body, one that is representative of the population in general, which includes individuals with disabilities. Programs can implement the recommendations listed in Box 4.4 to develop a more accessible admissions process.

Box 4.4 Recommendations for Admissions Committees and Admissions Offices
1. Be aware of the barriers for students with disabilities and provide training to assist admissions teams in reducing these barriers.
2. Clearly post the program's technical standards. This will allow prospective students with disabilities to make informed decisions about the "fit" of your program.

3. Designate a specialized disability resource professional (DRP) as the contact person for questions regarding accommodations. This will minimize unwanted disclosures and reduce the chance that a student's disability will become a consideration for admission.
4. Make sure your admissions materials and websites are accessible.
5. Make a statement. Clearly communicate the process to disclose a disability and to request accommodations, and state your commitment to inclusion.

Once a student with a disability is accepted and then matriculates to a program, the student should receive clear instruction that further guides them through the process of accessing the disability resource office. This guidance may come through the admissions office or other relevant office or directly from the disability resource office. This approach allows the disability resource professional (DRP) and student to work on accommodation requests prior to starting the health science program and enabling a smooth transition for the student with a disability.

Transparency of Disability Policies

It is important that accommodation policies and processes are clearly outlined in relevant admissions application, interview, and acceptance materials; this information should also be included in key locations on the website. The application process for accommodations and the steps of the disclosure and application process should be clearly outlined. A complicated or ill-defined process can serve as a disincentive to disclosure and may cause confusion for incoming students, faculty, and staff.

The entire accommodation process (request form, intake/interactive process, documentation review, accommodation creation, and implementation to faculty) should be transparent and should be available on the website for faculty, staff, prospective, and current students to review. Students should also know that they maintain full control of the process and can stop the interactive process at any time should they change their minds about disclosure or requesting accommodations.

Developing a Program

Program Infrastructure

Given the complexity of disability law and the level of nuance that is intrinsic to the provision of disability resources, institutions should develop a specialized disability resource office that addresses all aspects of disability – including accommodation requests, implementation, and the provision of programmatic and institutional guidance on accessibility. Within this structure, programs should hire a specialized disability resource professional (DRP) who is responsible for ensuring equal access for students with disabilities and for determining reasonable accommodations in accordance with federal laws. The parent institution should also provide scaffolding for the office by including disability in its diversity statement.

Hiring a Disability Resource Professional (DRP) for Health Science Programs

Specialization in the Field

Students requesting accommodations in health science programs (e.g., medicine, physical therapy, nursing, dentistry, pharmacology, occupational and physical therapy, and others) often encounter complexities that are unique to the course of study. DRPs must have a broad awareness of, and facility with, these areas. These complexities may include nuanced and variable clinical environments, restrictive or confusing technical standards, clinical competencies, and licensing requirements that result in varied thresholds of "reasonableness" when determining accommodations. In the clinical domain, as opposed to other environments, reasonable accommodations must not only consider program standards but must also take patient safety into consideration. In addition, clinical accommodations must not alter the essential functions of a course or program. DRPs must also have a clear understanding of board/licensing exams and state licensing agency criteria, which may vary considerably [11].

DRPs housed in traditional undergraduate programs may lack expertise in clinical curricula, clinical accommodations, specialized assistive and adaptive medical equipment and technology, clinical hierarchy, tailored professional communication, and electronic medical record systems, to name a few. They may also lack expertise in the Department of Education (DOE), the Department of Justice (DOJ), and the Office of Civil Rights (OCR) guidance or case law in health science education. Additionally, DRPs without extensive health science backgrounds will likely be unfamiliar with accommodating students in novel assessment environments such as clinical rotations, clerkships, internships, preceptorships, standardized patient exams, and objective-structured clinical examinations (OSCEs), which may make determinations about reasonable and effective accommodations in the clinical environment more challenging. In order to implement a thorough and well-informed interactive process, DRPs must develop expertise in the aforementioned clinical and legal domains and must spend considerable time learning about their respective health science programs. Rotating through their program's clerkships and other clinical experiences will provide DRPs with additional insight into, and understanding of, programmatic requirements and reasonable, applicable accommodations; this exposure will also help to spark creative solutions [3].

Competencies for Health Science Disability Service Professional

As noted, there is a sharp learning curve for traditional DRPs who seek to specialize in health science programs. Given the absence of formal credentialing and guidelines, programs may be challenged in the hiring process when attempting to determine the ideal background and experiences of a health science DRP, while the DRP themselves may face challenges in gaining the relevant experience and knowledge for the field. Core competencies begin with requirements for a generalist DRP (one who works with students in traditional undergraduate domains) who maintain competence and knowledge in three areas – the Americans with Disabilities Act (ADA), determination of reasonable accommodations, and reading and interpreting relevant documentation. In addition to this generalist knowledge, health science DRPs must also maintain information about and understanding of clinical assessments, clinical accommodations, modified equipment, assistive technology, and clinical culture.

Given the lack of formal credentialing for DRPs, qualified individuals may come from a variety of educational and experiential backgrounds including legal (Master in Law or Juris Doctorate of Law); educational (PhD or Masters in Education, a masters in learning disabilities or special education, school psychology, clinical or experimental psychology); or a degree in rehabilitation counseling (CRC). While the majority of individuals who come to this field do so through the educational pipelines mentioned above, there are an infinite number of pathways for entry. Regardless of the educational or experiential background, a health science DRP needs to develop and maintain specific expertise as outlined in the sample job descriptions (see Appendix A).

The need for specialization in health science disability services is clear. Programs that seek excellence and are committed to inclusion should train an individual to serve in the DRP role. While different programs may have varied needs, identifying a point person who can accurately and robustly represent the interactive process and the institution is required by the ADA.

Dual Roles in Disability Resources

As noted above, the institution must identify a point person for disability-related requests. The key contact in the accommodations process is ideally a neutral DRP. When a program does not have a DRP, the key contact should be someone who *does not* serve in an evaluative or academic decision-making role. To remove bias and the potential for discrimination, individuals who hold an evaluative faculty position, who serve in the role of admissions or student affairs dean, or who function as the director of the program should *not* be the points of contact for an accommodations request. It is important to note, however, that students often disclose first to faculty or to others with whom they feel comfortable. In these cases, the person to whom the student discloses should refer the student to the disability resource office and the DRP.

Key Point

Individuals who hold an evaluative faculty positions, who serve in the role of admissions or student affairs dean, or who function as the director of the program should *not* be the point of contact for an accommodations request. No diagnostic documentation should be shared with faculty or administrators in the process, and students should know that they can stop the interactive process at any time.

The Use of Committees for Decision-Making

Some schools utilize a committee approach in determining reasonable accommodations. When using a committee, a DRP should ideally lead the committee in order to reduce potential bias, to ensure a robust and fair process, and to inform best practice in the area of disability resources in health sciences. In these instances, the DRP can share the functional limitations and barriers experienced by the student, but *should not* share diagnostic documentation. The literature suggests a number of concerns regarding committees including the sharing of information and sensitive documentation among individuals who may, at some point, have an evaluative role [12]. Additionally, students may be hesitant to disclose disability or request accommodations if they know that a committee of faculty or deans will be making the determination. Even when steps are taken to protect privacy, the perception that a group of individuals will review their documentation may be enough to keep students from disclosing a disability. There are additional drawbacks to using a committee approach. When faculty members are involved with the committee, having prior knowledge of a disability can lead to unconscious bias and actions toward a student that may be expressed in more subjective evaluations or opportunities. Faculty may also unknowingly start to view the student in the role of a patient and unintentionally treat them differently. In addition to relational concerns, there may also be legal concerns about the use of a committee. For example, if a committee substitutes their clinical knowledge for the recommendations of the treating provider and fails to approve an accommodation request as a result, the required interactive process has not been followed. Committees may also meet at defined time intervals, such as monthly, which may result in delays for decision-making, which, in a fast-paced health science program, can prove costly to the student. The ADA requires that accommodation requests be reviewed and implemented within a reasonable amount of time. Finally, when students know that multiple parties are aware of their status as a person with a disability, fear of bias against them increases.

Building a Program for Access

There are several models of access followed at universities and health science campuses across the country. These include the centralized model, liaison model, health science model, and program model. The following models are offered as examples, but with an understanding that programs vary in their structure (e.g., stand-alone vs. large academic centers) and their resources. For programs that are in low-resource settings, administrators should attempt to align their procedures with best practices within the scope of their setting.

Models of Disability Access

Centralized Model

The centralized model is one that, in the absence of a formal liaison, utilizes a central campus disability resource office to receive and determine accommodations for all health science programs. In this model, the health science program relinquishes some decision-making to the central campus office, relying on the expertise of this centralized office. While relegating the process to a central campus expert may seem beneficial, if specific knowledge about individual programs is not robust, disability determinations may be negatively impacted and can result in an absence of clinical accommodations, unfairly limited clinical accommodations, or even unreasonably excessive and unnecessary or unreasonable accommodations. As an example, in the undergraduate domain, it may be appropriate to excuse absences for disability-related reasons. In health science programs, however, a careful evaluation of absence must be conducted.

Liaison Model

The liaison model utilizes the central campus disability access model but with the expertise of a formal liaison as a go-between. This liaison represents a particular health science program and serves as a conduit and center of expertise for the programs' essential functions and technical standards and helps to inform clinical accommodation decisions. At times, this model may include a specified point person within the centralized office who serves as the disability resource point person for students in a particular program. The centralized office contact works collaboratively with the program liaison to determine whether an accommodation is reasonable given specific program requirements, with the final decision made by the central office. One benefit of this model is that the centralized office contact gains additional expertise over time through the ongoing relationship, and exchange of information, with the program liaison. This model is the most common model and is in use at the University of Minnesota [13].

Health Science Campus Model

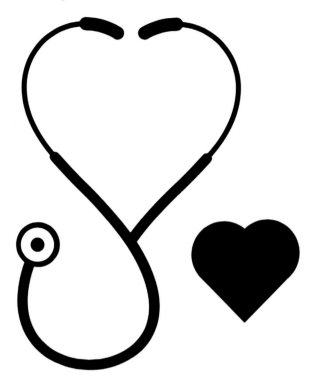

Free-standing health science institutions (e.g., the University of California, San Francisco; Rush University; and Oregon Health and Science University) often hire a DRP to provide services for the entire health science campus (including all health science and graduate programs). These institutions are not tethered to a primary undergraduate university or, if so, may opt out of central campus services and, instead, invest in specialized disability access by having a primary DRP for the health science programs. In this model, the specialized DRP maintains a point person in each individual health science program, who serves as a resource regarding program-specific questions and requirements (usually the dean of students). The DRP in this model also maintains a direct relationship with a variety of relevant constituents, including the wellness team, and simulation center team and faculty. This model includes numerous benefits for students and for the institution. First, the DRP is considered an "insider" vs. someone who is disconnected from the health science program. As part of the "team," the DRP often sits on committees, consults with faculty, conducts faculty trainings, and is able to consult on curricular and structural changes to the programs that impact accessibility. Being immersed in the programs has the added benefit of building further expertise in the health sciences and utilizing knowledge from these experiences across programs.

Program Model

A program-specific model represents the greatest example of expertise and efficacy. In the program-specific model, a health professions program hires a program-specific DRP (e.g., medicine, dentistry, nursing, pharmacy) and trains them in every aspect of the program. In this immersive model, the DRP becomes highly specialized and knowledgeable of program-specific requirements and nuance. When the DRP oversees a single program, they usually also have a lower student ratio, which provides greater opportunity to focus on critical programmatic development, faculty training, and curriculum. In addition, the resulting low student-to-DRP ratios allow the DRP more time to not only get to know the students and their needs in a more in-depth fashion but to also provide more enhanced services such as supporting applications for board exams, running affinity groups, conducting research, and developing policy. Under this model, requests for accommodation can usually be processed more quickly, decisions are well-informed, and stakeholders are well supported in implementing reasonable accommodations. In many cases the DRP in this model are also faculty members and may have other non-evaluative administrative roles.

Building an Office and Partnerships

Constituent departments must work together to ensure disability inclusion and awareness. DRPs must work with multiple offices on campus and must maintain knowledge of overarching institutional policies in order to identify potential barriers (Fig. 4.3).

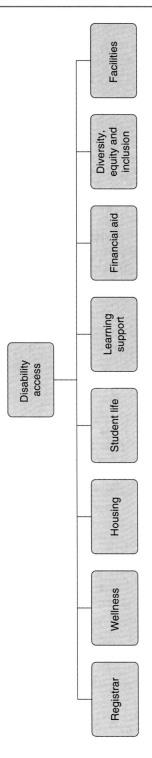

Fig. 4.3 Institutional partners in access

A DRP's work naturally intersects with other departments such as the registrar and financial aid. For example, policies for withdrawals or for taking a leave of absence may unintentionally and negatively impact students with disabilities. Financial aid offices may need to make alternations in loan disbursement for students with a disability-related cost. Working together helps to build trust and understanding and to further remove barriers.

The counseling center, student health center, student life, and housing offices are also important partners in working toward equal access. Policies in these offices should be reviewed through the lens of equal access to ensure that there are no unintended barriers for students with disabilities. For example, counseling centers, while offering a valued and needed resource for students, may have a policy of not providing documentation of psychological disability; this type of policy could hinder eligibility for accommodations on high stakes exams for a student with a psychological disability whose primary mental healthcare is provided by the institution. Lack of documentation can also hinder the ability of health professionals on campus to provide students with holistic and comprehensive care.

Finally, to ensure appropriate cross referrals between offices, including referrals for neuropsychological evaluations, and to ensure access to all available resources for students with learning disabilities, DRPs should have full knowledge of institutional learning resources and providers in the area for expedited referrals. DRPs must also work with facilities and maintenance to ensure physical access to buildings and to assure well-maintained walk ways, ramps, and building entrances.

Legal Partnerships

When possible, DRPs should maintain a close relationship with their in-house legal counsel. Alternatively, or additionally, the DRP might maintain a relationship an attorney, or a team of attorneys with specialization in either educational or medical law that are assigned to the institution or with the ADA coordinator for the institution.

Ideally, the DRP should have ongoing and regular appointments with the designated legal resource to keep apprised of legal trends and recommendations from relevant professional organizations. This also helps to develop a relationship and to strengthen rapport and trust between the DRP and the institutional official. When developing a program or evaluating an existing program, those in decision-making positions should ask and understand how pre-litigious or complicated requests for accommodations will be handled and should try to anticipate potential outcomes. These decision-makers should develop a protocol for understanding when and how to contact the appropriate legal resource and should work with the legal resource (counsel and the ADA coordinator) to establish a framework for addressing a DRP's questions or concerns.

Appropriately Staffing DS Offices in Health Science Education

Much nuance and complexity underlie the provision of disability services, and even skilled DRPs require significant time to implement their services. Time is required to appropriately determine, arrange, and communicate with relevant stakeholders in regard to disability accommodations and to support lengthy applications for high-stakes testing. DRPs also spend considerable time in documenting the accommodations process itself; in recording relevant, critical communications; and in documenting their own decision-making.

Appropriately, DRPs, or the individuals charged with fulfilling this role as part of their other duties, must have the protected time to appropriately manage these duties. A DRP (or equivalent) position-to-student ratio of 1–85 has been identified as best practice for health science-specific programs [15]. This allows a specialized professional or a team working within the program enough time to attend to the complexities disability inclusion and to proactively ensure effective service.

Disability Resource Policies and Procedures

Disability resource offices should write and maintain policies and procedures regarding requests for accommodations and should clarify and advertise processes for determining accommodations and how accommodations will be implemented. DRPs must also have processes in place for documentation of the accommodations process itself; for recording relevant, critical communications; and for documenting their decision-making. These processes should be written in tandem with the legal team to ensure that not only are federal requirements being met but that institutional policies and accreditation requirements are also being honored. Disability resource offices must also maintain and publish a grievance policy; institutions that receive federal funds are obligated to have a grievance procedure in place to address any complaints. The grievance policy should be posted on the disability resource webpages, and all students should receive a copy when they register for services (see Box 4.5).

Box 4.5 Grievance Procedures Rush University
Consistent with the spirit of the Americans with Disabilities Act (ADA), Rush determines disability accommodations through a deliberative and interactive process involving the appropriate members of the university community and, of course, the individuals with disabilities themselves.

We recognize that disagreements may occur about the appropriateness of accommodations. We also acknowledge that even with the best efforts a problem may occur. To this end, we recommend a range of options to resolve concerns about accommodation and eligibility decisions, services received, treatment by university staff and faculty, and university policies related to students with disabilities. Issues often occur as a result of misunderstandings, miscommunication, or lack of education around disability. In these instances, clarification and effective communication can lead to a quick and effective solution. If a problem arises regarding the delivery of your accommodations, determination about accommodations, or other issues of access, we encourage you to reach out to the director of student accessibility services immediately.

Rush University will attempt to serve our students' needs and concerns through internal resolution as a first step. Of course, students have multiple options available for grieving their concerns. Throughout any of these procedures, students can expect to be treated with respect, receive a timely response, not experience any form of retaliation, and have their concerns dealt with in a confidential manner to the greatest extent possible. The university encourages students to bring up any concerns early, give clear and detailed information, and alert the director of student disability services in writing.

Technical Standards

Technical standards are the essential abilities and characteristics required for graduation from a given program and are a standard part of health science programs (see Chap. 9 for a full review). DRPs, program/clerkship directors, and deans should have a robust knowledge of their program's technical standards and should regularly review them to identify potential barriers for students with disabilities and to be on the alert for potentially discriminatory language. Faculty and administrators reviewing and revising technical standards together with the DRP not only provides expertise from a disability professional but also presents an ideal opportunity for the DRP to gain more knowledge of a clinical program, to help add more inclusive language to the technical standards, and to further identify any barriers that may preclude accessibility to the program.

Faculty Training

Engaging with the faculty is vital in creating a collaborative and welcoming climate and culture for disability inclusion. As such, the DRP should be invited to relevant meetings with program/clerkship directors and core faculty meetings. This type of interaction will not only help to enrich the DRP's understanding of the program and its requirements but will also help faculty to better understand access and accommodation. Faculty, particularly those lacking exposure to current disability procedures, may be fearful of the process and reluctant to deviate from historical practices. Disability professionals should have prepared overviews of relevant topics such as the social justice approach to inclusion, legal obligations for inclusion, and an example of how functional limitations, essential competencies, and environmental barriers help inform determination of reasonable accommodations. They should also be prepared to answer questions about potential patient safety concerns and licensure (see Chaps. 10 and 12 for a detailed discussion of these respective issues). Faculty should be made aware of the disability resource website and the services offered and should understand the process for referring students.

Communication Regarding Approved Accommodations

Critical to the accommodations process is a standardized flow of information that communicates approved accommodations to the domain-specific stakeholders (e.g., faculty, academic support counselors, clinical placement coordinators, lab directors, clerkship directors). This standardized flow of information not only leads to timely facilitation of accommodations but also reduces the burden on students who may not be well-versed in communicating about their disability and who may feel intimidated at the prospect of communicating accommodation needs. To assist students and faculty with communication about accommodation needs, programs should share the free communication guide for students and faculty offered by Springer Publishing [17, 18]. This guide offers specific language for communicating about accommodations and disability and includes example emails (see Box 4.6) and general guidance on how to improve communication or how to approach delicate topics in a professional manner.

Box 4.6 Well-Written First Email from the Communication Guide (With Permission from Meeks and Jain (2015))

Example of a Well-Written First Email

Dear Professor Smith,

My name is XXXX and I am a student in your Adult Med/Surg course.[a] I am writing because you have received an e-mail from the nursing school liaison confirming my registration with Student Disability Services and outlining my approved accommodations for your course. I am hoping to speak to you to discuss how I will access my exam accommodations. Per my accommodations, I require 150% time for my exams, as well as a private room.[b]

Could you please advise me on when and where I should report for my exams?[c] If you would prefer, I would be happy to meet with you in person to discuss this. Generally, once we have finalized the plan, I send a reminder to my faculty of my needs 2 weeks in advance of my exams to confirm the arrangements.[d]

If you have a course coordinator or proctor whom you prefer I contact, or whom you would like copied on these e-mails, please let me know. I look forward to working together to facilitate these accommodations.
Thank you in advance for your assistance.
Best regards,

- [a]This introduction informs the professor who you are and introduces you as a current student first.
- [b]Reminding professors that they have already received communication about your circumstances will prompt them to look back in their emails to refresh their memory about your case.
- [c]You ask for the specific information needed to access your accommodations.
- [d]Taking responsibility to remind your professors that you require accommodations 2 weeks before an exam will help to avoid any confusion or miscommunication on the day of the exam, when you are hoping to stay focused on the exam material.

Stakeholders should also be mindful of students' privacy during such communications. Confidential information should not be transmitted via email, student names or IDs should not be used in subject lines, and student-specific disability information should never be shared with others who are not directly involved in the provision of accommodation, including other students, faculty, staff, or administrators [19].

The University of California, San Francisco, maintains guidance for faculty around student privacy. These guidelines are applicable to all program types and offers faculty clear direction on how to maintain confidentiality of student disability information (see Box 4.7).

It is important to remember that all forms of accommodations-related communication are subject to review by the student, who has the right to view their own education records, and that these records may be collected as part of the discovery[1] process during legal proceedings.

Legal Obligations for Funding Accommodations

Under the Americans with Disabilities Act (1990), institutions are required to provide reasonable accommodations to qualified students, except when the accommodation causes undue hardship [1]. This hardship is most often determined in terms of financial difficulty in paying for the accommodation and is assessed based on the institution's total financial resources (see Chap. 8 for full discussion of

---

[1] Discovery is a pre-trial procedure in a lawsuit in which each party can obtain evidence from the other party or parties including Requests for Production of Documents (RPD) – This means the other side may ask you to present copies of written documents, including emails.

Box 4.7 Maintaining Confidentiality of Student Disability Information (Used with Permission from UCSF SDS Office)

All disability-related information including documentation, accommodation letters, correspondence, and consultations are considered confidential and will be managed in accordance with the Family Educational Rights and Privacy Act (FERPA) regulations. Please read this carefully, as there are instances that may necessitate student documentation being released without consent. This includes electronic, paper, verbal, and any other types of communication. In addition to fulfilling legal obligations, maintaining a high standard of confidentiality also serves to maintain an environment in which students with disabilities feel respected, safe, supported, and protected. Breaches of confidentiality are taken very seriously by UCSF. Unauthorized disclosures of student information must be documented and can result in the University being in non-compliance with federal regulations. Additionally, such disclosures may violate state privacy laws and may subject the university and the individual to liability. Please contact Student Disabilities Services if there are any questions, issues, or concerns regarding maintaining confidentiality of information.

Student Disability Services offers the following guidelines for faculty, staff, and administrators to ensure that confidential student information is kept secure:

All information that a student shares with a faculty member is to be used specifically for arranging reasonable accommodations for the course of study.

Do not leave student disability information visible on your computer or in any printed format that others can see, and dispose of it securely at the end of the quarter.

Refrain from discussing a student's disability status and necessary accommodations within hearing range of fellow students, faculty, staff, or others who do not have an "educational need to know."

Do not assume that students registered with Student Disabilities Services are aware of other students' disability status. Blind copy (BCC) students so they are not privy to other student's information, or better yet, send separate emails to each student.

At no time should the class be informed that a student has a disability.

Discuss Accommodation Letters and logistics of implementing accommodations with students in private. Make yourself available by email, during office hours, or by appointment to discuss.

Requesting specific information about a student's disability is inappropriate. Requesting a letter from the student's physician is inappropriate. The Accommodation Letter is all that is needed to justify the accommodation.

If a student voluntarily discloses the nature of their disability to you, even if it is obvious, do not disclose it to others.

If a student tries to provide you with their primary disability documentation, refuse to read or accept it and refer the student to Student Disabilities Services. UCSF has designated Student Disabilities Services as the repository of all disability documentation for students with disabilities.

the law). However, the undue hardship exemption has almost never been successful in an educational context. Appropriately, institutions should be cautious about claiming undue hardship in defense of withholding a reasonable and appropriate accommodation. Two recent cases, both at the educational and employment level, demonstrate that even in the case of costly accommodations, undue hardship is generally not defensible [19, 20].

Funding Accommodations in Educational Programs

Health science programs take varied approaches to funding student accommodations, with approaches ranging from centralized institutional funding to program-specific funding. The challenges associated with obtaining accommodations can become even more complex for students when clear institutional protocols for funding are not in place. In most cases, the disability resource office will cover the expenses associated with accommodations by using the disability resource office budget or by tapping into a centralized institutional fund. This approach uses centralized institutional funds or "pooled funds," where each program contributes a set amount of money to the overall budget to cover accommodations for all health science programs. Under the centralized institutional model, nursing student accommodations would be covered by the same funding model as a medical student. This helps to reduce bias in decision-making at the admissions level and allows programs to determine the most appropriate and impactful accommodation without being influenced by the burden of cost (Fig. 4.4). Alternatively, program funding models rely on program-specific funds to cover accommodations for students. In a program-specific model, a nursing student's accommodation would be paid for by the nursing school, while a medical school student's accommodation would be paid for by the medical school.

Regardless of the funding format, institutions must remember that equal access through reasonable accommodation is an *institution-level responsibility* and that the cost of an accommodation, and responsibility for the accommodation, ultimately rests with the institution, regardless of the method of funding or budget structure.

Given that the institution is wholly responsible for ensuring equal access for qualified students, disability programs need to work with the institution to develop a budget that recognizes institutional responsibility for financing reasonable accommodations. While a disability resource budget may cover employee salaries, office space, equipment, and supplies, accommodation expenses should be added as a projection, but with the realization that reasonable accommodations (that do not cause an undue burden to the institution) must be provided.

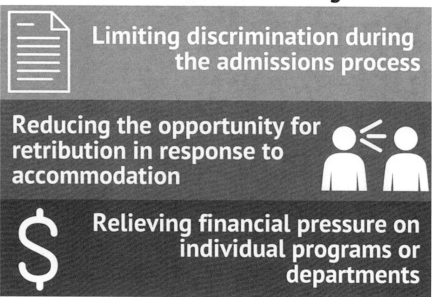

Fig. 4.4 Advantages of centralized accommodation funding in health professions and science higher education settings

Funding Accommodations in Training and Employment Settings

Responsibilities to provide reasonable accommodations are similar in healthcare employment settings to educational settings, though they fall under different titles of the law. Employees including fellows and other residents or "trainees" who receive paychecks from the institution are covered under title 1 of the ADA. As discussed above in the educational setting, institutional claims of undue hardship in the employment setting are rarely successful. While the ADA states that funding is an institutional responsibility, there is no stipulation about *who* within the employing entity actually pays for the accommodation. This means that while the calculation for determining undue hardship is assessed using the entity's overall budget (as it is in education), the cost of the accommodations is often decentralized and filtered

Box 4.8 Searls v. Johns Hopkins University
A lawsuit against Johns Hopkins Hospital (JHH) serves as an example of the challenges associated with decentralized accommodation funding. In this case, a deaf nursing student was offered a position at JHH. However, this offer was later rescinded, as JHH claimed that the cost of the American Sign Language (ASL) interpreter that the nurse had requested, estimated by JHH to be $120,000 per year, would be a financial hardship. JHH's operational budget at that time was approximately $1.7 billion, and that accommodation was just 0.007% of that budget. This means that while the cost of the accommodation may come from a much smaller divisional or departmental budget, the calculation for determining undue hardship is assessed using the entity's overall financial picture, $1.7 billion in Johns Hopkins' case, and no evidence of financial hardship was found. Johns Hopkins Hospital had filtered the cost of the nurse's accommodation down to the hiring department, which had an operational budget of $3.4 million in 2012, but the institution as a whole is responsible for ensuring equal access.

down to the department or program that hired the employee or trainee. These referrals to smaller departmental budgets can lead to difficulty in administration of the actual funding itself and can lead to vulnerability on the part of the employee who is asking for the accommodation. Misunderstandings, about the responsibility of employers, given these issues, occur as evidenced in the Searls v. Johns Hopkins University lawsuit (see Box 4.8).

Filtering the cost of an accommodation down to the hiring division or department can also have a severe impact on that unit or department's financial bottom line that, in turn, may lead to discriminatory hiring practices regarding those with known disabilities.

To combat this potential roadblock in the financing of accommodations, the United States Equal Employment Opportunity Commission (EEOC) [21] recommends the creation of centralized funding mechanisms. Under this guidance, the EEOC suggests that institutions pool resources to offset the costs of accommodations. The use of these centralized funds better aligns with the ADA calculation of undue hardship and allows for better protection from discrimination and bias for employees. There are many examples of employers [22], academic institutions [23], and state [24] and federal [25] government agencies successfully using centralized accommodation funding, and there are examples of how this type of funding can be created [26].

Programmatic Review for New and Existing DSP Offices

Whether your institution already has a DSP office/department or is considering opening a new one, the following section can provide guidance on how a new DSP can get up and running and/or provide touchstones for an established DSP office/

department. Similar methods of assessment can be employed for both new and pre-existing DSP offices. Periodic review of already-established DSP offices is important to ensure continued optimal access and streamlining of processes.

Know Your Institution: Start with an Assessment

Each institution has its own distinct culture, climate, mission, and philosophy. Understanding how these core values integrate helps to contextualize how accessibility and inclusion are viewed for each institution/program. This can aid in identifying opportunities for improvement.

Under the institutional umbrella, various health science programs operate differently with regard to requirements. Understanding how these core values interdigitate helps to contextualize how disability access and inclusion are best approached for each institution/program and helps to identify opportunities for improvement. Determining institutional needs and understanding the environment is critical for institutions which are either starting or seeking to improve a disability resource office. The following is a checklist of items that should be reviewed as part of a comprehensive programmatic review:

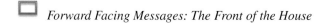 *Forward Facing Messages: The Front of the House*

Regardless of how well-developed internal processes are, DRPs and program administrators may have difficulty in objectively looking at the institution from the *outside*. Viewing the institution and its accessibility from the perspective of a *potential student/applicant, a new student, or even current student* is critical in identifying gaps in information and in highlighting opportunities for improving transparency and communication about disability. Taking this viewpoint is also important for new programs. In assessing this perspective, here are a few questions to ask:

1. *What message and/or vision does your institution send to its prospective students about disability inclusion? To its current students?*
2. *Does your institution's formal mission statement communicate an inclusive environment?*
3. *Is your admissions messaging welcoming? Do you communicate a commitment to accessibility in your technical standards? Do you provide information regarding how applicants can request accommodations or where they can ask questions?*
4. *Are your students with disabilities valued and included as part of a diversity, equity, and inclusion agenda?*

   Taking time to understand your institution's climate, culture, and messaging is vital in making forward progress and is critical to removing potential barriers for prospective applicants, new students, and current students.

☐ *Welcoming Language for DSP Offices*

An example of welcoming language is available on multiple websites. Below, we offer one example from Rush University. More examples can be found in the 2018 AAMC/UCSF report, Accessibility, Inclusion, and Action in Medical Education: Lived Experiences of Learners and Physicians with Disabilities [3].

☐ *Transparency Regarding Disability Resources and Accommodations*

Critical to the engagement of students with disabilities is the institution's transparency regarding the availability of accommodations and the process by which students can apply. Relevant and clear communication is critical in ensuring that the program follows disability law, as evidenced in *Chenari v. George Washington University,* 847 F.3d 740 (D.C.Cir 2017) (see Case Example 4.1).

Box 4.9 Rush University Statement of Disability Inclusion

"In keeping with its goal to promote diversity among its student population, Rush University is committed to attracting and educating students who will help to make the population of health care professionals reflective of the national population, including individuals with disabilities. In addition, Rush University is committed to ensuring equal access to its facilities, programs and services are available to students with disabilities."

Case Example 4.1 Chenari v. George Washington University [26]

Chenari was a medical student at George Washington University. While taking the surgery shelf exam, he failed to stop engaging with the exam once time was called, and he was subsequently brought up for dismissal under the school's code of conduct. Chenari claimed, among other things, that George Washington had refused him accommodation for his ADHD (which he claimed caused the behavior) and reported having shared his ADHD diagnosis with multiple faculty members. Although he admitted never requesting accommodations, he stated that his "repeated notifications to the administration created an obligation on [the University] to investigate and implement reasonable accommodations."

University officials had twice referred Chenari to counseling but he never followed up on the referrals. Chenari stated he did not have time to seek counseling, but he did not request time off in order to do so.

The court noted that in addition to the referrals, the University has an Office of Disability Support Services that is charged with reviewing requests for accommodation. The office also counsels all first-year students that "if they have a disability and need to request an accommodation, it is the student's responsibility to go to [the Office] to pursue that matter." Finally, the

University's "First Year Survival Guide" for medical students instructs "[s]tudents who suspect that they may have a disability which may require an accommodation" to contact the Office of Disability Support.

The Disability Support Services office maintains a website that guides students through the process for obtaining a reasonable accommodation, and that includes specific instructions about how students with ADHD can obtain accommodations.

The district court granted summary judgment to the University, deferring to the school's view that the appellant broke the honor code and finding no violation of relevant disability statutes.

Similar cases show that the courts uphold institutional decisions when schools provided clear steps for requesting accommodation. This includes identification of a point person to review requests for accommodation, having a defined process for determining disability accommodations, and ensuring that this process is available for students to review.

Metrics: Measuring Need, Growth, Retention, and Success

Metrics, or the collection of data, are an important consideration when developing a program. Data trends can help administrators identify peak times for services delivery, testing, and intakes, allowing for maximizing of staffing at these times. Data can assist administrators in identifying the need for additional positions, will show growth in the number of students engaging in services, and can even serve as outcome measures to evaluate the success of outreach programs or campaigns aimed at increasing the number of students with disabilities who access the office. Metrics are also important in developing a budget and in strengthening relationships with other related offices (e.g., Counseling, Veteran Services, Diversity, Equity and Inclusion offices). Tracking key data can also assist in providing demographic information to faculty, staff, and administrators. However, determining *what* to document can be overwhelming. The following boxes identify the most widely captured metrics, broken down into three categories: personnel/resources, growth and trajectory, and cyclic personnel or student support needs (see Boxes 4.10, 4.11, and 4.12).

Box 4.10 Data Needed to Document Need for Personnel/Resources
- Number of requests/inquiries for accommodations
- Number of accommodations approved
- Number of testing accommodations
- Accommodation requests that have been denied

Box 4.11 Data Needed to Document Population Growth and Trajectory
- Program/college of students enrolled in disability resource office
- Type of accommodation (clinical, didactic, lab, testing, housing, etc.)
- Disability or category of disability (e.g., psychological, physical, chronic health)
- Expected graduation date

Box 4.12 Data Needed to Document Cyclic Personnel or Student Support Needs
- Dates of initial student contact across specific programs
- Ancillary appointment or requests (e.g., help with step exams, choosing clerkship locations)
- Testing dates for specific programs/high-stakes licensing exam dates (∗this helps to plan staffing and time accordingly)
- Any program events that may cause an uptick in symptoms or flares for students

Table 4.1 Example of spreadsheet to track student data

Student ID	College/ program	Request date	Accommodation issued date	Accommodation	Grad date	Email	Notes
2018-1	CON-DNP	4/26/18	5/10/18	Time and one half for examinations	05/20	jane.doe@school.edu	
2018-2	MED-1st Year	4/28/18	5/12/18	Lifting restriction-15 lbs	05/22	janice.doe@schoo.edu	TEMP Expires 6/30/18

Storing Data

Once you identify metrics, a unified data collection plan should be created. Data collection of this nature can be as simple as an Excel spreadsheet or as robust as a more centralized database (e.g., Accommodate[2] or Titanium[3]). Partnering with the registrar for graduation information may also help the disability office to keep track of data such as graduation rates and time to graduation and for medicine, where a student matched, and into which specialty. An example of tracking key data can be seen in the table below (Table 4.1).

---

[2] https://www.symplicity.com/higher-ed/solutions/accommodate
[3] http://www.titaniumschedule.com/Main/

A Note About Privacy

Data tracking can be very helpful to disability resource professionals, but is designed to be an internal system. While there is great benefit in using the data to track growth of services, inform staffing, and to identifying the spectrum of trajectories and trends for students, this should all be accomplished within the office under strict privacy guidelines. Sharing this data in any identified way is discouraged. If used outside of the office or for research/publication, student identifiers should be removed, and information in research manuscripts should only be reported in aggregate. At no time is it acceptable to share lists of students and their private disability information outside of the disability office.

NIH Mandates for the Recruitment and Retention of Students with Disabilities

Federal funding agencies, including the National Institutes of Health (NIH) and National Science Foundation (NSF), maintain a commitment to attracting and retaining a diverse biomedical workforce [27–29]. For example, the NIH "encourages institutions to diversify their student and faculty populations to enhance the participation of individuals from groups identified as underrepresented in the biomedical, clinical, behavioral, and social sciences," which includes individuals with disabilities.

To help realize the NIH's mission to increase disability inclusion, Medical Scientist Training Programs (MSTP) and NIH training programs, including T-32 grants, are required to develop a plan to recruit and retain students with disabilities. To assist programs with meeting these NIH funding requirements, the University of California, San Francisco, has developed a guide to assist institutions with the recruitment and retention of students with disabilities; the guide is available on the NIH website [30].

External Resources for Health Science Programs

Several organizations exist that support the work of DRPs (see Table 4.2). Some are focused on generalist training, while others are specialized within specific educational programs such as medicine. These organizations work to support the ongoing efforts of disability inclusion in the health science professions, and many of them host yearly conferences or symposia (see Table 4.3) where resource specialists gather to discuss legal trends and best practices.

Table 4.2 External resources for disability resources

Organization	Website
The Coalition for Disability Access in Health Science Education (Coalition)	www.hsmcoalition.org
Association of Higher Education and Disability (AHEAD)	www.ahead.org
National Organization of Nurses with Disabilities (NOND)	https://nond.org
Association of Medical Professionals with Hearing Loss (AMPHL)	www.amphl.org
Society for Physicians with Disabilities	www.physicianswithdisabilities.org
Association of American Medical Colleges (AAMC)	www.aamc.org
Exceptional Nurse	http://exceptionalnurse.com
MDisability Program	https://medicine.umich.edu/dept/family-medicine/programs/mdisability

Table 4.3 Conference/symposium/webinars

Organization	Conference
The Coalition for Disability Access in Health Science Education (Coalition)	Every April
Association of Higher Education and Disability (AHEAD)	Every July
Association of Medical Professionals with Hearing Loss (AMPHL)	Every other June

Summary

Federal laws prohibit discrimination of persons with disabilities and require institutions to create transparent and informed processes to determine reasonable accommodations. The law, however, does not give guidance as to *how* an institution should create and implement disability inclusion processes, including how to process student requests. This lack of guidance can lead to legal liability for an institution and can lead to significant barriers for students with disabilities. Thoughtful analysis of pre-existing disability services and targeted strategies for establishment of new offices/services will help to mitigate these issues and will help to expand the definition of diversity while leading to greater success for students and for the institution as a whole.

Appendix A

Sample Job Description for a Health Science DRP

Health Science DRP [insert official institutional title]

The disability resource professional [or other title] is responsible for the comprehensive and timely coordination and delivery of accommodations to students with disabilities within the health science programs [list specific program].

Responsibilities include, but are not limited to, coordinating note-taking services, alternate format materials and equipment loans, CART and sign-language interpreting services, assistive technology assessments and training, as well as programmatic and collaborative outreach.

The [title] will serve as the primary resource to educate, train, and guide the schools of [insert program] in understanding disability access. As such, the [title] will facilitate reasonable accommodations for students with disabilities. The [title] will also interface regularly with faculty and provide ongoing technical assistance to faculty, deans, and other advisors regarding the [insert program] obligations to students with disabilities under the American with Disabilities Act As Amended.

The [title] will ensure that criteria and procedures for assessing accommodations are clearly identified and disseminated, assist students in understanding their rights and responsibilities related to reasonable accommodations, and provide additional assistance in ensuring equal access. The [title] must work within a highly confidential service delivery model that is fast-paced, is high-stakes, is detail-oriented, and promotes accountability and maturity.

Below are examples of job requirements regarding education, experience, and ability. Each skill can be modified to align with the hiring institutions mission, vision, and verbiage.

Education/Experience

- Master's degree in counseling, education, law, psychology/psychiatry, social work, and/or vocational rehab counseling
- A minimum of 3–5 years of experience in disability services, special education, counseling, or a closely related field or an equivalent combination of education and experience in the provision of disability services in a higher education setting
- Substantial knowledge of specific federal and state laws impacting the provision of federally mandated accommodations for individuals with disabilities
- Substantial knowledge of disability accommodations in a health science context
- Ability to handle complex and sensitive student issues and documentation
- Knowledgeable of HIPPA and FERPA requirements for the communication, handling, and storage of confidential documentation and information
- Substantial experience in planning and conducting consultations, in-service training/workshops, and other collaborative programming involving a variety of audiences, pertaining to but not limited to disability issues, accommodations, and instructional strategies
- Knowledge, expertise, and training in working with culturally/disability diverse populations
- Demonstrated management and supervisory experience
- Knowledge of assistive technology software and hardware, including Read and Write Gold, Dragon Naturally Speaking, Kurzweil 1000/3000, JAWS, CCTVs, and various applications for the iPad

- Proven ability to communicate clearly and interact effectively with students, faculty, and university staff
- Must possess attributes of compassion, patience, and respect for others as well as sensitivity to multicultural

Job Responsibilities

- Through the interactive process, create and implement (clinical, didactic, housing, etc.) accommodations for student's self-identifying as having a disability.
- Evaluate diagnostic documentation relating to the student's disability and address potential barriers students may encounter throughout educational experience.
- Facilitate implementation of clinical accommodation across schools and multiple clinical sites. This includes researching, identifying, ordering, and coordinating the installation of adaptive technology or modification of physical space or pathway.
- Collect, analyze, and maintain data regarding number of intakes, type of accommodation approved (clinical vs. didactic), program student is enrolled in, and expected graduation date.
- Supervise the development and implementation of policies and procedures related to disability services in compliance with *name of school* values, college rules, as well as state and federal laws.
- Work with campus departments to ensure that all academic programs, student activities, and facilities are accessible for students with disabilities.
- Develop and manage department budget and other fiscal resources.
- Serve as a resource for the college regarding accessibility, accommodations, and other disability-related issues.
- Coordinate captioning, sign language interpreting, and CART services.
- Remain current regarding national trends, issues, and literature related to students with disabilities and disability-related services, including participating in professional development activities, researching best practices, and addressing transition issues for students with disabilities entering postsecondary education.
- Evaluate services and prepare reports to assess and communicate DRC program activities, services, and outcomes.
- Administer and develop program services necessary for meeting the reasonable accommodation requests generated by students with disabilities and others identifying as needing services (alternative testing, interpreter and note-taking services, alternative format material production, and adaptive furniture/equipment).
- Maintain up-to-date case notes regarding interactions and coordination of accommodations for students.
- Evaluate diagnostic documentation and determine eligibility for reasonable academic accommodations on the basis of a disability in accordance with university policy and ADA as amended.

- Interpret documentation for students requesting academic accommodations on the basis of physical disabilities, sensory disabilities, chronic health conditions, learning disabilities, attention disabilities, and psychological disabilities.
- Accurately track and document requests; document actions taken to coordinate services (including time table) and delivery of notes to students.
- Excellent written, oral, interpersonal, analytical, and organizational skills required.
- Create and/or maintain departmental website.
  - Update information in a timely manner and ensure website links are updated and functioning.
  - Review and verify other campus websites relevant to SDS to ensure the information provided is accurate and reflects current policy.

References

1. 42 USC sec 12101 (1990).
2. 29 USC sec 794 (1973).
3. Meeks L, Jain NR. Accessibility, inclusion, and action in medical education: lived experiences of learners and physicians with disabilities. Association of American Medical Colleges: Washington, DC. 2018.
4. Zazove P, Case B, Moreland C, Plegue MA, Hoekstra A, Ouellette A, Sen A, Fetters MD. US medical schools' compliance with the Americans with Disabilities Act: findings from a national study. Acad Med. 2016;91(7):979–86.
5. McKee M, Case B, Fausone M, Zazove P, Ouellette A, Fetters MD. Medical schools' willingness to accommodate medical students with sensory and physical disabilities: ethical foundations of a functional challenge to "organic" technical standards. AMA J Ethics. 2016;18(10):993–1002.
6. Mehta L, Clifford G. Admissions as a facilitator of inclusion—not a gatekeeper. Disabil Compliance High Educ. 2017;22(12):7–7.
7. Meeks LM, Liao P, Kim N. Using Twitter to promote awareness of disabilities in medicine. Med Educ. 2019;53(5):525–6.
8. Meeks, LM. DocsWithDisabilities podcast. [cited 11 October]. Available from: https://podcasts.apple.com/us/podcast/docswithdisabilities/id1474844514.
9. General Medical Council. Able Medics podcast. [cited 11 October]. Available from: https://www.gmc-uk.org/education/standards-guidance-and-curricula/guidance/welcomed-and-valued/welcomed-and-valued-resources/able-medics-podcast.
10. Meeks LM. DocsWithDisabilities podcast. [internet] Dr. Marley Doyle [cited 11 October]. Available from: https://podcasts.apple.com/us/podcast/dr-marley-doyle-md/id1474844514?i=1000451888413.
11. Jain NR, Lewis C, Meeks LM. The process of requesting accommodations on certification, licensing, and board exams: assisting students through the application. The guide to assisting students with disabilities: equal access in health science and professional education. 2015 Aug 13:89.
12. Laird-Metke E. Disability decisions by committee: an increase in risk and decrease in student well-being. Disabil Compliance High Educ. 2016;21(7):8.
13. Blacklock B. Enhancing access in medical and health science programs: the college model. Disabil Compliance High Educ. 2016;21(10):7.
14. Meeks LM, Sullivan L. Appropriately staffing DS offices in health science education. Disabil Compliance High Educ. 2019;24(6):1–5.
15. Meeks LM, Sullivan L. Disability resource offices must also maintain and publish a grievance policy; institutions that receive federal funds are obligated to have a grievance procedure in place to address any complaints 2019.

16. Jain NR, Meeks LM. Professionalism in communication: a guide for graduate and professional health sciences students with disabilities. The guide to assisting students with disabilities: equal access in health science and professional education 2015 Aug 13:165.
17. Jain NR, Meeks LM. Supporting health science students' communication skills: avoiding pitfalls. Disabil Compliance High Educ. 2015;21(8):5.
18. Jain NR, Meeks LM. Privacy, disability, and health science students. Disabil Compliance High Educ. 2017;22(7):7–7.
19. Searls vs. Johns Hopkins Hospital (D. Maryland 1/21/16). Available at: https://www.leagle.com/decision/infdco20160121d03.
20. Argenyi vs. Creighton (2014 WL1838980, May 8, 2014) Available at: https://casetext.com/case/argenyi-v-creighton-university-10.
21. Hastings RR. Central accommodations pave the way. 2008. Available at: https://www.shrm.org/resourcesandtools/hr-topics/behavioral-competencies/global-and-cultural-effectiveness/pages/centralaccommodationfunds.aspx.
22. Hailey K. University continues to make critical improvements to enhance accessibility and inclusion across campus. 2017. Syracuse University Campus and Community. Available at: https://news.syr.edu/blog/2017/08/24/university-continues-to-make-critical-improvements-to-enhance-accessibility-and-inclusion-across-campus/.
23. Executive Office for the Administration of Finance. Establishing the reasonable accommodations capital reserve account. Regional Bulletin. December, 22, 2011. Available at: https://www.mass.gov/administrative-bulletin/establishing-the-reasonable-accommodations-capital-reserve-account-af-20.
24. Computer/Electronic Accommodations Program (CAP). Available at: https://www.cap.mil/AboutCAP/AboutCAP.aspx.
25. Orslene JA. Best practices in establishing a centralized accommodation fund. Job Accommodation Network. Available at: https://askjan.org/articles/Best-Practices-in-Establishing-a-Centralized-Accommodation-Fund.cfm.
26. Chenari v. George Washington University. 847 F.3d 740 (D.C.Cir 2017).
27. National Institute of General Medical Sciences. Enhancing diversity in training programs Available at: https://www.nigms.nih.gov/Training/Diversity/. Accessed 3 June 2019.
28. National Science Foundation. Programs for people with disabilities. Available at: https://www.nsf.gov/careers/life/disabilities.jsp. Accessed 3 June 2019.
29. National Institutes of Health. Notice of NIH's interest in diversity. Available at: https://grants.nih.gov/grants/guide/notice-files/NOT-OD-18-210.html.
30. Meeks LM, Jain NR. NIH T32 Grant/MSTP Program Guide for Recruitment and Retention of Students with Disabilities RETRIEVED MAY 11 https://www.nigms.nih.gov/training/diversity/Documents/Disabilities-recuitment-and-retention-MSTPs.pdf.

Wellness and Disability

5

Wei Wei Lee, Sharron Guillett, Joseph F. Murray, and Lisa M. Meeks

Introduction

Chris is a second-year health science student who begins his clinical rotations and finds himself "getting through" the day. Most days he leaves the wards after 10 h of working with patients and struggling with the electronic health record system. He is stressed knowing that his patient documentation will be heavily scrutinized by two preceptors who've noted Chris's struggles. When Chris leaves the wards, he goes directly home, crawls into bed falling asleep immediately, only to awaken at 5 in the morning and repeat the previous day. Two days ago, Chris started night float (a mandatory requirement in his program). After the 2 weeks of night float, Chris is finding it difficult to get into his old routine. He has trouble falling asleep, finds himself crying at the end of each evening, and has lost a total of 15 pounds since starting the program. Chris has withdrawn from his friends and his family and spends all of his non-clinical time in bed, sleeping. Chris is drowning in depression and is completely unaware of how to change his circumstances.

The original version of this chapter is revised and updated. The correction to this chapter can be found at https://doi.org/10.1007/978-3-030-46187-4_14

W. W. Lee (✉)
Assistant Dean of Students, Director, Wellness Programs, Assistant Professor Department of Medicine University of Chicago Pritzker School of Medicine, Chicago, IL, USA
e-mail: wlee3@medicine.bsd.uchicago.edu

S. Guillett
Eleanor Wade Custer School of Nursing, Shenandoah University, Winchester, VA, USA
e-mail: sguillet@su.edu

J. F. Murray
Associate Professor Department of Psychiatry, Former Associate Dean of Student Affairs, Weill Cornell Medical College, New York, NY, USA
e-mail: jfmurray@med.cornell.edu

L. M. Meeks
Assistant Professor, Department of Family Medicine, Director of MDisability Education, The University of Michigan Medical School, Ann Arbor, MI, USA
e-mail: meeksli@med.umich.edu

© Springer Nature Switzerland AG 2020
L. M. Meeks, L. Neal-Boylan (eds.), *Disability as Diversity*,
https://doi.org/10.1007/978-3-030-46187-4_5

Fig. 5.1 Drowning in depression illustrator: Amy Rutherford, 2019

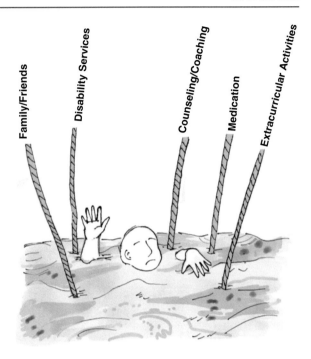

Chris's story is not unique: many health profession students experience depression. Chris may have poor insight into his level of depression and little energy to navigate a pathway to better functioning. The presentation of depression is sometimes compared to quick sand (Fig. 5.1). Students may not recognize the symptoms of depression, avoid seeking help, and sink deeper into the illness. Chris will need multiple mechanisms of support to improve his functioning and ensure full access to the curriculum. He requires support from his family and friends, faculty advisors, counseling services, and medical providers and would benefit from medication and reasonable accommodations from disability resources. How could things have gone better?

The Americans with Disabilities Act (ADA) [1] applies to students, trainees, and healthcare professionals. It is proposed that healthcare providers with disabilities, including psychological disabilities, provide excellent care for their patients and strengthen the healthcare workforce [2–5], yet health profession students still face challenging learning environments and high rates of mental health concerns. For students with psychological disabilities, robust support through thoughtful, student-centered policies and student disability resource offices can help students navigate health profession education to become valued and welcomed members of the workforce.

Rough Waters Ahead

Regardless of the type of health science program a student enters, they will have a high probability of experiencing a period of stress, burnout, anxiety, depression, or other mental health concerns. If the mental health condition is severe and the

Table 5.1 Prevalence of psychological diagnosis in health science students by program

	Nursing	Medicine
Burnout	15.6% [6]	44.2% [7]
Anxiety	60% [8]	7–65% [10]
Depression	34% [10, 11]	27% [9]
Suicidal ideation	14% [12]	11% [9]

student experiences significant functional limitations that interfere with their ability to engage in the curriculum without accommodations, classifying the student as having a psychological disability is appropriate. The impact of stress on health science students' mental health and well-being has been studied extensively, and studies have found high rates of student burnout, anxiety, depression, and suicidal ideation (see Table 5.1) [6–11]. These rates of distress are often higher than rates found in their US college graduates peers of similar age [12–13]. The need to promote well-being, increase resilience, and augment mechanisms of support has never been greater.

Wellness and Resilience in the Health Sciences

Given the high prevalence of mental health conditions in nursing and medicine, attention to the impact of the environment on students with psychological disabilities is important.

Wellness

The definition of wellness for health science students is not simply the absence of burnout or distress; it encompasses positive elements of professional fulfillment, resilience, meaning, and satisfaction with work, and both nursing and medical associations are building proactive responses to wellness [14–15]. The National Wellness Institute promotes six dimensions of wellness: emotional, occupational, physical, social, intellectual, and spiritual, which is defined as a holistic concept including an individual's state of being in good health (including mental health) [16]. The absence of wellness is often measured as a function of burnout. Indicators of burnout include a state of chronic stress that contributes to emotional and physical exhaustion and detachment [17].

To address burnout, depression, anxiety, and suicidality, many programs are implementing wellness initiatives. Despite the increasing prevalence of wellness programs at health professional schools, the research on effective interventions to promote student well-being is still at an early stage. Initial findings emphasize the importance of targeting both individual and systems' level interventions and studying the prevention of and recovery from distress, in addition to the promotion of engagement, meaning from work, and other positive aspects of well-being [18].

Resilience

According to the American Psychological Association, resilience is defined as:

> the process of adapting well in the face of adversity, trauma, tragedy, threats or significant sources of stress such as family and relationship problems, serious health problems or workplace and financial stressors. It means 'bouncing back' from difficult experiences and involves behaviors, thoughts and actions that can be learned and developed.

A review by Sanderson and Brewer resulted in a modified framework for examining the factors associated with resilience that includes personal traits, behaviors, and experiences (see Table 5.2) [19]. While these factors have been identified in the literature as being associated with resilience, there is insufficient evidence to suggest any one factor is the key. Several studies have reported low resilience scores among health science students especially in medicine and nursing and call for increased attention to this matter [20–21]. It has also been noted that a high percentage of students with disabilities have conditions that are not visible (i.e., psychological disabilities) [22] and that these students may not disclose those disabilities, especially if they feel they are functioning well [23]. Therefore, the importance of building an awareness of accommodations for psychological disabilities and embedding resilience initiatives and into student programming and culture is becoming increasingly evident.

Table 5.2 Overview of resilience factors [19]

Personal resources (22 factors)	Contextual resources (16 factors)	Strategies (7 factors)	Outcomes (5 factors)
Adaptability/flexibility	Leisure activity	Balance (work/life)	Connectedness
Agreeableness	Social activity	Coping	Employability
Commitment	Physical activity	Meaning making	Retention (in
Conscientiousness	Life experience	Problem-solving	course and
Courage	Mentorship	Reflection	profession)
Emotional intelligence	Organizational structure	Self-care	Satisfaction
Extraversion	Organizational culture	Taking action	Well-being
Hardiness	Team environment		
Mental stability	Social support		
Mindset (growth/open)	Family support		
Motivation	Peer support		
Personal confidence	Academic support		
Personal integrity	Financial support		
Proactive	Psychological support		
Robust/strong	Faculty support		
Self-awareness	Stable relationship		
Self-efficacy			
Self-esteem			
Sense of belonging			
Sense of control			
Spirituality			
Tenacity/persistence/grit			

In health science education, resiliency training has been incorporated into wellness programming as a way to help students develop and enhance skills to better manage stress and utilize a range of psychological and emotional support resources. Resiliency training often targets common cognitive distortions (i.e., catastrophizing), addresses problematic mindsets (i.e., maladaptive perfectionism), and aims to provide students with cognitive behavioral tools to challenge these faulty perceptions.

Resiliency interventions include peer support and robust faculty advising [24–27], cognitive behavioral techniques [28, 29], student wellness programs [18, 31], stress management training (i.e., mindfulness) [27, 30–34], and curricular changes that promote student collaboration (i.e., pass/fail grading) [18, 31, 35, 36]. Results of these interventions have generally been positive, and advising programs, peer support, and mindfulness programs have been found to improve resilience in medical students [25, 26]. In addition, a 2016 literature review found that using resilience workshops, cognitive behavioral training, or a combination of interventions (i.e., small group problem solving, reflection, mindfulness and relaxation training, and mentoring) was most effective in promoting resilience in health professionals [37–39].

Wellness in Nursing and Medicine

Medical and nursing programs are very demanding, both physically and mentally, and it is not surprising that studies report high levels of stress, anxiety, and depression among students especially during the clinical portion of their education [39, 40]. The stress and anxiety associated with health science education can impact student sleep patterns, physical and mental health, the ability to learn, and performance of health science students [41–43]. A systematic review notes a high prevalence of depression in both nursing (34%) [10] and medicine (27%) [9].

Health science programs are rigorous by design, and students often manage multiple didactics while also attending to clinical duties that can lead to 12-hour plus days. For nursing, the number of direct care clinical hours is often controlled by each state's board of nursing and can be as high as 900 clinical hours over the duration of the program in order to graduate, whereas in medicine the clinical hours vary by rotation and are more competency vs. time based.

Over the past decade, researchers have increased their focus on improving student and trainee well-being [44, 45]. Despite the increased focus on student well-being, the culture and practice of medicine continues to send mixed messages [46]. The research on well-being and resiliency initiatives in student and advanced education have found that "individual-level" interventions targeting personal resilience (i.e., reflection, meditation, etc.) are ineffective unless they also target organizational-level factors (i.e., scheduling concerns, curricular changes, etc.) and workplace or learning environment conditions (i.e., physical work environment) [47]. The culture, leadership, training systems, and curricula must align to support the educational, clinical, and personal development of students [46]. Since the

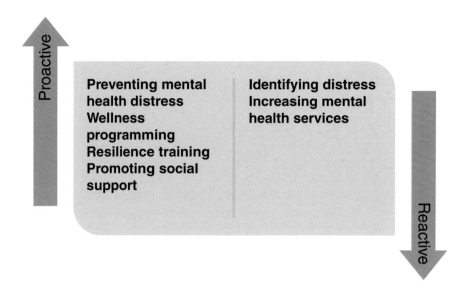

Fig. 5.2 Proactive vs. reactive approaches to medical student well-being [36]

causes of distress and mental health concerns in health science programs are multifactorial, approaches to improve student mental health should include a wide range of approaches. The different types of interventions can be categorized within a framework of reactive, proactive, or curricular initiatives (see Fig. 5.2) [18].

Reactive approaches include enhancing mechanisms to identify students in distress and bolstering referral to mental health services. Proactive approaches focus on preventing mental distress in medical school and typically focus on balancing out negative aspects of medical training and include wellness programming, resilience training, and promoting social support and learning communities [18]. Curricular initiatives focus on addressing structural contributors to student distress and include implementing pass/fail grading and team-based learning, providing more opportunities for connection and meaning in their educational experience (see Fig. 5.3) [18, 48].

Resilience in Medicine and Nursing

The intense, high-stress, and competitive environment of health science programs can erode student health and well-being. Studies have found that social support plays a critical role in student resiliency and high levels of perceived support from family, faculty, staff, and peers and a positive learning climate (i.e., collaborative environment, student education is priority for faculty members and overall learning environment) were protective against burnout [49]. Mindfulness interventions have also been found to reduce burnout and stress and improve mood and empathy in medical students [50, 51].

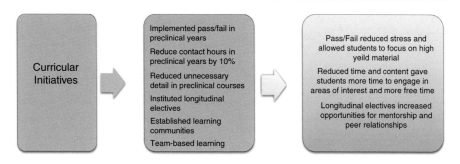

Fig. 5.3 Curricular initiatives and goals for improving wellness at Saint Louis University [36]

Students who develop resilience are more likely to adjust to the demands of professional practice and respond positively to academic and personal challenges [52, 53]. This is especially important when one considers the high incidence of suicides in nursing and medical trainees and professionals [9, 11].

Major barriers to promoting student well-being in health science programs relate to the challenging culture of medicine that rewards self-sacrifice and forgoing self-care and discourages trainees from asking for help for fear of appearing "weak." [54, 55] Thus, cultural changes, attention to the learning environment, and awareness of the detrimental effect of mixed messaging on well-being must be addressed in order to meaningfully address student distress.

A great deal of time, energy, money, and personal sacrifice is on the line for these students. While various stakeholders in nursing and medicine recommend the elimination of high stakes testing, they remain in effect and are often used as predictors of future success, such as passing the national exams like the National Council Licensure Examination for Registered Nurses (NCLEX) and the United States Medical Licensing Exams (USMLE) Step series [56, 57]. Health professional schools emphasize high pass rates for the standardized national exams, and high performance on these exams often correlates with success in the residency match for medical students and can bolster recruitment efforts for nursing and medical schools. In nursing education, schools that have persistently low NCLEX pass rates or a high number of students with repeated failures may lose accreditation and risk sanctions from the board of nursing including closure of the program. Unfortunately, the focus on high-stakes examinations causes unnecessary barriers for students with disabilities who may need additional time or alternative methods of assessment [58].

Disability in Health Science Education

When Do Symptoms Rise to the Level of Disability?

Let's revisit Chris, the student in our opening vignette:

Lately, when Chris leaves the wards he goes directly home, crawls into bed falling asleep immediately, only to awaken at 5 in the morning and repeat the previous day. Two days ago, Chris started night float (a mandatory requirement in his program). After the 2 weeks of night float end, Chris finds it difficult to get into his old routine. He has trouble falling asleep, finds himself crying at the end of each evening, and has lost a total of 15 pounds since starting the program. Chris has withdrawn from his friends and his family and spends all of his non-clinical time in bed, sleeping. Chris is drowning in depression and is completely unaware of how to change his circumstance.

You might be asking yourself, *"But these programs are stressful. Being a provider is stressful. Is Chris **really** a person with a disability or just another stressed out health science student?"*

There are times when every health science student will experience symptoms that can be very uncomfortable. For example, in clinical rotations with long days, students will experience fatigue and exhaustion. They will have trouble falling asleep; they may be anxious about presenting in front of their clinical team. These symptoms might occur during a stressful portion of a rotation or during exam week. However, when the stressor ends, the symptoms typically end, and with time and experiences, students' symptoms attenuate and become less pronounced in the clinical setting, their stress-related symptoms are time-limited, and they do not have a major impact on the students' overall functioning.

Other times when health sciences students experience fatigue, insomnia, and anxiety, among other symptoms, and they persist beyond a stress evoking event or a busy week or rotation, they should be guided to seek out a healthcare professional to diagnose potential mental health conditions and to help determine if the mental health condition should be considered a disability. During these times, the symptoms are negatively impacting the student's ability to function and are causing *functional limitations*—a key part of determining disability. When symptoms of impairment begin to impact the student's activities of daily life or interpersonal relationships, they may meet the threshold for disability.

Functional Limitations with Psychological Disabilities

Students with psychological disabilities may experience functional limitations in many areas including difficulty with sleeping, energy, eating, and concentrating [59]. In some cases, students with a psychological disability might be receiving medication treatment for their condition. Some medications to treat anxiety, bipolar disorder, and even the insomnia associated with depression can result in fatigue and some cognitive fogging [60].

Accommodations for Psychological Disabilities

Accommodations are designed to remove barriers to the educational, learning, or work environment and are determined based on an interactive process that looks at the functional limitation (e.g., impact of disability on the person in a specific context) and the barriers created in the learning environment.

Students with acute psychological distress should be immediately referred to counseling. For those who experience chronic, but well-managed, psychological disabilities, academic accommodations may ensure equitable access to educational programs and allow students to remain engaged with their support systems, attend to their wellness-related needs, and maintain their enrollment and continuation in health profession programs. Disability resource professionals (DRP) within the respective programs or another designated individual who oversees disability accommodations can work with students to establish a proactive accommodation plan that ensures access across all points in the curriculum, including clinical rotations.

Determining Reasonable Accommodations

Reasonable accommodations are the mechanism by which barriers in health science settings are removed. Like a key to a door, accommodations are designed to "open the door" to the program. Accommodations do not lower standards or lessen the amount of information a student must learn; instead they provide an equal opportunity to engage in the educational process or to perform the essential functions of a job by mitigating the impact of the functional limitation in a specific setting. For example, a student with a mental health condition whose medication is causing some cognitive difficulties may require more time in a standardized testing situation. The functional limitation would be the slowed processing caused by the cognitive difficulty, the environmental barrier would be the time constraints imposed on the examination, and the accommodation would be additional time (see Fig. 5.4 and Table 5.3).

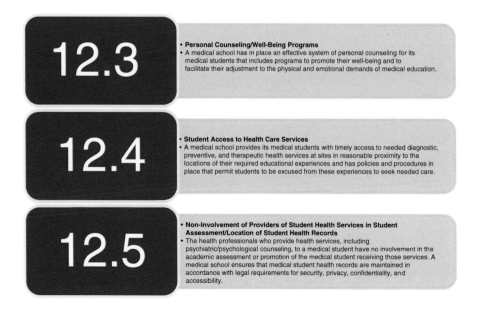

Fig. 5.4 LCME Requirements for Health Care Services and Well-Being Programs

Table 5.3 Common accommodations in clinical settings

Functional limitation	Accommodation
Slowed processing	Dragon dictate: Speech-to-text technology to assist with charting
	Assigned specific patients for presenting
	Reduced patient load
Difficulty with concentration	Smart pens for recording patient intake
	Reminders set on watch to direct use of time
	Noise-cancelling headphones for charting
Panic attacks	Laminated list of how to present patient worn on badge (to facilitate ease of reference)
	Pre-assigned patients for presenting
	Ability to take 10-minute breaks throughout the day to meditate and practice calming techniques
	Release from clinic for weekly therapy appointments
Anxiety	Release from clinic to go to weekly mental health appointments
	Request clinical rotations in geographical areas that allow continued therapy
	Completing competencies or clinical hours via simulation

Adapted from Meeks and Murray [61]

Table 5.4 Proactive accommodations for clinical placements

Need	Potential accommodation
Weekly appointments	Release from clinical duties to attend appointments. Time missed to be made up on alternative day
Continuous sleep	Weekend day call in lieu of overnight call
	Hard stop on wards by 10 pm
Getting to the clinical site: parking/driving	Designated parking or access to parking space to allow student to leave and return quickly from appointments
	Placement at clinical sites within a specified radius of a student's primary provider's location to facilitate weekly appointments
Clinical rotation order scheduling	Ordering of rotations to allow for break time between physically taxing rotations (surgery/medicine/Ob-gyn)
	Scheduling of rotations to provide equal distribution of physically taxing rotations (e.g., avoiding medicine and surgery back to back)
Release from specific clinical site	Thoughtful placement into clinical sites to avoid having student rotate at locations where they were admitted or evaluated (e.g., through ED, in-patient psychiatry, ICU)
Decompression of clinical rotations	Students may require a decompression of clinical rotations in one of the two models:
	Decompression by block with one block on/one block off
	Decompression by extending the length of individual clinical rotations

Adapted from Meeks and Murray [61]

Some of the most common accommodations to address psychological disabilities are proactively approached. These accommodations work to support the ongoing need for sleep, mental health appointments, decompression of curriculum, or clinical rotations (See Table 5.4).

Guidance from Accrediting Bodies

Nursing

The nursing profession is guided by multiple accrediting and state regulatory bodies, and to date none of these offer guidance or regulation on the creation of supports for student mental health or disability accommodation.

Medicine

The Liaison Committee on Medical Education (LCME) provides specific guidelines for Medical Student Health Services. The LCME lists three elements that medical schools must follow to maintain accreditation (see Fig. 5.5) [62]. Together, these three elements guide medical school programs in ensuring that counseling services are available in a timely manner, that wellness is promoted proactively, and that healthcare services are within reasonable proximity to the clinical rotations. Most importantly and in line with our recommendations in this chapter, the LCME requires medical schools to release students to seek needed care, including

Fig. 5.5 Depiction of student disability determination

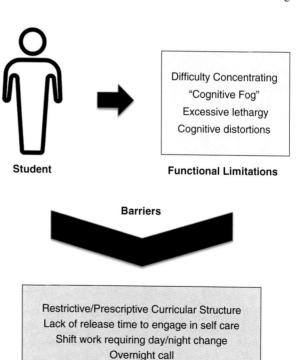

psychiatric and psychological care. Given the impact of stigma on the help-seeking behavior of students in health science programs, it is critical and recognized in the LCME element guidance that providers of mental health services do not retain any role in the academic assessment or promotion of the medical students and that all clinical notes and treatment records are held within legal requirements for security, privacy, and confidentiality.

Disability Insurance

The LCME requires medical schools offer disability insurance to each medical student. While all schools must be compliant with this guidance, the importance and attention given to electing disability insurance varies considerably. Consider the large number of students who acquire a psychological disability across all health science fields (see Table 5.1) and the consequences that can result from a new, acute onset of psychological disability. These might include the need to take a leave of absence, to decompress the curriculum (thus extending time in medical school), and to mobilize additional resources (e.g., therapy, hospitalization, medication.)

Disability insurance is one way that schools can help ensure that students who might need to take time off during their education can remain financially supported. Depending on a school's policies, when students are on a leave of absence, particularly an extended leave of absence, they might be taken off of their student health insurance. Some may have to leave school housing or lose financial aid. By providing all students with disability insurance, schools can ensure that students who may be at their lowest points do not also have to experience loss of care, loss of their providers, loss of housing, and loss of social supports due to financial difficulties.

The LCME standards for accreditation of medical schools require that a school must ensure that disability insurance is available to each medical student. The cost for disability insurance is low, as most students never use their disability insurance during their time in medical school. It is a worthwhile investment by schools to provide this for all students. Making it optional and leaving the cost to the student can result in students opting not to enroll. However, schools that require it and pay for it make a strong statement to their students: we want to support you throughout your educational time with us, and we want to make sure that if, due to your disability, you have to take a break from the curriculum, you will be financially supported to enable you to get care, to get better, and to get back to school.

Let's go back to our vignette in the beginning of the chapter. *Chris is drowning in depression and is completely unaware of how to change his circumstances.* Given the acute nature of Chris's predicament, surely exacerbated by his recent change in shift work, he will likely need to step out of his program for a period of time to attend to his health and wellness. Now imagine Chris attends school in a highly populated city that is also prohibitively expensive. Once Chris goes on leave, depending on the school's policies, he could lose access to housing, health insurance, and prescription coverage. For students who have psychological disabilities and need to take a leave of absence (LOA) or decompress the curriculum, the financial impact is a significant consequence and may serve as a disincentive to engage with services. Chris may need to take a 3-month leave of absence that would surely have financial consequences. If he does not have personal means to pay his rent, or other expenses, he may choose to forgo a LOA and "push through" his program, to the detriment of his health. If, on the other hand, Chris had elected into disability insurance, he may be eligible for coverage under the insurance, which would help offset his living cost, mitigating the financial concern and increasing the likelihood that Chris would put his health first.

Leave of Absence Policies

Leave of absence policies for students with disabilities can be unexpectedly and unintentionally harmful. Many administrators and faculty falsely believe that students with psychological disabilities have to take a leave of absence until they are clear of any symptoms or impairment. However, this belief and approach can be punitive and paternalistic. A leave of absence can be punitive in that it does not take into consideration the unintended consequences of a leave of absence (see Table 5.5). It can be paternalistic in that the belief that a student with a chronic psychological disability must be "fixed" fails to recognize that individuals live and thrive with chronic mental health conditions and are gainfully employed in all professions.

Nursing students have a unique stressor in that they matriculate in cohorts and proceed through the curriculum in a lock-step fashion (i.e., entering a future course is dependent on completion of the previous course). This leaves little flexibility in the system. Therefore, the unexpected need to take a leave would require the student to reenter a year later, even if they only require a week or two to address their disability-related needs.

Table 5.5 Potential consequences of leave of absence (LOA) and impact on students

Potential consequence of LOA
Loss of housing
Loss of revenue (in particular, are you referring to student loans or perhaps work study?) loss of income derived from scholarship, loan, or work study
Loss of student health services
Loss of health insurance
Loss of cohort/social support
Separation from medical or mental health provider
Loss of student status and need to repay student loans after 6 months as a non-student status
Impact on student
Removal from support system (especially critical for underrepresented minorities, first generation to college students, and socioeconomically disadvantaged students)
Separation from friends
Increased shame, feelings of worthlessness, "I can't cut it" or "Maybe I'm not cut out for this"
Exacerbation of symptoms/conditions
Lack of focus, "nothing to get up for"
Increased stressors from financial burden
Increased desire to act on suicidal thoughts feeling that all is lost

When determining fitness for health science schools and determining reasonable accommodations, we focus on functional limitation and whether or not accommodations can reasonably remove any barriers that are caused from the functional limitation (see Table 5.2). Students with chronic mental health disabilities (e.g., bipolar disorder, dysthymia, PTSD) can function well with appropriate accommodation and attention to their wellness.

Potential Consequences

A number of students with psychological disabilities face potential consequences of taking a leave of absence. As noted in Table 5.5, a leave of absence can have serious financial, social, medical, and psychological consequences for students. Knowing that these consequences exist can serve as a *strong disincentive* to seek help. Even for those students who wish to take a leave of absence, the financial and social impact may be enough to keep students in school to the detriment of their health.

Assumption of Support

When thinking about what a leave of absence might offer a student, administrators, disability professionals, and faculty should also be mindful not to assume privilege. It can be easy to imagine our students returning home to a supportive family with time to attend to the student's needs, good health insurance, access to providers, financial resources to support the student's health care bills and student debt, and ability to provide an ideal environment where the student can recover. This is not the experience of all students, and for some, the support network they have been building at their health professions school might offer more nurturing, more resources, more expertise, and more support for the student in need.

The Student Perspective

Students who are asked to take a leave of absence are fearful and can feel overwhelmed at the prospect of leaving their current environment, even if they are experiencing a mental health event. The power differential that naturally exists between faculty and students adds to the complexities of advising a student with students likely to "follow direction" even if they feel that with the proper accommodations or resources they could stay in a program.

When developing a leave of absence policy, institutions should be careful to allow for the modification of policies when appropriate and ensure that the leave of absence policy itself does not serve as a barrier (see Box 5.1).

Box 5.1 Potential Barriers to Leave of Absence
- Requiring multiple signatures prior to LOA
- Requiring diagnosis on provider letters vs an overall attestation that the student requires a leave
- Charging leave of absence administrative fees
- Requiring extensive "fitness for duty" exams upon reentry for students who took voluntary leave of absence in absence of any concerning behavior
- Re-enrollment fees upon reentry
- Immediate withdrawal of services (psychological, medical) upon leave of absence

---

Box. 5.2 Summary Best Practices for Leave of Absence Policies
- Know the accommodations and modifications often used in clinical programs
- Avoid the potential barriers to LOA (see Box 5.1)
- Only require a provider attestation for leave (exclude diagnosis, history, trajectory).
- Know the guidance for settlement agreements and FOLLOW it.
- Do not punish students for seeking help. Students are more likely to make good decisions when they are well supported.
- Assign a mental health contact for disability services.
- Fitness for duty should be clinician of student's choice. (Treating provider).

Best Practices for LOA

Know what you don't know! Schools may not be aware of their obligations to reasonably accommodate students with psychological disabilities. Multiple DOJ settlements offer school-specific guidance on important topics, and these can inform a best practice model for drafting leave of absence policies [63–66].

First, programs should be aware of the common reasonable accommodations afforded in health science programs (as listed in this chapter) and should make students aware that these accommodations are available to those who qualify under the ADA as a person with a disability.

Next, programs should understand the existing guidance to schools under various settlement agreements (see Box 5.2 Lessons learned from the UTHC settlement) and the codes that guide evaluation of direct threat (see Chap. 13). Schools should also ensure that the messaging they convey about mental health is not punitive, which may keep students from disclosing mental health concerns and seeking treatment. Indeed, schools should treat mental health leaves no differently than medical-based leaves of absences. Identifying a disability professional who can work directly with programs to identify reasonable accommodations for psychological disability ensures that regardless of program knowledge, best practice on the topic will be followed. Always defer to the students primary treating provider for fitness for duty. An established relationship with a foundation of trust is critical to a proper assessment.

Leave of Absence Language

Taking a leave of absence should be a simple process. Most students deciding whether or not to take a leave of absence are already burdened with the consequences and implications of doing so or may already have entered a program or treatment center and may not be able to complete a long to-do list independently. Programs can assist students in the process by streamlining communication, assigning a staff member to serve as a point person to collect any needed documents and to assist with reentry to the program. The process should be simple and the requirements to take a leave should be minimal. Most importantly, communication around taking a leave of absence should be supportive and recognize the legal protections for students with disabilities (see Box 5.3).

Health science programs should aim to craft leave of absence policies that should try to honor the following principles:

1. A leave of absence is for the benefit of the student; therefore, the process should be student-centered and easily navigable for a student in need. Think of it as a lifeline and not an obstacle course.
2. A leave of absence can entail some degree of social and financial disruption for a student, and it should be entered into thoughtfully by both the student and the school. Disability insurance can make leaves of absence go more smoothly for students and schools.

Box 5.3 Sample Language for a Leave of Absence Policy
- Students in [insert institution or program] often take time away from their studies to engage in personal reflection and to care for their physical and mental health. A request based on the need to attend to personal well-being is automatically approved for a period of up to 1 year.
- A provider's attestation of need should be submitted and accompanied by the Leave of Absence form. Once received, the program will take immediate action to support the student's leave of absence. In partnership with the [insert role or office], the program will create a plan to return in line with the academic and curricular structure of each program.
- Students should note that their well-being is our first priority and that we support reasonable accommodations to mitigate the impact of physical and psychological disabilities. Students can inquire about the availability of disability related accommodations by contacting [Name of person in office/email/or website for office].
- All students must continue to meet the program's technical standards with or without reasonable accommodations while enrolled in the program [insert technical standards link/ensure with or without language is included].

3. Students can often feel pressured or coerced into agreeing to go on a leave of absence. It is important for the school to recognize the power differential that exists between a struggling student and a large institution. At these vulnerable moments, students need their school to respect and support their personal autonomy. Assigning someone to advocate for the student is one way to help the student become an equal partner in the negotiations.
4. Mental health comes in gradations; it is not black and white, all or nothing, in or out. Schools should recognize the expertise of the student's own primary mental health provider in recommendations regarding leaves of absence.
5. Going on a leave of absence does not waive a student's right to privacy. Paperwork from the primary mental health provider should be simple and straightforward and should be seen by only those who need to see this (e.g., DSP and one school official).
6. Most mental health issues are manageable conditions, and many healthcare providers have had mental health issues and function at a very high level.

Conclusion

Part of building a culture of wellness in health science professions is the recognition that physicians, nurses, and other health professionals can simultaneously be highly competent and a person with a psychological disability. Indeed, some physicians, nurses, and medical students disclose chronic mental health disabilities and receive reasonable accommodations that, in conjunction with self-mitigating measures, ensure that they can balance their mental health and wellness needs with the duties of their role [2, 27].

Yet, high rates of burnout, depression, anxiety, and mental health concerns are present in medical and nursing students, and environmental contributors cannot be discounted. While efforts to promote wellness and foster resilience can help improve overall morale among students, they are not a substitute for taking an honest look at the often-toxic culture of our institutions and our professions. We must ensure that each student has access to high-quality mental health services and disability resources as needed and that skilled advisors and mentors are there to help all students process the many difficult and challenging situations they experience as health professions students. As educators, mentors, advisors, deans, and administrators, we have a responsibility to our students to help them become the healthcare workforce of the future.

References

1. Americans With Disabilities Act of 1990, Pub. L. No. 101–336, 104 Stat. 328. 1990.
2. Gupta R. I solemnly share. JAMA. 2018;319(6):549–50. https://doi.org/10.1001/jama.2017.22135.
3. Meeks LM, Herzer K, Jain NR. Removing barriers and facilitating access: increasing the number of physicians with disabilities. Acad Med. 2018;93(4):540–3.

4. McKee MM, Smith S, Barnett S, Pearson TA. Commentary: what are the benefits of training deaf and hard-of-hearing doctors? Acad Med. 2013;88(2):158.
5. Annonymous. In my experience. How educators can support a medical student with mental illness. Acad Med. 2019;94:1638. https://doi.org/10.1097/ACM.0000000000002953.
6. King and Bradley. PRC national nurse engagement report. Retrieved on 1 Oct 2019 from: https://prccustomresearch.com/wp-content/uploads/2019/PRC_Nursing_Engagement_Report/PRC-NurseReport-Final-031819-Secure.pdf.
7. Frajerman A, Morvan Y, Krebs MO, Gorwood P, Chaumette B. Burnout in medical students before residency: a systematic review and meta-analysis. Eur Psychiatry. 2019;55:36–42.
8. Wedgeworth M. Anxiety and education: An examination of anxiety across a nursing program. J Nurs Educ Pract. 2016;6(10):23–32.
9. Rotenstein L, Ramos M, Torre M, Segal J, Peluso M, Guille C, et al. Prevalence of depression, depressive symptoms, and suicidal ideation among medical students: a systematic review and meta-analysis. JAMA. 2016;316(21):2214–36.
10. Tung Y-J, Lo KKH, Ho RCM, Tam WSW. Prevalence of depression among nursing students: a systematic review and meta-analysis. Nurse Educ Today. 2018;63:119–29. https://doi.org/10.1016/j.nedt.2018.01.009. Epub 2018 Feb 9.
11. Chen D, Sun W, Liu N, Wang J, Guo P, Zhang X, Zhang W. Effects of nonpharmacological interventions on depressive symptoms and depression among nursing students: a systematic review and meta-analysis. Complement Ther Clin Pract. 2019;34:217–28.
12. Aradilla-Herrera A, Tomas-Sabado J, Gomez-Bonito J. Associations between emotional intelligence, depression and suicide risk in nursing students. Nurs Educ Today. 2018;34:520–52.
13. Dyrbye LN, West CP, Satele D, Boone S, Tan L, Sloan J, Shanafelt TD. Burnout among US medical students, residents, and early career physicians relative to the general US population. Acad Med. 2014;89(3):443–51.
14. https://www.americannursetoday.com/kicking-off-year-healthy-nurse/.
15. National Academy of Medicine. Clinician Resilience and Well-being – National Academy of Medicine. [online]. 2018. Available at: https://nam.edu/initiatives/clinician-resilience-and-well-being/. Accessed 28 Oct 2018.
16. https://www.nationalwellness.org.
17. Card AJ. Physician burnout: resilience training is only part of the solution. Ann Fam Med. 2018;16(3):267–70.
18. Slavin SJ, Schindler DL, Chibnall JT. Medical student mental health 3.0: improving student wellness through curricular changes. Acad Med. 2014;89:573–7.
19. Brewer M, Reubenson A, Donaldson M, et al. Building graduate resilience for the disrupted future of the 21st Century. Australian Technology Network (ATN) of Universities; 2018.
20. Ríos-Risquez MI, García-Izquierdo M, Sabuco-Tebar ED, Carrillo-Garcia C, Martinez-Roche ME. An exploratory study of the relationship between resilience, academic burnout and psychological health in nursing students. Contemp Nurse. 2016;52(4):430–9.
21. Dyrbye L, Shanafelt T. Nurturing resiliency in medical trainees. Med Educ. 2012;46(4):343.
22. Meeks L, Case B, Herzer K et al. Change in Prevalence of Disabilities and Accommodation Practices Among US Medical Schools, 2016 vs 2019. JAMA. 2019;322(20):2022–24.
23. Meeks L, Jain NR. Accessibility, inclusion, and action in medical education: lived experiences of learners and physicians with disabilities. Washington, DC: Association of American Medical Colleges; 2018.
24. Zhao F, Guo Y, Suhonen L-KH. Subjective well being and its association with resilience among nursing vs medical students: a questionnaire study. Nurse Educ Today. 2016;37:108–13.
25. Howe A, Smajdor A, Stöckl A. Towards an understanding of resilience and its relevance to medical training. Med Educ. 2012;46:349–56.
26. Moir F, Henning M, Hassed C, Moyes SA, Elley CR. A peer-support and mindfulness program to improve the mental health of medical students. Teach Learn Med. 2016;28:293–302.
27. Thomas LJ, Asselin M. Promoting resilience among nursing students in clinical education. Nurse Educ Pract. 2018;28:231–4.

28. Sood A, Prasad K, Schroeder D, Varkey P. Stress management and resilience training among Department of Medicine faculty: a pilot randomized clinical trial. J Gen Intern Med. 2011;26:858–61.
29. Mc CM, McKinnon J. The importance of teaching and learning resilience in the health disciplines: a critical review of the literature. Nurse Educ Today. 2009;29(4):371–9.
30. Drolet BC, Rodgers S. A comprehensive medical student wellness program–design and implementation at Vanderbilt School of Medicine. Acad Med. 2010;85:103–10.
31. Dyrbye LN, Thomas MR, Shanafelt TD. Medical student distress: causes, consequences, and proposed solutions. Mayo Clin Proc. 2005;80:1613–22.
32. Gordon JS. Mind-body skills groups for medical students: reducing stress, enhancing commitment, and promoting patient-centered care. BMC Med Educ. 2014;14:198.
33. Thomas SE, Haney MK, Pelic CM, Shaw D, Wong JG. Developing a program to promote stress resilience and self-care in first-year medical students. Can Med Educ J. 2011;2:32–6.
34. Aherne D, Farrant K, Hickey L, Hickey E, McGrath L, McGrath D. Mindfulness based stress reduction for medical students: optimising student satisfaction and engagement. BMC Med Educ. 2016;16:209.
35. Chen J. Problem based learning- developing resilience in nursing students. Kaohsiung J Med Sci. 2011;27(6):230–3.
36. Slavin SJ. Medical student mental health: culture, environment, and the need for change. JAMA. 2016;316(21):2195–6.
37. Jahanpour F, Azodi P, Azodi F, Khansir, A. Barriers to practical learning in the field: A qualitative study of Iranian Nursing Students' Experiences. Nurs Midwifery Stud. 2016;5(2):e26920.
38. Rogers D. Which educational interventions improve healthcare professionals' resilience? Med Teach. 2016;38:1236–41.
39. Liang H, Wu k, Hung C, Wang Y, Peng N. Resilience Enhancement among student nurses during clinical practices: A participatory action research study. Nurse Educ Today. 2019;75(4):22–7.
40. Ludwig A, Burton W, Weingarten J, Milan F, Myers D, Kligler B. Depression and stress amongst undergraduate medical students. BMC Med Educ. 2015;15(1):141. https://doi.org/10.1186/s12909-015-0425-z.
41. Grady F, Roberts LW. Sleep Depribed and overwhelmed: sleep behaviors of medical students in the USA. Acad Psychiatry. 2017;41:661. https://doi.org/10.1007/s40596-017-0804-3.
42. Melaku L, Mossie A, Negash A. Stress among medical students and its association with substance use and academic performance. J Biomed Educ. 2015;2015:1.
43. Akhu-Zaheya LM, Shaban IA, Khater WA. Nursing students' perceived stress and influences in clinical performance. Int J Adv Nurs Stud. 2015;4(2):44.
44. Lekan DA, Ward TD, Elliott AA. Resilience in baccalaureate nursing students: an exploration. J Psychosoc Nurs Ment Health Serv. 2018;56(7):46–55.
45. Shanafelt T, Trockel M, Ripp J, Murphy ML, Sandborg C, Bohman B. Building a program on Well-being: key design considerations to meet the unique needs of each organization. Acad Med. 2019;94(2):156–61.
46. Meeks LM, Ramsey J, Lyons M, Spencer AL, Lee WW. Wellness and work: mixed messages in residency training. J Gen Intern Med. 2019;34(7):1352–5.
47. Panagioti M, Panagopoulou E, Bower P, et al. Controlled interventions to reduce burnout in physicians: a systematic review and meta-analysis. JAMA Intern Med. 2017;177:195–205.
48. Slavin SJ, Hatchett L, Chibnall JT, Schindler D, Fendell G. Helping medical students and residents flourish: a path to transform medical education. Acad Med. 2011;86(11):e15.
49. Dyrbye LN, Power DV, Massie FS, Eacker A, Harper W, Thomas MR, Szydlo DW, Sloan JA, Shanafelt TD. Factors associated with resilience to and recovery from burnout: a prospective, multi-institutional study of US medical students. Med Educ. 2010;44(10):1016–26.
50. Dyrbye LN, Sciolla AF, Dekhtyar M, Rajasekaran S, Allgood JA, Rea M, Knight AP, Haywood A, Smith S, Stephens MB. Medical school strategies to address student Well-being: a National Survey. Acad Med. 2019;94(6):861–8.

51. Van der Riet P, Levett-Jones T, Aquino-Russell C. The effectiveness of mindfulness meditation for nurses and nursing students: An integrated literature review. Nurs Educ Today. 2018;65:211.
52. Amsrud KE, Lyberg A, Severinsson E. Development of resilience in nursing students: a systematic qualitative review and thematic synthesis. Nurse Educ Pract. 2019;17:102621.
53. Reyes AT, Andrusyszyn MA, Iwasiw C, Forchuk C, Babenko-Mould Y. Resilience in nursing education: an integrative review. J Nurs Educ. 2015;54(8):438–44.
54. Szymczak JE, Smathers S, Hoegg C, Klieger S, Coffin SE, Sammons JS. Reasons why physicians and advanced practice clinicians work while sick. A mixed-methods analysis. JAMA Pediatr. 2015;169(9):815–21.
55. Wallace JE, Kemaire JV, Ghali WA. Physician wellness: a missing quality indicator. Lancet. 2009;374:1714–21.
56. Spurlock D. The Promise and Perils of High Stakes Testing in Nursing Education. J Nurs Regul. 2013;4(1):4–8.
57. Moynahan KF. The current use of United States medical licensing examination step 1 scores: holistic admissions and student well-being are in the balance. Acad Med. 2018;93(7):963–5.
58. Jain NR, Lewis C, Meeks LM. The process of requesting accommodations on certification, licensing, and board exams: assisting students through the application. The Guide to Assisting Students With Disabilities: Equal Access in Health Science and Professional Education. 2015;13:89.
59. Malhi GS, Mann JJ. Depression. Lancet. 2018;392(10161):2299–312.
60. Santarsieri D, Schwartz TL. Antidepressant efficacy and side-effect burden: a quick guide for clinicians. Drugs Context. 2015;4:212290.
61. Meeks LM, Murray JF. Mental Health and Medical Education. In Medical Student Well-Being, Springer, Cham. 2019. p. 17–58.
62. Liaison Committee on Medical Education (LCME). Functions and Structure of a Medical School: Standards for Accreditation of Medical Education Programs Leading to the MD Degree. Washington, DC/Chicago, IL: LCME; 2016. Effective July 1, 2017. http://lcme.org/publications. Accessed 23 Oct 2019.
63. Princeton settlement U.S. Department of Justice.
64. UTHC U.S. Department of Justice.
65. Quinnipiac U.S. Department of Justice.
66. Northwern Michigan U.S. Department of Justice.

Realizing Academic Success Within the Health Science Learning Environment

6

Kristina H. Petersen, Charlotte O'Connor, Steve Ciesielski, and William Eidtson

Introduction

Rigorous health science programs require the use of different affective and cognitive skills than those applied in many undergraduate areas of study [1]. Demanding health science learning environments can present unique barriers for students with disabilities, particularly students with specific learning disorders (SLD) and attention-deficit/hyperactivity disorder (ADHD) who may find prior compensation techniques inadequate [2]. Students with SLD and ADHD require accommodations to fully access curriculum. These students also benefit from support in developing learning strategies and skills to help mitigate learning barriers and address the volume, pace, and complexity of health science curricula [3, 4]. Effective approaches to learning will vary based on context, content, and individual differences [5, 6].

The cognitive process of learning involves identifying new information and deciding what is important, organizing new information into meaningful and memorable patterns, and making connections between new information and existing knowledge in order to recall or apply it in the future [7]. This process is governed by a student's ability to monitor, control, and modify his/her learning (metacognition), as well as initiate and maintain goal-focused behaviors (motivation) [7]. Students

K. H. Petersen (✉)
Assistant Professor, Department of Biochemistry & Molecular Biology, Director, Academic Support Programs, New York Medical College, Valhalla, NY, USA
e-mail: k_harrispetersen@nymc.edu

C. O'Connor
Office of Medical Student Education, University of Michigan School of Medicine, Ann Arbor, MI, USA

S. Ciesielski
Assistant Dean for Student Success, MGH Institute of Health Professions, Boston, MA, USA

W. Eidtson
Geisel School of Medicine at Dartmouth, Hanover, NH, USA

© Springer Nature Switzerland AG 2020
L. M. Meeks, L. Neal-Boylan (eds.), *Disability as Diversity*,
https://doi.org/10.1007/978-3-030-46187-4_6

can learn the self-regulatory behaviors of metacognition and motivation, which are essential to the learning process and achieving academic success [3, 8, 9].

Section 1: The Learning Process

The Science of Learning

Learning has been defined in many ways, and there are numerous published theories. In this chapter, we will highlight enduring principles that are supported by published evidence and can be practically applied to support student learning. Most models of cognitive-information processing can be traced to the multistage theory of memory proposed by Atkinson and Shiffrin [10], which proposed that information goes through a series of transformations before it can be stored in long-term memory [10, 11]. Driscoll [11] proposed that sensory input is received, a select amount of which is deposited into temporary working memory, after which information must be encoded to be stored in long-term memory [11]. A subsequent retrieval process is necessary to access information stored in long-term memory.

The cognitive theory of multimedia learning is of particular relevance to modern health science program curricula because it focuses on content presented in visual and aural formats (e.g., PowerPoint in conjunction with a lecture). This theory proposes that meaningful learning occurs when students *select* relevant information received via dual-channel aural and visual sensory input, *organize* information into a coherent structure within temporary working memory, and *integrate* information with existing knowledge to encode it into long-term memory [12–15]. As students *select* relevant information, they attempt to determine the most important material presented and add it to working memory. In order for students to *organize* content, they must make connections within the selected content. As students *integrate*, they build connections between new and existing knowledge [14, 16]. When discussing the simultaneous use of the visual and aural sensory input channels, it is particularly important to understand cognitive load theory. The basis for this theory is that working memory has a limited capacity. When both channels (visual and aural) are used simultaneously, the working memory can be used to its full capacity, but if sensory information is received too quickly, a student can experience cognitive overload. It is possible for instructors to design curriculum with this in mind by making an effort to minimize extraneous information and taking frequent pauses during lectures to allow students time to fully process content (see Chap. 7) [17–20].

Broadbent [21] and Marton and Saljo [22] proposed a distinction between surface and deep learning: surface learning involves reproducing learned material, whereas deep learning involves attempting to understand the meaning of learned material [21–23]. Deep learning approaches are associated with success on subsequent examinations [22, 23] and include integration of knowledge, summary writing, and self-testing [24, 25]. The deep learning approach was supported by a recognition that students thrived when given opportunities to elaborate on their knowledge (e.g., allowing students to discover how learned material relates to other topics, particularly clinical applications) [26, 27]. Levin [28] defines "elaboration" as learning that "involves meaning-enhancing additions, constructions, or generations that improve one's memory for what is being learned" [28].

Problem-based learning curricula provide opportunities for students to "elaborate" by requiring them to formulate and criticize hypotheses about problems presented, discuss evidence to support or refute hypotheses, and generate summaries of information [29]. This applied approach particularly appeals to adult learners who prefer to learn information that is relevant and practically useful [30–34]. Elaborative study tasks promote effective information encoding and have been found to be important to successful learning [28, 35]. Elaboration tasks may include drawing diagrams, tables, pathways, or figures.

Generative learning occurs when learners generate relationships between presented information and their own experiences [7]. Examples of generative learning include generating summaries of content or notes that require connections with previous knowledge or experiences, making verbal and graphical connections with content, generating analogies while reading text, self-testing, self-explaining, and teaching [7, 36–43]. A common challenge learners face is transferring learned knowledge to a new situation. Whether or not successful transfer of problem-solving skills or knowledge occurs depends on the learner's use of cognitive and metacognitive strategies [44]. Mastering learning transfer is essential to succeeding on many health science program examinations, particularly questions that involve clinical applications of the basic sciences.

In this chapter, we will define learning as the process of creating meaning and understanding through individual experiences and interactions, which results in lasting changes and increases the likelihood of improved performance or learning in the future [45, 46]. Of particular importance in this definition are the assumptions that learning is a process not a product, although we can only infer successful learning by measuring learning outcomes; a lasting change in knowledge, beliefs, or skills; and accomplished by students' active engagement with knowledge and experiences, not something that is done *to* them [16, 46].

Self-Regulation, Motivation, and Metacognition

When students actively engage in the learning process, they are more likely to be intrinsically motivated to achieve learning objectives [5, 6, 47–50]. Student engagement is embedded within empirically proven active learning techniques, which require students to participate in meaningful activities that enlist critical thinking skills to apply concepts [51–53]. Active learning techniques are often discussed in the context of instruction (see Chap. 7). However, as students consider how to most effectively approach individual and group studying, the principles of engaged, active learning still hold true and should be infused into study plans. It is the responsibility of the student to actively engage in the learning process both in class and during individual study sessions.

Self-efficacy has been described as a person's beliefs concerning his/her ability to perform a given task successfully [54]. These beliefs can impact a student's actions, effort, perseverance, and resilience within an academic program [8, 55, 56]. Self-efficacy is related to academic performance and persistence [57] and is positively associated with course participation [3]. Self-efficacy beliefs develop over time and can be cultivated as goals are achieved and intrinsic interest increases [54]. Self-efficacy beliefs improve largely due to satisfaction derived from mastering a certain level of performance [58]. When students are confident in their abilities, they are more likely to reflect about how they best learn (referred to as metacognition) [59], manage time better through strong self-regulation techniques [60, 61], and stay motivated to persevere through difficulties to ultimately achieve their goals [3, 8, 9].

Self-regulated learning occurs when a student approaches his/her understanding of the learning process proactively and is motivated to take appropriate action to improve where necessary [60]. Self-regulated learners set goals and monitor progress while reflecting on their strategies. These learners tend to have strong self-efficacy beliefs, which may help them view learning tasks as interesting and worthwhile and allow them to continue utilizing learning strategies that maximize their success [60, 61]. Self-regulated learners are more likely to succeed academically and have a more optimistic view of the future [9]. As faculty and mentors meet with students, they should set goals to assist students in developing self-regulated learning skills. As students develop these skills, any resulting academic success can fuel more positive self-efficacy beliefs [57].

Students with SLD and ADHD: Variations in the Learning Process

The neurological variations that characterize SLD and ADHD can impact students' cognitive processing, motivation, and use of learning strategies in ways that pose barriers to academic achievement [17, 62] (Tables 6.1 and 6.2). Most often students with SLD are reported to have persistent deficiencies in phonological processing, which is defined as their ability to break down the sounds of language and match

Table 6.1 Specific learning disorders (SLD)

Specific learning disorder [71]	Possible barriers to learning	Potential functional limitations
With impairment in reading (dyslexia) [88, 89]	Comprehension, phonetic decoding, word recognition, and reading fluency	Slower reading rate Deficits in comprehension and retention Deficits in spelling Deficits in discerning main ideas Slower written expression
With impairment in math (dyscalculia) [90, 91]	Understanding mathematical concepts and using math skills to solve problems	Slower reading/processing Deficits in understanding symbols and alignment of numbers Deficits in understanding spatial concepts and math reasoning
With impairment in written expression (dysgraphia) [92, 93]	Letter formation, spacing, organization of the page, or speed of putting written information on paper; writing is laborious and messy	Deficits in motor coordination Barriers to effective note-taking, essay composition, and in-class writing

Table 6.2 Attention-deficit/hyperactivity disorder (ADHD) [71]

Types	Possible symptoms	Potential functional limitations
Inattentive	Lacks attention to detail Makes careless mistakes Lack of focus Doesn't seem to listen Doesn't understand or follow instructions Avoids tasks that involve effort Easily distracted Forgetful Loses things necessary to complete daily tasks	Organizing time and materials Sustaining attention Processing information Ignoring distractions Listening Following through on tasks Persistence of effort or response to tasks that have little intrinsic appeal or minimal immediate consequences
Hyperactive-impulsive	Fidgets, taps hands or feet Unable to stay seated Moves at inappropriate times Talks too much Talks out of turn Interrupts, intrudes, or takes over Often in a rush	Delaying a response Waiting for outcomes Regulation and inhibition of behavior Impulse control Interpersonal skills/relationships
Combined	Displays symptoms of both inattentive and hyperactive-impulsive types Most common type	Some combination of limitations listed above

sounds to written symbols [63, 64]. For this reason, students with SLD may have deficits in reading, reading fluency, reading comprehension, and memory [65] and thus require accommodations to access curriculum. These students can also benefit from developing learning strategies to address additional barriers [66, 67].

Students with ADHD may experience hyperactivity, impulsivity, inattention, or some combination of these symptoms which pose barriers to concentration and can affect academic performance [68–72]. When planning and implementing learning strategies, students with ADHD may encounter barriers determining relevant information and inhibiting impulsive responses [73]. Students with ADHD often encounter barriers when skills such as focused attention, planning, cognitive processing, and self-control are required to complete a task [74]. Wallace et al. [75] reported that college students with ADHD experienced barriers to persisting and enjoying learning [75].

Students with SLD and ADHD may encounter barriers when the learning tasks require them to select, identify, prioritize, organize, synthesize, or recall information, particularly within constraints, such as timed testing conditions or a fast-paced curriculum [76]. Research of students with and without disabilities has demonstrated that retention and understanding of material rapidly declines after about 15–20 minutes of uninterrupted lecture [77, 78] and that the number of students paying attention also drops dramatically after 15–20 minutes [79–81]. For students with processing and attention disabilities, attempting to staying engaged in a lecture that extends beyond 15–20 minutes can present a considerable barrier. Students with ADHD often experience barriers when engaged in note-taking, summarizing, and test-taking [82] and may demonstrate motivational barriers and a greater reliance on extrinsic advice rather than intrinsic insights to improve performance [75].

Students with SLD and ADHD may also experience barriers when they encounter learning tasks that require planning, monitoring, time management, or persistence of effort [83, 84]. Strategies that may benefit students with SLD and ADHD include the explicit use of metacognitive, self-regulatory, and behavioral learning methods [17, 62, 85, 86]. Metacognition is part of the "executive processes" [59] that include orientation and monitoring of comprehension task requirements, planning the steps involved in task processing, checking and regulating cognitive processing when it fails, and evaluating outcomes of processing [87]. Developing and strengthening metacognitive skills can support students with SLD and ADHD in mitigating barriers to learning [17, 62, 85, 86].

Section 2: Barriers to Learning in Health Science Programs

Students with disabilities encounter various barriers to learning in health science programs, which we categorize as either physical/environmental or attitudinal/behavioral [94]. Physical/environmental barriers in a learning environment can include those that are organizational, structural, and curricular. Attitudinal/behavioral barriers may be encountered as learners confront the beliefs, attitudes, misconceptions, biases, stereotypes, or discrimination of individuals (sometimes their own) operating within a learning environment. Table 6.3 describes some common barriers to learning in health science programs.

Although we have summarized some of the most common barriers to learning experienced by students with disabilities, they will vary from one program to another, and from one student to another. Section 3 presents strategies to mitigate various barriers to curricular content and negative self-judgment. Chapter 7 addresses instructional design barriers and negative beliefs of others.

Section 3: Strategies for Mitigating Barriers to Learning

Dyslexia in Medical School: A Case Study

Adam Atkins was diagnosed with dyslexia in third grade and achieved success with accommodations through high school. Adam went to college part-time and earned an associate's degree in radiation technology. After working for 2 years as a radiologic technologist in a large hospital system, he decided to get a bachelor's degree and pursue a career in medicine. He transferred to a 4-year public university, where he earned A's and B's in his pre-medicine coursework. By the time he applied and was accepted to an MD program, he was nearly convinced that he had "outgrown" his learning disability.

In the medical school program, clinical experiences went well for Adam; he was accustomed to working with patients and performing procedural and other

Table 6.3 Examples of Physical and Attitudinal Barriers to Learning

Potential physical/environmental barriers	
Curricular content	Large volumes of information [95, 96]
	Content that requires high levels of abstract thinking [97] or visual-spatial processing [98]
	Pre-class knowledge acquisition without scaffolding (e.g., flipped classrooms) [67, 99]
	Attendance requirements [100]
	Heavy memorization [101]
	Information presented at a fast pace [102]
	Heavy reading loads [102]
	Social/communication skill-based grading [103]
	Varied instructors with different styles/approaches [104]
	Learning experiences that require fine motor skills [98]
	Assessments provided in only one format [105] or given under timed conditions [106]
Instructional design [107]	Course materials contain lengthy paragraphs without headings
	Presentation slides with dense text, small or difficult to read fonts [67, 99, 108]
	Course materials given to students in an untimely fashion
	Blanket rules, such as no laptops in class [109–111]
	Uncaptioned videos [112]
	Text used without graphic examples and vice versa [99, 113, 114]
	Instructors who speak quickly and/or remove visual material before learners can process the information [77, 115]
	Materials that do not account for learners with color blindness or other visual impairment or are not compatible with assistive technology [112, 116]
	Numerous back-to-back, non-interactive lectures [77, 80, 81]
	Course content with metaphors, sarcasm, or frequent references to aspects of American culture with no additional explanation or background
Physical space [67, 117, 118]	Lack of ramps and/or elevators
	Doors that are heavy or difficult to open
	Classrooms with poor sight lines or acoustics
	Rooms with inflexible seating layout or lack of standing options
	Inaccessible restrooms
	Inaccessible library or study spaces
	Rooms with excessive noise
	Rooms with visual distractions, such as busy colored walls or floor coverings
Other considerations	Care of parents, children, significant others
	Outside employment
	Cost prohibitive resources, such as question banks and outside tutors
Attitudinal/behavioral barriers	
Negative beliefs of others [67, 119–122]	Unconscious and implicit bias
	Intolerance to difference
	Lowered expectations
	Stigma
	Discrimination
	Stereotypes
Negative self-judgment [95, 96]	Reluctance to seek support [69, 123, 124]
	Perfectionism [125]
	Competition [126]
	Fear of failure [126]
	Stereotype threat [127, 128]
	Impostor syndrome [125, 129, 130]

hands-on tasks. The reading, written work, and exams were challenging, however. Adam realized that he had not outgrown his dyslexia after all and decided to seek accommodations at his medical school.

Questions to consider:

- *What barriers to learning might exist for a student with a reading disability?*
- *Which strategies might you suggest for Adam if you were the Disability Resources Provider (DRP)?*
- *Are there any advantages to being a physician with a reading disability?*

Learning Strategies to Mitigate Common Curricular Barriers

Students in health science programs must develop strategies to conquer the intense workload [95]. Some students may believe the solution is to simply work harder, even at the expense of their emotional and physical well-being [131]. However, developing a more efficient study plan will be more effective and sustainable [59–61]. Studies have demonstrated that students with SLD and ADHD do not have strong self-regulation skills and, to compensate for the barriers they face, spend more time studying than students without disabilities [131–133]. Therefore, when working with students with SLD and ADHD, it is especially important to emphasize efficient study techniques and encourage the implementation of a balanced, self-regulated learning plan.

Among the student population in health science programs, there is often a tendency to avoid seeking help [69, 96, 123, 124, 134]. Students' past experiences can impact how they value and seek support from learning or disability resource professionals. Those who have previously encountered and overcome barriers with little or no support may attempt to address issues without making use of available support systems [120, 122, 134]. In addition, if a student's impression of support services is negative due to misconceptions or previous experiences, the student may be reluctant to use these resources. In some cases, students may fear using academic support or disability resources will further stigmatize them or worry that they will be perceived as taking advantage of the system [120, 122]. Although some health science programs include graduation competencies for developing help-seeking behaviors and maintaining self-care, much could be done to alter health science student culture to normalize and encourage help-seeking behaviors as a critical part of professionalism.

Students with disabilities require accommodations to fully access curriculum. In addition to accommodations, students with disabilities can benefit from developing learning strategies to address their specific needs. Learning strategies are the techniques or methods students use to select, organize, integrate, and apply new information [16, 135]. Students who successfully apply learning strategies can intentionally control, monitor, evaluate, and adapt their usage of techniques based on their real time needs [7, 59–61]. Successful students utilize various learning strategies and develop self-reflection and self-regulation skills to monitor their progress.

It is important to assist students in identifying learning barriers so they can be mitigated by a study plan. Every plan will be specifically tailored to the individual as learning strategies are selected to address each barrier. As students are encouraged to embark on the often challenging task of trying new study strategies, it is critical to help them focus on their motivation for success and to emphasize the importance of fully engaging in the agreed-upon study techniques to discover those that work best. When students fully engage and are motivated, they are more likely to see positive learning outcomes [5, 6, 47–50, 136].

Evidence-Based Learning Principles
As students discern which strategies to use and how to apply them to their study plans, it is important to highlight a few evidence-based learning principles that apply to students with and without disabilities.

Deliberate Practice
Studies have demonstrated a positive effect of regular, effortful practice on one's ability to achieve superior performance [137, 138]. The amount of practice required to master a particular skill varies, and while it is agreed that innate talent plays a role, even one with innate talent must deliberately commit time to regular practice to achieve expertise. To truly understand health science content to a mastery level, one must engage in repeated, effortful practice [139].

Spaced Repetition
The concept of spaced repetition, in contrast to massed repetition ("cramming"), involves multiple exposures to material with periods of time lapsing between sessions. Studies have demonstrated increased retention when material is reviewed repeatedly, with time between study sessions [140–143]. While there is general agreement that repetition is necessary to assimilate and retain new information, the optimal timing between repeated content exposures has been studied in various types of content, but consensus has not yet been reached.

Retrieval Practice/Testing Effect
Many students think of practice questions merely as a tool to assess knowledge just before an exam. However, research has demonstrated that students who regularly test themselves during study sessions retain information better, especially in the long-term. This is referred to as retrieval practice or the testing effect [144–147]. This type of learning also occurs during quizzes and examinations. Therefore, students should seize any opportunity to review exam questions, as learning from mistakes can support long-term retention for future cumulative final and board/certification examinations [144, 148, 149].

Active Recall
Often students will listen to lectures, read texts, and review notes. While these are important strategies for content acquisition, using them repeatedly without other active methods can lead to a passive study plan. Ideally students should interleave these strategies with active recall activities, such as drawing a pathway from

memory or writing a list of drugs that fall into a particular category [150]. Even when a student's recall (retrieval) attempts are unsuccessful, studies have demonstrated that active recall enhances future learning [151].

Strategies for Selecting and Organizing Information

Previewing Material and Preparation for Lectures

Preparation is particularly important for students with disabilities who may have a difficult time identifying the high-yield content in the lecture and/or may require more time to process content [152–154]. Previewing material before lecture can help students with disabilities prime themselves to tune in to the professor's cues during class [155]. Students should pay attention to course and lecture objectives, what is covered in course readings, and which clinical cases are assigned and how they relate to the material [156, 157]. If lecture outlines are available, they can be used as a starting point for note-taking during lecture [154, 158].

Reviewing assigned material before attending lectures primes students to actively learn and engage in material [155]. Taking notes, identifying and defining unfamiliar vocabulary, and writing down questions about content will facilitate active listening during lecture as students seek answers to their questions and take notes to stay engaged [159, 160].

Note-taking Strategies

It has been established that generative note-taking (e.g., paraphrasing, mapping) is more effective than non-generative note-taking (i.e., verbatim copying) [36–40]. Effective note-taking involves four broad skills: listening, cognitive processing, writing/recording, and reviewing noted information [161–164]. Cognitive processing requires students to discern important ideas, activate prior knowledge and associate it with new knowledge, retain information in short-term memory, paraphrase content, and elaborate on lecture ideas [165–167]. When students engage in a deeper level of processing during lecture, they are better able to record the most important ideas in their notes while making connections with prior knowledge [36, 168]. Given the density of content presented and time limitations of health science programs, taking time to create highly detailed notes is unrealistic. Notes must be written in such a way that the student can subsequently extract meaning, add or delete information, and review multiple times to facilitate retention [155].

During lecture, writing or typing notes in real time requires listening, cognitive processing, and writing/recording to occur simultaneously. Students with disabilities may find such complex multitasking activities difficult [115, 152, 154, 158, 169]. Some of the accommodations that reduce these barriers on a case-by-case basis include use of a note-taker or scribe, ability to review recorded lectures, use of a smart pen, and the use of handheld tablets or iPads [158, 170]. Suritsky [171] surveyed a group of 31 college students with learning disabilities who reported that their top five challenges with note-taking were speed of writing, attention span, making sense of notes, discerning important information, and understanding the professor [171].

Note-taking: Laptop Versus Longhand Notes

Laptops are critical tools for students with disabilities such as dyslexia, processing speed deficits, rheumatoid arthritis, or other conditions that may impair the ability to write longhand [89, 158, 172]. While professors often cite evidence suggesting that multitasking on laptops during class can be distracting [173], many students with disabilities rely on technology to fully access and participate in courses. Some professors have banned laptops from class, which forces students with disabilities to make a difficult choice: maintain their privacy as a person with a disability or fully access the curriculum (see Chap. 7 for a discussion of a more inclusive instructional approach to this issue) [109–111].

Professors who ban laptops often cite a study reported by Mueller and Oppenheimer [174] that suggests note-taking on laptops is less effective than using pen and paper, in part due to the study's report that students tend to type verbatim notes on a laptop even when instructed not to do so [174]. However, it is important to note that this study does not involve students enrolled in a graded course, used a pre-recorded TED Talk lecture, and paid some of the students to participate. Effective note-taking strategies within semester or year-long advanced health science courses may be considerably different than those employed while watching a single TED talk. In fact, many students taking advanced science courses use stylus pens in conjunction with their laptops to access digital images and write directly on complex pathways or diagrams in parallel with the lecturer. Bui, Myerson, and Hale [175] reported an advantage of laptop usage over longhand note-taking, although some of their methodologies were questioned in the Mueller and Oppenheimer study [174, 175]. Luo et al. [176] reported that the optimal note-taking medium will depend on the nature of the lectures and emphasized that retention is affected by whether or not a student reviews notes subsequent to the lecture [176, 177].

The lack of consensus in cited studies can be confusing. However, we know the cognitive processing step is critical to taking effective notes [36, 165–168]. We also know the cognitive processing step can be challenging for students with certain disabilities [115, 152, 154, 158, 169] and that many students with disabilities require laptop technology to fully access the curriculum [89, 158, 172]. Consequently, when discussing note-taking strategies for students with disabilities, emphasizing the cognitive processing step is critical, especially to students who use laptops. To be effective, students must not transcribe lectures; rather, they should listen to the lecturer and periodically summarize information in their own words, write questions when there are points that require subsequent clarification, and note areas that need further review. In addition to using assistive technology necessary for accommodations, laptop users may explore technology options to determine whether they can benefit from tools such as a stylus pen to facilitate a hybrid note-taking approach. Any lesson on effective note-taking should also emphasize the importance of reviewing notes, ideally multiple times in a spaced repetition manner, in order to achieve desired learning outcomes [140–143, 176, 177].

Summarizing

After a lecture session, students can generate an outline with a summary of key points and identify questions to answer before the exam. As part of this process, students with disabilities may utilize recordings of lectures to revisit material that was presented too quickly for them to fully process. These outlines are a starting point for regular review and should not cover every detail [165–167]. It should be noted that studies of students with SLD have demonstrated improved recall when material is organized into categories or "chunked" [178].

Mapping

Concept mapping is a method of elaboration that facilitates the encoding of meaningful relationships between concepts and guides the student to make connections with previously learned knowledge [179, 180]. Whether used individually or as a tool for group study, research has shown concept maps promote critical thinking by forcing students to view material holistically [181–183].

Teaching

Students who teach in peer-assisted learning (PAL) programs report increased confidence and understanding through the act of teaching [184]. In addition, studies have demonstrated that PAL tutors earn higher exam scores in the areas of content that they have taught [185, 186]. The idea that one solidifies understanding of knowledge by teaching should be emphasized as students consider working in study groups, where opportunities arise to teach one another [187, 188].

Self-Regulation Strategies and Time Management

To keep up with the new pace and volume of curricula presented in health science programs, time management and study efficiency are critical to student success [60, 61, 101, 189–191].

Setting Goals

While students usually have a clear long-term goal to become an excellent healthcare professional, they may have more difficulty recognizing the numerous small steps necessary to achieve that goal. Studies have reported that motivation is the strongest predictor of college GPA and is therefore a critical component of a self-regulated learning plan [192, 193]. To stay focused and motivated, students can be coached to break down their long-term goal into a series of manageable, achievable short-term goals [8, 191, 194–198].

A short-term goal should be specific and measurable, so students know when it has been achieved [199]. For example, "to achieve a score of 85 on my next biochemistry examination" is a specific, measurable goal, whereas "to do well in biochemistry" is not specific or measurable because it is left to the student to interpret if or when the goal has been achieved [195]. The act of writing down a goal may increase accountability [200]. Frequently viewing a written goal increases the likelihood the student will engage in practice activities to work toward accomplishing the goal [201].

Box 6.1 Creating a Study Schedule	
Identify obligated time.	Lectures, work, meetings, travel time, meals, laundry, sleep, medical appointments, etc.
Add any important dates.	Deadlines, exam dates, etc. [195, 196]
Identify available time.	Assess how much is left for studying and other balance activities
Add balance time.	Breaks, recreation, physical fitness, socializing, family time [6, 202, 203]
Prioritize individualized study techniques to populate the open time.	Various methods for content assimilation, study groups, practice questions, flashcards/memorization techniques, review sessions, etc. [101, 139, 141, 144, 145]

Creating a Plan

Advisors may work with students to create plans to achieve individual short-term goals. Academic plans are usually made in conjunction with a calendar but can also be done in a to-do list format with daily and weekly goals. Students should create a specific, step-by-step plan to guide them through the behaviors and strategies required to achieve the goal (Box 6.1) [195, 197, 198].

Quality, Not Quantity: Efficient Studying

Study strategies must be identified that contribute to the best outcomes for each individual student. A self-regulated approach to studying should include regular periods of self-reflection to determine what study strategies work best. Students should identify "time sinks" and form new habits that allow them to reinvest their time to better accomplish goals (Box 6.2) [60, 61, 190, 197]. As students improve their efficiency, self-efficacy beliefs improve, which has a positive effect on academic performance and persistence [9, 57, 204].

Accountability and Follow-Through

It can be easier to set and accomplish goals with support from others [214]. Students should be encouraged to participate in any existing mentoring programs on campus [215] or to select an accountability partner [214] who supports their goals (Box 6.3). Meeting with a mentor or accountability partner regularly is important while establishing new habits. An intervention referred to as "ADHD coaching" aims to assist students with ADHD and SLD in developing self-regulation and time management skills through regular meetings with a coach [205, 206]. Parker et al. [216] conducted a 1-year study at ten college campuses throughout the USA; students diagnosed with ADHD who participated in "ADHD coaching" felt their participation resulted in their development of self-regulated learning skills and positive academic experiences and outcomes [216]. Troiano et al. [217] reported that students with disabilities who regularly used academic support services were more likely to have higher grades and graduate than students with disabilities who did not use support services regularly [217]. Zwart and Kallemeyn [82] demonstrated that students with ADHD who accessed peer-led coaching sessions regularly earned higher grades

Box 6.2 Planning Efficient Study Time [205, 206]

Before – Set Yourself Up for Success

Find an appropriate place to study with minimal internal and external distractions [207]. Turn off your cell phone and disconnect from social media [190, 208].

Identify which topics you will cover, and estimate how long it will take you. Before starting, create realistic goals to set yourself up for success [195–197, 207].

During – Pay Attention to Progress

Keep track of the amount of time it takes to accomplish a goal (e.g., read 10 pages, watch a recorded lecture, etc.), by recording your start and stop times [209]. This will make future planning more accurate.

Take note of your distractors. If you become distracted, refocus as quickly as possible. If you struggle with sustaining attention, consider starting with shorter study sessions with more frequent breaks and working up to longer sessions [209–211].

When studying clinical material, use a book of patient cases as a reference. This is an example of anchored or situated learning; adult learners prefer to learn relevant and practically useful information [31–34]. This can help fuel motivation while also providing an opportunity to apply basic sciences to a clinical scenario.

If a technique isn't working, change it! Successful strategies will vary from course to course. Studying the same material using multiple modalities can help you see content from various perspectives, which reinforces learning. Strategies to try include group study, note-taking, practice questions, flashcards, mnemonics, reading, drawing diagrams and figures, concept maps, etc. [190, 210–212].

After – Assess Your Productivity

Pay attention to what worked, and take note of anything that could be improved or any strategy that did not help you achieve a goal [210–212].

Identify "time sinks," and commit to reinvesting lost time into actions that help you achieve your goals.

Create new habits, and be patient with yourself as you determine which study strategies work best for you. To create a new habit, repetition and self-acknowledgment are important [213].

Box 6.3 Planning Efficient Study Time [205, 206]

Meet regularly to set goals, and check in about progress.

Remind the student of goals even when challenges or feelings of disappointment surface.

Remain invested in the student's goal, and support accountability to the schedule and study plan.

Provide support, encouragement, and expertise to help the student achieve goals.

than those who did not [82]. ADHD coaching sessions align with principles covered in academic coaching sessions in the health sciences and can be used as a model to provide support to students with SLD and ADHD.

In the most extreme circumstances, e.g., when students are at risk of being dismissed from a program, an advisor may need to act as an accountability partner on a short-term basis and follow up periodically to ensure the student is taking actions to achieve academic goals.

Strategies for Self-Monitoring

When students are proactive and organized, they will be able to identify knowledge gaps early enough to fix them. Checkpoints, such as practice questions, group studying, and collaborative learning sessions, are helpful resources to identify weaknesses. Knowledge gaps represent areas where a student is most likely to lose points on an examination and should be prioritized in a study plan to maximize learning outcomes and exam performance [6, 60, 61].

Dyslexia in Medical School: Adam Atkins Case Discussion [88, 89, 183, 218–220]

The medical school DRP, Diego Gomez, interviewed Adam to determine how accommodations had supported him in high school and what learning strategies had worked for him in college. This became a starting point to identify barriers specific to the medical school curriculum.

As part of his medical school accommodations plan, a Livescribe® pen, which captures audio and visually records handwritten notes, was given to Adam to use during his time as a student. In addition, Adam was given speech-to-text and text-to-speech software to assist reading and writing tasks. To accommodate the great volume of reading, Diego worked with the DRP to locate audio text resources. When books were only available in print, the DRP scanned the text to convert it to audio format.

Diego was aware of many online study resources available to medical students. While many are free, others offer paid subscriptions. Adam had a strong preference for online lectures and animated videos. They discussed resources that seemed most likely to meet Adam's needs.

Students with reading disabilities often find it easier to make connections by drawing a concept map as an alternative or supplement to notes. Diego recommended Adam select one of several free online applications, paid subscriptions, or books of concept maps created specifically for medical and nursing students. A summary of Diego's recommendations to support Adam is included in Table 6.4.

Potential Benefits of Dyslexia

According to the British Medical Association, the following attributes, common among those with dyslexia, are beneficial for clinicians in health science professions [221]*:*

- *Innovative and lateral thinking*
- *Superior troubleshooting skills*
- *Intuitive problem solving*
- *Creativity*
- *Facility with hands-on learning*
- *Excellent verbal communication*

Table 6.4 Dyslexia in medical school: Adam Atkins [88, 89, 183, 218–220]

Barrier	Accommodation	Didactic	Clinical	Learning strategy
High volume of reading	Audio books Video content Text-to-speech software	x	x	Listen first without taking notes to increase comprehension, as time allows
Note-taking	Livescribe® pen to capture lectures/allow for re-listening/enhancing notes	x	x	Attend all lectures and experiences
High volume of memorization in a short timeframe		x	x	Use mnemonics Create concept maps Use color-coding to show relationships Use school tutors/study partners
Unfamiliar vocabulary	Phone application or online medical dictionary	x	x	Create flashcards to review regularly
Fast-paced curriculum		x	x	Use a planner or calendar Maintain a daily schedule Track how long it takes to do tasks, and plan accordingly
Handwriting deficit	Speech-to-text software, e.g., Dragon Dictate Medical Use laptop computer for note-taking	x	x	Develop a personal system of abbreviations
Slow speed performing calculations	Use a talking or other calculator	x	x	Check and double check numbers for accuracy
Composing SOAP notes	Use a laptop computer compatible with electronic medical record systems and confidentiality to type notes Speech-to-text software		x	Use Spellcheck and proofread for accuracy
Barriers to assessments				
Time constraints Spelling deficit	Extended time for exams 1.5x Smaller setting or private room for testing Use of spell check software for essay exams	x	x	Subvocalize (read out loud softly to self) Use Spellcheck and proofread for accuracy

*The barriers, accommodations, and strategies listed may not apply to every student with a similar diagnosis. Always follow an interactive process to determine specific barriers, accommodations, and learning strategies for the individual learner

Strategies for Mitigating Student's Attitudinal Barriers to Learning

Students may experience a number of intrinsic barriers to learning, which may be difficult to identify. We highlight a few of the most common student attitudinal barriers to learning and make suggestions for mitigating these barriers.

Impostor Syndrome

Some high achieving students question whether they deserve to be enrolled in their programs and may even believe their admission was an error [129, 130, 222]. This set of beliefs is referred to as impostor syndrome, which is prevalent among students in health science programs; students with these beliefs often desire perfection and put themselves down every time they do not achieve it [125, 130]. Impostor beliefs may be reinforced if a student fails an examination. Studies have reported that impostor syndrome is a barrier for college students with disabilities [131, 223].

Research suggests that the impostor phenomenon can be transitory and with the right support students can work to overcome this unhealthy mindset [125, 130]. When students have failed an examination and find themselves studying for a remediation while also trying to move forward with coursework, they are likely to spend a disproportionate amount of time studying and have less time with their primary support system, including friends and family. It is important for advisors to support these students in building their self-efficacy beliefs, assist them in developing a growth mindset, and help them acknowledge their accomplishments while assisting them in creating an effective study plan [55–57, 224, 225].

Lack of Attention to Wellness, Growth Mindset, and Self-Care

Students have acquired a variety of academic and non-academic skills and habits prior to their health science program matriculation. A student's inability to address and handle stress associated with academic challenges can have a devastating effect and leave him/her feeling dejected and overwhelmed [126, 202]. This can quickly lead to a feeling of powerlessness and helplessness and may contribute to a student's impostor syndrome. At this critical time, it is important for students to feel supported and focus on things within their control: personal wellness, developing a growth mindset, and, once they are well enough, developing a proactive academic plan for success in future courses [198, 224–226].

Mindset theory asserts that assumptions about talent and intelligence profoundly impact how students view mistakes and failures. Those with a fixed mindset view their abilities as static and believe that failure results from a lack of ability. Conversely, those with a growth mindset view ability as acquired through practice and effort; "failure" can therefore be viewed as an opportunity for improvement [225]. Fostering a growth mindset with students can help them reframe their academic challenges into an opportunity for growth [224, 225].

When creating study schedules, it is critical to help students set reasonable expectations, work toward efficiency, and include balance time [6, 202, 203]. Looking forward to balance activities can fuel motivation to accomplish study goals [227–229]. When addressing wellness, it may be helpful to explain Maslow's hierarchy of needs [230, 231] which prioritizes taking care of one's physiological and emotional needs before addressing difficult tasks. A discussion of this theory can serve as a blueprint to help students prioritize basic elements of self-care such as nutrition, sleeping well, and exercising [232]. When students feel well, they tend to have strong self-efficacy beliefs, which contribute to their ability to learn more effectively [57, 95, 204, 227–229, 233–236]. Many students also find that regularly using deep breathing, yoga, meditation, visualization, or another relaxation technique helps reduce anxiety and promote mindfulness [237, 238].

Addressing Test-taking Strategically

Although successful test-taking requires a combination of content mastery, strategy, and growth mindset, we included test-taking strategies in the attitudinal barriers section to emphasize the importance of a healthy mindset to an intentional, strategic approach (Box 6.4). If a student achieves content mastery, but does not enter the examination with a growth mindset and strategies to cope with anxiety, the examination score may not accurately represent his/her knowledge and study effort [224, 225, 239–242].

Successful students prepare for examinations well in advance, utilizing a plan informed by the type of examination. By understanding the format of the examination (e.g., short answer, essay, or multiple choice), study approaches and practice questions can address information from that vantage point [243]. Ideally a student will execute a study plan that allows for confidence as the examination begins, helping the student trust his/her knowledge, instincts, and answers selected. The student can further improve examination day confidence by establishing and honing stress management skills. While in the examination, it can help to reframe feelings of anxiety so it is no longer entirely a negative element, but instead may fuel success [213, 244–246].

Box 6.4 Common Test-taking Challenges and Strategies for Success

Challenge	Strategy for Success
Rushing through the exam – jumping to conclusions	Slow down; read questions thoroughly.
Changing answers – doubting instinct	Trust your first instinct; only change an answer you *know* is wrong.
Arriving late to the testing site	Plan ahead to avoid stress: pack your bag the night before, and allow more than enough time to get to the test location.
Looking to classmates for support and confirmation of ideas the day of the examination	Avoid talking with anxious students the day of the exam, as this behavior may increase personal stress.
Cramming material shortly before the exam; pulling an "all-nighter"	Pace studying and get a good night's sleep before the exam to allow for clear thinking [247–249].
Using ineffective study habits – e.g., memorizing facts without context or understanding	Study to attain a higher cognitive level by using strategies that require applying, analyzing, evaluating, and creating knowledge [250, 251].
Experiencing stress during the exam	Rehearse techniques for stress reduction and stress management prior to the exam [198].

Test Anxiety in Nursing School: A Case Study

Eun-Sook is a 29-year-old female from Seoul, South Korea, who is enrolled in the Direct Entry Master's Program in nursing. She arrived in the USA 8 weeks ago. Two faculty members referred Eun-Sook to the academic support office after the first round of examinations in two separate courses. Eun-Sook never used academic support services in Korea.

In the first meeting, Eun-Sook shared that she felt stressed and anxious, speaking about family pressures and her need to achieve. Eun-Sook reported that she does not have a medical diagnosis related to her test anxiety and so understands that she is not eligible for exam accommodations. She expressed that she has always been a bad test-taker and that she has struggled with mild test anxiety in the past, but it had never been this bad. While enrolled in high school and college, she experienced test anxiety but did not feel it impacted her grades.

Since enrolling in the nursing program, she has experienced considerable stress leading up to examinations, had difficulty sleeping the night before, and feels her scores do not reflect her study efforts. During the two recent examinations, her mind went blank, and she experienced rapid heart rate and increased breathing, felt sweaty, and was emotionally distressed. Eun-Sook's anxiety worsened as she saw students finish the examination and leave the classroom.

Questions to consider:

- *What barriers to learning might exist for a student who experiences test anxiety in nursing school?*
- *What learning strategies might you discuss with Eun-Sook?*

Strategies for Test Anxiety

Feeling a certain amount of anxiety or stress about an examination is normal [252, 253]. Some anxiety can help motivate students or catapult them into higher levels of achievement [213, 246, 254]. However, high levels of anxiety, often referred to as test anxiety, can interfere with learning and hinder examination performance [213, 244–246]. A student who experiences test anxiety, but does not have an underlying medically diagnosed disability, would not be eligible for accommodations. However, there are study skills and test-taking strategies that can help students prevent and cope with it. Students may experience test anxiety for many reasons including previous negative test-taking experience(s), lack of preparation, massed repetition ("cramming"), fear of failure, pressure to perform well, and focusing on negative outcomes rather than preparing for success [202, 204, 252, 254, 255]. Studies of students who experience test anxiety have demonstrated hindered examination performance [239–242]. People experience test anxiety differently, but in addition to physical, emotional, and behavioral symptoms, many experience cognitive symptoms including going blank, difficulty concentrating, negative self-talk, feelings of dread, comparing oneself to others, and racing or disorganized thoughts [236, 256, 257]. If any of these symptoms become pervasive, lost examination time may hinder optimal performance [239–242, 244, 245, 252, 254].

Mindfulness, or being in the moment, is a powerful tool that students can use during examinations [237, 258]. A stressed, exhausted student may adopt a disorganized, repetitive thought pattern of harsh self-criticism. In these moments, it is important for a student to stop, take note of the current thought pattern, and reset. Cognitive behavioral techniques, including reframing, recognizing locus of control, and controlled breathing can help a student re-group [259]. Most schools offer wellness workshops or programs to assist students in developing these and other useful stress management techniques. As students take charge of their test-taking strategies, they feel empowered to focus on the areas that are within their control (Box 6.5).

Box 6.5 Taking Charge of Examinations

Review your syllabus and course learning objectives
  What do I need to know?
  What do I already know?
  What don't I know – and what is my plan for assimilating that information? [260, 261]
Make a plan [57, 204, 235, 236, 190]
  Prepare and commit to a study plan.
  Develop reasonable expectations.
  Have a clear plan for exam day [237].
  Pack your bag the night before the exam.
  Plan for success.
Tap into your resources [134, 237, 258, 262–264]
  Seek assistance from your counselor, learning specialist, tutors, mental health and wellness staff, peer mentors, etc.
  Ask questions.
Test yourself
  Take a timed practice test under conditions that are as similar as possible to those of the actual test exam [257].
  Perform error analysis; prepare a strategy to preemptively combat errors [265].
  Seek help if necessary to address any shortcomings.
Practice wellness/be nice to yourself
  Develop and use relaxation techniques that work for you (yoga, deep breathing, imagery, visualization, etc.) [57, 204, 235, 236].
  Make a list of your successes, and read it during times of difficulty [57, 204, 235, 236].
    Keep things in perspective.
    Eat well, exercise, and get enough sleep.
    Reward yourself for meeting small and large goals [139].
    Change negative thinking patterns.
    Use positive self-talk.
Exam Day
    Eat a good breakfast. Take healthy snacks and water to the exam.
    Consider warming up your mind by reviewing material for 20 minutes.
    Arrive at the exam location no more than 10 minutes early (but don't be late!).
    Avoid discussing the exam with other students; consider wearing earphones.
    Keep track of your time during the exam.
    Keep calm, stay positive, and gather as many points as you can using the content knowledge and test-taking strategies you have acquired.

Self-Advocacy and Knowing When to Seek Help

Although many health science program administrators talk to students about the importance of self-care, much needs to be done to alter health science student culture to normalize these actions as components of professionalism [202, 203]. As program directors communicate expectations associated with professionalism, they should emphasize that reaching out for help to take care of one's own needs is critical to success as a health science professional [234, 266]. Particularly in light of these students being involved in future patient care, the message needs to be clear that clinicians must prioritize their own health if they are to be in a position to treat patients [267, 268]. Advisors must be familiar with campus support resources and encourage students to use them regularly to improve and strengthen their skill sets [120, 134, 269].

Test Anxiety in Nursing School: Eun-Sook Case Discussion
[213, 239–242, 244–246]

Although Eun-Sook experienced test anxiety, she did not have any underlying medical diagnosis that qualified her for accommodations. An academic support advisor helped Eun-Sook identify self-perceptions that hindered her from meeting her potential on examinations. By addressing her sense of "being a bad test taker," she was able to recognize her previous successes. When Eun-Sook realized that her anxiety was fueled by a pattern of thinking, she felt empowered to change. She carried a list of her top ten most significant accomplishments and started to journal her nursing school achievements.

Eun-Sook also started to use positive self-imaging. She imagined herself in the classroom taking the exam confidently, feeling good after the test, and also pictured what it would be like at graduation wearing her cap and gown, receiving her diploma. She learned how to anticipate and manage anxiety so she was no longer disempowered by it. If she felt anxious during an examination, she knew she could work through it by using mindful breathing techniques. A summary of the academic support advisor's recommendations to support Eun-Sook is included in Table 6.5.

Table 6.5 Test anxiety in nursing school: Eun-Sook [239–242, 244–246]

Barriers	Possible strategies
"Bad test-taker" self-perception	Take inventory of past successes
	Recognize that admission to the program requires previous academic success and test-taking aptitude
Anxiety impacting recall of facts	Practice using stress management techniques while studying
	Use deep breathing and visualization techniques
	Study in the room where the exam will be administered
	Practice self-care – including diet, exercise, and sleep
	Anticipate that stress will likely occur during the exam, and develop strategies to work through and manage it
	Reframe the importance of the exam
Fear of failure and low confidence in academic abilities	Change thinking patterns
	Develop reasonable expectations
	Make positive statements, even if at first they are hard to believe
	Reward dedication to the study plan
	Don't allow grades to become dependent on one exam
	Keep things in perspective

Section 4: Advising Students with SLD and ADHD in Need of Learning Support

Identifying Individual Learner Barriers

According to Crookston's developmental view of advising (1994), partnering with students to assess the barriers they are encountering is accomplished through an inquiry process that ideally takes place within an environment of "openness, acceptance, trust, sharing of data, and collaborative problem-solving, decision-making and evaluation" [270]. Advisors must attempt to ascertain what students are experiencing, filter that information through their knowledge and experience, and decide where, on a continuum, advising versus more student-discovered solutions are appropriate. Skillful navigation of this process not only is important in mitigating learning barriers but serves as an opportunity to model good interpersonal communication skills, a key competency for health science students [271, 272].

The One-on-One Student Meeting

Advisors can influence students' learning outcomes through a series of one-on-one interactions [273, 274]. Thus, advisors must have strong interpersonal and communication skills to build and maintain productive relationships with students [275]. Noel-Levitz [276] reported that college students consistently rated academic advising as an important part of their college experience [276]. If an advisor-student relationship is to be successful, students must feel heard and their questions must be answered [277]. Students guide these conversations, and advisors actively listen to understand the student's objective in the meeting. It is reasonable to ask the student "how can I help?" or "what are you hoping to get from this meeting?" To a student overwhelmed by details, such general questions may provide an opportunity for them to reassess their concerns while also demonstrating the advisor's openness and readiness to tailor a plan to their individual needs [278–281].

Historically, the advisor-student relationship can be described as "prescriptive" in that the advisor prescribed advice that the student received it [270]. However, as this relationship became viewed as an opportunity to facilitate and catalyze student growth and development, the newer model of "developmental" advising largely took the place of the prescriptive model [270, 282, 283]. Coll and Draves [284] reported that more effective advising outcomes resulted from developmental rather than prescriptive advising practices [284]. In a study of university students, Hale et al. [285] found that more than 95% of students preferred the developmental to the prescriptive advising approach [285]. Studies have connected postsecondary student retention to positive one-on-one relationships with professors or advisors [286]. Meeting individually with students is an effective way to build relationships, gather information, and assist students in creating study plans [212].

There are a few general considerations for proceeding with a one-on-one student encounter:

1. Prior to meeting, consider having the student fill out a questionnaire describing the learning strategies they are presently using. This engages the student in self-reflection and may also guide the initial conversation [60, 61, 210, 212].

2. Begin the meeting with a warm greeting to make it clear to students that they are in a supportive environment. Be ready to ask open-ended questions and listen empathetically.
3. Gather information to learn about the student.
   - Ask a general, open-ended question so the student can guide you toward what they most hope to discuss.
   - Ex.: How can I best be of support?
   - Ask questions to understand more about relevant prior experiences.
   - Ex.: What was your major in college? Tell me about your academic history.
   - Ask questions to better understand the student's current approach to studying.
   - Ex.: What strategies did you use to prepare for your exam? What do you feel worked and what could be improved [212]? What strategies have worked for you in the past?
   - Ask nonthreatening questions about personal wellness and work/life balance to assure the student you will be approaching the meeting holistically [202, 203]. Ex: Tell me about your support systems on and off campus. When you have free time, what do you like to do?
   - Ask reflective questions to ensure you understand what the student is expressing.
   - Ex: What I'm hearing you say is… Did I get that right?
4. After listening carefully to the student's self-reflections [212, 279–281], ask follow-up questions to better determine what specific learning strategies have and have not been working. Be sure to acknowledge his/her strengths and progress, and partner with the student to determine how to continue building on them.
5. Based on the information collected, share your assessment of what study strategies may support them. Try to lead students to discover their own plan. Sometimes students are considering a new plan or strategy and are seeking feedback.
   - Use language such as "My impression is____. Please tell me if I misunderstood." Or, "From what you've shared, it sounds like…" Or, "Based on what you shared, I wonder if ____ may be helpful?" [279, 280]
   - When helping the student create a plan, be sure to incorporate evidence-based learning principles previously discussed including deliberate practice, retrieval effect, spaced repetition, active recall, and generative learning.
6. Once you agree upon a plan, ask the student to share a study schedule with you by email within a day of the meeting, at which time you will review and reply with feedback [59–61, 210].
   - Support the development of a self-regulated learning approach by reminding the student that self-reflection is critical as the study plan is executed.
   - Guide the student to notice what is and is not working and to make appropriate adjustments. Discussing this information will help individualize the student's plan moving forward.
7. Schedule a follow-up meeting where the student can share experiences with the study plan and discuss any other concerns.
8. Send periodic emails during particularly stressful times (e.g., midterms and final examinations) to enrich students' feeling of support and continue to build the relationship [8, 55, 56, 210].

Questioning, Listening, and Intervening

To effectively identify barriers to learning, advisors must develop strong skills in posing nonthreatening questions, listening actively, and appropriately initiating and maintaining interventions [217, 279–281]. When done well, students will feel empowered to explore issues and develop appropriate solutions that encourage self-reflection, and advisors will view students and the barriers they face holistically [59–61]. Table 6.6 details advising skills necessary to effectively identify barriers to learning, as well as potential obstacles advisors may encounter.

Table 6.6 Interpersonal and communication skills of advisors: creating a safe space to assess student barriers to learning

Advisory skill	Ways to achieve	Positive outcomes	Obstacles to achieving	Negative outcomes if not achieved
Effective questioning/ probing [274, 279, 280]	Ask the reason for the meeting: What brings you here today? How can I best be of support? Ask about prior experiences: What was your major in college? Did you take time between college and professional school? Tell me about your academic history. Pose scaling questions: On a scale of 1 to 10, how confident are you that you can achieve your goal? Pose ideal case questions: In a perfect world, what would ____ look like? Ask about extracurricular factors: Tell me about the demands on your time outside of class	Provides an accurate picture of the various barriers a student faces [211] Encourages student self-reflection [211]	Taking incomplete history Making assumptions about students Believing a student's situation is the same as another student's	Rushed/ premature solutions Less transferrable solutions
Active listening [278–281]	Pay attention to verbal and non-verbal cues Make eye contact Reflect back to confirm understanding: What I'm hearing you say is… Have students explain their process in detail: Walk me through how you prepare for class	Builds trust Creates opportunity for student to open up Lessens likelihood of "one-size-fits-all" plans Student can appreciate the value of metacognition [59, 85]	Being distracted/ not in the moment Being too prescriptive	Blanket solutions Hearing what one wants to or expects to hear

Table 6.6 (continued)

Advisory skill	Ways to achieve	Positive outcomes	Obstacles to achieving	Negative outcomes if not achieved
Maintaining consistency between words and actions [274, 287, 288]	Be honest about how much time you have with the student Only share details of interactions with the student's permission Follow up promptly, especially if promised	Builds trust Sets reasonable expectations Models character	Not maintaining confidentiality Not following through as promised	Erosion of trust May confirm negative beliefs about support services
Using a developmental advising approach [270, 289, 290]	Ask the student to propose a solution to the concern or issue Emphasize the difference in learning approaches when students are looking for prescriptive advice If the student is reluctant or appears to have misguided beliefs/habits, share that what you are suggesting has worked for others: I have seen ___work for other students and you may consider trying ___. Then encourage them to bring individualized feedback to the next meeting for further evaluation of the method	Allows students to appreciate value of self-reflection Students are partners in the process Increases the likelihood of a tailored solution addressing specific needs	Being too prescriptive Not being assertive when a student is making a clear error in judgment Being too friendly or too stern	Solutions may not be useful for the student Student may feel pushed in an uncomfortable direction Student may feel advisor wasn't listening or wasn't helpful
Maintaining accountability [274]	Ask students to email a proposed plan by a specific date Follow up with students if you don't hear from them Set reminders to periodically check in with students via email	Fosters trust Maintains relationship Demonstrates caring Opens door to modify existing plan or address new concerns Models self-regulation	Disorganization Large caseload Inadequate student encounter tracking methods	Advisor can lose track of students' progress Difficult to know if suggestions are effective without student feedback

Awareness of the Institution's Policy for Students with Disabilities

Faculty, staff, and advisors must be aware of the institution's process for disclosure of disabilities and applying for accommodations. It is important to emphasize that only the institution's DRP should seek information from a student regarding any specific diagnosis. In the event that a student discloses a disability to anyone other than the institution's DRP, the student should be informed immediately in a supportive manner that all accommodation plans are determined by the DRP. No other faculty or staff member should engage in discussions about what accommodations may be appropriate to address the barriers faced by the student. Faculty and staff should encourage students with disabilities to see the DRP and, once an accommodation plan has been communicated by the DRP, take action as directed to ensure the plan is fully executed [120, 122, 134].

Some students who are registered for and receive accommodations may choose to share their diagnosis when seeking specific supportive strategies from a faculty member or learning support professional. If you find yourself in this position, there are a few things to consider:

- *First, confirm that the student has gone through the institutional procedure for obtaining accommodations.* If not, send them to the appropriate office on campus to do so. Invite them to continue a discussion of study strategies with you at a later time [120].
- *Only with the students' permission, consult the DRP.* Whenever possible, follow up with the DRP to get more information about the specific functional limitations associated with the student's disability and any recommended learning strategies.
- *Be aware of the various support services on campus.* A student with a learning disability may need disability resources but may also benefit from learning support, tutoring, mentoring, counseling, wellness, or other support programs [122, 134, 269].

Is It a Learning Disability?

Faculty members and learning support providers are often in a position to provide deep insight into a student's learning behaviors and experiences with barriers and thus can be an integral partner with the DRP in referring students when appropriate. As mentioned in the previous section, it is critical that all members of the institution understand that they should never ask about a diagnosis or attempt to diagnose a student. However, when students reach out for academic support from a faculty member or learning specialist, these advisors may notice a pattern of behavior that could be consistent with a SLD or ADHD. The faculty or mentor may consider suggesting that a conversation with the DRP might be beneficial if a number of the following characteristics and behaviors are observed in a student:

- Has experienced a learning deficit, such as slow reading, for many years [88, 89, 291, 292]
- Experiences barriers using learning or cognitive strategies or is not seeing improvement after a few diligent attempts to apply new strategies [69–72]

- Is forgetful consistently, disorganized, and unable to break projects into steps or displays other deficits related to executive functioning [69, 70]
- Expresses the need for more time to collect thoughts [69–72]
- Runs out of time while taking examinations [69–72]
- Experiences barriers memorizing course content, despite considerable effort [69–72]
- Gets bored easily and distractible and starts many projects but does not complete them [69–72]
- Appears to have deficits in auditory perception [63, 64] and/or gross motor skills [98, 293]
- Displays a significant or consistent gap between academic potential and achievement [294, 295]
- Doesn't pick up on social, emotional, or communication cues [296–298]
- Shyness, hyperactivity, or impulsivity [69–72]

Developing an Integrated Longitudinal Plan

After identifying barriers and recommending evidence-based strategies, the advisor partners with the student to create a study plan to address the individual learner's needs. It is important to encourage the student to monitor progress regularly and for advisors to follow up in order to troubleshoot and enhance plans as students reflect on strategies that have and have not been successful [60, 61, 145, 147, 187]. As students continue through the program, study strategies may need to be altered based on the type of content, the student's prior knowledge of the content, and real-time strengths and weaknesses.

When students develop the ability to reflect on challenges, adjust accordingly, and refocus their goals, they are more likely to succeed academically [145, 147, 205, 206, 217]. It is the responsibility of the advisor to support the student in optimizing the learning process, effectively serving in the role of a teacher by providing periodic feedback to assist the student's development into a self-regulated learner.

Conclusion

Students with SLD and ADHD encounter barriers in health science learning environments beyond those addressed by accommodations [17, 62, 67, 75, 83, 84]. Curricular and attitudinal barriers to learning can be mitigated with support. After identifying individual student barriers, a study plan can be created that incorporates evidence-based learning strategies to reduce barriers and meets individual needs. Advisors are in a position to support students in developing self-regulated learning skills by following up regularly, keeping students accountable to achieving their goals, and longitudinally monitoring their academic progress. Advisors should always use a holistic approach to assist students in creating study plans and prioritize balance and wellness.

References

1. Scheffer BK, Rubenfeld MG. A consensus statement on critical thinking in nursing. J Nurs Educ. 2000;39(8):352–9.
2. Rosebraugh CJ. Learning disabilities and medical schools. Med Educ. 2000;34(12):994–1000.
3. Stegers-Jager KM, Cohen-Schotanus J, Themmen APN. Motivation, learning strategies, participation and medical school performance. Med Educ. 2012;46(7):678–88.
4. Walters JA, Croen LG. An approach to meeting the needs of medical students with learning disabilities. Teach Learn Med. 1993;5(1):29–35.
5. Curry L. Individual differences in cognitive style, learning style and instructional preference in medical education. In: Norman GR, van der Vleuten CPM, Newbie DI, editors. International handbook of research in medical education. Dordrecht: Springer; 2002.
6. Brown PC, Roediger HL III, McDaniel MA. Make it stick: The science of successful learning. 1st ed. Cambridge, MA: Belknap Press: An Imprint of Harvard University Press; 2014. 336 p.
7. Fiorella L, Mayer RE. Learning as a generative activity: Eight learning strategies that promote understanding. New York: Cambridge University Press; 2015. 218 p.
8. Zimmerman BJ. A social cognitive view of self-regulated academic learning. J Educ Psychol. 1989;81(3):329–39.
9. Zimmerman BJ. Becoming a self-regulated learner: An overview. Theory Pract. 2002;41(2):64–70.
10. Atkinson RC, Shiffrin RM. Human memory: a proposed system and its control processes. Psychol Learn Motiv. 1968;2:89–195.
11. Driscoll MP. Psychology of learning for instruction. A Division of Paramount Publishing, Inc: Allyn & Bacon; 1994.
12. Wittrock MC. Generative learning processes of the brain. Educ Psychol. 1992;27(4):531–41.
13. Mayer RE. Applying the science of learning to medical education. Med Educ. 2010;44(6):543–9.
14. Mayer RE, Fay AL. A chain of cognitive changes with learning to program in Logo. J Educ Psychol. 1987;79(3):269–79.
15. Mayer RE. Multimedia learning. 2nd ed. New York: Cambridge University Press; 2009.
16. Mayer RE. Learning strategies for making sense out of expository text: The SOI model for guiding three cognitive processes in knowledge construction. Educ Psychol Rev. 1996;8(4):357–71.
17. Trainin G, Swanson HL. Cognition, metacognition, and achievement of college students with learning disabilities. Learn Disabil Q. 2005;28(4):261–72.
18. Ben-Yehudah G, Banai K, Ahissar M. Patterns of deficit in auditory temporal processing among dyslexic adults. Neuroreport. 2004;15(4):627–31.
19. Sweller J. Cognitive load during problem solving: Effects on learning. Cognit Sci. 1988;12(2):257–85.
20. Sweller J. Instructional design in technical areas. Australian Council for Educational Research: Camberwell; 1999.
21. Broadbent DE. The well ordered mind. Am Educ Res J. 1966;3(4):281–95.
22. Marton F, Säaljö R. On qualitative differences in learning–I Outcome and process. Br J Educ Psychol. 1976;46(1):4–11.
23. Marton F, Säaljö R. On qualitative differences in learning–II Outcome as a function of the learner's conception of the task. Br J Educ Psychol. 1976;46(2):115–27.
24. Groves M. Problem-based learning and learning approach: is there a relationship? Adv Health Sci Educ Theory Pract. 2005;10(4):315–26.
25. McParland M, Noble LM, Livingston G. The effectiveness of problem-based learning compared to traditional teaching in undergraduate psychiatry. Med Educ. 2004;38(8):859–67.
26. Stein BS, Littlefield J, Bransford JD, Persampieri M. Elaboration and knowledge acquisition. Mem Cognit. 1984;12(5):522–9.
27. Coles CR. Elaborated learning in undergraduate medical education. Med Educ. 1990;24(1):14–22.

28. Levin JR. Elaboration-based learning strategies: Powerful theory = powerful application. Contemp Educ Psychol. 1988;13(3):191–205.
29. Schmidt HG. The rationale behind problem-based learning. In: Schmidt HG, Lipkin M, de Vries MW, Greep JM, editors. New directions for medical education: Problem-based learning and community-oriented medical education [Internet]. New York: Springer; 1989. 105–111. [cited 2019 Nov 15]. (Frontiers of Primary Care). Available from: https://doi.org/10.1007/978-1-4612-3472-2_8.
30. Maudsley G, Strivens J. Promoting professional knowledge, experiential learning and critical thinking for medical students. Med Educ. 2000;34(7):535–44.
31. Lave J, Wenger E. Situated learning: Legitimate peripheral participation. Cambridge, UK: Cambridge University Press; 1991. 138 p.
32. Knowles MS. The modern practice of adult education: From pedagogy to andragogy. Englewood Cliffs: Cambridge Adult Education; 1970.
33. Kolb DA. Experiential learning: Experience as the source of learning and development. 1st ed. Englewood Cliffs: Prentice Hall; 1983.
34. Young MF. Instructional design for situated learning. Educ Technol Res Dev. 1993;41(1):43–58.
35. Craik FIM, Tulving E. Depth of processing and the retention of words in episodic memory. J Exp Psychol Gen. 1975;104(3):268–94.
36. Craik F, Lockhart R. Levels of processing: A framework for memory research. J Verbal Learn Verbal Behav. 1972;11(6):671.
37. Kiewra KA. Investigating notetaking and review: A depth of processing alternative. Educ Psychol. 1985;20(1):23–32.
38. Di Vesta FJ, Gray GS. Listening and note taking: II. Immediate and delayed recall as functions of variations in thematic continuity, note taking, and length of listening-review intervals. J Educ Psychol. 1973;64(3):278–87.
39. Slotte V, Lonka K. Review and process effects of spontaneous note-taking on text comprehension. Contemp Educ Psychol. 1999;24(1):1–20.
40. Igo LB, Bruning R, McCrudden MT. Exploring differences in students' copy-and-paste decision making and processing: A mixed-methods study. J Educ Psychol. 2005;97(1):103–16.
41. Peper RJ, Mayer RE. Note taking as a generative activity. J Educ Psychol. 1978;70(4):514–22.
42. Kourilsky M, Wittrock MC. Verbal and graphical strategies in the teaching of economics. Teach Teach Educ. 1987;3(1):1–12.
43. Wittrock MC, Alesandrini K. Generation of summaries and analogies and analytic and holistic abilities. Am Educ Res J. 1990;27(3):489–502.
44. Mayer RE, Wittrock MC. Problem-solving transfer. In: Berliner DC, Calfee RC, editors. Handbook of educational psychology. 1st ed. New York: Routledge; 1996. p. 47–62.
45. Ertmer PA, Newby TJ. The expert learner: Strategic, self-regulated, and reflective. Instr Sci. 1996;24(1):1–24.
46. Ambrose SA, Bridges MW, DiPietro M, Lovett MC, Norman MK. How learning works: Seven research-based principles for smart teaching. San Francisco: Jossey-Bass; 2010. xxii, 301.
47. Zepke N, Leach L. Improving student engagement: ten proposals for action. Act Learn High Educ. 2010;11(3):167–77.
48. Carini RM, Kuh GD, Klein SP. Student engagement and student learning: Testing the linkages. Res High Educ. 2006;47(1):1–32.
49. Appleton JJ, Christenson SL, Kim D, Reschly AL. Measuring cognitive and psychological engagement: Validation of the student engagement instrument. J Sch Psychol. 2006;44(5):427–45.
50. Kuh GD. What we're learning about student engagement from NSSE: Benchmarks for effective educational practices. Change Mag High Learn. 2003;35(2):24–32.
51. Bonwell CC, Eison JA. Active learning: creating excitement in the classroom. [Internet]. Vols. 1991 ASHE-ERIC Higher Education Report. ERIC Clearinghouse on Higher Education, The George Washington University; 1991 [cited 2019 Aug 12]. Available from: https://eric.ed.gov/?id=ED336049.

52. Prince M. Does active learning work? A review of the research. J Eng Educ. 2004;93(3):223–31.
53. Kimonen E, Nevalainen R. Active learning in the process of educational change. Teach Teach Educ. 2005;21:623–35.
54. Bandura A. Self-efficacy: The exercise of control. New York: W H Freeman; 1997. ix, 604.
55. Bandura A. The explanatory and predictive scope of self-efficacy theory. J Soc Clin Psychol. 1986;4(3):359–73.
56. Bandura A, Schunk DH. Cultivating competence, self-efficacy, and intrinsic interest through proximal self-motivation. J Pers Soc Psychol. 1981;41(3):586–98.
57. Multon KD, Brown SD, Lent RW. Relation of self-efficacy beliefs to academic outcomes: A meta-analytic investigation. J Couns Psychol. 1991;38(1):30–8.
58. Locke EA, Latham GP. Work motivation and satisfaction: Light at the end of the tunnel. Psychol Sci. 1990;1(4):240–6.
59. Brown AL. Metacognition, executive control, self-regulation, and other more mysterious mechanisms. In: Weinart FE, Fluwe RH, editors. Metacognition, motivation, and understanding. Hillsdale: Lawrence Erlbaum; 1987. p. 65–116.
60. Zimmerman BJ. Investigating self-regulation and motivation: Historical background, methodological developments, and future prospects. Am Educ Res J. 2008;45(1):166–83.
61. Pintrich PR, Smith DAF, Garcia T, Mckeachie WJ. Reliability and predictive validity of the motivated strategies for learning questionnaire (MSLQ). Educ Psychol Meas. 1993;53(3):801–13.
62. Reaser A, Prevatt F, Petscher Y, Proctor B. The learning/study strategies of college students with ADHD. Psychol Sch. 2007;44(6):627–38.
63. Scarborough HS. Continuity between childhood dyslexia and adult reading. Br J Psychol. 1984;75(3):329–48.
64. Bruck M. Persistence of dyslexics' phonological awareness deficits. Dev Psychol. 1992;28(5):874–86.
65. Ransby MJ, Lee SH. Reading comprehension skills of young adults with childhood diagnoses of dyslexia. J Learn Disabil. 2003;36(6):538–55.
66. Lefly DL, Pennington BF. Spelling errors and reading fluency in compensated adult dyslexics. Ann Dyslexia. 1991;41(1):141–62.
67. Fuller M, Healey M, Bradley A, Hall T. Barriers to learning: A systematic study of the experience of disabled students in one university. Stud High Educ. 2004;29(3):303–18.
68. Barkley RA, Murphy KR. Attention-deficit hyperactivity disorder: A clinical workbook. 3rd ed. New York: The Guilford Press; 2005.
69. Allsopp DH, Minskoff EH, Bolt L. Individualized course-specific strategy instruction for college students with learning disabilities and ADHD: Lessons learned from a model demonstration project. Learn Disabil Res Pract. 2005;20(2):103–18.
70. Flannery AJ, Luebbe AM, Becker SP. Sluggish cognitive tempo is associated with poorer study skills, more executive functioning deficits, and greater impairment in college students. J Clin Psychol. 2017;73(9):1091–113.
71. American Psychiatric Association. Diagnostic and statistical manual of mental disorders. 5th ed. Washington, D.C: American Psychiatric Publishing; 2013.
72. Lerner JW, Kline F. Learning disabilities and related disorders: Characteristics and teaching strategies. 10th ed. Boston: Wadsworth Publishing; 2005.
73. Reardon SM, Naglieri JA. PASS cognitive processing characteristics of normal and ADHD males. J Sch Psychol. 1992;30(2):151–63.
74. Fraser C, Belzner R, Contec R. Attention deficit hyperactivity disorder and self-control: A single case study of the use of a timing device in the development of self-monitoring. Sch Psychol Int. 1992;13(4):339–45.
75. Wallace BA, Winsler A, NeSmith P. Factors associated with success for college students with ADHD: Are standard accommodations helping? In Montreal, Quebec: Canada; 1999. [cited 2019 Nov 15]. Available from: https://eric.ed.gov/?id=ED431350.
76. Simmons F, Singleton C. The reading comprehension abilities of dyslexic students in higher education. Dyslexia. 2000;6(3):178–92.

77. McKeachie WJ. Improving lectures by understanding students' information processing. New Dir Teach Learn. 1980;1980(2):25–35.

78. Verner C, Dickinson G. The lecture: an analysis and review of research. Adult Educ. 1967;17(2):85–100.

79. Hartley J, Cameron A. Some observations on the efficiency of lecturing. Educ Rev. 1967;20(1):30–7.

80. Thomas EJ. The variation of memory with time for information appearing during a lecture. Stud Adult Educ. 1972;4(1):57–62.

81. Stuart J, Rutherford RJ. Medical student concentration during lectures. Lancet. 1978;2(8088):514–6.

82. Zwart LM, Kallemeyn LM. Peer-based coaching for college students with ADHD and learning disabilities. J Postsecond Educ Disabil. 2001;15(1):1–15.

83. Schirduan V, Case K, Faryniarz J. How ADHD students are smart. Educ Forum. 2002;66(4):324–8.

84. Richard MM. Pathways to success for the college student with ADD: Accommodations and preferred practices. J Postsecond Educ Disabil. 1995;11(2–3):16–30.

85. Wong BYL. The relevance of metacognition to learning disabilities. In: Learning about learning disabilities. San Diego: Academic Press; 1991. p. 231–58.

86. Harris KR, Reid RR, Graham S. Self-regulation among students with LD and ADHD. In: Wong B, Butler D, editors. Learning about learning disabilities [Internet]: Academic Press; 2004. p. 167–95. [cited 2019 Nov 15]. Available from: https://asu.pure.elsevier.com/en/publications/self-regulation-among-students-with-ld-and-adhd.

87. Veenman M, Elshout JJ. Changes in the relation between cognitive and metacognitive skills during the acquisition of expertise. Eur J Psychol Educ. 1999;14(4):509–23.

88. Nielsen K, Abbott R, Griffin W, Lott J, Raskind W, Berninger VW. Evidence-based reading and writing assessment for dyslexia in adolescents and young adults. Learn Disabil Multidiscip J. 2016;21(1):38–56.

89. Mckendree J, Snowling MJ. Examination results of medical students with dyslexia. Med Educ. 2011;45(2):176–82.

90. Rourke BP. Arithmetic disabilities, specific and otherwise: A neuropsychological perspective. J Learn Disabil. 1993;26(4):214–26.

91. Munro J. Dyscalculia: A unifying concept in understanding mathematics learning disabilities. Aust J Learn Difficulties. 2003;8(4):25–32.

92. Berninger VW. A developmental approach to learning disabilities. In: Damon W, Lerner RM, Renninger KA, Siegel IE, editors. Handbook of child psychology [Internet]. American Cancer Society; 2007 [cited 2019 Nov 15]. Available from: https://onlinelibrary.wiley.com/doi/abs/10.1002/9780470147658.chpsy0411

93. Simner M, Eidlitz M. Work in progress towards an empirical definition of developmental dysgraphia: Preliminary findings. Can J Sch Psychol. 2000;16(1):103–10.

94. Learning disabilities and the Americans with Disabilities Act (ADA) [Internet]. National Joint Committee on Learning Disabilities; 1992. Available from: http://www.ldonline.org/?module=uploads&func=download&fileId=594.

95. Dyrbye LN, Thomas MR, Shanafelt TD. Medical student distress: Causes, consequences, and proposed solutions. Mayo Clin Proc. 2005;80(12):1613–22.

96. Dyrbye LN, Eacker A, Durning SJ, Brazeau C, Moutier C, Massie FS, et al. The impact of stigma and personal experiences on the help-seeking behaviors of medical students with burnout. Acad Med J Assoc Am Med Coll. 2015;90(7):961–9.

97. Krawec JL. Problem representation and mathematical problem solving of students of varying math ability. J Learn Disabil. 2014;47(2):103–15.

98. Pieters S, Desoete A, Roeyers H, Vanderswalmen R, Van Waelvelde H. Behind mathematical learning disabilities: What about visual perception and motor skills? Learn Individ Differ. 2012;22(4):498–504.

99. Hmelo-Silver C, Duncan R, Chinn C. Scaffolding and achievement in problem-based and inquiry learning: A response to Kirschner, Sweller, and Clark (2006). Educ Psychol. 2007;42(2):99–107.

100. Eisen DB, Schupp CW, Isseroff RR, Ibrahimi OA, Ledo L, Armstrong AW. Does class attendance matter? Results from a second-year medical school dermatology cohort study. Int J Dermatol. 2015;54(7):807–16.
101. Afzal H, Afzal S, Siddique SA, Naqvi SAA. Measures used by medical students to reduce test anxiety. JPMA J Pak Med Assoc. 2012;62(9):982–6.
102. Paul G, Hinman G, Dottl S, Passon J. Academic development: A survey of academic difficulties experienced by medical students and support services provided. Teach Learn Med. 2009;21(3):254–60.
103. Gibson S, Leinster S. How do students with dyslexia perform in extended matching questions, short answer questions and observed structured clinical examinations? Adv Health Sci Educ. 2011;16(3):395–404.
104. Pinto A. Variability in the formal and informal content instructors convey in lectures. J Math Behav. 2019;54:100680.
105. Ricketts C, Brice J, Coombes L. Are multiple choice tests fair to medical students with specific learning disabilities? Adv Health Sci Educ. 2010;15(2):265–75.
106. Colker R. Extra time as an accommodation. Univ Pittsburgh Law Rev. 2008;69:413–74.
107. Scott SS, McGuire JM, Foley TE. Universal design for instruction: A framework for anticipating and responding to disability and other diverse learning needs in the college classroom. Equity Excell Educ. 2003;36(1):40–9.
108. Comp G, Comp C. A guide to providing alternate formats. West Columbia: Center for Rehabilitation Technology Services; 1995. Report No.: ERIC document no ED 405689.
109. Colker R. Universal Design: Stop banning laptops! Cardozo Law Rev. 2017;39(2):483–93.
110. Murray KE. Let them use laptops: Debunking the assumptions underlying the debate over laptops in the classroom. Okla City Univ Law Rev. 2011;36:185–229.
111. Pryal KRG. Trust disabled students and their technology. Women High Educ. 2018;27(7):8–15.
112. Kenney MJ, Jain NR, Meeks LM, Laird-Metke E, Hori J, McGough JD. Learning in the digital age: Assistive technology and electronic access. In: Meeks LM, Jain NR, editors. The guide to assisting students with disabilities: Equal access in health science and professional education. 1st ed. New York: Springer Publishing Company; 2016. p. 119–40.
113. Rose DH, Meyer A. Teaching every student in the digital age: universal design for learning. Alexandria: Association for Supervision & Curriculum Development; 2002.
114. Rose DH, Meyer A. A practical reader in universal design for learning. Cambridge, MA: Harvard Education Press; 2006.
115. Piolat A, Olive T, Kellogg RT. Cognitive effort during note taking. Appl Cogn Psychol. 2005;19(3):291–312.
116. Greer D, Rowland AL, Smith SJ. Critical considerations for teaching students with disabilities in online environments. Teach Except Child. 2014;46(5):79–91.
117. Mace RL. Universal design: Barrier-free environments for everyone. Des West. 1985;33(1):147–52.
118. Steinfeld E, Schroeder S, Bishop M. Accessible buildings for people with walking and reaching limitations [Internet]. Department of Housing and Urban Development; 1979 Apr [cited 2019 Dec 17]. Report No.: PDR-397`. Available from: https://eric.ed.gov/?id=ED184280.
119. Neal-Boylan L, Miller M. Treat me like everyone else: The experience of nurses who had disabilities while in school. Nurse Educ. 2017;42(4):176–80.
120. Meeks LM, Jain NR. Accessibility, inclusion, and action in medical education: Lived experiences of learners and physicians with disabilities [Internet]. Washington, D.C: Association of American Medical Colleges; 2018. Available from: https://store.aamc.org/accessibility-inclusion-and-action-in-medical-education-lived-experiences-of-learners-and-physicians-with-disabilities.html.
121. Houck CK, Asselin SB, Troutman GC, Arrington JM. Students with learning disabilities in the university environment: A study of faculty and student perceptions. J Learn Disabil. 1992;25(10):678–84.
122. Stergiopoulos E, Fernando O, Martimianakis MA. "Being on both sides": Canadian medical students' experiences with disability, the hidden curriculum, and professional identity construction. Acad Med. 2018;93(10):1550–9.

123. Chew-Graham CA, Rogers A, Yassin N. "I wouldn't want it on my CV or their records": Medical students' experiences of help-seeking for mental health problems. Med Educ. 2003;37(10):873–80.

124. Winter RI, Patel R, Norman RI. A qualitative exploration of the help-seeking behaviors of students who experience psychological distress around assessment at medical school. Acad Psychiatry J Am Assoc Dir Psychiatr Resid Train Assoc Acad Psychiatry. 2017;41(4):477–85.

125. Henning K, Ey S, Shaw D. Perfectionism, the imposter phenomenon and psychological adjustment in medical, dental, nursing and pharmacy students. Med Educ. 1998;32(5):456–64.

126. Slavin SJ, Schindler DL, Chibnall JT. Medical student mental health 3.0: Improving student wellness through curricular changes. Acad Med. 2014;89(4):573–7.

127. Steele CM. A threat in the air. How stereotypes shape intellectual identity and performance. Am Psychol. 1997;52(6):613–29.

128. Pennington CR, Heim D, Levy AR, Larkin DT. Twenty years of stereotype threat research: A review of psychological mediators. PLoS One. 2016;11(1):e0146487.

129. Clance P, Imes S. The imposter phenomenon in high achieving women: dynamics and therapeutic intervention. Psychother Theory Res Pract. 1978;15(3):241–7.

130. Prata J, Gietzen J. Imposter phenomenon in physician assistant education. J Am Acad Physician Assist. 2007;20(7):32–3.

131. Denhart H. Deconstructing barriers: perceptions of students labeled with learning disabilities in higher education. J Learn Disabil. 2008;41(6):483–97.

132. Barga NK. Students with learning disabilities in education: Managing a disability. J Learn Disabil. 1996;29(4):413–21.

133. Reis SM, Neu TW. Factors involved in the academic success of high ability university students with learning disabilities. J Second Gift Educ. 1994;5(3):60–74.

134. Vogan CL, McKimm J, Da Silva AL, Grant A. Twelve tips for providing effective student support in undergraduate medical education. Med Teach. 2014;36(6):480–5.

135. Pressley M, McCormick CB. Advanced educational psychology for educators, researchers, and policymakers. New York: Allyn & Bacon; 1997.

136. Benner P, Sutphen M, Leonard V, Day L, Shulman LS. Educating nurses: A call for radical transformation. 1st ed. San Francisco: Jossey-Bass; 2009.

137. Chi MTH, Glaser R, Farr MJ, editors. The nature of expertise. 1st ed. Hillsdale: Psychology Press; 1988.

138. Ericsson KA, Smith J, editors. Toward a general theory of expertise: Prospects and limits. 1st ed. New York: Cambridge University Press; 1991.

139. Ericsson KA, Krampe RT, Tesch-Römer C. The role of deliberate practice in the acquisition of expert performance. Psychol Rev. 1993;100(3):363–406.

140. Ericsson KA, Chase WG, Faloon S. Acquisition of a memory skill. Science. 1980;208(4448):1181–2.

141. Dempster FN. Effects of variable encoding and spaced presentations on vocabulary learning. J Educ Psychol. 1987;79(2):162–70.

142. Dempster FN. Spacing effects and their implications for theory and practice. Educ Psychol Rev. 1989;1(4):309–30.

143. Cepeda NJ, Pashler H, Vul E, Wixted JT, Rohrer D. Distributed practice in verbal recall tasks: A review and quantitative synthesis. Psychol Bull. 2006;132(3):354–80.

144. Roediger HL, Karpicke JD. Test-enhanced learning: Taking memory tests improves long-term retention. Psychol Sci. 2006;17(3):249–55.

145. Larsen DP, Butler AC, Roediger HL. Repeated testing improves long-term retention relative to repeated study: A randomised controlled trial. Med Educ. 2009;43(12):1174–81.

146. Roediger HL, Butler AC. The critical role of retrieval practice in long-term retention. Trends Cogn Sci. 2011;15(1):20–7.

147. Karpicke JD, Blunt JR. Retrieval practice produces more learning than elaborative studying with concept mapping. Science. 2011;331(6018):772–5.

148. Larsen DP, Butler AC, Roediger HL. Test-enhanced learning in medical education. Med Educ. 2008;42(10):959–66.

149. Deng F, Gluckstein JA, Larsen DP. Student-directed retrieval practice is a predictor of medical licensing examination performance. Perspect Med Educ. 2015;4(6):308–13.
150. Morris PE, Fritz CO, Jackson L, Nichol E, Roberts E. Strategies for learning proper names: Expanding retrieval practice, meaning and imagery. Appl Cogn Psychol. 2005;19(6):779–98.
151. Kornell N, Hays MJ, Bjork RA. Unsuccessful retrieval attempts enhance subsequent learning. J Exp Psychol Learn Mem Cogn. 2009;35(4):989–98.
152. Boyle JR. Note-taking skills of middle school students with and without learning disabilities. J Learn Disabil. 2010;43(6):530–40.
153. Maydosz A, Raver SA. Note taking and university students with learning difficulties: What supports are needed? J Divers High Educ. 2010;3(3):177–86.
154. Boyle JR, Rivera TZ. Note-taking techniques for students with disabilities: A systematic review of the research. Learn Disabil Q. 2012;35(3):131–43.
155. Suritsky SK, Hughes CA. Notetaking strategy instruction. In: Deshler DD, Ellis ES, Lenz BK, editors. Teaching adolescent with learning disabilities. 2nd ed. Denver: Love; 1996. p. 267–312.
156. Titsworth S. The effects of teacher immediacy, use of organizational lecture cues, and students' notetaking on cognitive learning. Commun Educ. 2001;50(4):283–97.
157. Titsworth S, Kiewra K. Spoken organizational lecture cues and student notetaking as facilitators of student learning. Contemp Educ Psychol. 2004;29(4):447–61.
158. Boyle JR, Forchelli GA, Cariss K. Note-taking interventions to assist students with disabilities in content area classes. Prev Sch Fail. 2015;59(3):186–95.
159. Andersen MS, Gicheva D, Sarbaum J. Requiring versus recommending preparation before class: Does it matter? South Econ J. 2018;85(2):616–31.
160. Popkess AM, McDaniel A. Are nursing students engaged in learning? A secondary analysis of data from the National Survey of Student Engagement. Nurs Educ Perspect. 2011;32(2):89–94.
161. Lebauer RS. Using lecture transcripts in EAP lecture comprehension courses. TESOL Q. 1984;18(1):41–54.
162. Peck KL, Hannafin MJ. The effects of notetaking pretraining and the recording of notes on the retention of aural instruction. J Educ Res. 1983;77(2):100–7.
163. Einstein GO, Morris J, Smith S. Note-taking, individual differences, and memory for lecture information. J Educ Psychol. 1985;77(5):522–32.
164. Smith PL, Tompkins GE. Structured notetaking: A new strategy for content area readers. J Read. 1988;32(1):46–53.
165. Anderson TH, Armbruster BB. The value of taking notes during lectures. Champaign: University of Illinois at Urbana-Champaign, Center for the Study of Reading; 1986. Report No.: Technical Report No. 374.
166. Di Vesta FJ, Gray GS. Listening and note taking. J Educ Psychol. 1972;63(1):8–14.
167. Peper RJ, Mayer RE. Generative effects of note-taking during science lectures. J Educ Psychol. 1986;78(1):34–8.
168. Ladas HS. Note taking on lectures: An information-processing approach. Educ Psychol. 1980;15(1):44–53.
169. Meltzer L, Krishnan K. Executive functioning difficulties and learning disabilities: Understandings and misunderstandings. In: Meltzer L, editor. Executive Function in Education: From Theory to Practice. New York: Guilford Press; 2007. p. 77–105.
170. Stachowiak JR. Universal design for learning in postsecondary institutions. New Horiz Learn [Internet]. 2010; s8(1). Available from: http://jhepp.library.jhu.edu/ojs/index.php/newhorizons/article/view/68.
171. Suritsky SK. Note-taking approaches and specific areas of difficulty reported by university students with learning disabilities. J Postsecond Educ Disabil. 1992;10:3–10.
172. Adams SJ. Leveling the floor: Classroom accommodations for law student with disabilities. J Leg Educ. 1998;48(2):273–96.
173. Sana F, Weston T, Cepeda NJ. Laptop multitasking hinders classroom learning for both users and nearby peers. Comput Educ. 2013;62(1):24–31.

174. Mueller PA, Oppenheimer DM. The pen is mightier than the keyboard: Advantages of long-hand over laptop note taking. Psychol Sci. 2014;25(6):1159–68.

175. Bui D, Myerson J, Hale S. Note-taking with computers: Exploring alternative strategies for improved recall. J Educ Psychol. 2013;105(2):299–309.

176. Luo L, Kiewra KA, Flanigan AE, Peteranetz MS. Laptop versus longhand note taking: Effects on lecture notes and achievement. Instr Sci Int J Learn Sci. 2018;46(6):947–71.

177. Hartley J, Davies IK. Note-taking: A critical review. Program Learn Educ Technol. 1978;15(3):207–24.

178. Wong B. The effects of directive cues on the organization of memory and recall in good and poor readers. J Educ Res. 1978;72(1):32–8.

179. Novak JD. Concept maps and Vee diagrams: Two metacognitive tools to facilitate meaningful learning. Instr Sci. 1990;19(1):29–52.

180. Novak JD. Results and implications of a 12-year longitudinal study of science concept learning. Res Sci Educ. 2005;35(1):23–40.

181. Guerrero AP. Mechanistic case diagramming: A tool for problem-based learning. Acad Med J Assoc Am Med Coll. 2001;76(4):385–9.

182. Fischer K, Sullivan AM, Krupat E, Schwartzstein RM. Assessing the effectiveness of using mechanistic concept maps in case-based collaborative learning. Acad Med J Assoc Am Med Coll. 2019;94(2):208–12.

183. Baugh NG, Mellott KG. Clinical concept mapping as preparation for student nurses' clinical experiences. J Nurs Educ. 1998;37(6):253–6.

184. Bentley BS, Hill RV. Objective and subjective assessment of reciprocal peer teaching in medical gross anatomy laboratory. Anat Sci Educ. 2009;2(4):143–9.

185. Sobral DT. Cross-year peer tutoring experience in a medical school: Conditions and outcomes for student tutors. Med Educ. 2002;36(11):1064–70.

186. Wong JG, Waldrep TD, Smith TG. Formal peer-teaching in medical school improves academic performance: The MUSC supplemental instructor program. Teach Learn Med. 2007;19(3):216–20.

187. Chi MTH, De Leeuw N, Chiu M-H, Lavancher C. Eliciting self-explanations improves understanding. Cognit Sci. 1994;18(3):439–77.

188. Sobral DT. Improving learning skills: A self-help group approach. High Educ. 1997;33(1):39–50.

189. Schunk DH, Zimmerman BJ, editors. Self-regulated learning: From teaching to self-reflective practice. 1st ed. New York: The Guilford Press; 1998.

190. Plant EA, Ericsson KA, Hill L, Asberg K. Why study time does not predict grade point average across college students: Implications of deliberate practice for academic performance. Contemp Educ Psychol. 2005;30(1):96–116.

191. Schunk DH, Zimmerman BJ. Self-regulation of learning and performance. Hillsdale: Routledge; 1994. 342 p.

192. Prus J. The learning and study strategies inventory (LASSI) as a predictor of first-year college academic success. J Freshm Year Exp. 1995;7(2):7–26.

193. Rugsaken KT, Robertson JA, Jones JA. Using the learning and study strategies inventory scores as additional predictors of student academic performance. NACADA J. 1998;18(1):20–6.

194. Schunk DH. Social cognitive theory and self-regulated learning. In: Zimmerman BJ, Schunk DH, editors. Self-regulated learning and academic achievement: Theory, research, and practice. New York: Routledge; 1989. p. 83–110.

195. Locke EA, Latham GP. Building a practically useful theory of goal setting and task motivation: A 35-year odyssey. Am Psychol. 2002;57(9):705–17.

196. Schunk DH. Participation in goal-setting: Effects of self-efficacy and skills of learning disabled children. J Spec Educ. 1985;19:307–17.

197. Bandura A, Cervone D. Self-evaluative and self-efficacy mechanisms governing the motivational effects of goal systems. J Pers Soc Psychol. 1983;45(5):1017–28.

198. MacLeod A. Goals and plans: Their relationship to well-being. In: Efklides A, Moraitou D, editors. A positive psychology perspective on quality of life social indicators research series

[Internet]. Dordrecht: Springer; 2012. (Social Indicators Research Series; vol. 51). Available from: https://doi.org/10.1007/978-94-007-4963-4_3.

199. Locke EA, Latham GP. The application of goal setting to sports. J Sport Exerc Psychol. 1985;7(3):205–22.

200. Shapiro ES. Self-monitoring procedures. In: Ollendick TH, Hersen M, editors. Child behavioral assessment: Principles and procedures. New York, NY: Pergamon; 1984. p. 148–65.

201. Weinberg R, Morrison D, Loftin M, Horn T, Goodwin E, Wright E, et al. Writing down goals: doses it actually improve performance? Sport Psychol. 2019;33(1):35–41.

202. Dyrbye LN, Thomas MR, Shanafelt TD. Systematic review of depression, anxiety, and other indicators of psychological distress among U.S. and Canadian medical students. Acad Med J Assoc Am Med Coll. 2006;81(4):354–73.

203. Goldman ML, Shah RN, Bernstein CA. Depression and suicide among physician trainees: Recommendations for a national response. JAMA Psychiat. 2015;72(5):411–2.

204. Chemers M, Hu L, Garcia B. Academic self-efficacy and first-year college student performance and adjustment. J Educ Psychol. 2001;93(1):55–64.

205. Swartz SL, Prevatt F, Proctor BE. A coaching intervention for college students with Attention Deficit/Hyperactivity Disorder. Psychol Sch. 2005;42(6):647–56.

206. Parker DR, Boutelle K. Executive function coaching for college students with learning disabilities and ADHD: A new approach for fostering self-determination. Learn Disabil Res Pract. 2009;24(4):204–15.

207. Alvarez MC, Risko VJ. Motivation and study strategies. In: Flippo RF, Caverly DC, editors. Handbook of college reading and study strategy research. 2nd ed. New York: Routledge; 2008. p. 199–216.

208. Kirschner PA, Karpinski AC. Facebook® and academic performance. Comput Hum Behav. 2010;26(6):1237–45.

209. Zadina JN, Smilkstein R, Daiek D. Anter. College reading: The science and strategies of expert readers. 1st ed. Boston: Wadsworth; 2014.

210. Artino AR, Hemmer PA, Durning SJ. Using self-regulated learning theory to understand the beliefs, emotions, and behaviors of struggling medical students. Acad Med J Assoc Am Med Coll. 2011;86(10):S35–8.

211. Boud D, Keogh R, Walker D. Reflection: Turning experience into learning [Internet]. 1st ed. London: Routledge; 1985. [cited 2019 Nov 15]. Available from: http://www.123library.org/book_details/?id=110587.

212. Guerrasio J, Nogar C, Rustici M, Lay C, Corral J. Study skills and test taking strategies for coaching medical learners based on identified areas of struggle. MedEdPORTAL. 2017;13:10593.

213. Yerkes RM, Dodson JD. The relation of strength of stimulus to rapidity of habit-formation. J Comp Neurol Psychol. 1908;18(5):459–82.

214. Chou C-Y, Lin P-H. Promoting discussion in peer instruction: Discussion partner assignment and accountability scoring mechanisms. Br J Educ Technol. 2015;46(4):839–47.

215. Akinla O, Hagan P, Atiomo W. A systematic review of the literature describing the outcomes of near-peer mentoring programs for first year medical students. BMC Med Educ. 2018;18(1):98.

216. Parker DR, Hoffman SF, Sawilowsky S, Rolands L. An examination of the effects of ADHD coaching on university students' executive functioning. J Postsecond Educ Disabil. 2011;24(2):115–32.

217. Troiano PF, Liefeld JA, Trachtenberg JV. Academic support and college success for postsecondary students with learning disabilities. J Coll Read Learn. 2010;40(2):35–44.

218. Dupler AE, Allen C, Maheady DC, Fleming SE, Allen M. Leveling the playing field for nursing students with disabilities: Implications of the amendments to the Americans with Disabilities Act. J Nurs Educ. 2012;51(3):140–4.

219. Tee SR, Owens K, Plowright S, Ramnath P, Rourke S, James C, et al. Being reasonable: Supporting disabled nursing students in practice. Nurse Educ Pract. 2010;10(4):216–21.

220. Aiken F, Dale C. A review of the literature into dyslexia in nursing practice. London: Royal College of Nursing; 2007.

221. British Medical Association – Studying with dyslexia [Internet]. [cited 2019 Nov 15]. Available from: https://www.bma.org.uk/advice/career/studying-medicine/common-challenges-while-studying/studying-with-dyslexia/impact-of-dyslexia.
222. Villwock JA, Sobin LB, Koester LA, Harris TM. Impostor syndrome and burnout among American medical students: A pilot study. Int J Med Educ. 2016;7:364–9.
223. Lightner KL, Kipps-Vaughan D, Schulte T, Trice AD. Reasons university students with a learning disability wait to seek disability services. J Postsecond Educ Disabil. 2012;25(2):145–59.
224. Whittington RE, Rhind S, Loads D, Handel I. Exploring the link between mindset and psychological well-being among veterinary students. J Vet Med Educ. 2017;44(1):134–40.
225. Klein J, Delany C, Fischer MD, Smallwood D, Trumble S. A growth mindset approach to preparing trainees for medical error. BMJ Qual Saf. 2017;26(9):771–4.
226. Nugent PM, Vitale BA. Test success: Test-taking techniques for beginning nursing students. 7th ed. Philadelphia, PA: F.A. Davis Company; 2016.
227. Aspinwall LG, Taylor SE. Modeling cognitive adaptation: A longitudinal investigation of the impact of individual differences and coping on college adjustment and performance. J Pers Soc Psychol. 1992;63(6):989–1003.
228. Scheier MF, Carver CS. Effects of optimism on psychological and physical well-being: Theoretical overview and empirical update. Cogn Ther Res. 1992;16(2):201–28.
229. Stewart SM, Betson C, Lam TH, Marshall IB, Lee PW, Wong CM. Predicting stress in first year medical students: A longitudinal study. Med Educ. 1997;31(3):163–8.
230. Maslow AH. A theory of human motivation. Psychol Rev. 1943;50(4):370–96.
231. Maslow AH. Motivation and personality. New York: Harper and Row; 1954.
232. Hale AJ, Ricotta DN, Freed J, Smith CC, Huang GC. Adapting Maslow's hierarchy of needs as a framework for resident wellness. Teach Learn Med. 2019;31(1):109–18.
233. Eisenberg D, Gollust SE, Golberstein E, Hefner JL. Prevalence and correlates of depression, anxiety, and suicidality among university students. Am J Orthopsychiatry. 2007;77(4):534–42.
234. Wallace JE, Lemaire JB, Ghali WA. Physician wellness: A missing quality indicator. Lancet Lond Engl. 2009;374(9702):1714–21.
235. Nelson DW, Knight AE. The power of positive recollections: Reducing test anxiety and enhancing college student efficacy and performance. J Appl Soc Psychol. 2010;40(3):732–45.
236. Powell DH. Treating individuals with debilitating performance anxiety: An introduction. J Clin Psychol. 2004;60(8):801–8.
237. Saunders PA, Tractenberg RE, Chaterji R, Amri H, Harazduk N, Gordon JS, et al. Promoting self-awareness and reflection through an experiential mind-body skills course for first year medical students. Med Teach. 2007;29(8):778–84.
238. Gonzalez HP. Systematic desensitization, study skills counseling, and anxiety-coping training in the treatment of test anxiety. In: Spielberger CD, Vagg PR, editors. Test anxiety: Theory, assessment, and treatment. Washington, D.C: Taylor & Francis; 1995. p. 117–32.
239. Tobias S. Test anxiety: Interference, defective skills, and cognitive capacity. Educ Psychol. 1985;20(3):135–42.
240. Hembree R. Correlates, causes, effects, and treatment of test anxiety. Rev Educ Res. 1988;58(1):47–77.
241. Zeidner M. Does test anxiety bias scholastic aptitude test performance by gender and socio-cultural group? J Pers Assess. 1990;55(1–2):145–60.
242. Onwuegbuzie AJ, Daley CE. The relative contributions of examination-taking coping strategies and study coping strategies to test anxiety: A concurrent analysis. Cogn Ther Res. 1996;20(3):287–303.
243. Scouller K. The influence of assessment method on students' learning approaches: Multiple choice question examination versus assignment essay. High Educ. 1998;35(4):453–72.
244. Frierson HT, Hoban JD. The effects of acute test anxiety on NBME Part I performance. J Natl Med Assoc. 1992;84(8):686–9.
245. Farooqi YN, Ghani R, Spielberger CD. Gender differences in test anxiety and academic performance of medical students. Int J Psychol Behav Sci. 2012;2(2):38–43.

246. Hardy L, Parfitt G. A catastrophe model of anxiety and performance. Br J Psychol Lond Engl 1953. 1991 May;82(2):163–78.
247. Harrison Y, Horne JA. Sleep loss and temporal memory. Q J Exp Psychol A. 2000;53(1):271–9.
248. Gohar A, Adams A, Gertner E, Sackett-Lundeen L, Heitz R, Engle R, et al. Working memory capacity is decreased in sleep-deprived internal medicine residents. J Clin Sleep Med JCSM Off Publ Am Acad Sleep Med. 2009;5(3):191–7.
249. Alhola P, Polo-Kantola P. Sleep deprivation: Impact on cognitive performance. Neuropsychiatr Dis Treat. 2007;3(5):553–67.
250. Krathwohl DR. A revision of bloom's taxonomy: An overview. Theory Pract. 2002;41(4):212–8.
251. Anderson LW, Krathwohl DR, Airasian PW, Cruikshank KA, Mayer RE, Pintrich PR, et al. A taxonomy for learning, teaching, and assessing: A revision of Bloom's taxonomy of educational objectives, abridged edition. 1st ed. New York: Pearson; 2000.
252. Spielberger CD, Vagg PR. Test anxiety: A transactional process model. In: Spielberger CD, Vagg PR, editors. Test anxiety: Theory, assessment, and treatment. Washington, DC: Taylor & Francis; 1995. p. 1–14.
253. Lyndon MP, Strom JM, Alyami HM, Yu T-C, Wilson NC, Singh PP, et al. The relationship between academic assessment and psychological distress among medical students: A systematic review. Perspect Med Educ. 2014;3(6):405–18.
254. Spielberger CD, Anton WD, Bedell J. The nature and treatment of test anxiety. In: Zuckerman M, Spielberger CD, editors. Emotions and anxiety: New concepts, methods, and applications. New York, NY: Psychology Press; 2016. p. 317–46.
255. Calabrese R, Roberts B. Character, school leadership, and the brain: Learning how to integrate knowledge with behavioral change. Int J Educ Manag. 2002;16:229–38.
256. LeBlanc VR. The effects of acute stress on performance: Implications for health professions education. Acad Med. 2009;84(10 Suppl):S25–33.
257. Powell DH. Behavioral treatment of debilitating test anxiety among medical students. J Clin Psychol. 2004;60(8):853–65.
258. Pritchard ME, Wilson GS. Using emotional and social factors to predict student success. J Coll Stud Dev. 2003;44(1):18–28.
259. Delany C, Miller KJ, El-Ansary D, Remedios L, Hosseini A, McLeod S. Replacing stressful challenges with positive coping strategies: A resilience program for clinical placement learning. Adv Health Sci Educ Theory Pract. 2015;20(5):1303–24.
260. West C, Sadoski M. Do study strategies predict academic performance in medical school? Med Educ. 2011;45(7):696–703.
261. Williams CA. Exam wrappers: It is time to adopt a nursing student metacognitive tool for exam review. Nurs Educ Perspect [Internet]. 2019 Nov. 8 [cited 2019 Nov 14]; Available from: https://journals.lww.com/neponline/Abstract/publishahead/Exam_Wrappers__It_Is_Time_to_Adopt_a_Nursing.99624.aspx.
262. Robinson E, Niemer L. A peer mentor tutor program for academic success in nursing. Nurs Educ Perspect. 2010;31(5):286–9.
263. Spivey-Mooring T, Apprey CB. University of Virginia Graduate Mentoring Institute: A model program for graduate student success. Peabody J Educ. 2014;89(3):393–410.
264. Vora RS, Kinney MN. Connectedness, sense of community, and academic satisfaction in a novel community campus medical education model. Acad Med J Assoc Am Med Coll. 2014;89(1):182–7.
265. Winston KA, Van Der Vleuten CPM, Scherpbier AJJA. At-risk medical students: Implications of students' voice for the theory and practice of remediation. Med Educ. 2010;44(10):1038–47.
266. Barnett JE, Baker EK, Elman NS, Schoener GR. In pursuit of wellness: The self-care imperative. Prof Psychol Res Pract. 2007;38(6):603–12.
267. Shanafelt TD, West C, Zhao X, Novotny P, Kolars J, Habermann T, et al. Relationship between increased personal well-being and enhanced empathy among internal medicine residents. J Gen Intern Med. 2005;20(7):559–64.

268. Firth-Cozens J, Greenhalgh J. Doctors' perceptions of the links between stress and lowered clinical care. Soc Sci Med. 1997;44(7):1017–22.
269. McGough JD, Murray JF. Know your campus resources. In: Meeks LM, Jain NR, editors. The guide to assisting students with disabilities: Equal access in health science and professional education. 1st ed. New York: Springer Publishing Company; 2016. p. 1–14.
270. Crookston BB. A developmental view of academic advising as teaching. NACADA J. 1994;14(2):5–9.
271. Webb L. Nursing: Communication skills in practice. 1st ed. Oxford: Oxford University Press; 2011.
272. Rider EA, Keefer CH. Communication skills competencies: Definitions and a teaching toolbox. Med Educ. 2006;40(7):624–9.
273. Hughey JK, Hughey KF. The changing workplace: Implications for academic and career advising. Acad Advis Today. 2006;29(3):1.
274. Hughey JK. Strategies to enhance interpersonal relations in academic advising. NACADA J. 2011;31(2):22–32.
275. Habley W. Advisor training in the context of a teaching enhancement center. In: Glennen RE, Vowell FN, editors. Academic advising as a comprehensive campus process (Monograph Series No 2). Manhattan, KS: National Academic Advising Association; 2005. p. 75–9.
276. Noel-Levitz. National student satisfaction and priorities report. Coralville, IA: Author; 2009. p. 2009.
277. Nadler S, Simerly RL. Effects of listening on the formation of students trust and commitment in academic advising: A study of a United States university. Int J Manag. 2006;23:215–21.
278. Fox R. Delivering one-to-one advising: Skills and competencies. In: Gordon VN, Habley WR, Grites TJ, editors. Academic advising: A comprehensive handbook. San Francisco, CA: Jossey-Bass; 2008. p. 342–55.
279. Imhof M. What makes a good listener? Listening behavior in instructional settings. Int J List. 1998;12(1):81–105.
280. Rautalinko E. Reflective listening and open-ended questions in counselling: Preferences moderated by social skills and cognitive ability. Couns Psychother Res. 2013;13(1):24–31.
281. Huerta-Wong JE, Schoech R. Experiential learning and learning environments: The case of active listening skills. J Soc Work Educ. 2010;46(1):85–101.
282. Ivey AE, Morrill WH. Career process: A new concept for vocational behavior. Pers Guid J. 1968;46(7):644–9.
283. Oetting ER. Developmental definition of counseling psychology. J Couns Psychol. 1967;14(4):382–5.
284. Coll JE, Draves P. Traditional age students: Worldviews and satisfaction with advising; A homogeneous study of student and advisors. Coll Stud Aff J. 2009;27(2):215–23.
285. Hale MD, Graham DL, Johnson DM. Are students more satisfied with academic advising when there is congruence between current and preferred advising styles? Coll Stud J. 2009;43(2):313–24.
286. Habley W, McClanahan R. What works in student retention? All survey colleges. Iowa City, IA: ACT, Inc.; 2004.
287. Rogers CR. Person to person: The problem of being human, a new trend in psychology. 1st ed. Lafayette, Calif: Real People Press; 1967.
288. McClellan JL. Promoting trust through effective advising administration. Mentor Acad Advis J. 2014;16. https://doi.org/10.26209/MJ1661261.
289. Brown T, Rivas M. The prescriptive relationship in academic advising as an appropriate developmental intervention with multicultural populations. NACADA J. 1994;14(2):108–11.
290. Fielstein LL. Developmental versus prescriptive advising: Must it be one or the other? NACADA J. 1994;14(2):76–9.
291. Child J, Langford E. Exploring the learning experiences of nursing students with dyslexia. Nurs Stand R Coll Nurs G B 1987. 2011;25(40):39–46.
292. Shaw SCK, Anderson JL. The experiences of medical students with dyslexia: An interpretive phenomenological study. Dyslexia Chichester Engl. 2018;24(3):220–33.

293. Stoodley CJ, Harrison EPD, Stein JF. Implicit motor learning deficits in dyslexic adults. Neuropsychologia. 2006;44(5):795–8.
294. Vogel SA, Adelman PB. The success of college students with learning disabilities: Factors related to educational attainment. J Learn Disabil. 1992;25(7):430–41.
295. Wilczenski FL. Comparison of academic performances, graduation rates, and timing of drop out for LD and non-LD college students. Coll Stud J. 1993;27(2):184–94.
296. Tantam D, Holmes D, Cordess C. Nonverbal expression in autism of Asperger type. J Autism Dev Disord. 1993;23(1):111–33.
297. Nowinski LA, Milot A, Gold A, McDougle CJ. Efficacious treatments for common psychiatric challenges in adolescents with autism spectrum disorder. In: Gelbar NW, editor. Adolescents with autism spectrum disorder: A clinical handbook [Internet]. New York: Oxford University Press; 2017. p. 30–66. [cited 2019 Nov 15]. Available from: https://www.oxfordclinicalpsych.com/view/10.1093/med-psych/9780190624828.001.0001/med-9780190624828-chapter-2.
298. Mann CC, Karsten AM. Efficacy and social validity of procedures for improving conversational skills of college students with autism. J Appl Behav Anal. 2019;22:402–21.

Increasing Accessibility Through Inclusive Instruction and Design

Kristina H. Petersen

What Is Inclusive Instruction?

Faculty members wholeheartedly engaged in teaching are dedicated to utilizing instructional methods that best help students achieve learning outcomes. While students must actively engage in courses to succeed (see Chap. 6) [1–4], dedicated instructors make every effort to provide all students opportunities to meet their potential [5–8]. Inclusive instruction derives from universal design principles as applied to education: course design and instruction should be planned strategically to ensure students from diverse backgrounds can fully access course curriculum [6, 9–12].

Examples of Barriers to Inclusive Instruction and Design

Pedagogical methods with empirically proven efficacy may still pose barriers for students with disabilities if lessons are not designed using an inclusive approach. For example, problem-based learning sessions, which require quick assessments of problems followed by time sensitive oral responses, may present barriers for students with processing difficulty or other disabilities [13, 14]. The flipped classroom and problem-based learning formats can present barriers for students with learning, visual, and attentional disabilities unless accessible digital content is provided and appropriate guidance, directions, or scaffolds are implemented [15–20].

As courses are designed, deliberate choices should be made to prevent barriers for students with disabilities. A "one-size-fits-all" instructional model will not work, as inflexible curricula pose barriers for students with disabilities [21–24].

K. H. Petersen (✉)
Assistant Professor, Department of Biochemistry & Molecular Biology, Director, Academic Support Programs, New York Medical College, Valhalla, NY, USA
e-mail: k_harrispetersen@nymc.edu

© Springer Nature Switzerland AG 2020   143
L. M. Meeks, L. Neal-Boylan (eds.), *Disability as Diversity*,
https://doi.org/10.1007/978-3-030-46187-4_7

For example, when instructors ban laptops from class, students with various disabilities (e.g., students with rheumatoid arthritis, dyslexia, visual disabilities, etc.) cannot fully access material without an accommodation plan [14, 25]. This forces students to choose between fully accessing the curriculum or maintaining their privacy. If a laptop ban is in place, students who identify themselves as requiring laptop use due to a disability will be outed to their instructor and classmates. Another potential barrier to consider involves textbook selection; instructors should confirm the availability of alternative digital formats. If such formats are unavailable, students with visual or reading disabilities may not be able to fully access the course curriculum [17, 18]. Deliberate, inclusive choices made by the instructor can ensure all students have full access to course content, regardless of disability [6, 9, 26, 27].

This chapter will discuss considerations for implementing inclusive instruction in health science programs including basic principles of universal design in education, strategies for securing faculty buy-in, strengths and barriers associated with the most commonly utilized instructional methods, and recommendations for removing instructional and curriculum design barriers.

Optimizing Instruction for Diverse Student Learners

Learning has been defined as a process of creating meaning and building personal interpretations of the world based on an individual's experiences and interactions [28, 29]. The collective work of Sweller (1988), Miller (1956), and Halford et al. (2005) helped us understand that a limited amount of cognitive information can be processed when presented in a single modality (e.g., visual only) [30–32]. Paivio's dual-coding theory (1980) suggested that material presented in two modalities simultaneously (e.g., audio and visual) allows learners to process information more efficiently [33, 34]. Building on these theories, Mayer's cognitive theory of multimedia learning (2009) asserts that learning is most efficient when both sensory modalities are utilized in instruction: visually presented material (e.g., pictures, animations, videos) and auditorily presented material (e.g., narration and background sounds) [35].

When students with or without disabilities actively engage in the learning process, they are more likely to be intrinsically motivated to achieve learning objectives [1–4, 36, 37]. Students who are fully engaged generally have a strong sense of self-efficacy, and many have determined their individualized approach to learning [38–42]. Many learning style models have been published that claim to assist individuals in considering their approach to understanding, learning, and applying information [43–45]. Proponents of learning styles research assert that optimal instruction should align with an individual's learning style, but evidence has not supported this theory [46, 47]. Studies suggest that learning styles are fluid; that is, students' approaches to learning may change as new skills are developed or as different types of material are presented [48, 49]. Given the variation of psychometric approaches, and in some cases the absence of validation, if learning style inventories are used, they should only catalyze an individualized discussion about learning approaches [46, 47]. Although learning styles theory will not inform our discussion of instructional methods, we must acknowledge that approaches to learning will vary based on context, content, and individual differences (see Chap. 6) [36, 37].

Instructors will teach groups of students who have varied learning approaches, diverse experiences upon which to build, varying abilities to self-reflect, and different approaches to feedback and communication. In order to reach a diverse group of students, inclusive instructors must utilize multiple strategies.

Universal Design Principles in Classroom Instruction

The concept of universal design (UD) originated in the field of architecture through the work of Ronald Mace (1985) who aimed to design buildings that are "usable to the greatest extent possible by everyone, regardless of age, ability, or situation." [50, 51] Concepts of universal design applied to learning environments are referred to as universal design for learning (UDL), while those associated with instruction are referred to as universal design for instruction (UDI) or universal instructional design (UID) [6, 9, 18, 52–55]. All three of these interrelated universal design concepts in education place high value on student learner diversity and inclusion [6, 9, 56]. Although there are distinctions between UDL, UDI, and UID, in this chapter we will follow the method of Rao et al. (2014) and refer to all three models collectively as "UD in education." [57]

Concepts of UD in education (UDE) are focused on intentional accessibility, not accommodation. Whereas accommodations are prescriptive, specifically tailored to support the needs of each individual, the intentional and anticipatory design of UDE aims to meet the varied needs of all students [12, 19, 54, 58]. UDE acknowledges that students learn in a variety of ways and seeks to meet diverse student needs by ensuring curricula include multiple means of representation (perception, language and symbols, and comprehension), multiple means of expression and action (physical action, expression and communication, and executive function), and multiple means of engagement (recruiting interest, sustaining effort and persistence, and self-regulation) [55, 59, 60]. According to UDL researchers, this method was developed using scientific insight into the human learning process. The method targets three neural networks: the affective network, the recognition network, and the strategic network ("the why," "the what," and "the how," respectively). An UDE approach seeks to activate these different neural networks, allowing diverse learners to fully engage in content. The method also encourages resourcefulness, self-expression of knowledge, and self-directed learning [21, 53, 55, 56, 60].

Instructors utilizing UDE are encouraged to use all four modalities in lessons and assignments: visual, aural, read-write, and kinesthetic. Multimodal teaching methods are designed to prevent barriers to learning from the outset and allow flexibility for a diverse group of learners [21, 53, 55, 56, 60]. This can be done by varying the course structure (e.g., lecture, small group, think-pair-share, hands-on activities, fieldwork, or discussion boards), including scaffolding (e.g., posting copies of outlines/summaries or guiding groups through team assignments with a list of questions) [20], and by providing multiple options for assimilating content (e.g., videos, podcasts, on-demand lectures, reading materials, or online resources) [17, 35]. The use of technology is fundamental to successfully implementing UDE [17–19]. Faculty instructors may consider accessing resources available through CAST (Center for Applied Special Technology), a not-for-profit organization dedicated to promoting the use of technology to increase access and opportunities for all, including those with disabilities [21].

UDE embraces the inclusion of a range of student assessment techniques [61, 62]. To be clear, the goal is not for all students to pass examinations but rather for all to have an opportunity to demonstrate their knowledge and skills without barriers [61]. Inclusive instructors develop examinations to provide a broad range of diverse learners with varied opportunities to demonstrate learning competencies [61, 62]. For example, in addition to written examinations, students may demonstrate proficiency in competencies by doing group projects or a hands-on simulation or by writing a reflection on a patient case. In Dolan et al. (2005), examination software was created with read-aloud capability; high school students with *and* without disabilities scored higher using the examination software than using pen and paper [62]. As written examinations are formatted, it is critical for an inclusive instructor to consider the print size and font and the amount of space between letters and lines [61, 63, 64]. In addition to students with disabilities, other at-risk student populations, including English language learners, slow readers, and students from diverse socioeconomic backgrounds, have benefited from universally designed assessments [65]. Students with disabilities often require extra examination time as part of their accommodation plan. Instructors may opt to give untimed examinations (i.e., unlimited time) as a way of implementing UDE principles, but it is important to recognize that if any time limit is set, students with accommodations are entitled to additional examination time as specified in their plan.

Published postsecondary education UDE studies show great promise, particularly for learner engagement, satisfaction, and/or self-efficacy [66–69]. One such study involved a first year undergraduate nursing course; students responded positively to the UDE course design and perceived increased flexibility and social presence, reduced stress, and felt it facilitated enhanced success [68]. In addition, positive effects have been reported for instructors who attended UDE training sessions [70, 71], student engagement in courses taught by UDE-trained instructors [26], and student-perceived value of UDE-based components of an online course [66, 72]. A positive impact on undergraduate students was reported when they had access to UDE-aligned technology [73]. Studies have not yet empirically examined UDE's impact on postsecondary student learning outcomes. However, there are examples of UDE-aligned innovations being implemented in higher education science courses [8, 68, 69, 73]. One example is the work done by Reglinksi (2007): pictorial representations of chemistry concepts were utilized on an assessment which asked students to "give a detailed explanation of the diagram." The study reported increased student performance with this assessment format [74].

More research needs to be conducted to gain a full perspective of UDE's potential influence on learning outcomes in health science program curricula.

When discussing UDE with faculty, administration, and stakeholders, it is important to emphasize the aim of UDE: to benefit all students [6, 9, 75, 76]. In addition, since many students with disabilities utilize varied learning approaches, the adoption of these practices may serve the needs of many students with disabilities without the need for further individualized accommodations [58, 68, 77]. For instance, students with ADHD may find the multimodal and hands-on approach of an inclusively designed flipped classroom more engaging and easier to follow than a traditional lecture. Students with processing delays may prefer watching videos and reading material prior to class so they can pace themselves and reread as needed [13, 14, 63]. In line with the student-centered approach of UDE [78], providing multimodal instruction and resources empowers students to use a method that works best for them, regardless of disability. Providing such options may prevent students from experiencing disability-related barriers [21, 53, 56]. Although UDE increases the accessibility of instruction for all students, often reducing the need for some accommodations, it does not eliminate the need for all accommodations, and students should continue to be referred to the appropriate office to ensure all barriers are identified and appropriately addressed.

UDE is not a radical new approach to classroom instruction. UDE principles are built on evidence from research and practice about how to create an accessible learning environment while optimizing instructional methods. Long before UD was applied to education, many individual instructors were incorporating UDE principles. However, a deliberate, comprehensive UDE approach is necessary to ensure full inclusion across health science program curricula [6, 9, 22, 75]. Instructional changes require buy-in from faculty, as heavy workloads are already a considerable barrier. Whenever possible, a team approach should be implemented, where librarians, academic support, educational technology, assistive technology, and departmental and other staff members play a supportive role in assisting faculty as they make changes to instructional materials. Instructors and stakeholders may consider using resources available on the University of Connecticut's Center on Postsecondary Education and Disability website, which include information about UDE [79].

Many of the pedagogical techniques commonly used in health science programs can and should be adapted and supplemented to align with a comprehensive implementation of UDE principles across the curriculum. UDE brings discussions of potential barriers and accessibility road blocks into the curriculum and instructional planning processes. Intentional inclusion and varied methods for accessing and connecting with content are designed into learning experiences [10, 19, 56]. This student-centered approach [78] not only helps students with disabilities access the curriculum but also aims to support all students with diverse learning approaches [6, 9, 75, 80]. As UDE principles are implemented, all students can experience instructional access and equity, thereby affording all students the opportunity to achieve their potential [78].

Sending a Curricular Message: The Process of Learning Is Critical to Student Success

Many students entering health science programs could benefit from developing stronger study strategies and academic self-efficacy. Although academic support services are offered on many campuses to teach study skills, they are not generally integrated with course content. In 1993, Rye et al. reported the success of offering optional integrated learning skills instruction in medical school courses; the program offered real-time, peer-guided opportunities for applications of various study strategies and learning principles within course content [81]. With recent calls to apply the science of learning to medical education [82–84], discussions about other professional programs incorporating lessons in metacognition for first year students [14] evidence to suggest metacognition assists students with disabilities [85], and the assertion that disability resource providers should advocate for instruction on learning strategies [86], it is time for the science of learning to be valued and integrated as a mandatory part of health science program curricula for all students. Although many health science program curricula include courses on pedagogical methods to build students' teaching skills, very few incorporate opportunities for a student to consider and improve his or her own learning process.

Since 1986, the Higher Education for Learning Problems Center (H.E.L.P. Center) at Marshall University has offered a Medical H.E.L.P. Program which teaches medical students about study strategies, executive functioning, test-taking strategies, and more [87]. Of course, this is not a curricular requirement and not every student is in a position to be able to attend. Many institutions rely on academic support program infrastructure to offer optional workshops or one-on-one study skills meetings. While these are important programs which have helped many students, they are not part of mandated curricula.

As many medical schools have been revising and integrating curricula, some have adopted an integrated course at the beginning of medical school where principles of the science of learning are explored and applied. These integrated courses are often paired with themes of professionalism, team building, and career advising. From the learning standpoint, the focus is generally on the science of learning, study resources, applying study strategies to basic science course content, and discussing the importance of receiving and implementing feedback. One such course, offered at the University of Texas Medical Branch School of Medicine, is referred to as Mindfully Evolving, Thriving and Advocating [88]. Another example at Virginia Tech Carilion School of Medicine is entitled Interprofessional Teamwork & Roles for Collaborative Practice [89].

The inclusion of these types of courses in the required medical school program curricula is one example of the implementation of UDE. Rather than waiting to identify students in need of learning support on the basis of examination failures, this proactive approach sends a message to all students about the value of reflecting on how they best learn, becoming receptive to instructor feedback, and not being afraid to seek support. Indeed, evidence has shown that as students develop academic self-efficacy and optimism about their abilities, their performance improves

[42, 90, 91]. It makes sense to preemptively ensure all students in health science programs receive instruction about the science of learning and how it may inform their own studying and future professional development.

Dispelling Myths and Gaining Allies

In 2012, a nationwide survey of baccalaureate nursing programs reported that nurse educators preferred able-bodied students [92, 93]. In 2014, a study was done on higher education faculty that revealed faculty attitudes still create barriers to an equitable learning environment for students with disabilities [27]. Fortunately, other studies reported more positive nursing faculty attitudes [94, 95], more positive higher education faculty attitudes [7], and mixed higher education faculty attitudes [63]. In order to foster an inclusive learning environment, it is critical to address attitudinal barriers pervasive among some faculty members who lack awareness of issues related to disabilities, access, and inclusion [22, 96].

Faculty members play a critical role in setting the tone in a learning environment that is already stressful for students [97–100]. In order to foster an environment where students can learn effectively, attention must be paid to ensure all members of the learning environment feel valued and accepted; this allows members of the learning community to form a "connectedness" that contributes to overall student well-being [101, 102]. Through multipronged education and awareness efforts, faculty with attitudinal barriers can change [103–105].

Spreading awareness and gaining allies within an educational program is essential to affect change [106]. Some potential barriers to faculty members embracing inclusive instructional methods include lack of understanding why students with disabilities require accommodations, a perception that inclusive instructional methods will create more work for faculty, lack of understanding of how certain current instructional methods present barriers for some students, and lack of understanding that inclusive instruction could benefit all students [22, 96, 107]. These barriers, as well as strategies and tools for addressing them to recruit faculty allies, are explored further in Table 7.1.

A team approach is necessary to best serve student needs; thus faculty buy-in is critical to implementing inclusive accessibility and instructional changes [84, 112–115]. Studies have suggested that faculty training sessions in UDE principles have yielded student-perceived improvements in instruction [26, 116], which is one of the many steps necessary to lead the charge in support of inclusive instruction. In order to affect lasting change, it is important to spread the message with a sense of urgency while building a team of allies [106]. Utilizing some of the strategies highlighted in Table 7.1, work to find others who share your common mission and enlist them in the cause.

Once allies are identified, seek their support in spreading the message; consider working with faculty allies to lead seminars explaining why accommodations and instructional changes are critical to providing inclusive access. It may be helpful to enlist the ADA compliance officer, general legal counsel, disabilities resource

Table 7.1 Barriers, strategies, and tools for gaining allies

Barrier to faculty buy-in	Strategy	Tools for removing/mitigating barrier
Perception that accommodations and/or changing of instructional methods will give a student an unfair advantage [103, 105, 107]	Distinguish equality from equity; help faculty understand that accommodations remove barriers to access for students with functional limitations	Post information on the institution's webpage about the interactive process and criteria used to determine reasonable accommodations [22] Provide access to best practices for inclusion of students with disabilities [22] Provide evidence using studies in the primary literature
Lack of knowledge of ADA requirements and/or best practices [22, 96, 103, 105, 107]	Bridge the knowledge gap; then focus on compliance with the law	Work with your ADA compliance officer to lead faculty development workshops on accessibility and accommodation best practices, citing primary literature and case law [22] Include expert guest speakers on the topic of disability as a mechanism of improving knowledge and climate Engage students in a student-run organization that advocates for accessibility and awareness [22] Encourage faculty and administration partnerships with the student group [104] Share success stories of health science and clinical accommodations at other, similar institutions
Personal experience[s] and/or cultural beliefs may lead to bias [92, 108–111]	Dispel myths with facts and published best practices	Provide evidence using studies in the primary literature Share other faculty members' successes to motivate a change in perspective Enlist help from faculty allies to help promote awareness separate from your efforts Discuss common myths and misconceptions during faculty trainings Publicly recognize faculty who develop inclusive practices for students with disabilities in their courses

Table 7.1 (continued)

Barrier to faculty buy-in	Strategy	Tools for removing/mitigating barrier
Lack of awareness or understanding of learning and other disabilities and how certain instructional methods may present barriers for students [103, 105]	Bridge the knowledge gap; then enlist their help in a common mission	Educate about learning disabilities Using examples, educate how specific instructional methods pose barriers for students with disabilities [104] Share personalized testimonies from students with and without disabilities who have experienced barriers and benefited from inclusive instructional methods [22, 104] Provide evidence using studies in the primary literature
Lack of awareness that all students can benefit from multimodal instructional methods [103, 105]	Focus on how the multimodal approach of UDE can assist faculty in achieving their teaching goals	Educate about multiple modalities and the individualized nature of learning Educate about UDE and how it can benefit students Share personalized testimonies from students who have benefited from UDE Share the experiences of instructors who have successfully implemented UDE Making instruction more inclusive positively affects all students, which may impact student course evaluations and learning outcomes Provide evidence using studies in the primary literature
Perception that instructional changes and/or accommodations are costly and require more work by faculty [107]	Speak to their personal stake in the strength of the program, institution, and student body	Educate that providing inclusive instructional methods may lessen the need for some classroom accommodations, which could result in an overall reduction in cost [58, 68] Share the experiences of instructors who have successfully implemented UDE Emphasize that any additional work or resource investment necessary in the short-term will benefit the institution in the long-term As students' needs are addressed satisfaction increases [84], an important factor in recruiting new students and maintaining accreditation

professional, and/or the equity and inclusion office to provide further expertise regarding the institutional policies and governing laws that support this approach [22, 107].

Active Learning Methods for Lecture Instruction

Although the lecture format may allow instructors to transmit large amounts of information to students, this instructional method alone does not foster deep student content understanding. Research has demonstrated that retention and understanding of material rapidly declines after about 15–20 minutes of uninterrupted lecture [117, 118]. For students with processing and attentional disabilities, staying engaged in a lecture that extends beyond 15–20 minutes can be especially challenging. In addition, research has demonstrated that the number of students paying attention also drops dramatically after 15–20 minutes, further contributing to the lower retention rates [119–121].

When students are engaged in the learning process, they are more motivated to achieve learning objectives [1, 2]. Infusing active learning strategies into lectures can help students stay engaged [122, 123]. For example, a lecturer intentionally pausing to allow students to review their notes can help all students, including those with processing disabilities, stay engaged in the content [124]. Research has demonstrated an increase in short-term and long-term retention when such lecture pauses are implemented [125, 126]. When lecturers speak and move through slides and concepts quickly, students, especially those with processing and attentional disabilities, may have a difficult time keeping up [127–130]. Inserting a pause and slowing the pace of the lecture allow students the time necessary to process content [63, 131, 132]. A similarly helpful tool is inserting an interactive question using an audience response system.

Active learning strategies have been shown to improve retention of knowledge, allow for deeper content understanding, and foster engagement through self-directed learning [123, 133–136]. By utilizing active learning techniques during lectures, material can be contextualized [137–140] allowing student learning to shift from simply remembering to applying and analyzing, a much deeper form of learning [141]. In line with UDE principles, active learning shifts the responsibility of organizing learning from the teacher to the student, which allows for a diverse range of student approaches to learning [142–144].

Retaining attention and facilitating deeper student understanding during lectures can be accomplished using various tools spanning multiple modalities. One tool often utilized is the wireless laptop computer, where software allows the instructor and student to interact in real time [134]. Studies on the use of laptops as tools for active learning in the classroom have yielded positive results including increased student motivation and collaboration, strengthened connections between disciplines, and improved problem-solving skills [145–148]. For example, one study reported that students used laptops in class to access virtual patient cases, allowing each student to make individual patient care decisions in real time;

learning outcomes were significantly improved when compared to a traditional lecture format [134].

Laptops are critical tools for students with disabilities; students with rheumatoid arthritis, dyslexia, processing, or other disabilities may require a laptop to fully access the curriculum [14, 25]. Given the laptop's potential power as an active learning tool, as well as its essential supportive role for students with various disabilities, it is surprising that many university and graduate schools have experimented with banning laptops from classrooms [149–153]. When laptops are allowed in class, the student with a disability who requires specific accommodation software can blend in with members of the class, rather than being singled out and involuntarily identified as requiring accommodations.

A laptop ban forces students with disabilities to choose between fully accessing the curriculum or maintaining their privacy [113, 154–156]. Arguments in support of laptop bans seem to disregard the impact on students with disabilities as an unimportant consequence of the professor's attempt to manage the classroom by preventing distractions [149, 151–153]. While evidence has been published to suggest multitasking on laptops during class can be distracting for the laptop user [151], many have noted a lack of empirical evidence to support the premise that the majority of students using laptops in class are, in fact, multitasking. However, evidence has been published that laptop multitasking can also distract neighboring students [151].

Some professors have attempted to address these concerns without banning laptops from class. Approaches range from the professor walking around the classroom (to disincentivize multitasking) to implementing rules that laptop users must sit in either the front few rows (to reduce the temptation to multitask) [149, 153] or the back few rows (to minimize distractions to other students) [149]. Bearing in mind that students with visual or hearing impairments often require front row seating and/ or assistive technology, the front row seating rule is more in line with UDE principles.

Arguments made in support of laptop bans often cite Mueller and Oppenheimer's study (2014) on note-taking, which asserts that handwritten notes are more effective for a learner than typed notes [157]. This issue was addressed in depth in Chap. 6 along with suggestions as to how this and other studies can inform an effective approach to note-taking using a laptop. Luo et al. (2018) published a study specifically addressing note-taking in science instruction. They concluded that optimal note-taking formats depend on the nature of the lecture content and whether or not the material in the notes is learned depends on subsequent review by the student [158].

Arguments made in support of allowing laptops in class assert that the use of technology can be supportive of each individual's learning, and note that no empirical evidence has been published to suggest the use of laptops is causal of decreased classroom engagement [154–156]. However, there is anecdotal evidence to suggest classroom engagement can decrease when students multitask on laptops, with some faculty members noting lack of eye contact or decreased class participation.

Aligning courses with UDE principles can be inconvenient. Nevertheless, it is important to consider if there are ways to increase student engagement while also taking into account all students' needs. Instructors can include active learning peda-gogical techniques and use technology within their lessons to facilitate interaction. As student engagement increases, intellectual excitement in the classroom can eclipse many distractions [134, 145–148, 159]. Classroom distractions are not a new phenomenon, and regardless of any classroom policy, the learning environment will never be distraction-free [154–156, 160].

Some of the most effective active learning techniques for large lectures are included in Table 7.2 [161, 162].

Table 7.2 Active learning techniques for lectures

Technique	Description	Notes
Interactive lecture demonstrations [163]	Students predict the outcome of a demonstration individually, then interact with small groups, view the demonstration, and describe the results, and finally the instructor integrates concepts together in a large group discussion	Demos can be viewed using multiple monitors, wireless laptops, and/or a computer projector to ensure all can see in a large lecture hall
Clarification pause [124, 125, 131, 132]	An intentional pause in lecture to allow students time to review notes, process, and assimilate information	Instructor(s) can circulate the room and answer questions, allowing them to assess student understanding
One-minute paper pause [164, 165]	The instructor asks a question; students write a one-minute reflection	Can be done during or at the end of class; if turned in, instructor can assess student understanding
Think-pair-share [125, 166]	Individual students consider a question, then talk about their responses, and reach consensus with a peer, after which the instructor calls on pairs to share with the larger group	Can be thought of as a way to infuse a small amount of problem-based learning into a lecture format
Case-based learning [167, 168]	A patient case vignette is described and discussed within the lecture. Another technique, such as think-pair-share, could be employed to facilitate discussion of the case among students	An example of "anchored" or "situated" learning, which puts information in context [137–140]
Concept maps [169, 170]	A diagram depicting relationships between concepts. Can be created individually or in pairs/groups, depending on the layout of the lecture hall	Instructor can distribute a partially completed concept map to provide scaffolding and/or if time is limited [20]
Role-play/ Thinking hats [135, 171, 172]	Most commonly, students take a particular viewpoint or act out a specific role. This technique can also be used by professors to illustrate different viewpoints: the instructor literally puts on different hats during lecture to signal students which viewpoint is being represented	Often used in lessons on interprofessional and patient communication or to facilitate debates
Commitment activities [134, 173, 174]	Activities that force students to make decisions (e.g., practice questions with responses) which can be done individually or in pairs/groups	An audience response system is commonly used

Table 7.2 (continued)

Technique	Description	Notes
Problem-based review sessions [161]	Students are divided into pairs or triads and must solve a series of problems together, interspersed with full class discussions of the problems [a]see PBL recommendations for ensuring inclusion and accessibility when using this technique	Choose problems with ambiguous solutions so students have to debate which answer is best
The muddiest point pause [175]	Students reflect on and share areas of confusion either in writing or verbally through class discussion	Allows instructor to assess student understanding of content
Fish bowl [161]	At the end of class, students are given index cards and asked to bring written questions to the next class. Questions are drawn from the fish bowl; students must answer questions within an instructor facilitated discussion	Allows students to ask and answer questions about weaknesses or areas of confusion

Problem-Based Learning (PBL)

Problem-based learning (PBL) is a method of instruction that anchors learning experiences in investigations of complex problems or scenarios which require students to engage in collaborative application of content [139, 176–181]. Learning is self-directed and student-centered and occurs in small groups, and instructors serve as active learning facilitators [177–179]. Students with disabilities have benefited from contextual learning of scientific concepts [140], so the PBL method has great potential in an inclusive UDE instructional model.

In the health sciences, PBL sessions can involve patient or laboratory cases that require analysis of a real or simulated patient, experimental or clinical laboratory data, images such as X-rays, video clips, newspaper articles, scientific journal articles, genetic information such as a pedigree chart, and more [182]. Noting the multiple modalities represented by this list, it is clear the PBL format can be designed in alignment with the principles of UDE. In order to bring this to fruition, the curriculum of each PBL session must provide "multiple means of representation" of content, allow "multiple means of engagement" as students work toward understanding and applying content, and allow "multiple means of expression and action" as students communicate their content understanding [55, 59, 60, 183]. As discussed in the UDE section, inclusive instruction is designed to provide learning opportunities for as many students as possible [59].

PBL has been widely used in health science education since its introduction to medical education by McMaster University in 1969 [180, 184]. Due in part to the lack of uniformity in the definition of "PBL curriculum" and widely varying outcome measurements, there is still a debate over what effect PBL has on learning outcomes [181, 184–186]. Mixed results have been reported for how medical school PBL curricula affect USMLE board examination scores [187, 188]; fairly recently, one single medical school's 10-year study reported significant increases in scores after PBL curricula were implemented [189]. Graduates from medical schools with PBL curricula have demonstrated equivalent or superior performance in the following physician competencies: coping with uncertainty [190], communication skills [190, 191], appreciation of legal and ethical aspects of health care [190], and self-directed continuing learning [190, 191]. In nursing, Kong et al.'s (2014) systematic meta-analysis of the literature suggested that PBL sessions support nursing students in improving critical thinking skills [192]. Other nurse education studies have demonstrated student satisfaction with PBL sessions [193–195] and an increase in knowledge after attending PBL sessions [195]. Calls in nursing education to move toward a concept-based curriculum have resulted in increased usage of PBL sessions [196, 197].

Faculty members engaged in PBL generally report an advantage in observing how students think through complex issues, which allows instructors to identify struggling students and intervene early [177]. Many faculty instructors in medical education were positive about the opportunities PBL afforded them to personally interact with students [198, 199]. Some barriers to the use of PBL sessions include the number of instructors available to teach small group sessions, the time required to create and implement problem-based sessions, and a need for faculty development to shift from an instructor- to a learner-centered approach to instruction.

PBL sessions, where scenarios are presented in real time, present barriers for students with various types of disabilities often due to limited processing time and the need for simultaneous real-time note-taking [13, 14, 63]. Students who are unable to simultaneously engage in discussion and note-taking tasks may not be able to achieve the desired learning outcome(s). Appropriate accommodation plans should be communicated to faculty by the institution's disability resource professional on a case-by-case basis and may include the use of a smart pen or a digital recorder. In addition to the accommodation, an inclusive instructor could identify one note-taker in each group and assign the student to share notes with the entire group at the end of the session [13, 15, 16]. If the assigned note-taker learns well through the process of writing, this student's experience could also be optimized by taking on the responsibility of note-taking for the group [43–45]. Many of the barriers students may face in PBL sessions are presented in Table 7.3, with potential accommodation and UDE recommendations to remove or mitigate the barriers [13].

In order to further mitigate barriers and facilitate full inclusion of students with disabilities in PBL sessions, appropriate faculty guidance and scaffolding resources should be provided [13, 63]. Hmelo-Silver et al. (2007) highlighted three categories of PBL scaffolding that can benefit all students: making disciplinary thinking and strategies explicit, embedding expert guidance, and structuring complex tasks or reducing the cognitive load [20]. Many studies of PBL sessions have successfully utilized scaffolds, which may include supplementary resources or real-time faculty guidance [20, 200–203].

Some students with disabilities have difficulty presenting orally in front of peers. In this real-time PBL session format, students who already find this challenging may be put on the spot without the benefit of preparation. Students'

Table 7.3 Potential approaches to small group barriers [13]

Small group barrier	Potential accommodation	UDE approach
Taking notes while simultaneously listening and participating in discussion	Note-taker for learner Livescribe pen recording small group	Provide written case materials with outline Small group leader creates an audio recording of pen (e.g., Livescribe) and makes available to all students Class notes available to all learners via volunteer note-takers Assign one student in each class to take photos of any items on board and upload to class content via learning management system
Information and discussions presented verbally	Note-taker for learner Instructors present concepts in charts, graphs, or photos as appropriate to student with disability	Provide charts, graphs, photos, or videos that depict relevant concepts to all students Diagram concepts on a whiteboard; upload photos of diagram to LMS
Not enough time to process information and participate in meaningful discussion—especially if the case is presented in group	Provide the learner with a disability with the case at least 1 week in advance Leader calls on learner last to allow more time to develop feedback	Open case prior to small group to allow for thoughtful reading and reflection Students contribute at their comfort level. Leaders ensure equal participation for all Incorporate observational learning methods; allow learners to observe how other groups deduce and formulate a differential diagnosis
Anxiety about contributing to discussion	Assign learners specific parts of case so they can practice their contribution	Allow different forms of contributions for learners (e.g., taking notes for the group, providing an outline in advance, explaining a concept in detail verbally, drawing a representation of the concept or process for visual input)
Attendance difficulties due to chronic health conditions	Provide note-taker Alternate assignment if allowed by faculty	Stream small group via Skype or Google Hangout, allowing students to attend remotely Record small group Post case materials on LMS
Synthesizing information	Provide note-taker	Incorporate reflection process (e.g., journaling, papers) after the small group session

LMS learning management system
[a]Reproduced and slightly re-formatted with permission from Sullivan and Meeks [13]

anxiety can worsen due to a fear of being judged and stigmatized if symptoms of their disability are viewed by others [22, 24, 63, 204, 205]. Without allowing any preparation time prior to the session, students who already struggle with oral presentations may find themselves much less able to meet their potential. A more inclusive approach to the design of a PBL small group session may include providing a written copy and/or a video of the scenario prior to the session, which would allow students time to process the material before engaging in discussions or presentations in front of peers [13].

Table 7.4 Scaffolding ideas for PBL sessions [20, 182, 206–208]

Formats	Examples
Images	X-rays, graphs, histology/anatomy images, lab test images (e.g., gel electrophoresis, ELISA, etc.)
Diagrams	Data tables, pathways, procedures, processes, genetic pedigrees
Graphic organizers	Flow charts, concept maps, visualizations of the problem at multiple stages of the solution
List of questions	Questions that help students think through the important points of the case in a step-by-step manner
Videos	Animations of cellular processes or drug mechanisms, simulated patient interviews, instructional videos on relevant concepts
Laboratory demonstrations	Dissections, minimum inhibitory concentrations (MIC), in-class microscopy, use of an ultrasound machine
Real-time standardized patient interviews	Use to enhance a case discussion and/or to allow students to practice interviewing skills in groups
Podcasts	Can be used in class or pre-/post-class to highlight important content or key points

Inclusive curriculum design for PBL sessions will ensure all students have the same learning goals while allowing some flexibility in the learning process (e.g., use of time, groupings, offering a variety of materials for content acquisition) [13, 19, 70]. Identifying groups in advance and assigning roles to each member may decrease student anxiety. Materials presented could include images, diagrams, graphic organizers/flow charts/concept maps, scaffolded questions to guide students through important points of the scenario, video or laboratory demonstrations, visualizations of the problem at multiple stages of its solution, real-time standardized patient interviews, and podcasts to emphasize certain points prior to or after the session [206–208]. To illustrate how scaffolding may assist learners, the same ideas presented in the previous text-dense sentence have been converted into table format with examples (Table 7.4). Any diagrams or information written on the board in PBL sessions should be captured as photographs and posted to the learning management system for all students to access. Providing students time to reflect after the small group session before submitting a graded assignment can also assist students in processing the content and performing to their potential [13].

As inclusive PBL session materials are created, it is important to be certain students with visual or reading disabilities who utilize screen readers or other assistive software have access to digital copies of any hard copy materials distributed in class. Ideally copies should be provided in advance of the class session, and all students should be allowed to use laptops in class. Any documents created by an inclusive instructor will include fonts that are text-to-speech technology friendly. For students with hearing impairments, it is important to know that FM systems work best in traditional lecture halls, so the disabilities resource professional may need to consider an alternate option such as such as a personal assistive listening system (e.g., pocket talker, MINI IR system, soundAMP-R app) [113]. When an instructor chooses a PBL classroom, the acoustics of the room should be considered to ensure multiple groups can talk simultaneously without hindering the participation of a student with a hearing impairment. In addition, inclusive PBL design will include considerations of how students with chronic health conditions, who may require leniency in attendance policies, may be able to participate remotely or in an asynchronous alternative format (e.g., a read-and-respond written assignment) [13, 19, 146]. As instructors make deliberate choices in alignment with UDE principles, the PBL classroom becomes fully inclusive, making it a positive learning environment where students can meet their full potential.

The Flipped Classroom Instructional Model

The instructor-centered traditional lecture model places students into a passive learning mode [209, 210]. As higher education classrooms utilize student-centered active learning strategies such as problem-based learning sessions to supplement traditional lectures, content isn't always removed to compensate for the additional sessions [196, 211]. Adding sessions without removing contact hours may hinder students' ability to fully engage in and appreciate supplemental active learning experiences [82, 83, 211]. The student-centered active learning model of a flipped classroom intentionally changes the curricular and pedagogical structure to allow time for students to engage in content acquisition activities outside of class, using assigned course materials such as videos, podcasts, or readings [211–214]. Class time is focused on engagement in higher-order cognition, such as case-based or problem-based exercises or discussions [15, 141, 212, 215, 216]. Application of content within small groups is common in flipped classroom sessions, making them similar to PBL sessions.

Although the "flipped classroom" model was first published in 2012 and originated in secondary education [212], there is a fair amount of evidence to support health science program students' satisfaction with flipped classrooms [211, 214, 217–220] and some evidence to suggest increased learning outcomes when compared to a traditional lecture classroom [217, 221, 222] or when compared to benchmark and formative assessments [214]. Hew and Low (2018) conducted a meta-analysis on the literature addressing flipped classrooms in health professions education (including medicine, nursing, dental, pharmacy, and public health) which reported a significant improvement in student learning in the flipped classroom when compared to traditional teaching methods [223]. In addition to the growing body of supportive literature specifically addressing the flipped classroom model, the method's alignment with active, experiential, and self-directed learning strategies further supports the rationale for its use in health science programs [224–227].

Despite its apparent benefits, the flipped classroom model may present barriers for students with disabilities unless it is designed using UDE principles. Similar to the issues raised for PBL sessions, traditional didactic accommodations may be harder to implement in the inherently dynamic environment of the flipped classroom [13, 15, 16]. The barriers and suggestions enumerated in the PBL section should be considered when planning inclusive flipped classroom sessions. In 2017, a review of medical student perceptions of flipped classrooms noted a student concern that aligns with one addressed in the PBL section: direction and structure was insufficient during activity learning sessions [220]. To reiterate what was previously discussed, in a student-centered learning format, it is critical for instructors to provide scaffolds and guidance to ensure learning objectives are met [20].

Selection and Development of Pre-class Content and Materials

Instructors must be proactive and strategic when determining what pre-class content and materials to provide for students. It is important to create and/or locate resources and materials that are engaging, manageable, and accessible [1–4, 82]. Materials posted on the institution's learning management system, including PowerPoints and other supplemental materials, should be provided in a digitally accessible format for use with assistive technology such as screen readers, Kurzweil, Read and Write Gold, and other learning software [113, 228].

Universally designed content and materials will allow students to explore and review information using various methods [216, 229]. Many instructors will use some combination of the following materials for pre-class content acquisition: video lectures, narrated PowerPoints, chapter readings, journal articles, videos, podcasts, and websites [214]. It has been proposed that short 10-minute videos could be utilized, although most studies do not specify the duration of their pre-class materials [211].

As videos, podcasts, and other multimedia items are selected or created, instructors should verify accurate captioning and/or provide descriptive transcripts. In this process, it may be helpful to meet with the institution's disability resource and learning technology service professionals to discuss available captioning and transcription services. As resources are created, instructors should be cognizant of turnaround times for captioning and transcription services to ensure all materials are accessible when they are released to students. In the case of internally produced videos, vodcasts, or podcasts, scripting in advance of recording can help instructors consider how to describe and refer to on-camera elements such as charts, diagrams, procedure demonstrations, or on-screen text notations. Once the video is created, the script can be edited to include any necessary descriptions of images and released to students [113].

An inclusively designed flipped classroom allows all students to pace themselves in their self-directed knowledge acquisition processes, potentially reviewing multimodal content many times while utilizing instructor guidelines and scaffolds to prepare for the active class session. This flexibility can support all students, particularly those with processing, attentional, or other disabilities.

Peer Assisted Learning (PAL)

Peer-assisted learning (PAL) is an educational method where students learn from other students [230]. PAL is used in many health science programs for pre-clinical and clinical courses, but the program design, reason for implementation, and method of evaluation often differ. In near-peer tutoring, the tutor is more advanced in training compared to the tutee(s) [231]; in reciprocal-peer tutoring, students within the same year of training and course alternate between serving as the tutor and tutee [231]; in peer-to-peer tutoring, stronger students are designated tutors, and those in need of support are designated tutees while simultaneously taking a course [232]. Some PAL programs involve one-on-one sessions, while most implement small groups or larger lectures. Program heterogeneity makes it difficult to compare efficacy and outcomes across institutions. The goals of PAL programs often differ and can be multifaceted. Some PAL programs are implemented to help struggling students [233], some to supplement the limited number of faculty available [234], some to teach students clinical skills [235, 236], and others to train student tutors how to teach [237–239].

Published PAL studies largely report qualitative program outcomes [231, 236, 240, 241]. Overall, PAL programs instituted in health science programs demonstrate qualitative benefits for both tutors and tutees in basic science [242, 243] and clinical environments [235, 236, 244, 245]. Strengths of these programs include promoting a safe learning environment, applicable discussions of study strategies, mentorship about difficulties in medical school, and improving teaching and communication skills [246–249]. Many studies provide evidence to quantitatively support the improved performance of participant tutors [231, 243, 250–252]. However, more quantitative studies are necessary to draw a definitive conclusion as to the impact of PAL programs on academic outcomes of tutees. Some studies suggest tutee participation plays a role in increasing grades and/or examination scores in the classroom and clinic, particularly among those who are at risk of failing a course [253–256].

Sufficient training of peer tutors is necessary to ensure program outcomes are achieved [257, 258]. Peer tutors must be trained to understand the importance of supporting students with accommodations, and any knowledge they obtain regarding a student's accommodation must be kept strictly confidential. Any student with attitudinal barriers to inclusion of students with disabilities [22] should be educated before being considered to serve as a PAL tutor. In order to ensure students with disabilities can fully access PAL sessions, peer tutor trainings should cover UDE methods to enhance peer tutors' awareness and ability to present content using multiple modalities [259, 260]. Training sessions should also include a variety of study strategy methods that can be implemented to address various academic challenges including distractibility, executive functioning, time management, test-taking strategies, and test anxiety (see Chap. 6) [261]. Street et al. (2012) reported preliminary positive academic outcomes for student tutees with disabilities in an undergraduate STEM PAL program; this program's extensive peer tutor trainings emphasized principles of UDE and specific strategies to support students with learning disabilities and ADHD [261].

PAL programs are offered in many health science programs. As institutions make strides toward providing more inclusive instructional methods and resources, simple alterations or additions to PAL tutor trainings could positively impact all students who participate in the program.

Conclusion

It is critical that inclusive instructional methods become the norm among faculty in health science programs, as adapting these practices can help instructors meet their teaching goals by ensuring *all* students have full access to the curriculum and the opportunity to demonstrate competency in course learning objectives. Although UDE increases the accessibility of instruction, it does not eliminate the need for all accommodations, and students should continue to be referred to the appropriate office to ensure all barriers are identified and appropriately addressed. Many learning barriers can be removed through a thoughtful UDE approach to curriculum and instructional design. A few deliberate alterations of many commonly used pedagogical techniques can afford many students, particularly those with disabilities, the opportunity to achieve their full potential.

Acknowledgments The author would like to express appreciation to Erika Maikish, Grace C. Clifford, Adele Shenoy, and Kellen K. Petersen for their support at various stages of this project.

References

1. Zepke N, Leach L. Improving student engagement: ten proposals for action. Act Learn High Educ. 2010;11(3):167–77.
2. Carini RM, Kuh GD, Klein SP. Student engagement and student learning: testing the linkages. Res High Educ. 2006;47(1):1–32.
3. Appleton JJ, Christenson SL, Kim D, Reschly AL. Measuring cognitive and psychological engagement: validation of the student engagement instrument. J Sch Psychol. 2006;44(5):427–45.
4. Kuh GD. What we're learning about student engagement from NSSE: benchmarks for effective educational practices. Change Mag High Learn. 2003;35(2):24–32.
5. Norman K, Caseau D, Stefanich GP. Teaching students with disabilities in inclusive science classrooms: survey results. Sci Educ. 1998;82(2):127–46.
6. Silver P, Bourke A, Strehorn KC. Universal instructional design in higher education: an approach for inclusion. Equity Excell Educ. 1998;31(2):47–51.
7. Leyser Y, Greenberger L. College students with disabilities in teacher education: faculty attitudes and practices. Eur J Spec Needs Educ. 2008;23(3):237–51.
8. Kumar K. A journey towards creating an inclusive classroom: how universal design for learning has transformed my teaching. Transform Dialogues Teach Learn J. 2010;4(2):1–5.
9. Scott SS, Mcguire JM, Shaw SF. Universal design for instruction: a new paradigm for adult instruction in postsecondary education. Remedial Spec Educ. 2003;24(6):369–79.
10. Pliner SM, Johnson JR. Historical, theoretical, and foundational principles of universal instructional design in higher education. Equity Excell Educ. 2004;37(2):105–13.
11. Mace RL, Hardie GJ, Place JP. Accessible environments: toward universal design. Raleigh, NC: North Carolina State University: The Center for Universal Design; 1996.
12. Scott SS, McGuire JM, Foley TE. Universal design for instruction: a framework for anticipating and responding to disability and other diverse learning needs in the college classroom. Equity Excell Educ. 2010;36(1):40–9.
13. Sullivan L, Meeks LM. Big solutions for small groups in health science programs. Disabil Compliance High Educ. 2018;23(8):1–7.
14. Adams SJ. Leveling the floor: classroom accommodations for law student with disabilities. J Leg Educ. 1998;48(2):273–96.

15. Milman NB. The flipped classroom strategy: what is it and how can it best be used? Dist Learn. 2012;9(3):85–7.
16. Sullivan L. Flip, don't flop: ensuring accessibility of the flipped classroom. Disabil Compliance High Educ. 2018;23(9):6–7.
17. Rose DH, Hasselbring TS, Stahl S, Zabala J. Assistive technology and universal design for learning: two sides of the same coin. In: Edyburn D, Higgins K, Boone R, Langone J, editors. Handbook of special education technology, research and practice. Whitefish Bay: Knowledge by Design; 2005. p. 507–18.
18. Abell MM, Bauder DK, Simmons TJ. Access to the general curriculum: a curriculum and instruction perspective for educators. Interv Sch Clin. 2005;41(2):82–6.
19. Basham JD, Israel M, Graden J, Poth R, Winston M. A comprehensive approach to RtI: embedding universal design for learning and technology. Learn Disabil Q. 2010;33(4):243–55.
20. Hmelo-Silver C, Duncan R, Chinn C. Scaffolding and achievement in problem-based and inquiry learning: a response to Kirschner, Sweller, and Clark (2006). Educ Psychol. 2007;42(2):99–107.
21. CAST (Center for Applied Special Technology): About Universal Design for Learning, "UDL at a Glance" video [Internet]. [cited 2019 Aug 14]. Available from: http://www.cast.org/our-work/about-udl.html.
22. Meeks LM, Jain NR. Accessibility, inclusion, and action in medical education: lived experiences of learners and physicians with disabilities. [Internet]. Washington, D.C: Association of American Medical Colleges; 2018. Available from: https://store.aamc.org/accessibility-inclusion-and-action-in-medical-education-lived-experiences-of-learners-and-physicians-with-disabilities.html.
23. Neal-Boylan L, Smith D. Nursing students with physical disabilities: dispelling myths and correcting misconceptions. Nurse Educ. 2016;41(1):13–8.
24. Neal-Boylan L, Miller M. Treat me like everyone else: the experience of nurses who had disabilities while in school. Nurse Educ. 2017;42(4):176–80.
25. Mckendree J, Snowling MJ. Examination results of medical students with dyslexia. Med Educ. 2011;45(2):176–82.
26. Schelly CL, Davies PL, Spooner CL. Student perceptions of faculty implementation of universal design for learning. J Postsecond Educ Disabil. 2011;24(1):17–30.
27. Black RD, Weinberg LA, Brodwin MG. Universal design for instruction and learning: a pilot study of faculty instructional methods and attitudes related to students with disabilities in higher education. Except Educ Int. 2014;24(1):48–64.
28. Ertmer PA, Newby TJ. Behaviorism, cognitivism, constructivism: comparing critical features from an instructional design perspective. Perform Improv Q. 2013;26(2):43–71.
29. Ertmer PA, Newby TJ. The expert learner: strategic, self-regulated, and reflective. Instr Sci. 1996;24(1):1–24.
30. Sweller J. Cognitive load during problem solving: effects on learning. Cogn Sci. 1988;12(2):257–85.
31. Miller GA. The magical number seven plus or minus two: some limits on our capacity for processing information. Psychol Rev. 1956;63(2):81–97.
32. Halford GS, Baker R, McCredden JE, Bain JD. How many variables can humans process? Psychol Sci. 2005;16(1):70–6.
33. Paivio A. Mental representations: a dual coding approach. Oxford, UK: Oxford University Press; 1990. 336 p.
34. Paivio A, Desrochers A. A dual-coding approach to bilingual memory. Can J Psychol. 1980;34(4):388–99.
35. Mayer RE. Multimedia learning. 2nd ed. New York: Cambridge University Press; 2009. 320 p.
36. Curry L. Individual differences in cognitive style, learning style and instructional preference in medical education. In: Norman GR, van der Vleuten CPM, Newbie DI, editors. International handbook of research in medical education. Dordrecht: Springer; 2002.
37. Brown PC, Roediger HL III, McDaniel MA. Make it stick: the science of successful learning. 1st ed. Cambridge, MA: Belknap Press: An Imprint of Harvard University Press; 2014.

38. Bandura A. The explanatory and predictive scope of self-efficacy theory. J Soc Clin Psychol. 1986;4(3):359–73.
39. Bandura A, Schunk DH. Cultivating competence, self-efficacy, and intrinsic interest through proximal self-motivation. J Pers Soc Psychol. 1981;41(3):586–98.
40. Zimmerman BJ. A social cognitive view of self-regulated academic learning. J Educ Psychol. 1989;81(3):329–39.
41. Multon KD, Brown SD, Lent RW. Relation of self-efficacy beliefs to academic outcomes: a meta-analytic investigation. J Couns Psychol. 1991;38(1):30–8.
42. Stegers-Jager KM, Cohen-Schotanus J, Themmen APN. Motivation, learning strategies, participation and medical school performance. Med Educ. 2012;46(7):678–88.
43. Kolb DA. Experiential learning: experience as the source of learning and development. 1st ed. Englewood Cliffs: Prentice Hall; 1983.
44. Felder R. Learning and teaching styles in engineering education. Eng Educ. 1988;78(7):674–81.
45. Fleming ND, Mills C. Not another inventory, rather a catalyst for reflection. Improve Acad. 1992;11(1):137–55.
46. Mayer RE. Does styles research have useful implications for educational practice? Learn Individ Differ. 2011;21(3):319–20.
47. Pashler H, McDaniel M, Rohrer D, Bjork R. Learning styles: concepts and evidence. Psychol Sci Public Interest. 2009;9(3):105–19.
48. Fleming S, Mckee G, Huntley-Moore S. Undergraduate nursing students' learning styles: a longitudinal study. Nurse Educ Today. 2011;31(5):444–9.
49. Gurpinar E, Bati H, Tetik C. Learning styles of medical students change in relation to time. Adv Physiol Educ. 2011;35(3):307–11.
50. Center for Universal Design NCSU - About the Center - Ronald L. Mace [Internet]. [cited 2019 Aug 14]. Available from: http://www.ncsu.edu/ncsu/design/cud/about_us/usronmace.htm.
51. Mace RL. Universal design: barrier-free environments for everyone. Des West. 1985;33(1):147–52.
52. Orkwis R, McLane K. A curriculum every student can use: design principles for student access. [Internet]. Reston: Council for Exceptional Children; 1998 [cited 2019 Aug 14]. Available from: https://eric.ed.gov/?id=ED423654
53. Rose DH, Meyer A. Teaching every student in the digital age: universal design for learning. Alexandria: Association for Supervision & Curriculum Development; 2002.
54. McGuire JM, Scott SS, Shaw SF. Universal design and its applications in educational environments. Remedial Spec Educ. 2006;27(3):166–75.
55. Rose DH, Harbour WS, Johnston CS, Daley SG, Abarbanell L. Universal design for learning in postsecondary education: reflections on principles and their application. J Postsecond Educ Disabil. 2006;19(2):135–51.
56. Hall TE, Meyer A, Rose DH, editors. Universal design for learning in the classroom: practical applications. 1st ed. New York: The Guilford Press; 2012.
57. Rao K, Ok MW, Bryant BR. A review of research on universal design educational models. Remedial Spec Educ. 2014;35(3):153–66.
58. Brinckerhoff LC, McGuire JM, Shaw SF. Postsecondary education and transition for students with learning disabilities. 2nd ed. Austin: PRO-ED; 2002.
59. UDL Guidelines [Internet]. National Center on Universal Design for Learning (NCUDL). 2010 [cited 2019 Aug 12]. Available from: http://www.udlcenter.org/aboutudl/udlguidelines.
60. Rose DH, Gravel JW. Universal design for learning. In: Peterson P, Baker E, McGaw B, editors. International encyclopedia of education. 3rd ed. Oxford: Elsevier; 2010. p. 119–24.
61. Ketterlin-Geller LR, Johnstone C. Accommodations and universal design: supporting access to assessments in higher education. J Postsecond Educ Disabil. 2006;19(2):163–72.
62. Dolan R, Hall TE, Banerjee M, Chun E, Strangman N. Applying principles of universal design to test delivery: the effect of computer-based read-aloud on test performance of high school students with learning disabilities. J Technol Learn Assess. 2005;3(7):4–32.

63. Fuller M, Healey M, Bradley A, Hall T. Barriers to learning: a systematic study of the experience of disabled students in one university. Stud High Educ. 2004;29(3):303–18.

64. Comp G, Comp C. A guide to providing alternate formats. West Columbia: Center for Rehabilitation Technology Services; 1995. Report No.: ERIC document no ED 405689.

65. Johnstone CJ. Improving validity of large-scale tests: universal design and student performance. Minneapolis: National Center on Educational Outcomes; 2003.

66. Rao K, Tanners A. Curb cuts in cyberspace: universal instructional design for online courses. J Postsecond Educ Disabil. 2011;24(3):211–29.

67. Smith FG. Analyzing a college course that adheres to the universal design for learning (UDL) framework. J Scholarsh Teach Learn. 2012;12(3):31–61.

68. Kumar KL, Wideman M. Accessible by design: applying UDL principles in a first year undergraduate course. Can J High Educ. 2014;44(1):125–47.

69. Miller DK, Lang PL. Using the universal design for learning approach in science laboratories to minimize student stress. J Chem Educ. 2016;93(11):1823–8.

70. Spooner F, Baker JN, Harris AA, Ahlgrim-Delzell LA, Browder DM. Effects of training in universal design for learning on lesson plan development. Remedial Spec Educ - REM SPEC EDUC. 2007;28(2):108–16.

71. McGhie-Richmond D, Sung AN. Applying universal design for learning to instructional lesson planning. Int J Whole Sch. 2013;9(1):43–59.

72. Parker DR, Robinson LE, Hannafin RD. "Blending" technology and effective pedagogy in a core course for preservice teachers. J Comput Teach Educ. 2008;24(2):49–54.

73. Watt S, Vajoczki S, Voros G, Vine MM, Fenton N, Tarkowski J. Lecture capture: an effective tool for universal instructional design? Can J High Educ. 2014;44(2):1–29.

74. Reglinski J. Unlocking knowledge we know the students know. J Chem Educ. 2007;84(2):271.

75. Hall TE, Meyer A, Rose DH. Universal design for learning in the classroom: practical applications, What Works for Special-Needs Learners Series. Guilford Press; 2012. p. 1–8.

76. Meloy F, Gambescia SF. Guidelines for response to student requests for academic considerations: support versus enabling. Nurse Educ. 2014;39(3):138–42.

77. Heelan A, Halligan P, Quirke M. Universal design for learning and its application to clinical placements in health science courses (practice brief). J Postsecond Educ Disabil. 2015;28(4):469–79.

78. Mino J. Planning for inclusion: using universal instructional design to create a learner-centered community college classroom. Equity Excell Educ. 2004;37(2):154–60.

79. University of Connecticut Center on Postsecondary Education and Disability [Internet]. 2013 [cited 2019 Oct 12]. Available from: https://cped.uconn.edu/.

80. Riviou K, Kouroupetroglou G, Oikonomidis N. A network of peers and practices for addressing Learner Variability: UDLnet. Stud Health Technol Inform. 2015;217:32–9.

81. Rye PD, Wallace J, Bidgood P. Instructions in learning skills: an integrated approach. Med Educ. 1993;27(6):470–3.

82. Mayer RE. What neurosurgeons should discover about the science of learning. Clin Neurosurg. 2009;56:57–65.

83. Mayer RE. Applying the science of learning to medical education. Med Educ. 2010;44(6):543–9.

84. Vogan CL, McKimm J, Da Silva AL, Grant A. Twelve tips for providing effective student support in undergraduate medical education. Med Teach. 2014;36(6):480–5.

85. Wong BYL. The relevance of metacognition to learning disabilities. In: Learning about learning disabilities. San Diego: Academic Press; 1991. p. 231–58.

86. Shaw SF, Dukes LL. Program standards for disability services in higher education. J Postsecond Educ Disabil. 2001;14(2):81–90.

87. Marshall University Medical H.E.L.P. Program [Internet]. [cited 2019 Sep 30]. Available from: https://www.marshall.edu/medhelp/.

88. Year 1 & 2 Course Information ǀ UTMB School of Medicine ǀ UTMB [Internet]. [cited 2019 Aug 14]. Available from: https://som.utmb.edu/som-educational-affairs/instructional-management-office/year-1-2-course-information.

89. Phase I (Years 1 and 2) [Internet]. [cited 2019 Aug 14]. Available from: https://medicine.vtc. vt.edu/content/medicine_vtc_vt_edu/en/academics/phase1.html.

90. Chemers MM, Hu L, Garcia BF. Academic self-efficacy and first year college student performance and adjustment. J Educ Psychol. 2001;93(1):55–64.

91. Zimmerman BJ. Becoming a self-regulated learner: an overview. Theory Pract. 2002;41(2):64–70.

92. Aaberg VA. A path to greater inclusivity through understanding implicit attitudes toward disability. J Nurs Educ. 2012;51(9):505–10.

93. Frank B. Facilitating learning for students with disabilities. In: Billings DM, Halstead JA, editors. Teaching in nursing: a guide to faculty [Internet]. 5th ed. St. Louis: Elsevier; 2016 [cited 2019 Oct 1]. Available from: https://www.elsevier.com/books/teaching-in-nursing/billings/978-0-323-29054-8.

94. Wood D, Marshall ES. Nurses with disabilities working in hospital settings: attitudes, concerns, and experiences of nurse leaders. J Prof Nurs. 2010;26(3):182–7.

95. Dupler AE, Allen C, Maheady DC, Fleming SE, Allen M. Leveling the playing field for nursing students with disabilities: implications of the amendments to the Americans with Disabilities Act. J Nurs Educ. 2012;51(3):140–4.

96. Neal-Boylan L, Miller M, Bell J. Building academic communities to support nursing students with disabilities: an integrative review. Build Healthy Acad Communities J. 2018;2(1):60–73.

97. LeBlanc VR. The effects of acute stress on performance: implications for health professions education. Acad Med. 2009;84(10 Suppl):S25–33.

98. LeBlanc VR, McConnell MM, Monteiro SD. Predictable chaos: a review of the effects of emotions on attention, memory and decision making. Adv Health Sci Educ Theory Pract. 2015;20(1):265–82.

99. Evans W, Kelly B. Pre-registration diploma student nurse stress and coping measures. Nurse Educ Today. 2004;24(6):473–82.

100. Gibbons C, Dempster M, Moutray M. Stress and eustress in nursing students. J Adv Nurs. 2008;61(3):282–90.

101. Konopasek L, Slavin S. Addressing resident and fellow mental health and well-being: what can you do in your department? J Pediatr. 2015;167(6):1183–4.

102. Goldman ML, Bernstein CA, Konopasek L, Arbuckle M, Mayer LES. An intervention framework for institutions to meet new ACGME common program requirements for physician well-being. Acad Psychiatry. 2018;42(4):542–7.

103. Harrisson EG. Working with faculty toward universally designed instruction: the process of dynamic course design. J Postsecond Educ Disabil. 2006;19(2):152–62.

104. Tee S, Cowen M. Supporting students with disabilities--promoting understanding amongst mentors in practice. Nurse Educ Pract. 2012;12(1):6–10.

105. Harris J, Ho T, Markle L, Wessel R. Ball State University's faculty mentorship program: enhancing the first-year experience for students with disabilities. Campus. 2011;16(2):27–9.

106. Kotter JP. Leading change, with a new preface by the author. 1st ed. Boston: Harvard Business Review Press; 2012. 208 p.

107. Montgomery T, Meeks LM, Laird-Metke E. Debunking myths and addressing legitimate concerns. In: Meeks LM, Jain NR, editors. The guide to assisting students with disabilities: equal access in health science and professional education. 1st ed. New York: Springer Publishing Company; 2016. p. 213–21.

108. Munyi CW. Past and present perceptions towards disability: a historical perspective. Disabil Stud Q [Internet]. 2012 [cited 2019 Oct 12];32(2). Available from: http://dsq-sds.org/article/view/3197.

109. Dalal AK. Social interventions to moderate discriminatory attitudes: the case of the physically challenged in India. Psychol Health Med. 2006;11(3):374–82.

110. Etieyibo E, Omiegbe O. Religion, culture, and discrimination against persons with disabilities in Nigeria. Afr J Disabil. 2016;5(1):192.

111. O'Hara J. Learning disabilities and ethnicity: achieving cultural competence. Adv Psychiatr Treat. 2003;9(3):166–74.

112. McGough JD, Murray JF. Know your campus resources. In: Meeks LM, Jain NR, editors. The guide to assisting students with disabilities: equal access in health science and professional education. 1st ed. New York: Springer Publishing Company; 2016. p. 1–14.
113. Kenney MJ, Jain NR, Meeks LM, Laird-Metke E, Hori J, McGough JD. Learning in the digital age: assistive technology and electronic access. In: Meeks LM, Jain NR, editors. The guide to assisting students with disabilities: equal access in health science and professional education. 1st ed. New York: Springer Publishing Company; 2016. p. 119–40.
114. DeLee B. Academic support services for college students with disabilities. J Appl Learn Technol. 2015;5(3):39–48.
115. Tee SR, Owens K, Plowright S, Ramnath P, Rourke S, James C, et al. Being reasonable: supporting disabled nursing students in practice. Nurse Educ Pract. 2010;10(4):216–21.
116. Davies PL, Schelly CL, Spooner CL. Measuring the effectiveness of universal design for learning intervention in postsecondary education. J Postsecond Educ Disabil. 2013;26(3):195–220.
117. McKeachie WJ. Improving lectures by understanding students' information processing. New Dir Teach Learn. 1980;1980(2):25–35.
118. Verner C, Dickinson G. The lecture, an analysis and review of research. Adult Educ. 1967;17(2):85–100.
119. Hartley J, Cameron A. Some observations on the efficiency of lecturing. Educ Rev. 1967;20(1):30–7.
120. Thomas EJ. The variation of memory with time for information appearing during a lecture. Stud Adult Educ. 1972;4(1):57–62.
121. Stuart J, Rutherford RJ. Medical student concentration during lectures. Lancet. 1978;2(8088):514–6.
122. Chickering AW, Gamson ZF. Seven principles for good practice in undergraduate education. Am Assoc High Educ Bull. 1987;3:7.
123. Prince M. Does active learning work? A review of the research. J Eng Educ. 2004;93(3):223–31.
124. Rowe MB. Getting chemistry off the killer course list. J Chem Educ. 1983;60(11):954–6.
125. Ruhl KL, Hughes CA, Schloss PJ. Using the pause procedure to enhance lecture recall. Teach Educ Spec Educ. 1987;10(1):14–8.
126. Di Vesta FJ, Smith DA. The pausing principle: increasing the efficiency of memory for ongoing events. Contemp Educ Psychol. 1979;4(3):288–96.
127. Maydosz A, Raver SA. Note taking and university students with learning difficulties: what supports are needed? J Divers High Educ. 2010;3(3):177–86.
128. Suritsky SK. Note-taking approaches and specific areas of difficulty reported by university students with learning disabilities. J Postsecond Educ Disabil. 1992;10:3–10.
129. Boyle JR, Forchelli GA, Cariss K. Note-taking interventions to assist students with disabilities in content area classes. Prev Sch Fail. 2015;59(3):186–95.
130. Piolat A, Olive T, Kellogg RT. Cognitive effort during note taking. Appl Cogn Psychol. 2005;19(3):291–312.
131. Ruhl KL, Hughes CA, Gajar AH. Efficacy of the pause procedure for enhancing learning disabled and nondisabled college students' long- and short-term recall of facts presented through lecture. Learn Disabil Q. 1990;13(1):55–64.
132. Ruhl KL, Suritsky S. The pause procedure and/or an outline: effect on immediate free recall and lecture notes taken by college students with learning disabilities. Learn Disabil Q. 1995;18(1):2–11.
133. Littlewood KE, Shilling AM, Stemland CJ, Wright EB, Kirk MA. High-fidelity simulation is superior to case-based discussion in teaching the management of shock. Med Teach. 2013;35(3):e1003–10.
134. Subramanian A, Timberlake M, Mittakanti H, Lara M, Brandt ML. Novel educational approach for medical students: improved retention rates using interactive medical software compared with traditional lecture-based format. J Surg Educ. 2012;69(4):449–52.
135. Bonwell CC, Eison JA. Active learning: creating excitement in the classroom. 1991 ASHE-ERIC Higher Education Reports [Internet]. ERIC Clearinghouse on Higher Education,

The George Washington University; 1991 [cited 2019 Aug 12]. Available from: https://eric.ed.gov/?id=ED336049.

136. Kimonen E, Nevalainen R. Active learning in the process of educational change. Teach Teach Educ. 2005;21:623–35.

137. Lindsey L, Berger N. Experiential approach to instruction. In: Reigeluth CM, Carr-Chellman AA, editors. Instructional design theories and models, volume III: building a common knowledge base. 1st ed. New York: Routledge; 2009. p. 117–42.

138. Knowles MS. The modern practice of adult education: from pedagogy to andragogy. Cambridge: Englewood Cliffs; 1970.

139. Young MF. Instructional design for situated learning. Educ Technol Res Dev. 1993;41(1):43–58.

140. Gersten R, Baker S. Real world use of scientific concepts: integrating situated cognition with explicit instruction. Except Child. 1998;65(1):23–35.

141. Anderson LW, Krathwohl DR, Airasian PW, Cruikshank KA, Mayer RE, Pintrich PR, et al. A taxonomy for learning, teaching, and assessing: a revision of Bloom's taxonomy of educational objectives, abridged edition. 1st ed. New York: Pearson; 2000.

142. Keyser MW. Active learning and cooperative learning: understanding the difference and using both styles effectively. Res Strateg. 2000;17(1):35–44.

143. Niemi H. Active learning: a cultural change needed in teacher education and schools. Teach Teach Educ. 2002;18:763–80.

144. Johnson DW, Johnson RT, Smith KA. Active learning: Cooperation in the College Classroom. Edina, MN: Interaction Book Company; 1998.

145. Kiaer L, Mutchler D, Froyd J. Laptop computers in an integrated first-year curriculum. Commun ACM. 1998;41(1):45–9.

146. MacKinnon GR, Vibert C. Judging the constructive impacts of communication technologies: a business education study. Educ Inf Technol. 2002;7(2):127–35.

147. Siegle D, Foster T. Laptop computers and multimedia and presentation software: their effects on student achievement in anatomy and physiology. J Res Comput Educ. 2001;34(1):29–37.

148. Barak M, Lipson A, Lerman S. Wireless laptops as means for promoting active learning in large lecture halls. J Res Technol Educ. 2006;38(3):245–63.

149. Yamamoto K. Banning laptops in the classroom: is it worth the hassles? J Leg Educ. 2007;57(4):477–520.

150. Cismaru R, Cismaru M. Laptop use during class: a review of Canadian universities. J Coll Teach Learn TLC. 2011;8(11):21–8.

151. Sana F, Weston T, Cepeda NJ. Laptop multitasking hinders classroom learning for both users and nearby peers. Comput Educ. 2013;62(1):24–31.

152. DeGroff EA. The dynamics of the contemporary law school classroom: looking at laptops through a learning style lens. Univ Dayt Law Rev. 2014;39(2):201–28.

153. Eisenstat S. A game changer: assessing the impact of the Princeton/UCLA Laptop study on the debate to ban law student use of laptops during class. Univ Detroit Mercy Law Rev. 2015;92(2):83–114.

154. Colker R. Universal design: stop banning laptops! Cardozo Law Rev. 2017;39(2):483–93.

155. Murray KE. Let them use laptops: debunking the assumptions underlying the debate over laptops in the classroom. Okla City Univ Law Rev. 2011;36:185–229.

156. Pryal KRG. Trust disabled students and their technology. Women High Educ. 2018;27(7):8–15.

157. Mueller PA, Oppenheimer DM. The pen is mightier than the keyboard: advantages of longhand over laptop note taking. Psychol Sci. 2014;25(6):1159–68.

158. Luo L, Kiewra KA, Flanigan AE, Peteranetz MS. Laptop versus longhand note taking: effects on lecture notes and achievement. Instr Sci Int J Learn Sci. 2018;46(6):947–71.

159. Ehrlick SP. Managing digital distraction: a pedagogical approach for dealing with wireless devices in the classroom. J Teach Educ. 2014;3(3):207–16.

160. Wright R, Perry PJ, Yoshizuka K. In Reply to "Why We Banned Use of Laptops and 'Scribe Notes' in Our Classroom". Am J Pharm Educ. 2011;75(2):1–2.

161. Paulson DR. Active learning and cooperative learning in the organic chemistry lecture class. J Chem Educ. 1999;76(8):1136–40.

162. Wolff M, Wagner MJ, Poznanski S, Schiller J, Santen S. Not another boring lecture: engaging learners with active learning techniques. J Emerg Med. 2015;48(1):85–93.
163. Sokoloff DR, Thornton RK. Using interactive lecture demonstrations to create an active learning environment. Phys Teach. 1997;35(6):340–7.
164. Harwood WS. The one-minute paper: a communication tool for large lecture classes. J Chem Educ. 1996;73(3):229–30.
165. Wilson RC. Improving faculty teaching: effective use of student evaluations and consultants. J High Educ. 1986;57(2):196–211.
166. Estes TH, Mintz SL, Gunter MA. Instruction: A models approach. Upper Saddle River, NJ: Pearson; 2015.
167. Brown G, Manogue M. AMEE Medical Education Guide No. 22: refreshing lecturing: a guide for lecturers. Med Teach. 2001;23(3):231–44.
168. Chamberlain NR, Stuart MK, Singh VK, Sargentini NJ. Utilization of case presentations in medical microbiology to enhance relevance of basic science for medical students. Med Educ Online. 2012;17.
169. Cutrer WB, Castro D, Roy KM, Turner TL. Use of an expert concept map as an advance organizer to improve understanding of respiratory failure. Med Teach. 2011;33(12):1018–26.
170. Kumar S, Dee F, Kumar R, Velan G. Benefits of testable concept maps for learning about pathogenesis of disease. Teach Learn Med. 2011;23(2):137–43.
171. Resnick M, Wilensky U. Diving into complexity: developing probabilistic decentralized thinking through role-playing activities. J Learn Sci. 1998;7(2):153–72.
172. Duncombe S, Heikkinen MH. Role-playing for different viewpoints. Coll Teach. 1988;36(1):3–5.
173. Gauci SA, Dantas AM, Williams DA, Kemm RE. Promoting student-centered active learning in lectures with a personal response system. Adv Physiol Educ. 2009;33(1):60–71.
174. Nelson C, Hartling L, Campbell S, Oswald AE. The effects of audience response systems on learning outcomes in health professions education. A BEME systematic review: BEME Guide No. 21. Med Teach. 2012;34(6):e386–405.
175. Angelo TA, Cross KP. Classroom assessment techniques: a handbook for college teachers. 2nd ed. San Francisco: Jossey-Bass; 1993.
176. Berkson L. Problem-based learning: have the expectations been met? Acad Med. 1993;68(10 Suppl):S79–88.
177. Barrows HS. Problem-based learning in medicine and beyond: a brief overview. New Dir Teach Learn. 1996;1996(68):3–12.
178. Barrows HS. The essentials of problem-based learning. J Dent Educ. 1998;62(9):630–3.
179. Rideout E, Carpio B. The problem-based learning model of nursing education. In: Rideout E, editor. Transforming nursing education through problem-based learning. Mississauga: Jones & Bartlett Publishers; 2001. p. 21–49.
180. Barrows HS. How to design a problem-based curriculum for the preclinical years. New York: Springer Publishing Co.; 1985. 148 p.
181. Barrows HS. A taxonomy of problem-based learning methods. Med Educ. 1986;20(6):481–6.
182. Wood DF. Problem based learning. BMJ. 2003;326(7384):328–30.
183. Rose DH, Meyer A. A practical reader in universal design for learning. Cambridge: Harvard Education Press; 2006.
184. Neville AJ. Problem-based learning and medical education forty years on. A review of its effects on knowledge and clinical performance. Med Princ Pract Int J Kuwait Univ Health Sci Cent. 2009;18(1):1–9.
185. Dolmans DHJM, De Grave W, Wolfhagen IHAP, van der Vleuten CPM. Problem-based learning: future challenges for educational practice and research. Med Educ. 2005;39(7):732–41.
186. Hartling L, Spooner C, Tjosvold L, Oswald A. Problem-based learning in pre-clinical medical education: 22 years of outcome research. Med Teach. 2010;32(1):28–35.
187. Vernon DT, Blake RL. Does problem-based learning work? A meta-analysis of evaluative research. Acad Med. 1993;68(7):550–63.

188. Kasim RM. What can studies of problem-based learning tell us? Synthesizing and modeling PBL effects on National Board of Medical Examination performance: hierarchical linear modeling meta-analytic approach. Adv Health Sci Educ Theory Pract. 1999;4(3):209–21.

189. Hoffman K, Hosokawa M, Blake JR, Headrick L, Johnson G. Problem-based learning outcomes: ten years of experience at the University of Missouri-Columbia School of Medicine. Acad Med. 2006;81(7):617–25.

190. Koh GC-H, Khoo HE, Wong ML, Koh D. The effects of problem-based learning during medical school on physician competency: a systematic review. Can Med Assoc J. 2008;178(1):34–41.

191. Schmidt HG, Vermeulen L, van der Molen HT. Longterm effects of problem-based learning: a comparison of competencies acquired by graduates of a problem-based and a conventional medical school. Med Educ. 2006;40(6):562–7.

192. Kong L-N, Qin B, Zhou Y, Mou S, Gao H-M. The effectiveness of problem-based learning on development of nursing students' critical thinking: a systematic review and meta-analysis. Int J Nurs Stud. 2014;51(3):458–69.

193. Cooke M, Moyle K. Students' evaluation of problem-based learning. Nurse Educ Today. 2002;22(4):330–9.

194. Morales-Mann ET, Kaitell CA. Problem-based learning in a new Canadian curriculum. J Adv Nurs. 2001;33(1):13–9.

195. Gandhi S, Dass DP. A study to evaluate the effectiveness of problem based learning (PBL) module on knowledge and attitude among nursing students. Int J Nurs Educ. 2019;11(3):101–6.

196. Giddens JF, Brady DP. Rescuing nursing education from content saturation: the case for a concept-based curriculum. J Nurs Educ. 2007;46(2):65–9.

197. Baron KA. Changing to concept-based curricula: the process for nurse educators. Open Nurs J. 2017;11:277–87.

198. Maxwell JA, Wilkerson L. A study of non-volunteer faculty in a problem-based curriculum. Acad Med. 1990;65(9 Suppl):S13–4.

199. Bernstein P, Tipping J, Bercovitz K, Skinner HA. Shifting students and faculty to a PBL curriculum: attitudes changed and lessons learned. Acad Med. 1995;70(3):245–7.

200. Hmelo-Silver C, Barrows H. Goals and strategies of a problem-based learning facilitator. Interdiscip J Probl-Based Learn. 2006;1(1):21–39.

201. Bell P. Using argument representations to making thinking visible for individuals and groups. In: Koschmann T, Hall RP, Miyake N, editors. CSCL 2: carrying forward the conversation. 1st ed. Mahwah: Routledge; 2002.

202. Duncan RG. The role of domain-specific knowledge in promoting generative reasoning in genetics. In: Garab SA, Ha KE, Hickey DT, editors. Proceedings of the 7th international conference on Learning sciences: making a difference. Mahwah: Erlbaum; 2006. p. 147–54.

203. Schwartz DL, Bransford JD. A time for telling. Cogn Instr. 1998;16(4):475–522.

204. Houck CK, Asselin SB, Troutman GC, Arrington JM. Students with learning disabilities in the university environment: a study of faculty and student perceptions. J Learn Disabil. 1992;25(10):678–84.

205. Stergiopoulos E, Fernando O, Martimianakis MA. "Being on both sides": Canadian medical students' experiences with disability, the hidden curriculum, and professional identity construction. Acad Med. 2018;93(10):1550–9.

206. Fischer K, Sullivan AM, Krupat E, Schwartzstein RM. Assessing the effectiveness of using mechanistic concept maps in case-based collaborative learning. Acad Med. 2019;94(2):208–12.

207. Dymond SK, Renzaglia A, Rosenstein A, Chun EJ, Banks RA, Niswander V, et al. Using a participatory action research approach to create a universally designed inclusive high school science course: a case study. Res Pract Pers Sev Disabil RPSD. 2006;31(4):293–308.

208. Kennedy MJ, Thomas CN, Meyer JP, Alves KD, Lloyd JW. Using evidence-based multimedia to improve vocabulary performance of adolescents with LD: a UDL approach. Learn Disabil Q. 2014;37(2):71–86.

209. Mazur E. Education. Farewell, lecture? Science. 2009;323(5910):50–1.

210. Ferreri SP, O'Connor SK. Redesign of a large lecture course into a small-group learning course. Am J Pharm Educ. 2013;77(1):1–9.
211. Prober CG, Khan S. Medical education reimagined: a call to action. Acad Med. 2013;88(10):1407–10.
212. Bergmann J, Sams A. How the flipped classroom is radically transforming learning [Internet]. The Daily Riff. 2012 [cited 2019 Aug 15]. Available from: http://www.thedailyriff.com/articles/how-the-flipped-classroom-is-radically-transforming-learning-536.php.
213. Lage MJ, Platt GJ, Treglia M. Inverting the classroom: a gateway to creating an inclusive learning environment. J Econ Educ. 2000;31(1):30–43.
214. Pierce R, Fox J. Vodcasts and active-learning exercises in a "flipped classroom" model of a renal pharmacotherapy module. Am J Pharm Educ. 2012;76(10):1–5.
215. Prober CG, Heath C. Lecture halls without lectures — a proposal for medical education. N Engl J Med. 2012;366(18):1657–9.
216. Kavanagh L, Reidsema C, McCredden J, Smith N. Design considerations. In: Reidsema C, Kavanagh L, Hadgraft R, Smith N, editors. The flipped classroom: practice and practices in higher education. Puchong: Springer Singapore; 2017. p. 15–35.
217. McLaughlin JE, Griffin LM, Esserman DA, Davidson CA, Glatt DM, Roth MT, et al. Pharmacy student engagement, performance, and perception in a flipped satellite classroom. Am J Pharm Educ. 2013;77(9):1–8.
218. Critz CM, Knight D. Using the flipped classroom in graduate nursing education. Nurse Educ. 2013;38(5):210–3.
219. Young TP, Bailey CJ, Guptill M, Thorp AW, Thomas TL. The flipped classroom: a modality for mixed asynchronous and synchronous learning in a residency program. West J Emerg Med. 2014;15(7):938–44.
220. Ramnanan CJ, Pound LD. Advances in medical education and practice: student perceptions of the flipped classroom. Adv Med Educ Pract. 2017;8:63–73.
221. Missildine K, Fountain R, Summers L, Gosselin K. Flipping the classroom to improve student performance and satisfaction. J Nurs Educ. 2013;52(10):597–9.
222. Geist MJ, Larimore D, Rawiszer H, Sager AWA. Flipped versus traditional instruction and achievement in a baccalaureate nursing pharmacology course. Nurs Educ Perspect. 2015;36(2):114–5.
223. Hew KF, Lo CK. Flipped classroom improves student learning in health professions education: a meta-analysis. BMC Med Educ. 2018;18(1):38.
224. McCoy L, Pettit RK, Kellar C, Morgan C. Tracking active learning in the medical school curriculum: a learning-centered approach. J Med Educ Curric Dev. 2018;5:2382120518765135.
225. Taylor DCM, Hamdy H. Adult learning theories: implications for learning and teaching in medical education: AMEE Guide No. 83. Med Teach. 2013;35(11):e1561–72.
226. Graffam B. Active learning in medical education: strategies for beginning implementation. Med Teach. 2007;29(1):38–42.
227. Della Ratta CB. Flipping the classroom with team-based learning in undergraduate nursing education. Nurse Educ. 2015;40(2):71–4.
228. Greer D, Rowland AL, Smith SJ. Critical considerations for teaching students with disabilities in online environments. Teach Except Child. 2014;46(5):79–91.
229. Phillips CR, Trainor JE. Milennial students and the flipped classroom. Proc ASBBS Annu Conf. 2014;21(1):519–30.
230. Olaussen A, Reddy P, Irvine S, Williams B. Peer-assisted learning: time for nomenclature clarification. Med Educ Online. 2016;21:30974.
231. Ten Cate O, Durning S. Dimensions and psychology of peer teaching in medical education. Med Teach. 2007;29(6):546–52.
232. Provencio AB, Garcia CM, Roesch J. Peer-to-peer tutoring: reducing failure rates in medical school. Med Educ. 2018;52(11):1183.
233. Jayakumar N, Albasha D, Annan D. One-to-one peer tutoring for failing medical students: a novel intervention. Med Teach. 2015;37(5):498.

234. Durán CEP, Bahena EN, de Rodríguez M, LÁG, Baca GJ, Uresti AS, Elizondo-Omaña RE, et al. Near-peer teaching in an anatomy course with a low faculty-to-student ratio. Anat Sci Educ. 2012;5(3):171–6.
235. Field M, Burke JM, McAllister D, Lloyd DM. Peer-assisted learning: a novel approach to clinical skills learning for medical students. Med Educ. 2007;41(4):411–8.
236. Henning J, Weidner TG, Snyder M. Peer assisted learning in clinical education: literature review. Athl Train Educ J. 2008;3:84–90.
237. Evans DJR, Cuffe T. Near-peer teaching in anatomy: an approach for deeper learning. Anat Sci Educ. 2009;2(5):227–33.
238. Burgess A, McGregor D, Mellis C. Medical students as peer tutors: a systematic review. BMC Med Educ. 2014;14:115.
239. Clarke B, Feltham W. Facilitating peer group teaching within nurse education. Nurse Educ Today. 1990;10(1):54–7.
240. Williams B, Reddy P. Does peer-assisted learning improve academic performance? A scoping review. Nurse Educ Today. 2016;42:23–9.
241. Secomb J. A systematic review of peer teaching and learning in clinical education. J Clin Nurs. 2008;17(6):703–16.
242. Sobral DT. Peer tutoring and student outcomes in a problem-based course. Med Educ. 1994;28(4):284–9.
243. Agius A, Stabile I. Undergraduate peer assisted learning tutors' performance in summative anatomy examinations: a pilot study. Int J Med Educ. 2018;9:93–8.
244. Nestel D, Kidd J. Peer assisted learning in patient-centred interviewing: the impact on student tutors. Med Teach. 2005;27(5):439–44.
245. Silbert BI, Lake FR. Peer-assisted learning in teaching clinical examination to junior medical students. Med Teach. 2012;34(5):392–7.
246. Gottlieb Z, Epstein S, Richards J. Near-peer teaching programme for medical students. Clin Teach. 2017;14(3):164–9.
247. Shankar PR, Singh B, Singh AK, Karki BS, Thapa TP. Student perception about peer-assisted learning sessions in a medical school in Nepal. WebmedCentral Med Educ. 2011;2(11):WMC002459.
248. Erie AJ, Starkman SJ, Pawlina W, Lachman N. Developing medical students as teachers: an anatomy-based student-as-teacher program with emphasis on core teaching competencies. Anat Sci Educ. 2013;6(6):385–92.
249. Lockspeiser TM, O'Sullivan P, Teherani A, Muller J. Understanding the experience of being taught by peers: the value of social and cognitive congruence. Adv Health Sci Educ Theory Pract. 2008;13(3):361–72.
250. Sobral DT. Cross-year peer tutoring experience in a medical school: conditions and outcomes for student tutors. Med Educ. 2002;36(11):1064–70.
251. Wong JG, Waldrep TD, Smith TG. Formal peer-teaching in medical school improves academic performance: the MUSC supplemental instructor program. Teach Learn Med. 2007;19(3):216–20.
252. Knobe M, Münker R, Sellei RM, Holschen M, Mooij SC, Schmidt-Rohlfing B, et al. Peer teaching: a randomised controlled trial using student-teachers to teach musculoskeletal ultrasound. Med Educ. 2010;44(2):148–55.
253. Alcamo AM, Davids AR, Way DP, Lynn DJ, Vandre DD. The impact of a peer-designed and -led USMLE Step 1 review course: improvement in preparation and scores. Acad Med. 2010;85(10 Suppl):S45–8.
254. Turk SA, Mousavizadeh A, Roozbehi A. The effect of peer assisted learning on medical students' learning in a limbs anatomy course. Res Dev Med Educ. 2015;4(2):115–22.
255. Swindle N, Wimsatt L. Development of peer tutoring services to support osteopathic medical students' academic success. J Am Osteopath Assoc. 2015;115(11):e14–9.
256. Sawyer SJ, Sylvestre PB, Girard RA, Snow MH. Effects of supplemental instruction on mean test scores and failure rates in medical school courses. Acad Med. 1996;71(12):1357–9.

257. Reyes-Hernández CG, Carmona Pulido JM, De la Garza Chapa RI, Serna Vázquez RP, Alcalá Briones RD, Plasencia Banda PM, et al. Near-peer teaching strategy in a large human anatomy course: perceptions of near-peer instructors. Anat Sci Educ. 2015;8(2):189–93.
258. Horneffer A, Fassnacht U, Oechsner W, Huber-Lang M, Boeckers TM, Boeckers A. Effect of didactically qualified student tutors on their tutees' academic performance and tutor evaluation in the gross anatomy course. Ann Anat. 2016;208:170–8.
259. Parker DR, Getty M. PLTL and universal design for instruction: Investigating wider access for students with disabilities. Progress Newsl. 2009;10(1).
260. Parker DR, White CE, Collins L, Banerjee M, McGuire JM. Learning technologies management system (LiTMS): a multidimensional service delivery model for college students with learning disabilities and ADHD. J Postsecond Educ Disabil. 2009;22(2):130–6.
261. Street CD, Koff R, Fields H, Kuehne L, Handlin L, Getty M, et al. Expanding access to STEM for at-risk learners: a new application of universal design for instruction. J Postsecond Educ Disabil. 2012;25(4):363–75.

Health Professions and the Law

8

Samuel Bagenstos

Full and equal participation of disabled persons in the health professions is a moral and ethical imperative. Programs training health professionals provide important opportunities for social and economic advancement, and individuals with disabilities should not be shut out of those opportunities. As the professions become increasingly committed to promoting diversity, they must recognize disability as a significant axis along which to pursue that effort. They should do so not just because disability representation is good for health professionals with disabilities. They should do so because it is good for patients as well. "An accumulating body of evidence suggests that the lack of exposure to persons with disabilities as peers inhibits the ability of physicians to provide effective medical care to patients with disabilities" [1, p. 1011].

Moral and ethical reasons aside, programs training health professionals have a legal obligation to ensure that people with disabilities can fully and equally participate. Both the Americans with Disabilities Act (enacted in 1990 and strengthened by the ADA Amendments Act of 2008) and the Rehabilitation Act (enacted in 1973) prohibit discrimination against disabled individuals [2, 3]. Importantly, these statutes are not limited to barring animus-based exclusion. They also require reasonable accommodations for people with disabilities. And they define the failure to provide those accommodations as unlawful discrimination.

This chapter outlines the legal responsibilities that health sciences education programs have to prevent inappropriate exclusion of participants with disabilities. This chapter will review the statutes that impose these responsibilities and then discuss the question of how to determine whether an individual has a "disability" as defined by the statute. The question of what constitutes a reasonable accommodation or

S. Bagenstos (✉)
Professor, University of Michigan Law School, Ann Arbor, MI, USA
e-mail: sambagen@umich.edu

© Springer Nature Switzerland AG 2020
L. M. Meeks, L. Neal-Boylan (eds.), *Disability as Diversity*,
https://doi.org/10.1007/978-3-030-46187-4_8

modification is pervasive within academic communities and will also be addressed. Judicial decisions in cases brought both inside and outside of the health professions context will help illustrate these points.

Coverage of the Disability Discrimination Statutes

Two major federal statutes protect individuals with disabilities against discrimination: the Americans with Disabilities Act and the Rehabilitation Act. Virtually all institutions that provide health care or train healthcare providers are covered by one or both of these statutes. The statutes impose broadly similar requirements. But the precise rights of disabled individuals, and the remedies available to them if those rights are violated, depend on which statute applies.

The Rehabilitation Act

Section 504 of the Rehabilitation Act was the first general federal disability rights statute [16, p. 901]. It provides, in pertinent part, that "[n]o otherwise qualified individual with a disability" shall, "solely by reason of her or his disability, be excluded from the participation in, be denied the benefits of, or be subjected to discrimination under any program or activity receiving Federal financial assistance" [3]. The statute defines "program or activity" very broadly, to include the entire government department, university, or other entity that receives federal dollars, even if those dollars go only to one particular part of the entity [3]. "Federal financial assistance" includes Medicaid, Medicare Part A (hospital insurance), and federal education loans and grants. As a result, Section 504 covers nearly all colleges, universities, and hospitals in the United States. And its prohibitions of discrimination extend to any individual with a disability with whom a covered entity deals, including employees, independent contractors, students, and patients.

Section 504 prohibits discrimination against "otherwise qualified individual[s] with a disability." That means that covered entities are forbidden to engage in *intentional* or *disparate treatment* discrimination—refusing to hire, admit, or serve a person just because that person has a disability. The courts have also read that language to mean that covered entities have an affirmative obligation to make changes to their policies and practices to ensure that disabled persons have equal access to their programs. As the Supreme Court explained in the leading case of *Alexander v. Choate*, "to assure meaningful access, reasonable accommodations in the grantee's program or benefit may have to be made" ([4], p. 301). But the court also explained that the reasonable accommodations requirement has limits: "while a grantee need not be required to make 'fundamental' or 'substantial' modifications to accommodate the handicapped, it may be required to make 'reasonable' ones" ([4], p. 300).

Section 504 of the Rehabilitation Act was a model for the Americans with Disabilities Act (ADA). The ADA, like Section 504, imposes nondiscrimination and accommodation requirements. But while Section 504 applies only to those entities that receive federal funds, the ADA applies broadly to all state and local governments and to most nonprofits and private businesses.

The ADA

The ADA is divided into three substantive titles. Title I prohibits discrimination in employment. It applies to any entity—public or private—that employs 15 or more people in any given year. Employees of healthcare providers—including many participants of residency programs—are covered by this title.

Title II prohibits discrimination by state and local government entities. It applies to everything that any agency or office of any state or local government does [5]. If a state university operates a hospital or a training program for healthcare professionals, those who work at the hospital or participate in the program will be covered by Title II. That is true whether or not those individuals have the status of "employees" under the law. Even if they are independent contractors or students, they will be protected by this title.

Title III prohibits discrimination by privately operated places of public accommodation. Unlike more traditional public accommodations statutes, Title III does not apply simply to restaurants, inns, public conveyances, and auditoriums. It extends broadly to virtually all sellers of goods and services to the public. Notably, Title III specifically includes the "professional office of a health care provider" and a "hospital" as examples of "public accommodations" covered by the statute [6]. It also lists "a nursery, elementary, secondary, undergraduate, or postgraduate private school, or other place of education" [7].

Title III generally protects only customers or clients of a place of public accommodation. The statute, for example, bars hospitals from turning away otherwise qualified patients because of their disabilities. (In the 1998 case of *Bragdon v. Abbott*, e.g., the Supreme Court applied Title III to protect a patient with HIV who had been denied dental treatment [7–9]). It also bars private educational institutions from discriminating against disabled students or applicants for admission. Title III may also protect doctors, physician assistants, and nurse practitioners from being denied hospital admitting privileges based on their disabilities. A leading case from the federal Third Circuit Court of Appeals, *Menkowitz v. Pottstown Memorial Medical Center*, applied the statute to such a fact pattern [9]. In *Menkowitz*, an orthopedic surgeon sued a hospital that suspended his admitting privileges; he alleged they did so because of his diagnosis of ADHD. Although the surgeon was not an employee of the hospital, the court allowed his case to proceed based on its conclusion that admitting privileges were privileges offered by a place of public accommodation and thus covered under Title III.

Like the Rehabilitation Act, each of the ADA's three titles prohibits disability-based discrimination against qualified individuals. As with the Rehabilitation Act, the prohibition of discrimination includes both intentional discrimination and the failure to make reasonable accommodations or modifications. Although each statute uses slightly different wordings to describe its accommodations requirement, the crucial difference between these statutes lies in the remedies available to those whose rights have been violated.

Disabled individuals who prove a violation of their rights under Section 504 of the Rehabilitation Act may recover money damages to compensate them for the harms they suffered, at least so long as the defendant engaged in intentional discrimination or acted with "deliberate indifference"—essentially, recklessness—in violating the statute. Whether an individual may recover damages under the ADA depends on the title under which the individual sues.

An employee who prevails under ADA Title I in a lawsuit against a private entity or a local government may recover back pay. Employees of these entities who prove intentional discrimination, or who can show that their employer acted in bad faith in denying a reasonable accommodation, may also recover damages for emotional distress and out-of-pocket costs. A disabled individual who prevails against a local government under ADA Title II may also recover damages for intentional discrimination or deliberate indifference—the same rules that apply under the Rehabilitation Act. But where a state government (as opposed to a local government) is the defendant, constitutional principles of sovereign immunity bar any monetary remedy. The disabled person's remedy is limited to an injunction fixing the problem and preventing discrimination in the future. A plaintiff who prevails in a lawsuit against a private entity under ADA Title III is also limited to injunctive relief.

Definition of Disability

The ADA and the Rehabilitation Act prohibit discrimination on the basis of "disability." That means that these statutes require plaintiffs first to show that they are members of the protected class. In this respect, the disability discrimination laws are different than other antidiscrimination laws. Everybody—regardless of their race or sex—is protected against race and sex discrimination. But only those who have a disability as defined in the statute are protected against disability discrimination. That makes the definition of disability crucial in the application of the ADA and Rehabilitation Act.

The ADA and the Rehabilitation Act share the same three-pronged definition of disability. They define a disability as either (A) "a physical or mental impairment that substantially limits one or more major life activities" (often called the "actual disability" prong); (B) "a record of such an impairment" (often called the "past disability" or "record of" prong); or (C) "being regarded as having such an impairment" (often called the "perceived disability" or "regarded as" prong) [10].

Congress used this three-pronged definition in the Rehabilitation Act, but the presence of a disability was not contested in many cases decided under that statute before 1990. When it enacted the ADA in that year, congress simply used the same definition as it had used in the prior statute. Many members of congress appear to have believed that the question of who has a disability would not often arise in litigation under the ADA. But they were soon proven incorrect, as courts frequently rejected ADA claims on the ground that the plaintiff did not have a disability as defined in the statute. In its 1999 *Sutton* trilogy of cases—which rejected ADA claims brought by individuals with poor vision, high blood pressure, and amblyopia—the Supreme Court endorsed the restrictive jurisprudence of the lower courts [11–14]. And in its 2002 *Toyota* decision—which rejected an ADA claim brought by an individual with carpal tunnel syndrome and tendinitis—the court said that the statute's definition "need[s] to be interpreted strictly to create a demanding standard for qualifying as disabled" ([11], p. 197).

In 2008, congress sought to reverse the courts' restrictive interpretations of the disability definition. It passed, and President George W. Bush signed, the ADA Amendments Act [15]. The new statute left the three-prong definition of disability in place, but it substantially expanded the reach of that definition. In contrast to the *Toyota* decision, the ADA Amendments Act declared that the definition of disability must "be construed in favor of broad coverage" to "the maximum extent permitted" by the statutory text. And the new statute fleshed out the disability definition in ways that underscored its breadth. Because the ADA Amendments Act provides the framework that currently governs entities covered by the ADA and the Rehabilitation Act, the remainder of this section describes that framework in detail.

"Actual Disability"

Recall that the "actual disability" prong requires an individual to have a physical or mental "impairment" that "substantially limits" one or more "major life activities." Each of these three terms is important in applying the disability definition.

What is an "impairment"? The statute does not specifically define the term. Department of Justice regulations define "impairment" as "[a]ny physiological disorder or condition, cosmetic disfigurement, or anatomical loss affecting one or more body systems" or "[a]ny mental or psychological disorder" [16]. The regulations offer a nonexhaustive list of impairments embraced by that definition:

> Orthopedic, visual, speech and hearing impairments, and cerebral palsy, epilepsy, muscular dystrophy, multiple sclerosis, cancer, heart disease, diabetes, intellectual disability, emotional illness, dyslexia and other specific learning disabilities, Attention Deficit Hyperactivity Disorder, Human Immunodeficiency Virus infection (whether symptomatic or asymptomatic), tuberculosis, drug addiction, and alcoholism [16].

As the regulatory definitions and examples indicate, "impairment" is a very broad term. It reaches essentially any condition that would receive a medical or psychiatric diagnosis. It does not, however, include "simple physical characteristics, such as blue eyes or black hair"; "environmental, cultural, economic, or other disadvantages, such as having a prison record, or being poor"; or "common personality traits such as poor judgment or a quick temper where these are not symptoms of a mental or psychological disorder" [17]. The issue of whether an individual has an "impairment" does not often arise in ADA cases, but it comes up occasionally. For example, a number of courts have concluded that extreme obesity is not an "impairment" unless it is caused by some identifiable organic etiology [18]. One might question whether the line drawn by these courts makes sense: "Given the evolving state of medical knowledge, doctors still do not know the precise etiology of any number of conditions that they diagnose and treat. What normative theory would exclude people with these conditions from the protection of the ADA?" [19, p. 50]. But these cases usefully highlight the distinction courts draw between an "impairment" and a mere physical characteristic.

An impairment alone is not enough, however. To be a disability, the impairment must "substantially limit" a "major life activity." So what do these terms mean? The ADA Amendments Act added the following language defining "major life activity":

(A) In General
         For purposes of [the definition of "disability"], major life activities include, but are
         not limited to, caring for oneself, performing manual tasks, seeing, hearing, eating,
         sleeping, walking, standing, lifting, bending, speaking, breathing, learning, reading,
         concentrating, thinking, communicating, and working.
(B) Major Bodily Functions
         For purposes of [the definition of "disability"], a major life activity also includes
         the operation of a major bodily function, including, but not limited to, functions of the
         immune system, normal cell growth, digestive, bowel, bladder, neurological, brain,
         respiratory, circulatory, endocrine, and reproductive functions [20].

Under this definition, a "major life activity" might be defined socially (in subsection A, as an activity of everyday life) or medically (in subsection B, as a "major bodily function").

The statute does not specifically define "substantially limits." But the rule of broad construction means that the term "is not meant to [impose] a demanding standard" [16]. The ADA Amendments Act makes clear that the substantial limitation determination must "be made without regard to the ameliorative effects of mitigating measures" such as medication, prosthetics, or assistive technology [21]. Thus, if a person has epilepsy or diabetes that is being successfully controlled by medication, the person still has a disability under the statute—in the absence of the treatment, the condition would substantially limit many major life activities. And even if an impairment is "episodic or in remission," the statute explains, it "is a disability if it would substantially limit a major life activity when active" [21].

Before congress adopted the ADA Amendments Act, courts often refused to find a statutory disability unless individual plaintiffs provided detailed evidence that their impairments significantly affected their lives. Under the new statute, that sort of detailed, individualized proof is less necessary. As the Department of Justice explains in its regulations, many diagnoses now satisfy the criteria for disability under the statute "in virtually all cases" [16]. The regulations offer the following examples:

(A) Deafness substantially limits hearing.
(B) Blindness substantially limits seeing.
(C) Intellectual disability substantially limits brain function.
(D) Partially or completely missing limbs or mobility impairments requiring the use of a
         wheelchair substantially limit musculoskeletal function.
(E) Autism substantially limits brain function.
(F) Cancer substantially limits normal cell growth.

(G)   Cerebral palsy substantially limits brain function.
(H)   Diabetes substantially limits endocrine function
(I)   Epilepsy, muscular dystrophy, and multiple sclerosis each substantially limits neurological function.
(J)   Human immunodeficiency virus (HIV) infection substantially limits immune function.
(K)   Major depressive disorder, bipolar disorder, post-traumatic stress disorder, traumatic brain injury, obsessive-compulsive disorder, and schizophrenia each substantially limits brain function [16].

Healthcare entities can safely presume that any individual who has one of the conditions enumerated in this list has a "disability" under the "actual disability" prong. Such an individual is entitled to the protection of the nondiscrimination and reasonable accommodation requirements of the ADA and the Rehabilitation Act.

Controversies frequently arise regarding the amount of documentation an employer, school, or other covered entity may demand before it grants a request for an accommodation. The relevant legal rule is simple to state but not always easy to apply. An entity covered by the ADA or the Rehabilitation Act is entitled to make reasonable requests for information to ensure that an individual in fact has a covered disability and to determine what accommodations are necessary. But it must ensure that the documentation requests are appropriately tailored to the question at hand and do not impose unnecessary burdens [17]. And a covered entity that rejects a claim of disability does so at its peril; if a court later determines that the individual who sought an accommodation does in fact have a disability, the entity will be liable for violating the disability rights laws.

"Past Disability"

The "record of" prong of the statute's disability definition does not often come up in the cases. This prong protects individuals who once had conditions that substantially limited major life activities but which have now been fully cured. A hospital thus may not discriminate against a nurse because she has a history of cancer, for example, even if the nurse has been deemed cancer-free. (A nurse who still has cancer would be protected against discrimination under the "actual disability" prong.)

"Perceived Disability"

The "regarded as" or "perceived disability" prong of the disability definition is particularly important. That prong protects individuals who do not in fact have an impairment that substantially limits major life activities but who are perceived by others as having such an impairment. The individuals might have no impairment at all but be mistakenly believed to have a disabling condition like HIV or epilepsy. Or they might have an impairment that does not in fact impose substantial limitations but that others believe to be more debilitating than it in fact is.

By protecting people who are merely regarded as having disabilities, the ADA guards against irrational discrimination. Prior to the ADA Amendments Act, however, the courts read the "perceived disability" prong extremely narrowly. That trend reached its apotheosis in the 1999 *Sutton* decision [11]. United Airlines rejected the application of two sisters with vision impairments to be global airline pilots. After concluding that the vision impairments were not sufficiently limiting to satisfy the "actual disability" prong, the Supreme Court went on to reject the "regarded as" claim. United thought that the sisters' impairments disqualified them from the pilot jobs they sought. At a minimum, then, it "regarded" their impairments as imposing some limitation on their ability to work. But the court held that the sisters had not satisfied their burden to show that United thought their impairments *substantially* limited their ability to work. There was no evidence, the court said, that United believed that the sisters' visual impairments prevented them from working at other jobs for other employers. Because employers rarely, if ever, consider whether applicants are qualified for jobs other than the ones for which they applied, the *Sutton* decision took a major bite out of the "regarded as" prong of the disability definition.

In the ADA Amendments Act, congress rejected *Sutton*'s reading. To invoke the coverage of the "regarded as" prong, individuals now need show only that the defendant discriminated against them "because of an actual or perceived physical or mental impairment whether or not the impairment limits or is perceived to limit a major life activity" [22]. They no longer need to show that the defendant thought their condition was more broadly disabling, though the perceived impairment must be something more than "transitory and minor" [22].

Although the ADA Amendments Act broadened the "regarded as" prong, it did impose one significant limit: if an individual is covered by the statute under the that prong only, the individual will be protected against disparate-treatment discrimination but will not be entitled to reasonable accommodation [23]. To invoke the reasonable accommodations mandate of the ADA or the Rehabilitation Act, an individual must satisfy the requirements of the "actual disability" or "past disability" prongs of the disability definition.

Reasonable Accommodations in the Healthcare Setting

One of the key innovations of disability discrimination law is its broad definition of discrimination. Under the ADA and the Rehabilitation Act, discrimination includes both the singling out of people with disabilities for disfavored treatment and the failure to make changes to general policies or practices that exclude particular disabled people without a good reason. The former category is referred to as disparate treatment or intentional discrimination; the latter is referred to as the failure to make reasonable accommodations or reasonable modifications.

The insight behind the reasonable accommodation mandate is easy to understand. Physical facilities, job responsibilities, educational requirements, and other social and economic structures were designed with the reflexive background premise that the people who would use them would be nondisabled. If architects assumed that their buildings would be patronized by people with mobility impairments, they would design them with ramps instead of stairs at their front entrances. If web designers assumed that blind people would visit their Internet sites, they would include image descriptions rather than simply posting photographs without captions. The reasonable accommodation mandate rectifies these sorts of "stereo-typical thought processes" and "thoughtless actions" that "far too often bar those with disabilities from participating fully in the nation's life, including the work-place" [24, p. 401]. If a workplace, school, or other covered entity includes physical structures or policies or practices that gratuitously exclude individuals with disabili-ties, the law requires the entity to modify them to eliminate the exclusion.

The precise wording of the statutory accommodation requirement is different in the employment context than in other contexts, but the substance is essentially the same. In making employment decisions, an entity must make "reasonable accom-modations to the known physical or mental limitations of an otherwise qualified individual with a disability who is an applicant or employee, unless such covered entity can demonstrate that the accommodation would impose an undue hardship" on the enterprise [25]. In making other sorts of decisions (such as those involving students, independent contractors, or non-employee interns with disabilities), an entity must make "reasonable modifications" in its "policies, practices, and proce-dures" unless it can show that doing so would "fundamentally alter the nature" of its program or services [26, 27].

The accommodation requirement is broad, but it is not unlimited. The law requires entities to make accommodations even if doing so imposes some increased cost and even if it means that, in some sense, disabled individuals get a form of "preferential" treatment [24]. However, the law does not require entities to make accommodations unless they are generally "reasonable." And even if an accommo-dation is reasonable "in the run of cases" [24, p. 401], the entity need not provide it if doing so would impose an "undue" burden in a particular case or make a "funda-mental" change in the service it provides or the program it operates.

The reasonable accommodation inquiry is highly fact specific. What accommo-dations are required depends on the particular limitations imposed by an individu-al's disabilities, as well as on the means that are available for serving a particular covered entity's legitimate interests. As a result, there is no way to generalize about what the disability discrimination laws require. The possible scenarios are virtually limitless. But there are some types of accommodation issues that recur frequently in health professions programs. The remainder of this section discusses those common scenarios.

Accommodation of Technical Standards

Virtually all American health sciences programs impose "technical standards" for admission. Typically, accreditation requirements demand that the program impose some technical standards, though schools retain substantial discretion regarding how to frame them. These standards "often require students to demonstrate motor functions, intellectual abilities, and the capacities for observation and communica-tion." They are based on the "premise that all health sciences graduates should have the basic skills and abilities to enter any setting within their health care discipline—that is, that they should be 'undifferentiated graduates'" [1, p. 1012]. Because the inflexible application of these sorts of standards will screen out many individuals with disabilities [28], a number of prominent disability rights cases have sought accommodations to them. In these cases, courts and other adjudicators have been called upon to decide whether health sciences programs have a sufficiently strong interest in ensuring that each and every graduate can work in each and every practice setting.

Two leading cases on technical standards point in opposite directions. In its 2014 decision in *Palmer College of Chiropractic v Davenport Civil Rights Commission*, the Iowa Supreme Court rejected the overbroad application of technical standards [29]. The case was initiated by a blind man who had applied to, and been rejected from, Palmer College's chiropractic program. The school rejected the applicant because he could not meet its technical standard for "sufficient use of vision" to perform "the review of radiographs." But the court noted that many chiropractors do not in fact have to review radiographs in their practices. It also noted that other medical schools had admitted blind students who had been successful. The court accordingly held that Palmer College was required to make a reasonable modification to its technical standards to permit the blind applicant to matriculate.

By contrast, in a decision the same year, the United States Court of Appeals for the Tenth Circuit approved the exclusionary application of technical standards. The case was *McCulley v University of Kansas School of Medicine* [30]. The plaintiff, Emily McCulley, had spinal muscular atrophy. McCulley had applied, and been admitted, to the defendant medical school. But the school rescinded her admission when it learned of her disability. It relied on the school's "Motor Technical Standard, which mandates that students 'be physically able to . . . carry out diagnostic procedures' and 'provide general care and emergency treatment to patients,' including CPR, opening obstructed airways, and 'obstetrical maneuvers.'" The school determined that McCulley's disability would keep her from lifting and positioning patients, stabilizing elderly patients, and providing basic life support. And the court held that the school was not required to modify its standard to permit McCulley to matriculate. Even though there are practice settings that do not require doctors to engage in demanding physical activity, and McCulley said that she did "not intend to pursue a physically demanding specialty," the court concluded that a modification of the technical standard would constitute a fundamental alteration of the school's "broad, undifferentiated medical curriculum that prepares students to serve as physicians in a wide range of practice areas."

The *McCulley* decision has echoes of the very first decision in which the Supreme Court interpreted the disability discrimination laws. In the 1979 case of *Southeastern Community College v. Davis*, the court rejected a deaf applicant's challenge to a nursing program's denial of admission [31, 32]. The school argued that there were many work settings in which lip-reading would be impractical for a nurse and that "the purpose of its program was to train persons who could serve the nursing profession in all customary ways." The court agreed that it would not be reasonable to force the program to depart from this purpose—though it noted that technological and other changes might make accommodations for deaf students more reasonable in the future.

The world of medical and nursing practice is very different than it was in 1979. Many health sciences programs now have a record of successfully accommodating individuals with all sorts of disabilities. Nonetheless, as the *McCulley* decision indicates, the law in this area remains unsettled. General principles of reasonable accommodation would tend to require programs to come forward with some justification for imposing exclusionary technical standards that are not strictly necessary to success as a healthcare professional. But some adjudicators, like the court in *McCulley*, will find themselves hesitant to second-guess the professional decisions made by presumably expert academic institutions.

Communications Assistance

Many disability accommodation issues involve requests by blind or deaf students and professionals for assistance in communication. The ADA specifically requires covered entities to provide "auxiliary aids and services" to ensure effective communication with disabled individuals, at least where doing so would not cause a fundamental alteration or undue burden [26, 31]. As more blind and deaf students have been admitted to health professions programs in recent years, courts have increasingly been called upon to decide what burdens those programs must assume to provide communications assistance. The courts have imposed significant obligations on those programs.

The leading case is *Argenyi v. Creighton University* [33]. Michael Argenyi was a medical student with a serious hearing impairment. He found that he could not participate effectively in many of his classes without computer-assisted real-time transcription (CART)—an accommodation in which a stenographer types out all of the words spoken in a conversation so that they can be projected onto a computer screen in real time. He asked the school to provide CART for him, as well as a cued speech interpreter for clinical settings. The university refused to provide CART services— though it allowed Argenyi to pay for those services himself, at a cost of more than $50,000 each year—and it refused to allow him even to use his own interpreter in clinical settings. A jury ultimately concluded that the school violated the ADA by refusing to pay for CART and the interpreter, notwithstanding the significant cost.

Featherstone v. Pacific Northwest University of Health Sciences was a similar case [34]. Zachary Featherstone was a deaf osteopathic student. He asked his school to provide him an interpreter in his classes and clinical and laboratory settings. The university refused, on the grounds that the addition of an interpreter would fundamentally alter encounters with patients and that it was too burdensome to find and pay for an interpreter in Yakima, Washington. The federal district court for the Eastern District of Washington rejected the school's arguments and granted a preliminary injunction to Featherstone requiring the university to provide the interpreter.

These decisions highlight the importance of communications assistance to individuals with disabilities. They demonstrate that health professions programs will be required to assume substantial burdens to provide communications assistance where that is necessary to provide disabled individuals equal access to their curricula.

Accommodations of Testing and Curricular Requirements

Many ADA and Rehabilitation Act cases in the health professions setting involve requests by disabled students to modify testing or curricular requirements. The easiest cases involve offering an examination in a different format—such as a Braille test in lieu of one that uses printed text. Such an accommodation is virtually always required. A more controversial set of cases involves requests for additional time on speeded tests. Individuals with disabilities have sought extra time on admissions examinations, on tests administered by their schools, and on licensing examinations. In general, courts will require these extra time accommodations where the individual has a disability as defined by the law, where that disability prevents the individual from demonstrating the knowledge and ability tested by the examination in the time permitted, and where the purpose of the examination is to test for substantive knowledge rather than processing speed—that is, where the examination is timed largely for administrative reasons. A 2011 settlement agreement between the United States Department of Justice and the National Board of Medical Examiners incorporates these principles [35]. It requires extra time accommodations on the United States Medical Licensing Examination for individuals with disabilities, and it requires the NBME, in deciding an individual's request for such an accommodation, to give "considerable weight" to the accommodations the individual has received on other exams.

Where disabled individuals seek to change the *type* of examination their schools administer, they are far less likely to be successful than when they merely seek extra time. The 1992 decision of the United States Court of Appeals for the First Circuit in *Wynne v. Tufts University School of Medicine* is exemplary [36]. Steven Wynne, a medical student with a learning disability, challenged the school's use of multiple-choice examinations in his biochemistry class. As an accommodation for his disability, he asked for the school to ask him the exam questions orally instead. Although the court acknowledged that "at least one other medical school and a national testing service occasionally allow oral renderings of multiple-choice examinations in respect to dyslexic students," it held that Tufts was not required to provide the accommodation. The court recognized that there was more than one way to test biochemistry knowledge, but it concluded that the school had adequately explained why it believed that multiple-choice examinations were the fairest way to do so. "The point," the court said, "is that Tufts, after undertaking a diligent assessment of the available options, felt itself obliged to make 'a professional, academic judgment that [a] reasonable accommodation [was] simply not available.'"

Disabled students and residents also ask for changes to curricular requirements. In particular, in a number of cases, medical students who have had difficulty passing all of their courses have asked to take them on a decelerated schedule. In *Minaei v. University of Washington School of Medicine*, the school allowed Minaei to take her second-year courses over 2 years, as an accommodation for attention deficit disorder and anxiety [37, 38]. When she failed multiple courses during that 2-year period, the school dismissed her. The United States District Court for the Western District of Washington upheld the dismissal on the ground that the school had worked hard to accommodate Minaei, including by decelerating her second year of medical school. And in *Dean v. University at Buffalo School of Medicine*, the United States Court of Appeals for the Second Circuit held that there was at least a triable question whether the defendant medical school was required to give a student with depression a 3-month leave of absence to study for Step One of the USMLE [38, 39].

In *Shaikh v. Lincoln Memorial University*, by contrast, the school refused to allow a student with dyslexia and ADD to take his courses over 5 years instead of 4 [38]. The United States Court of Appeals for the Sixth Circuit held that the decelerated curriculum was not a "reasonable" accommodation, because it would have imposed significant administrative burdens on the school. And in *Powell v. National Board of Medical Examiners*, the Second Circuit held that a medical school was free to dismiss a student who had failed the USMLE Step One exam three times; the school was not required to allow her a fourth try as a reasonable accommodation for her dyslexia and ADD [40, 41]. These cases underscore the deference that academic institutions often receive in reasonable-accommodations decisions.

Similar issues can arise when an individual with a disability is working in a health sciences position—whether as an employee or in a clinical rotation as a student or resident. In *Samper v. Providence St. Vincent Medical Center*, for example, the plaintiff had fibromyalgia, which limited her sleep and left her in chronic pain [17]. As a result of her symptoms, she had numerous unplanned absences from her job as a nurse in a neonatal intensive care unit. The hospital eventually dismissed her, and the United States Court of Appeals for the Ninth Circuit rejected her ADA claim. The court held that no accommodation would have been reasonable, because regular attendance was an essential function of the job of NICU nurse.

The Accommodations Process

As the *Minaei* decision discussed in the previous section highlights, entities that engage openly and in good faith in attempting to find reasonable accommodations for disabled individuals are likely to be in the strongest position once litigation arises [37]. Many cases say that both the individual with the disability and the covered entity have an obligation undertake an *interactive process* to identify an accommodation. The individual must identify the limitations imposed by the disability and, if possible, suggest ways of accommodating it. And the entity must problem-solve if possible to either make the individual's proposed accommodation work or to find something else that does. If either party fails to engage in that process in good faith, a court is less likely to endorse that party's position should litigation arise.

Where a government entity with more than 50 employees is concerned, the procedural obligations take on a more formal cast. The Department of Justice's regulations require such an entity to "adopt and publish grievance procedures providing for prompt and equitable resolution of complaints" alleging violations of the disability discrimination laws [42, 43]. Individuals with disabilities are not required to exhaust these internal grievance processes before bringing a lawsuit under the ADA, but doing so may provide an opportunity to get relief without the time and expense of litigation.

Conclusion

Health sciences programs have a legal obligation to avoid discriminating against individuals with disabilities and to provide reasonable accommodations for their disabilities. This obligation requires programs to examine their policies and practices—across all of their operations—to ensure that they do not needlessly exclude disabled persons.

As the various cases discussed in this chapter demonstrate, cost alone is not a defense to a claim of accommodation under the disability discrimination laws. Where an accommodation is necessary to provide a disabled individual access to opportunities, a program or employer may be required to provide that accommodation even if it carries a substantial cost. Recall *Argenyi*, in which the medical school violated the ADA by refusing to pay for transcription and interpretive services that cost more than $50,000 per year. The question in disability accommodation cases is whether the cost is so great as to make the accommodation "unreasonable," an "undue hardship," or a "fundamental alteration." By erecting a very high standard for cost defenses, the disability discrimination laws underscore the commitment to eliminate practices that exclude talented disabled individuals from opportunities.

References

1. Bagenstos S. Technical standards and lawsuits involving accommodations for health professions students. AMA J Ethics. 2016;18(10):1010–6.
2. 42 USC sec 12101 (1990).
3. 29 USC sec 794 (1973).
4. Gildin G. Dis-qualified immunity for discrimination against the disabled. U Ill L Rev. 1999;1999(3):897.
5. Alexander v Choate, 469 US 287 (1985).
6. Pennsylvania Dept of Corrections v Yeskey, 524 US 206 (1998).
7. 42 USC sec 12181(7)(F).
8. 42 USC sec 12181(7)(J).
9. Bragdon v Abbott, 524 US 624 (1998).
10. Menkowitz v Pottstown Memorial Medical Center, 154 F3d 113 (3d Cir 1998).
11. 42 USC sec 12102(1).
12. Sutton v United Air Lines, Inc, 527 US 471 (1999).
13. Murphy v United Parcel Service, Inc, 527 US 516 (1999).
14. Albertsons, Inc v Kirkingburg, 527 US 555 (1999).
15. Toyota Motor Mfg, Ky, Inc v Williams, 534 US 184 (2002).
16. ADA Amendments Act of 2008, codified in scattered sections of 42 USC.
17. 29 CFR sec 35.108 (2016).
18. 29 CFR part 35 App (2016).
19. Richardson v Chicago Transit Auth, 926 F3d 881 (7th Cir 2019).
20. Bagenstos S. Disability rights law: cases and materials. 2nd ed. St. Paul: Foundation Press; 2014.
21. 42 USC sec 12102(2).
22. 42 USC sec 12102(4).
23. 42 USC sec 12102(3).
24. 42 USC sec 12201(h).

25. US Airways, Inc v Barnett, 535 US 391 (2002).
26. 42 USC sec 12112.
27. 42 USC sec 12182.
28. 28 CFR sec 35.130 (2011).
29. Ouellette A. Patients to peers: barriers and opportunities for doctors with disabilities. Nev Law J. 2013;13(3):645–67.
30. Palmer College of Chiropractic v Davenport Civil Rights Commn, 850 NW2d 326 (Iowa 2014).
31. McCulley v Univ of Kansas Sch of Medicine, 591 Fed Appx 648 (10th Cir 2014).
32. SE Comm Coll v Davis, 442 US 397 (1979).
33. 28 CFR sec 35.160 (2011).
34. Argenyi v Creighton Univ, 703 F3d 441 (8th Cir 2013).
35. Featherstone v Pac NW Univ of Health Sci, 2014 WL 3640803 (ED Wash 2014).
36. Settlement Agreement Between United States of America and National Board of Medical Examiners (Feb 23, 2011), https://www.ada.gov/nbme.htm.
37. Wynne v Tufts Univ Sch of Medicine, 976 F2d 791 (1st Cir 1992).
38. Minaei v Univ of Wash Sch of Medicine, 2018 WL 1508976 (WD Wash 2018).
39. Dean v Univ at Buffalo Sch of Medicine, 804 F3d 178 (2d Cir 2015).
40. Shaikh v Lincoln Mem Univ, 608 Fed Appx 349 (6th Cir 2015).
41. Powell v Natl Bd of Medical Examiners, 364 F3d 79 (2d Cir 2004).
42. Samper v. Providence St Vincent Medical Ctr, 675 F3d 1233 (9th Cir 2012).
43. 28 CFR sec 35.107 (2011).

Technical Standards

9

Michael M. McKee, Steven Gay, Sarah Ailey,
and Lisa M. Meeks

> Technical Standards are neither technical, nor standard
>   –Dr. Kurt Herzer, lamenting on the lack of utility and intentionality in most technical standards

What Are Technical Standards?

The term '*technical standards*' refers to all non-academic admission criteria that are essential to participation in the program in question." [1]. In Southeastern Community College v. Davis [2], the US Supreme Court considered a case where an

The original version of this chapter is revised and updated. The correction to this chapter can be found at https://doi.org/10.1007/978-3-030-46187-4_14

M. M. McKee (✉)
Department of Family Medicine, The University of Michigan Medical School,
Ann Arbor, MI, USA
e-mail: mmmckee@med.umich.edu

S. Gay
Assistant Dean for Admissions, Associate Professor of Internal Medicine, The University of Michigan Medical School, Ann Arbor, MI, USA
e-mail: sgay@med.umich.edu

S. Ailey
Professor, Department of Community, Systems and Mental Health Nursing, College of Nursing, Rush University Medical Center, Chicago, IL, USA
e-mail: Sarah_H_Ailey@rush.edu

L. M. Meeks
Assistant Professor, Department of Family Medicine, Director of MDisability Education,
The University of Michigan Medical School, Ann Arbor, MI, USA
e-mail: meeksli@med.umich.edu

© Springer Nature Switzerland AG 2020
L. M. Meeks, L. Neal-Boylan (eds.), *Disability as Diversity*,
https://doi.org/10.1007/978-3-030-46187-4_9

already licensed practical nurse, with bilateral, sensorineural hearing loss, was denied admission to a professional (registered) nursing program that received federal funds and that was required under Section 504 of the Rehabilitation Act of 1973 to provide reasonable accommodations [1]. An audiologist's report indicated that even with a hearing aid, the respondent could not understand speech directed to her except through lip-reading; the program rejected the respondent's application for admission because it believed her disability made it impossible for her to participate safely in the normal clinical training program or to care safely for patients.

The court held that the respondent was not an *otherwise qualified individual* protected by Section 504, and that the decision to exclude her was not discriminatory, and that in determining whether respondent was "otherwise qualified," the program must confine its inquiry to her *academic and technical qualifications*." The term "technical standards," thereafter, has been used to refer to the non-academic requirements articulated by most health professions schools that delineate the physical and other requirements for entry into a clinical program. Technical standards should not be conflated with *essential functions*, a term related to employment, not education.

Importantly, on appeal in Southeastern Community College v. Davis, the Supreme Court stated that:

> It is possible to envision situations where an insistence on continuing past requirements and practices might *arbitrarily deprive genuinely qualified* handicapped persons of the *opportunity to participate* in a covered program. Technological advances can be expected to enhance opportunities … Thus, situations may arise *where a refusal* to modify an existing program *might become unreasonable and discriminatory*.

Technical standards, the non-academic abilities required prior to entering a program, such as the ability to effectively communicate with members of a healthcare team, differ from a program's core competencies, which include the knowledge, skills, and abilities that a student must demonstrate in order to persist or graduate. Examples of these acquired skills include conducting a physical exam. Core competencies should be both measurable and observable and vary based on the health professional education program. Technical standards and core competencies are often conflated with one another and with the essential functions of employment, which are job-specific duties that an employee must be able to perform.

History of Technical Standards

In 1979, the American Association of Medical Colleges (AAMC) [3] put forward five key areas for technical standards including having abilities and skills in the following areas: [1] intellectual-conceptual abilities; [2] behavior and social attributes; [3] communication; [4] observation; and [5] motor capabilities. Since that time many programs have added a behavioral or professionalism category. The AAMC technical standards were intended to specify the minimum physical and mental abilities that were thought to be necessary to function as a physician. Candidates who were unable to meet these requirements could be denied admission to or graduation from a program. In medicine, the Liaison Committee on Medical Education

> **Box 9.1 Liaison Committee on Medical Education Standard Number 10.5**
> 10.5 Technical standards: A medical school develops and publishes technical standards for the admission, retention, and graduation of medical students, in accordance with legal requirements.

(LCME) (see Box 9.1) provides guidance to programs stating that all medical schools must maintain technical standards; however, the specific technical standards wording is left up to each school [4].

Candidates who are unable to meet the technical standards of a program have been denied admission to health professions programs, and the courts have held that schools are able to develop technical standards that are in keeping with their educational program goals as long as they are justifiable. In the case of McCulley v. University of Kansas School of Medicine [5], the court held that McCulley did not have the physical or motor capacity to execute emergency treatment (e.g., performing CPR) rendering her unable to meet the technical standards for admission to the University of Kansas School of Medicine. The court deferred to the school's assertion that the motor technical standards were an essential requirement for participation in a medical education at the University of Kansas School of Medicine.

The Law and Technical Standards

When developing technical standards for a program, the ADA (1990) regulations provide some guidance stating that a public accommodation [school]"shall not impose or apply eligibility criteria that screen out or tend to screen out an individual with a disability or any class of individuals with disabilities from fully and equally enjoying any goods, services, facilities, privileges, advantages, or accommodations, unless such criteria can be shown to be necessary for the provision of the goods, services, facilities, privileges, advantages, or accommodations being offered [6]."

Screening out someone with a disability occurs when a program applies a technical standard to a programs admissions standard that is not grounded in actual competencies required by the health professional education program, accrediting body, or that does not consider potential accommodations for meeting the standard. The communication domain of technical standards offers the most salient example. While the ability to communicate is certainly necessary to provide health care, a healthcare professional who is deaf or hard of hearing may communicate differently, but the ability to communicate can be equivalent to their peers with the provision of reasonable accommodations, including sign language interpreters or assistive devices. Based on this example, the following technical standard would impose or apply eligibility criteria that screen out or tend to screen out an individual with a disability (see Examples 9.1 and 9.2).

In contrast, in the following example, qualified individuals who are deaf or hard of hearing are provided an opportunity to meet the technical standards through reasonable accommodations.

> **Example 9.1 Prohibitive Language in Technical Standards**
> *Communication:* A candidate should be able to ***speak, to hear***, and to observe patients in order to elicit information, describe changes in mood, activity, and posture, and perceive nonverbal communications. A candidate must be able to communicate effectively and sensitively with patients. Communication includes not only ***speech*** but reading and writing. The candidate must be able to communicate effectively and efficiently in ***oral*** and written form with all members of the healthcare team.

> **Example 9.2 Inclusive Technical Standards Language**
> *Communication:* Students should be able to ***communicate*** with patients in order to elicit information, to detect changes in mood and activity, and to establish a therapeutic relationship. Students should be able to communicate effectively and sensitively with patients and all members of the healthcare team both in person and in writing.

Organic Versus Functional Technical Standards

Organic Technical Standards

A review of existing US medical and nursing programs' technical standards demonstrates a reliance largely on an ***organic*** approach or one that requires the student be able to demonstrate certain physical, cognitive, behavioral, and sensory abilities without assistance [7–9]. Examples of this would be that a student must be able to *hear*, *see*, and *speak clearly* and be able to *stand* for long periods of time and move in tight spaces. The use of organic technical standards emphasizes how a student goes about completing a task, over the skill-based competency. Organic technical standards serve as barriers for qualified students with disabilities through multiple mechanisms. In doing so, they contribute to the inequitable number of students with disabilities in health professional programs and promote and reinforce negative views of people with disabilities. *Organic* technical standards are grounded in false assumptions that center around concerns for patient safety, the cost of accommodations, and false information about the availability of accommodations in employment or on licensing exams. The majority of health professions programs continue to utilize organic technical standards that highlight students' limitations or deficits rather than their abilities [10].

Functional Technical Standards

In contrast to organic technical standards, a more progressive view is based on *functional* technical standards that focus on the students' *abilities*, with or without the use of accommodations or assistive technologies [9–11]. Reichgott suggests categorizing health professional technical standards into the following five domains: [1] acquiring fundamental knowledge; [2] developing communication skills; [3] interpreting data; [4] integrating knowledge to establish clinical judgment; and [5] developing appropriate professional attitudes and behaviors [9]" In a recent article, Kezar and colleagues developed a model for functional technical standards using Reichgott's categorization [9] (see Fig. 9.1 Reichgott Functional Model for Revised Technical Standards for MD and DO programs).

The use of functional technical standards can assist in removing barriers that prevent students with disabilities from entering into health professional education programs and then into health professions, improving the diversity of the healthcare professional workforce. Functional technical standards allow students with disabilities to include rapidly developing, cutting-edge assistive technologies (e.g., amplified stethoscopes, specialized motorized wheelchairs, magnifying devices) and accommodations (e.g., extended test times) to meet technical standards of the health professional school or training program [9]. Examples of these accommodations include allowing a DHoH applicant to meet the communication standard through the use of an American Sign Language (ASL) Interpreter or allowing a student who is a wheelchair user to meet the standards for motor skills, recognizing that the ability to walk or stand is discriminatory and that the actual standard is to be able to navigate a clinic or hospital space in order to provide patient care. Programs across the country are successfully implementing this approach, and stories of these successes are making their way to the literature [12–14].

A "Failure to Communicate"

Unfortunately, many programs' technical standards failed to adequately address the notion that these standards must be met with or without accommodations. A recent study by Zazove and colleagues suggests that 67% of medical schools do not explicitly state that they allow for accommodations to meet technical standards, while 7% of schools fail to publicize their technical standards [8].

Failure to publicize technical standards may serve as a disincentive to students with disabilities, keeping them from applying to a program for lack of information about whether or not they would be eligible. Zazove's study also highlighted the lack of transparency in communicating technical standards. Of the schools who posted technical standards, almost half (42%) were not easily located. Finally, technical standards that are available (or obtained) may utilize language that communicates a legalistic approach to working with students with disabilities. In many technical standards, the communication is very clear and suggestive that students with disabilities are not welcome (see Example 9.3).

A Functional Model for Revised Technical Standards (TS) for MD and DO Medical Education Programs, Using Michael Reichgott's Categories[46]

[School name] seeks to produce highly skilled and compassionate doctors. Students are expected to develop a robust medical knowledge base and the requisite clinical skills, with the ability to appropriately apply their knowledge and skills, effectively interpret information, and contribute to patient-centered decisions across a broad spectrum of medical situations and settings. The following technical standards, in conjunction with the academic standards, are requirements for admission, promotion, and graduation. The term "candidate" refers to candidates for admission to medical school as well as current medical students who are candidates for retention, promotion, or graduation. These requirements may be achieved with or without reasonable accommodations. Candidates with disabilities are encouraged to contact [disability office or position] early in the application process to begin a confidential conversation about what accomodations they may need to meet these standards. Fulfillment of the technical standards for graduation form medical school does not guarantee that a graduate will be able to fulfill the technical requirements of any specific residency program.

Category	Technical standard
Acquiring fundamental knowledge	Candidates must be able to learn through a variety of modalities, including, but not limited to, classroom instruction; laboratory instruction, including cadaver lab; physical demonstrations, small-group, team, and collaborative activities; individual study; preparation and presentation of reports; and use of computer technology.
Developing communication skills	Candidates must exhibit interpersonal skills to accurately evaluate patient conditions and responses and enable effective caregiving of patients. Candidates must be able to clearly and accurately record information and accurately interpret patients' verbal and nonverbal communication. Candidates must demonstrate effective communication, participation, and collaboration with all members of a multidisciplinary health care team, patients, and those supporting patients, in person and in writing.
Interpreting data	Candidates must effectively interpret, assimilate, and understand the complex information required to function within the medical school curriculum, including, but not limited to, the ability to comprehend three-dimensional relationships and understand the spatial relationships of structures; synthesize information both in person and via remote technology; interpret causal connections and make accurate, fact-based conclusions based on available data and information; formulate a hypothesis and investigate the potential answers and outcomes; and reach appropriate and accurate conclusions. Candidates must be able to correctly interpret diagnostic representations of patients' physiologic data.
Integrating knowledge to establish clinical judgment	Candidates must conduct routine physical examinations and diagnostic maneuvers to form an accurate and comprehensive assessment of relevant patient health, behavioral, and medical information. Candidates must be able to provide or direct general care and emergency treatment for patients and respond to emergency situations in a timely manner. Candidates must meet applicable safety standards for the environment and follow universal precaution procedures.
Developing appropriate professional attitudes and behaviors	Candidates must exercise good judgment; promptly complete all responsibilites attendant to the diagnosis and care of patients; and develop mature, sensitive, and effective relationships with patients. The skills required to do so include the ability to effectively handle and manage heavy workloads, function effectively under stress, adapt to changing environments, display flexibility, and learn to function in the face of uncertainties inherent in the clinical problems of patients. Candidates are expected to exhibit professionalism, personal accountability, compassion, integrity, concern for others,and interpersonal skills including the ability to accept and apply feedback and to respect boundaries and care for all individuals in a respectful and effective manner regardless of gender identity, age, race, sexual orientation, religion, disability, or any other protected status. Candidates should understand, and function within, the legal and ethical aspects of the practice of medicine and maintain and display ethical and moral behaviors commensurate with the role of a physician in all interactions with patients, faculty, staff, students, and the public. Interest and motivation throughout the educational processes are expected of all candidates.

Fig. 9.1 Reichgott functional model for revised technical standards for MD and DO programs used with permission from Kezar et al. [9]

Example 9.3 Introductory Language for Technical Standards that Dissuade Students with Disabilities

The College of Medicine has an ethical responsibility for the safety of patients with whom students and graduates will come in contact. Although students learn and work under the supervision of the faculty, students interact with patients throughout their medical school education. *Patient safety and well-being are therefore major factors in establishing requirements involving the physical, cognitive, and emotional abilities of candidates for admission, promotion, and graduation.*[1] As a result, the medical education process, which focuses so largely on patients, differs markedly from postsecondary education in fields outside of the health sciences.

Candidates must have the *physical and emotional stamina to function in a competent and safe manner in settings that may involve heavy workloads, long hours, and stressful situations.*[2] All candidates should be aware that the academic and clinical responsibilities of medical students may, at times, require their *presence during day and evening hours, any day of the week, at unpredictable times and for unpredictable durations of time. Individuals who constitute a direct threat to the health and safety of others are not suitable candidates for admission, promotion, or graduation.*[3]

Delineation of technical standards *is required for the accreditation of US medical schools*[4] by the Liaison Committee on Medical Education.

Candidates must possess the capability to complete the entire medical curriculum, achieve the degree Doctor of Medicine, and practice medicine with or without reasonable accommodations.[5]

---

[1] Begins discussion of technical standards with a repetitive and strong statement about patient safety, suggesting that the concern about inclusion of students with disabilities may be focused on safety.

[2] Communication regarding physical abilities of candidates. Although health science programs are difficult, the approach in this wording could be perceived as attempting to elicit fear and doubt in the minds of any candidate with a chronic health or mental health disability.

[3] This sentence can be perceived as a disincentive for any candidate who may require an adjustment to the schedule as a reasonable accommodation, for example, weekend vs. night call. On top of the aggressive language about availability, the statement includes another reminder (with some assumptions implied) that a student who is incapable of all of the above is a direct threat to patient safety.

[4] Compliance-driven statement, as if to say "we have to do this."

[5] While this includes the mandatory statement "with or without accommodations," it assumes ability before even entering medical school, notwithstanding that students without disability are, at times, unable to achieve the MD degree or chose, without disability, not to practice medicine once completing their degree.

> *Technological accommodations can be made for some handicaps in certain areas of the curriculum, but a candidate must meet the essential technical standards so that he or she will be able to perform in a reasonably independent manner.*[6] *The need for personal aids, assistance, caregivers, readers, and interpreters, therefore, may not be acceptable in certain phases of the curriculum, particularly during the clinical years.*[7]
>
> *In accordance with law*[8] and the College of Medicine policy, no qualified individual with a disability shall, on the basis of that disability, be excluded from participation in College of Medicine programs or activities. The College of Medicine will provide reasonable accommodation to a qualified individual with a disa`bility. *Candidates must also be aware that approval for and provision of reasonable accommodations do not mean that similar accommodations would be granted elsewhere by postgraduate clinical training sites or by national licensing review boards.*[9]
>
> A candidate who is unable to meet these technical standards with or without a reasonable accommodation may *be denied admission or may be dismissed from the MD program. Should a candidate pose a significant risk to health and safety of patients, self, or others that cannot be eliminated with a reasonable accommodation, the candidate may be denied admission or may be dismissed from the MD program.*[10]

In the example above, any candidate with a disability would be dissuaded from applying to this institution, which may, in fact, be the reason the language is written as presented. Oftentimes, bias and fear are the driver of an institution's communication about disability inclusion. In the example above, the institution mentions the legal obligation to accommodate, quickly followed by multiple reminders of all

---

[6] The use of the term handicaps is outdated and to some, offensive.

[7] The statement that suggests interpreters may not be acceptable in the clinical years is legally unsound. As well caregivers are appropriate at any time for someone who requires assistance with personal management (catherization). The expense of a personal caregiver may not be borne by the institution, but cannot be barred by it either.

[8] Compliance-driven statement, quickly mitigated by statement about what is not allowed.

[9] Language that suggests "even if we give you an accommodation, you won't make it past medical school." While it is certainly true that a medical school cannot predict nor be accountable for downstream decisions, this reads as more of a deterrent than a true disclosure.

[10] Another statement regarding patient safety, presuming a person with a disability pose a threat to patient safety. Strong language about dismissal or failure to accept.

reasons why they will exclude a person with a disability and three separate mentions of patient safety (beginning, middle, and end) subtly communicating their belief that a person with a disability should not be in their program.

In contrast to Example 9.3, some programs are working to ensure that students with disabilities understand the entry requirements but also feel welcomed and valued as a part of a diverse cohort of incoming students. Keep in mind the legal premise of accommodation and the legal requirement to accommodate is not tempered by the language used. The use of language only serves as a disincentive or incentive to apply. Take, for example, a starkly different and inviting set of language leading up to the technical standards in Example 9.4.

Example 9.4 Introductory Language for Technical Standards that Encourage Disclose of Disability

The school of nursing is *committed to diversity*[11] and to attracting and educating students who will make the population of healthcare professionals' representative of the national population. We *actively collaborate with students*[12] to develop *innovative ways to ensure accessibility*[13] and create a *respectful accountable culture through our confidential and specialized disability support.*[14]We are *committed to excellence in accessibility*[15]; we *encourage students with disabilities to disclose and seek accommodations.*[16]

The College of Nursing provides the following sample description/examples of technical standards to *inform incoming and enrolled students of the performance abilities and characteristics that are necessary to successfully complete the requirements of the nursing curriculum and provide effective and safe health care.*[17] To matriculate (enroll) the student must meet technical standards *with or*

---

[11] The first statement makes clear that disability is viewed as part of diversity.

[12] Actively collaborating with students is a description of the interactive process and is presented positively in this example.

[13] This statement suggests that the institution is aware of the technological advances available to aid in meeting technical standards and that they are willing to engage them.

[14] This statement communicates to the student or applicant that their disability-related items will be confidential and respected and that specialized support for accommodations is available.

[15] A statement of commitment to inclusion.

[16] A statement encouraging students with disabilities to disclose and seek accommodations.

[17] A statement about meeting the competencies and providing safe patient care, vastly different from that in Example <InternalRef RefID="FPar3">9.2.

> *without reasonable accommodations and maintain related satisfactory demonstration of these standards for progression through the program.*[18]
>
> We wish to *ensure that access to our facilities, programs, and services*[19] are available to students with disabilities. *The university provides reasonable accommodations to students on a nondiscriminatory basis consistent with legal requirements as outlined in the Americans with Disabilities Act (ADA) of 1990, the Americans with Disabilities Act Amendments ACT (ADAAA) of 2008, and the Rehabilitation Act of 1973.*[20]

As you can see, for the student reviewing programs technical standards, the choice of which program has a better culture of people with disabilities is clear. A side-by-side comparison of two of the elements provides greater clarity about the differences. In Example 9.5 you can see the comparison of statements regarding the legal requirement for inclusion.

As you will notice, these read quite differently, with option A and option B (see footnotes for specific notes). As well, the statements about inclusion of students with disabilities are vastly different in these two sets of technical standards language, which becomes very clear with a side-by-side comparison (see Example 9.6).

When directly compared there is little question about the differences in concern, and desire for inclusion, between the two programs. As discussed, there are several specific barriers in technical standards that work against schools wishing to recruit and retain students with disabilities. Two of the biggest barriers are failure to publish technical standards and overly legalistic language as highlighted below.

When schools fail to update their standards, many potential and current students resort to litigation. Examples of legal challenges from medical students with disabilities include *Argenyi* vs *Creighton* [15], *Featherstone* vs *Pacific Northwest University of Health Sciences,* [16] *and Palmer College of Chiropractic v. Davenport Civil Rights Commission* [17]. These cases favored the student's inclusion, in part due to the expansion of accessible technology and accommodations in use nationally and the prior successes of clinicians with hearing and vision loss.

The Critical Nature of Inclusive Technical Standards

Social justice and the need for full inclusion of students with disabilities in the health professions add compelling ethical reasons for inclusive technical standards, thereby improving the likelihood of admission to health professions programs and greater inclusion and provision of accommodations for applicants and students with disabilities. Students and professionals with disabilities are underrepresented in health care. Despite >20% of patients reporting a disability [18], the prevalence of medical students with disabilities remains low (4.7%) [19]. Patients with disabilities struggle to access equitable healthcare services in many cases due to providers who

Example 9.5 Direct Comparison of Statement Regarding the Legal Requirement for Inclusion

Option A:

In accordance with law[21] and the College of Medicine policy, no qualified individual with a disability shall, on the basis of that disability, be excluded from participation in College of Medicine programs or activities. The College of Medicine will provide reasonable accommodation to a qualified individual with a disability. Candidates must also be aware that approval for and provision of reasonable accommodations does not mean that similar accommodations would be granted elsewhere by postgraduate clinical training sites or by national licensing review boards.[22]

Option B:

We wish to ensure that access to our facilities, programs, and services[23] are available to students with disabilities. The university provides reasonable accommodations to students on a nondiscriminatory basis consistent with legal requirements as outlined in the Americans with Disabilities Act (ADA) of 1990, the Americans with Disabilities Act Amendments ACT (ADAAA) of 2008, and the Rehabilitation Act of 1973.[24]

do not understand the experience of disability, have insufficient knowledge about the impact of disability on health, and lack training specific to caring for people with disabilities, resulting in health and healthcare disparities [20–26]. The life experiences of health sciences students and professionals with disabilities may better equip them to not only understand but also to care for patients with disabilities more effectively and compassionately than their counterparts without disabilities but also help educate the health professions in general, changing attitudes through close associations with people with disabilities working alongside one another

---

[18] The standard "with or without accommodations statement."

[19] Another statement of inclusion to access.

[20] A compliance statement that comes after all of the language to invite inclusion and is written in a pro-student manner.

[21] Compliance-driven statement, quickly mitigated by statement about what is not allowed.

[22] Language that suggests, "even if we give you an accommodation, you won't make it past medical school." While it is certainly true that a medical school cannot predict, nor be accountable for downstream decisions, this reads as more of a deterrent than a true disclosure.

[23] Another statement of inclusion to access.

[24] A compliance statement that comes after all of the language to invite inclusion and is written in a pro-student manner.

Example 9.6 Direct Comparison of Inclusive Wording in Opening Paragraph of Technical Standards

Option A:

The College of Medicine has an ethical responsibility for the safety of patients with whom students and graduates will come in contact. Although students learn and work under the supervision of the faculty, students interact with patients throughout their medical school education. Patient safety and well-being are therefore major factors in establishing requirements involving the physical, cognitive, and emotional abilities of candidates for admission, promotion, and graduation.[25] As a result, the medical education process, which focuses so largely on patients, differs markedly from postsecondary education in fields outside of the health sciences.

Option B:

The school of nursing is committed to diversity[26] and to attracting and educating students who will make the population of healthcare professionals' representative of the national population. We actively collaborate with students[27] to develop innovative ways to ensure accessibility[28] and create a respectful accountable culture through our confidential and specialized disability support.[29]We are committed to excellence in accessibility[30]; we encourage students with disabilities to disclose and seek accommodations.[31]

[12, 27–30]. Disability is a valuable form of diversity. Health professions students with disabilities offer enriching perspectives from whom their peers can learn about the experience of disability. This can help address the gaps in disability awareness and disability health training in most programs' curricula [31–33].

---

[25] Begins discussion of technical standards with a repetitive and strong statement about patient safety, suggesting that the concern about inclusion of students with disabilities may be focused on safety.

[26] The first statement makes clear that disability is viewed as part of diversity.

[27] Actively collaborating with students is a description of the interactive process and is presented positively in this example.

[28] This statement suggests that the institution is aware of the technological advances available to aid in meeting technical standards and that they are willing to engage them.

[29] This statement communicates to the student or applicant that their disability-related items will be confidential and respected and that specialized support for accommodations is available.

[30] A statement of commitment to inclusion.

[31] A statement encouraging students with disabilities to disclose and seek accommodations.

Example 9.7 Two Largest Barriers Regarding Technical Standards
Barrier 1: Failure to Publicize Technical Standards
   Students with disabilities who cannot obtain information about a programs' technical standards will struggle in determining eligibility. When schools are not transparent with their technical standards, it discourages applications from potential students with disabilities. This reduces the overall representation of disability in the student population and reinforces negative stereotypes of disabilities in general.

Barrier 2: Overly Legalistic Language in Technical Standards
   Technical standards are often framed in a legalistic or unwelcoming manner. This may intimidate students with disabilities, disincentivizing their willingness to disclose their disabilities when applying.

Revising Technical Standards

Programs that seek to improve their technical standards can use the following sections as a guide to revision. The process of revising technical standards offers a unique opportunity for the program to reevaluate the mission, curricular competencies, and the essential components required to earn a degree in the health professions discipline. A periodic review of technical standards also allows the program to review the appropriate use of language and to ensure that program practices are in keeping with recent courts decisions. Importantly, reviewing and updating the standards help programs reflect on the mission for disability inclusion and improve the engagement of learners with disabilities.

Current Best Practice in the Field

Advances in technologies, recent case law, and a growing cohort of health science professionals with disabilities in practice have challenged programs to rethink their technical standards. Modern technologies such as high-frequency audio and visual output stethoscopes, standing wheelchairs, and voice-to-text technologies allow individuals with disabilities to perform the same tasks asked of their peers with equal competence. By focusing on the final competency, not the method a student uses, programs measure the "what" and not the "how."

   Recent commentaries in the literature warn of the legal implications of maintaining organic technical standards, while others suggest that outdated and discriminatory technical standards that do not accurately reflect the technical skills needed in the twenty-first century may negatively affect learners. Best practice, therefore, necessitates that schools revise their technical standards to align with *functional technical standards* that focus on students' ability to perform with or without the use of accommodations or assistive technologies. The distinct difference in functional technical standards is the lack of a motor skills category that is replaced by language that represents what a clinician does versus how they do it (see Examples 9.8 and 9.9).

Example 9.8 Acquiring Fundamental Knowledge
Candidates must be able to learn through a variety of modalities, including but not limited to laboratory instruction, including cadaver lab; physical demonstrations, small group, team, and collaborative activities; individual study; preparation and presentation of reports; and use of computer technology.

Example 9.9 Integrating Knowledge to Establish Clinical Judgment
Candidates must conduct routine physical examinations and diagnostic maneuvers to form an accurate and comprehensive assessment of relevant patient health, behavioral, and medical information. Candidate must be able to provide or direct general patient care and emergency treatment for patients and respond to emergency situations in a timely manner. Candidates must meet applicable safety standards for the environment and follow universal precaution procedures.

Experts support the move to functional technical standards and recommend that explicit information about the school's compliance with the ADA and the process for requesting accommodations be *clearly articulated on the website and other program communication*[8] Programs should ensure, through technical standards, that applicants and matriculated students understand the process for requesting accommodations. It should be clear to the current and prospective student that the program *encourages disclosure* of disability and maintains a commitment to students with disabilities.

Information about the process may look different for different programs, but at a minimum, technical standards should contain three fundamental elements (see Example 9.10).

- A statement that encourages disclosure
- A statement that communicates a confidential process
- A statement that directs students to the office for disability resources

By proactively communicating a commitment to prospective and current students with disabilities, programs may reduce stigma, encourage disclosure of disability, and increase opportunities to ensure learner access.

Conclusion

A diverse health professional team that includes those with disabilities may improve our ability to care for our increasingly diverse patient population. With the move to competency-based education, one might question the very need for technical

> **Example 9.10 Technical Standards Disability Statements**
>
> [Name of program] maintains a strong institutional commitment to equal educational opportunities for qualified students with disabilities who apply for admission to [degree program] or who are already enrolled. The technical standards are not intended to deter any candidate for whom reasonable accommodation will allow the fulfillment of the complete curriculum. Admitted candidates with disabilities are confidentially reviewed by the [name of office] to determine whether there are any reasonable accommodations or alternative mechanisms that would permit the candidate to satisfy the standards. This process is informed by the knowledge that students with varied types of disability have the ability to become successful health professionals. If you are an applicant with a disability who may require accommodations in our program, we encourage you to contact [name of person] at [email and phone number] for a confidential consultation.

standards. Advances in assistive technologies, recent case law, and a growing cohort of healthcare professionals in practice, representing multiple categories of disability, challenge health programs to rethink the applicability and necessity of technical standards. In the interim, the move from organic to functional technical standards will help facilitate the inclusion of individuals with disabilities into their educational programs.

Appendix A: Self-Assessment of Technical Standards

Programs should review the following questions to determine if their technical standards require revision.

1. Do your Technical Standards include language encouraging disclosure of disability?
   Students may be reticent to seek accommodations when they feel the environment is hostile or non-inclusive. Students should be *actively encouraged* to disclose disability and seek accommodations from the beginning of the program. These early requests for accommodations are known facilitators of success and help prevent last minute disclosures that may occur when a student has performed poorly.
2. Do your Technical Standards include welcoming language?
   Welcoming language is critical to encouraging disclosure of applicants. Check your technical standards for language that might be viewed as micro-aggressions. Framing accommodations in a positive manner encourages early disclosure of disability. A shift to more welcoming language does not change the laws that govern inclusion, the reasonable nature of an accommodation, or what

constitutes an undue burden. However, changing a program's language *does* communicate to applicants that your institution is a safe place to disclose a disability where the student and the program can engage in a meaningful interactive process. By proactively communicating a commitment to students with disabilities through their technical standards language, programs can reduce stigma and proactively address learner access.

3. Do your Technical Standards communicate a process for disclosing disability and requesting accommodations?

Programs must endeavor that applicants and matriculated students understand the process for requesting accommodations and have the information necessary to do so. In keeping with OCR recommendations, that programs provide clear notice of these requirements in order to prevent misunderstandings about the expectations for the program [34].

4. Are Your Technical Standards free of discriminatory language that screens out people with disabilities?

Technical standards that impose or apply eligibility criteria that screen out or tend to screen out an individual with a disability or any class of individuals with a disability are prohibited unless proven that they are essential for performing the tasks of the profession. Words like *hear, speak, or walk* are likely not appropriate for the technical standards of a health professions program.

If you found yourself answering any of these four questions with a *NO*, you should reassess your technical standards to align with the current best practices. Appendix A and B of this chapter provides a step-by-step approach to revising technical standards. Appendix C offers a set of general technical standards as a guide.

Appendix B: How to Approach a Review

Programs should periodically review their technical standards to ensure that these accurately reflect advancements in technology and align with the *actual* abilities needed to learn and master the competencies of the program. This appendix is designed for health professions programs that determine their technical standards warrant revision. The process can help health professional schools move toward more functional and inclusive technical standards. It is recommended that those revising the technical standards be aware of current advancements in assistive technologies and disability law.

Step 1: Identify a Team

Identify key stakeholders for a council or committee to review technical standards.

Team members should include:

- Experts in health science disability inclusion and the best practices on accommodation.
- Faculty who understand clinical curricula

- Simulation center experts
- Assessment deans or directors
- Student representative, preferably someone with a disability

Step 1: Identify Philosophy of School or Program
Schools should consider their philosophy and its implications on students with disabilities. It is helpful to review program goals to get a clear vision of how these goals align with equal access of students with disabilities. You should also gather all forward-facing messaging to review for inclusive language. Finally, you'll need to review all program competencies and accreditation requirements in order to identify the specific technical skills and abilities necessary for inclusion in the technical standards.

- What is the mission and vision of the program?
- What does the non-discrimination or inclusion statement say about people with disabilities?
- Does the school's philosophy reflect the current technological advances for the inclusion of people with disabilities?
- What are the competencies necessary for promotion and graduation? What, if any, competencies are required by the accrediting organization.

Now you and your team are ready to *begin revising technical standards!*
The Five-Step Process for Technical Standards Revision
Once you have developed your team and have gathered your forward-facing messaging and program competencies, you are prepared to begin the process of revising your technical standards. The following five 1–2 hour-long meeting structure is offered to assist programs with the revision process. The process may vary given the amount of revision needed or the unique structure of a specific program.

First Meeting
During the first meeting, programs should discuss the need for revision of the technical standards based on the above step 1, which are usually grounded in three items: [1] a need to comport with legal guidance, case law [2] desire to approach technical standards from a functional v. organic perspective, and [3] a desire to expand the diversity agenda to include disability.

This meeting should include a philosophical discussion about the program's commitment to inclusion. The committee members should determine how the program wishes to communicate their willingness to work with students with disabilities, with the understanding that the technical standards must meet the basic tenants of legal accessibility. In this first meeting, you may want to ask the following questions to get a better idea of the goals of the technical standards revision.

Committee questions:

1. What is the philosophy of the program or university?
2. Do our technical standards align with our mission statement?
3. Why do we have technical standards?

4. What are the expectations of oversight agencies regarding technical standards?

Questions 3 and 4 require committee members to have a basic understanding of expectations from accrediting agencies, state boards of licensure and professional organizations. Committee members should be able to articulate the need for technical standards, how they are used, and how to apply them in schools and programs. For example, the LCME provides general guidance to medical schools through their elements. See Example 9.11.

Example 9.11 LCME Guidance

The Liaison Committee for Medical Education (LCME) is recognized by the US Department of Education and World Federation for Medical Education (WFME) as the reliable authority for the accreditation of medical education programs leading to the MD degree. In order to carry LCME accreditation, a school must maintain a list of technical standards. Therefore, maintaining technical standards is critical to maintaining accreditation.

LCME Element 10.5 Technical Standards

A medical school develops and publishes technical standards for the admission, retention, and graduation of applicants or medical students with disabilities, in accordance with legal requirements.

Second Meeting

This meeting will be focused on identifying the goals of the technical standards revision and include a review of existing technical standards in comparison with other programs.

After reviewing all of the items mentioned above (language, mission/vision, and requirements for technical standards), the committee should focus on identifying the goal of revising the technical standards. For example, is the goal to become more inclusive, to improve the use of language in the technical standards, to develop functional technical standards, or to ensure alignment with the legal obligations. It could be that all four are drivers for a technical standards revision. Sometimes this exercise is time-consuming. People may be confused about the need for technical standards and how they are actually used. If this is the case, you should allow for an additional meeting to address any confusion.

The second half of this meeting can be spent comparing existing technical standards to other technical standards in the same or similar type of health professions program. Remember that other programs technical standards may not be well-written. Part of the comparison is to help the committee crystalize the difference between well-written and poorly written technical standards.

This exercise is helpful in identifying the range of language and technical requirements used in the field. The program gets to decide the essential competencies of the program and has this reflected in the technical standards, as long as they are in keeping with legal guidance and grounded in program or accreditation standards.

The committee should make a list of the items they liked from other program technical standards, and they should conduct a critical "first pass" of their own technical standards to identify nonconformity with the critical four questions:

- Do your technical standards language encouraging disclosure of disability?
- Do your technical standards include welcoming language?
- Do your technical standards communicate a process for disclosing disability and requesting accommodations?
- Are your technical standards free of discriminatory language that screens out people with disabilities?

Homework Review existing technical standards and note items that need to be removed and language that should be added.

Third Meeting

Here is where your committee will do a lot of the actual changing of the technical standards. This meeting may need to be longer than the other meetings to allow for the critical rewriting and revision of the standards. The committee members should come to table having completed the homework of identifying needed change in the program's technical standards and developing recommendations for new language. These recommendations can be funneled to one person who can create a master document that can be reviewed during the third meeting. At the end of this meeting, there should be a working document with all edits included. The committee members should review these recommended edits between the third and the fourth meetings.

Fourth Meeting

At this meeting, committee members will work to refine and finalize the technical standards. Once finalized, these standards are usually forwarded to a faculty committee or leadership for final approval. It may be helpful to provide a written summary of the process you followed to other stakeholders. It is also helpful to include any exemplar technical standards from similar programs. The next meeting should follow the final approval of the standards or a returned set of standards with queries from the leadership.

Fifth and Final Meeting

Once the technical standards are approved, the committee should work to implement them.

The committee should propose how the school's faculty, including the admission committee and disability resources professionals, will be informed of the revised technical standards.

We recommend a close collaboration between the office of disability resources and the school's faculty and admission committee members during the rollout of the technical standards. It may be helpful to have a question and answer session for those who have questions about the process or changes in technical standards. Importantly, all references to the old technical standards should be removed in writing and on the institutional and program website.

Finally, when possible, the disability office should conduct a training to remind faculty and leadership about the resources available, current best practices, and the mission and vision that informed the technical standards.

Appendix C: Example Technical Standards

[University] is committed to diversity and to attracting and educating students who will make the population of healthcare professionals' representative of the national population. We provide confidential and specialized disability support and are committed to excellence in accessibility; we encourage students with disabilities to disclose and seek accommodations.

Technical (Non-academic) Standards

- *Observation*: Students should be able to obtain information from demonstrations and experiments in the basic sciences. Students should be able to assess a patient and evaluate findings accurately. These skills require the use of vision, hearing, and touch or the functional equivalent.
- *Communication*: Students should be able to communicate with patients in order to elicit information, to detect changes in mood and activity, and to establish a therapeutic relationship. Students should be able to communicate via English effectively and sensitively with patients and all members of the healthcare team both in person and in writing.
- *Motor*: Students should, after a reasonable period of time, possess the capacity to perform a physical examination and perform diagnostic maneuvers. Students should be able to execute some motor movements required to provide general care to patients and provide or direct the provision of emergency treatment of patients. Such actions require some coordination of both gross and fine muscular movements balance and equilibrium.
- *Intellectual, conceptual, integrative, and quantitative abilities*: Students should be able to assimilate detailed and complex information presented in both didactic and clinical coursework, engage in problem-solving. Candidates are expected to possess the ability to measure, calculate, reason, analyze, synthesize, and transmit information. In addition, students should be able to comprehend three-dimensional relationships and to understand the spatial relationships of structures and to adapt to different learning environments and modalities.
- *Behavioral and social abilities*: Students should possess the emotional health required for full utilization of their intellectual abilities, the exercise of good judgment, the prompt completion of all responsibility's attendant to the diagnosis and care of patients, and the development of mature, sensitive, and effective relationships with patients, fellow students, faculty, and staff. Students should be able to tolerate physically taxing workloads and to function effectively under stress. They should be able to adapt to changing environments, to display flexibility, and to learn to function in the face of uncertainties inherent in the clinical problems of many patients. Compassion, integrity, concern for others,

interpersonal skills, professionalism, interest, and motivation are all personal qualities that are expected during the education processes.

• *Ethics and professionalism*: Students should maintain and display ethical and moral behaviors commensurate with the role of a physician in all interactions with patients, faculty, staff, students, and the public. The candidate is expected to understand the legal and ethical aspects of the practice of medicine and function within the law and ethical standards of the medical profession.

The technical standards delineated above must be met with or without accommodation.

Students who, after review of the technical standards determine that they require accommodation to fully engage in the program, should contact the [insert disability contact information] and [insert website] to confidentially discuss their accommodations needs. Given the clinical nature of the program, additional time may be needed to implement accommodations. Accommodations are never retroactive; therefore, timely requests are essential and encouraged.

References

1. Section 504 Federal Guidance, 45 CFR pt. 84, App. A, p. 405. 1978.
2. Powell, Lewis F., Jr, and Supreme Court of The United States. U.S. Reports: Southeastern Community College v. Davis, 442 U.S. 397. 1978. Periodical. Retrieved from the Library of Congress, www.loc.gov/item/usrep442397/.
3. Association of American Medical Colleges. Special Advisory Panel on Technical Standards for Medical School Admission. Washington, DC: Association of American Medical Colleges; 1979.
4. Liaison Committee on Medical Education. Functions and structures of a Medical School, standards for accreditation of medical education programs leading to the MD Degree. 2019. Retrieved from: lcme.org/publications.
5. McCulley v. The University of Kansas School of Medicine, Case No. 13–3299 (10th Cir. 2014).
6. 42 U.S.C. § 12182(b)(2)(A)(i); 28 CFR § 36.301(a).
7. Marks B, Ailey S. White paper on inclusion of students with disabilities in nursing educational programs for the California committee on the employment of people with disabilities. Chicago: American Association of Colleges of Nursing; 2014. Available at: https://www.aacnnursing.org/Portals/42/AcademicNursing/Tool%20Kits/Student-Disabilities-White-Paper.pdf.
8. Zazove P, Case B, Moreland C, Plegue MA, Hoekstra A, Ouellette A, Sen A, Fetters MD. U.S. medical schools' compliance with the Americans with disabilities act: findings from a national study. Acad Med. 2016;91(7):979–86. https://doi.org/10.1097/ACM.0000000000001087.
9. Kezar LB, Kirschner KL, Clinchot DM, Laird-Metke E, Zazove P, Curry RH. Leading practices and future directions for technical standards in medical education. Acad Med. 2019;94(4):520–7. https://doi.org/10.1097/ACM.0000000000002517.
10. McKee M, Case B, Fausone M, Zazove P, Ouellette A, Fetters MD. Medical schools' willingness to accommodate medical students with sensory and physical disabilities: ethical foundations of a functional challenge to 'organic' technical standards. AMA J Ethics. 2016;18(10):993–1002.
11. Argenyi M. Technical standards and deaf and hard of hearing medical school applicants and students: interrogating sensory capacity and practice capacity. AMA J Ethics. 2016;18(10):1050–9. https://doi.org/10.1001/journalofethics.2016.18.10.sect1-1610.

12. Meeks LM, Poullos P, Swenor BK. Creative approaches to the inclusion of medical students with disabilities. AEM Education and Training. Advance online publication. 2019. https://doi.org/10.1002/aet2.10425.
13. Jauregui J, Strote J, Addison C, Robins L, Shandro J. A novel medical student assistant accommodation model for a medical student with a disability during a required clinical clerkship. AEM Education and Training. Advance online publication. 2019. https://doi.org/10.1002/aet2.10426.
14. Herzer KR. Moving from disability to possibility. JAMA. 2016;316(17):1767–8.
15. Argenyi v. Creighton University, 703 F. 3d 441 (8th Cir. 2013).
16. Featherstone v. Pacific Northwest University of Health Sciences, No. 1:CV-14-3084-SMJ (E.D. Wash. 2014).
17. Palmer College of Chiropractic v. Davenport Civil Rights Commission, 850 NW2d 326. 2014.
18. Okoro CA, Hollis ND, Cyrus AC, Griffin-Blake S. Prevalence of disabilities and health care access by disability status and type among adults—United States, 2016. Morb Mortal Wkly Rep. 2018;67(32):882.
19. Meeks LM, Case B, Herzer K, Plegue M, Swenor BK. Change in prevalence of disabilities and accommodation practices among US medical schools, 2016 vs 2019. JAMA. 2019;322(20):2022–4.
20. Agaronnik ND, Pendo E, Campbell EG, Ressalam J, Iezzoni LI. Knowledge of practicing physicians about their legal obligations when caring for patients with disability. Health Aff. 2019;38(4):545–53.
21. Chapman EN, Kaatz A, Carnes M. Physicians and implicit bias: how doctors may unwittingly perpetuate health care disparities. J Gen Intern Med. 2013;28:1504–10.
22. Peacock G, Iezzoni LI, Harkin TR. Health care for Americans with disabilities—25 years after the ADA. N Engl J Med. 2015;373(10):892–3.
23. Iezzoni LI, Wint AJ, Smeltzer SC, Ecker JL. "How did that happen?" public responses to women with mobility disability during pregnancy. Disabil Health J. 2015;8(3):380–7.
24. Iezzoni LI, Kurtz SG, Rao SR. Trends in mammography over time for women with and without chronic disability. J Women's Health. 2015;24(7):593–601.
25. Wu J, McKee K, Meade M, McKee M, Sen A. Contraceptive use among women with vision or hearing loss: a secondary analysis of the National Survey of Family Growth, 2011–2013. Contraception. 2016;94(4):431.
26. McKee MM, Winters PC, Sen A, Zazove P, Fiscella K. Emergency department utilization among deaf American sign language users. Disability Health J. 2015;8(4):573–8.
27. DeLisa JA, Lindenthal JJ. Commentary: reflections on diversity and inclusion in medical education. Acad Med. 2012;87(11):1461–3.
28. McKee MM, Smith S, Barnett S, Pearson TA. Commentary: what are the benefits of training deaf and hard-of-hearing doctors? Acad Med. 2013;88(2):158–61.
29. Meeks LM, Herzer K, Jain NR. Removing barriers and facilitating access: increasing the number of physicians with disabilities. Acad Med. 2018;93(4):540–3.
30. Meeks LM, Maraki I, Singh S, Curry R. The new normal: global commitments to disability inclusion in health professions. The Lancet. (accepted).
31. Byron M, Cockshott Z, Brownett H, Ramkalawan T. What does "disability" mean for medical students? An exploration of the words medical students associate with the term "disability". Med Educ. 2005;39(2):176–83.
32. Symons AB, Fish R, McGuigan D, Fox J, Akl EA. Development of an instrument to measure medical students' attitudes toward people with disabilities. Intellect Dev Disabil. 2012;50(3):251–60.
33. Ailey SH, Marks B. Technical standards for nursing education programs in the 21st century. Rehabil Nurs. 2017;42(5):245–53. https://doi.org/10.1002/rnj.278.
34. OCR Letter to Appalachian State University, Case No. 11-05-2085; 2006.

Clinical Accommodations and Simulation

10

Christopher J. Moreland, Maureen Fausone, James Cooke,
Christopher McCulloh, Maureen Hillier, Grace C. Clifford,
and Lisa M. Meeks

This chapter is divided into four distinct sections. Section 1 focuses on determining accommodations, section II on accommodating different types of assessments, section III on accommodations common to various categories of disabilities, and section IV on the use of simulation labs for determining effective accommodations or modifications as well as piloting adaptive and assistive technologies.

The original version of this chapter is revised and updated. The correction to this chapter can be found at https://doi.org/10.1007/978-3-030-46187-4_14

C. J. Moreland (✉)
Associate Professor, Department of Medicine; Associate Director Internal Medicine
Residency, Dell Medical School at the University of Texas at Austin, Austin, TX, USA
e-mail: christopher.moreland@austin.utexas.edu

M. Fausone
University of Michigan Medical School, Ann Arbor, MI, USA
e-mail: fausone@umich.edu

J. Cooke
Executive Director, Clinical Simulation Center, Associate Professor, Department of Family
Medicine, University of Michigan Medical School, Ann Arbor, MI, USA
e-mail: cookej@med.umich.edu

C. McCulloh
Department of Pediatric Surgery, Nationwide Children's Hospital, Columbus, OH, USA
e-mail: Christopher.McCulloh@nationwidechildrens.org

M. Hillier
School of Nursing, MGH Institute of Health Professions, Boston, MA, USA
e-mail: mhillier@mghihp.edu

G. C. Clifford
Cleveland State University, Department of Student Affairs, Cleveland, OH, USA
e-mail: G.clifford@csuohio.edu

L. M. Meeks
Assistant Professor, Department of Family Medicine, Director of MDisability Education,
The University of Michigan Medical School, Ann Arbor, MI, USA
e-mail: meeksli@med.umich.edu

Section I. Determining Accommodations

Determining accommodations in health science programs is a highly nuanced process and requires an advanced understanding of health professions education, assistive technology, knowledge of safely modified procedural approaches, and a solid knowledge of the legal requirements for accommodation under the Americans with Disabilities Act. In Chap. 4, a full review of the qualifications for a disability resource professional (DRP) are outlined. This chapter will focus on [1] the process that is required under the law and how to ensure a good faith effort that is taken to investigate potential clinical accommodations, and [2] reasonable accommodations that have been vetted by health science faculty, trainees, and students and that are safely in practice nationwide. The aim of this chapter is to provide the reader with a holistic understanding of the process for determining equal access to the curriculum and the reasonable adjustments that mitigate barriers to learning, assessment, and clinical practice.

Section 504 of the Rehabilitation Act of 1973 [1] requires institutions who receive federal funds to provide reasonable accommodations to students that have disabilities. While reasonable is not outwardly defined, it is generally considered anything that is possible, within reason, that does not constitute a financial hardship for the institution nor fundamentally alter the nature of a program. To determine whether a request is reasonable, institutions appoint a representative to serve as a facilitator of the interactive process. This role is often titled the disability resource professional (DRP). This responsibility may also be relegated to a student affairs officer, many times a Dean of Students or a similar role in education oversight.

The *interactive process* is a term used to describe the interactions that occur when a student discloses a disability and either requests accommodation or expresses their need for an accommodation to mitigate a specific barrier in the environment as outlined in the Association of American Medical Colleges report on Disability (see Fig. 10.1) [2]. The institution or program reviews the student's *functional limitations* (restrictions that prevent one from fully performing an activity) and the activity that is serving as a barrier and the core competencies of the program or a specific course to identify any barriers to the curriculum or clinical experience. *Barriers* may be educational, physical, or attitudinal in nature. Finally, the program, in partnership with the student and faculty/administrators, determines *reasonable accommodations,* modifications, or adjustments that serve as mechanisms for removing or reducing the barrier.

One of the most common examples would be a student with a functional limitation of processing or reading fluency. In this case, items that have a component of time would serve as barriers to the student. In many cases, students would be afforded a percentage of additional time (as an accommodation) to mitigate the barrier caused by the functional limitation. For a person who is a wheelchair user, the functional limitation may be the inability to stand independently. This would cause a barrier in a clinical rotation that was surgical in nature and required the learner to be at standing height to observe a surgical procedure. A standing or hydraulic wheelchair, remote visual access to the operation via a monitor (for students who do

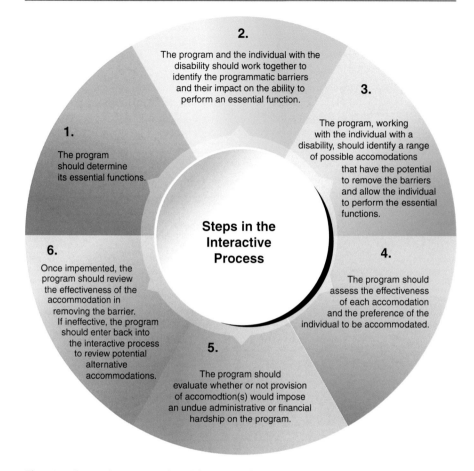

Fig. 10.1 Interactive process adapted from AAMC Report

not need to be intimately involved in the surgery), or the modification of having all parties sit during surgery (something that actually occurs in practice) [3] are all mechanisms of mitigating the barrier to the surgical learning environment. These are modifications of the original approach to the surgical experience and would be formalized through an interactive process that deems these accommodations reasonable.

In order to engage in an informed interactive process, disability resource professionals (DRPs), program administrators, and faculty must have a clear understanding of program requirements including the technical standards and clinical competencies. This requires a well-informed understanding of: the program's structure; the individual student's functional limitations as they occur in learning, clinical, and assessment settings; and current best practices regarding reasonable clinical accommodations, including an understanding of assistive and adaptive technologies [4].

Program Structure

The first step for determining accommodations in a clinical setting is to understand the program structure and requirements. Disability resource professionals (DRPs) or the appointee for disability access must have a clear understanding of the program and the clinical placement sites. DRPs can utilize the questions outlined in the clinical accommodation programmatic query (see Table 10.1) to build their programmatic knowledge.

A seasoned DRP will have a good command of the program's technical standards (see Chap. 9); maintain partnerships with program directors, clinical rotation directors, and clinical coordinators; and will have visited clinical sites for firsthand knowledge of potential barriers that exist for students with each category of disability.

Students' Functional Limitations

Accommodation decisions are not made based on diagnosis, per se. Indeed, within a specific diagnosis, there are a myriad of *functional limitations* that may occur (see Fig. 10.2). That is why the second step for determining reasonable accommodations

Table 10.1 Clinical accommodations programmatic query

Program of study: _____ (i.e., medicine, dentistry, nursing)
Are there a minimum number of clinical hours required to complete the program?
Of these, how many can be met using simulation?
Where are the clinical sites for each clerkship/rotation? (we recommend making a chart that depicts the availability of each clerkship for various blocks or rotations.)
Is each clerkship/rotation available at each site?
Are there physical barriers at specific sites?
Are the clinical sites at a major medical center or community-based hospital?
1. Understand the hours of operation for each site. (critical for students requiring additional time post clinic or shift to complete notes.)
2. What electronic health record (EHR) is used at each site? (important for accessibility to the EHR and compatibility with assistive technology.)
3. What are the distances for each site, and is there a public transportation option available? (important for those who have weekly primary care close to the main school location or who have limitations on driving.)
Have students with disabilities rotated through these sites?
Have there been any positive or negative experiences with students with disabilities?
Are the satellite sites part of the same hospital/educational system, or are they independently operated?
Do your affiliate agreements include a statement about ensuring full access to students with disabilities?
Does the program maintain a liaison at the clinical site who can facilitate or implement approved accommodations?
Do you have a copy of the technical standards (TS) for the program? (see Chap. 9 on TS for a full review of best practices.)
Do the TS contain any outdated or discriminatory language?
Do the TS direct students to the process for disclosing a disability and requesting reasonable accommodations?
DRPs should be aware of the technical standards for all program and any changes needed.

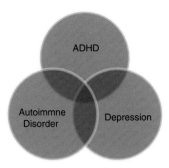

ADHD	Autoimmune Disorder	Depression	Potential Accommodation
Difficulty with focusing	Difficulty with focusing	Difficulty with focusing	Structured setting; checklists for procedures; noise-cancelling headphones while charting
Slowed processing	Slowed Processing	Slowed processing	Additional time to chart; pre-assignment of patients for early preparation; additional time on written examinations
Need to reread material		Need to reread material	Extra time on written assessments; use of text to speech technology for easier processing
	Lethargy	Lethargy	Limited time days (8-10 hours); no overnight call or night float (day time/weekend call instead); use of mobility device for wards
	Need for weekly appointments	Need for weekly appointments	Release from clinicals for weekly appointments
Forgetfulness	Forgetfulness		Checklists

Fig. 10.2 Mapping functional limitations to reasonable accommodations

is to identify the student's functional limitations and any barriers to program access that result from these limitations.

As you can see, many diagnoses share symptoms that lead to similar functional limitations and accommodations; however, barriers, and the accompanying accommodations, are often dependent on the distinct portion of the curriculum (e.g., didactic, clinical, simulation). For example, a student with ADHD whose symptoms result in the functional limitations of slowed processing and inattention may experience several barriers on timed exams in the didactic setting. While this is easily mitigated with extended time on examinations and a reduced distraction location, those same limitations in a clinical setting or simulation lab will not be mitigated through the same accommodations. That is not to say that extra time is always inappropriate in a clinical setting – it is not – but rather, it is less likely that extra time will be the primary accommodation in such cases. In a clinical setting, where a student is responsible for patient care, it is more likely that assistive technology and structural accommodations will be most effective and safe.

Determining Accommodations

After the DRP or appointee understands the program and identifies the functional limitations, it is time to determine reasonable accommodations. This section will review the process (see Fig. 10.3 flow chart), review widely utilized accommodations for specific functional limitations, offer options for assistive technology, and offer resources for gathering additional information.

As outlined by Laird-Metke and colleagues, the process for determining non-standard reasonable accommodations in a clinical setting involves asking four questions (see Box 10.1) [5].

If the request for a specific accommodation does not challenge any of the questions, then it is likely a reasonable request. Some accommodations have been in use at the educational level for over a decade, for example, daytime-weekend call in lieu of overnight call or night float. As well, release from clinic once weekly (for medically necessary care) is a vetted accommodation at many health science campuses; some even proactively set up a system whereby any student can seek care weekly without the need to register their disability with an office [6]. Importantly, accrediting bodies like the Liaison Committee for Medical Education require programs to adhere to a set of elements relevant to these issues. For example, element 12.4 (Student Access to Health Care Services) mandates that "a medical school provides its students with timely access to needed diagnostic, preventive, and therapeutic health services at sites in reasonable proximity to the locations of their required educational experiences and has policies and procedures in place that *permit students to be excused from these experiences to seek needed care*" [7] (emphasis ours; see Chap. 5 for detailed information on psychological disabilities). For a full review of the determination process, we recommend reading Laird-Metke and colleagues' full chapter on the topic [5].

Box 10.1 Four Questions as Proposed by Laird-Metke and Colleagues
- Would the proposed accommodation result in a failure to meet the program's technical standards?
- Would the accommodation legitimately jeopardize patient safety?
- Would the proposed accommodation fundamentally alter the program?
- Would the proposed accommodation pose an undue hardship on the institution? (using institutional vs. programmatic budgets).

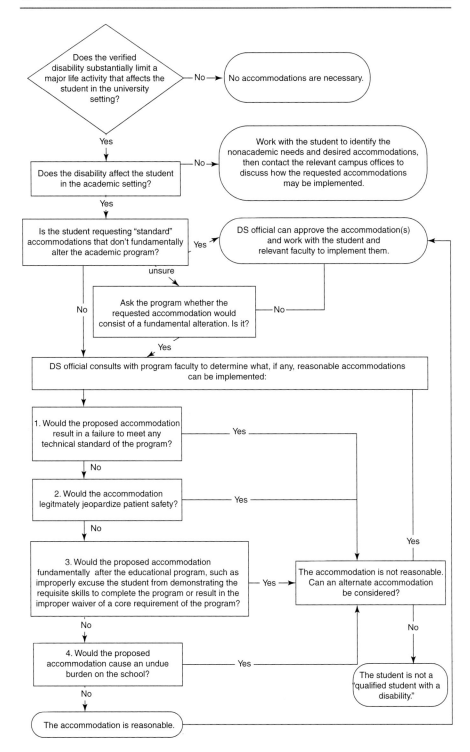

Fig. 10.3 Clinical accommodations flow chart with permission from Meeks/Jain

Table 10.2 Ten initial questions for guiding the student intake

1. How does your disability impact you in daily life (e.g., socially, academically, with work, and with self-care)?
2. How do you mitigate the impact independently and how have you mitigated this impact in an educational setting?
3. What, if anything, exacerbates or worsens your disability?
4. Do you have a history of needing to receive treatment, or do you anticipate needing to receive treatment such that you may need to "step out" of the curriculum at some point to attend to disability-related needs?
5. Have you ever worked in a clinical setting, or do you anticipate additional barriers during the clinical portion of your education? (may need to prompt with example competencies)
6. Have you reviewed the technical standards of the program and the competencies for each rotation? If not, we can do this together to identify any potential barriers.
7. Have you ever used assistive technology to mitigate the impact of your disability on a task (e.g., writing, reading)?
8. Have you ever used adaptive equipment? If the student has never been in a clinical setting it may be helpful to ask how they interact with everyday items (depending on the disability), like listening to music, using the phone, or cooking. This can prompt a discussion about how one might navigate the clinic, for example, a deaf or hard of hearing student using a pager system or a student with mobility disabilities navigating clinical spaces with multiple medical tools or devices
9. Do you take any medication that impacts (positively or negatively) your ability to function (e.g., medication that causes drowsiness or that allows a student to focus for a sustained about of time)?
10. What are your biggest concerns about entering this program?

While the questions in Table 10.2 will not address every need or inquiry regarding a student's disability-related needs, it provides the DRP with a starting point. Remember, most students will lack considerable experience in the clinical setting and will not truly understand all of the potential barriers of this environment. It is incumbent upon the DRP to have an appreciable knowledge of the program, the clinical rotations, and all skills and competencies required for graduation, including any high-stakes examinations.

Section II. Accommodating Assessments

Accommodations are designed to ensure accessibility of the curriculum, including assessments. Health science programs utilize several forms of assessments and all must be considered for accommodation. In most cases, using the flow chart for determining reasonable accommodations (see Fig. 10.2) will result in a well-informed decision about when to accommodate assessments.

Formative and Summative Assessments

Formative assessments are often thought of as having little impact on a student's overall performance and as such may be overlooked in the accommodation process.

On the contrary, formative assessments must be accessible to students and must be appropriately accommodated.

Formative assessments measure clinical skills and knowledge and provide important feedback for students, giving them critical data about their performance and deficits in knowledge or skill. When these assessments are inaccessible, students may not be able to accurately assess their level of competency and will be ill-equipped to refine their skills [8].

Practical Exams (Anatomy Labs)

Health science educators may falsely believe that accommodations are not possible in practical labs. In cases where a student requires extra time, a faculty member may raise concern about scheduling and modified approaches to a practical exam or simulation and/or may raise questions about a fundamental alteration.

Lab practical exams are often administered in groups, whereby the group size is equal to the number of stations. Each student stands at a station and rotates to a new station in a prescribed amount of time, making the addition of extra time complex. Meeks and Jain (2017) noted two distinct approaches to accommodating students in practical exams where extra time was the approved accommodation (see Box 10.2) [9].

Standardized Patient Exams

Objective Structured Clinical Exams (OSCEs) are clinical encounters utilizing standardized patients (trained actors) to measure a student's clinical and communication skills (e.g., taking a history and physical, developing a differential diagnosis) as

---

Box 10.2 Approaches to Accommodating Lab Examinations [9]

Example: A student who receives time and one half with lab stations that allow 5 minutes per station.

Option 1. Students with disabilities requiring extended time rotate through the final testing group of the day with classmates who do not require extended time. At the end of the standard time, all students are dismissed and students requiring extended time receive a 5-minute bathroom break. This break allows all students to exit the lab together, reducing the possible identification of students receiving accommodations. Students with extended time return to the lab after the break and rotate through all stations again to receive their allotted extended time (e.g., 2.5 additional minutes per station).

Option 2. Students with disabilities requiring extended time rotate through the exam as the final group of the day, with all stations timed on the 1.5x schedule (e.g., 7.5 min/station). For students receiving additional extended time (e.g., double time), the procedures in option 1 can be followed to allow the additional 2.5 minutes.

they progress in the program. Programs assert that, because this exercise is meant to mimic a clinical encounter, no accommodations can be provided. Some have even stated, in policy, that students are not accommodated on OSCE exams or in clinical environments. This statement is not in keeping with legal requirements. Programs must engage in an interactive process to determine the reasonable nature of an accommodation. Despite a program's or individual's belief about the reasonableness of an accommodation in any portion of the curriculum, there must be a robust discussion on the matter. As for OSCEs, programs around the country have determined, after careful consideration, that OSCEs should be accommodated when appropriate [10].

For any assessment, the DRP must understand what is being measured in order to determine if an accommodation fundamentally alters the program. In the case of OSCEs, which are timed, a program must determine whether or not time is a variable being assessed. In their article on the topic, Meeks and Jain outline the items a DRP must understand in order to determine reasonable accommodations in a clinical setting (see Box 10.3).

Most OSCEs are broken down into discrete parts, all measuring different aspects of a clinical encounter. For example, most students, regardless of program, begin by reading some general information about the standardized patient before entering the room. These might be referred to as door notes, as they were historically the notes in the patient's file that was placed in the door, ready for the provider to enter the room. This task requires reading and processing. What is being measured, if anything, is the ability to take the chief complaint of the patient and any test results and use this information to aid in developing a differential diagnosis. For a student with a disability, the act of reading and processing the information may require accommodation to fully access the materials. In an outpatient clinic setting, this activity may take a provider 2 minutes, or up to 5 minutes, depending on the complexity of the case. This portion of an OSCE is almost always amenable to reasonable accommodation.

The second part of any OSCE is the patient encounter. In this section, the student performs a history and physical on the patient, develops a differential

---

Box 10.3 Considerations to Determine Appropriate Nature of Accommodations
1. *What will the student be required to do?*
2. *Does it consist of several discrete tasks?*
3. *Is the exam timed, and if so, how much time is given for each part of the exam?*
4. *What is the exam designed to assess, and how is performance measured?*
5. *How important is timing to the purpose of the assessment? Is the goal to assess a student's performance in assessing the patient or the quality of her clinical skills within a specific time?*

diagnosis and treatment or follow-up plan, and communicates this to the patient. Technical skills, patient interviewing technique, and communication are being assessed during this portion of the OSCE. Accommodations on this section might be reasonable and necessary for students with specific disabilities including (but not limited to) physical disabilities and chronic health disabilities and the need for specialized equipment; sensory disabilities and the need for an interpreter; a communication disability (e.g., stuttering, expressive language disorder) and the need for additional time or a checklist of the steps for patient interaction as a prompt; and a student with a visual disability who utilizes assistive technology or a scribe.

The final portion of an OSCE usually involves a written assessment of the interaction, called SOAP (Subjective Objective Assessment Plan) notes. This section may also have an oral presentation of the patient. This portion does not have a patient interaction and instead draws on the student's ability to crystallize and organize their thoughts in writing or orally. For a student with a disability that causes functional limitations in the ability to write (or type) or to communicate using spoken language, this section may require accommodation.

Each portion of the OSCE should be evaluated independently for accommodation. Not all disability types will require accommodation on all portions of the exam. Take for example, a student with dyslexia, whose functional limitation includes slowed reading speed and comprehension (see Example 10.1).

In this scenario we might gather that Chris has more flexibility with time on the wards and in outpatient clinics. This 2–3 minute of additional time allow Chris to fully comprehend the patient's history and presenting issues. In a time-restricted setting, Chris is missing critical portions of the patient information. Let's do an analysis of Chris's disability, the functional limitations, the barrier to the OSCE, and what is being measured in that portion of the OSCE (see Box 10.4).

Now let's take a step back. Does Chris's disability and the associated functional limitations lead to any additional barriers for the two remaining portions of the OSCE, the patient interaction and the reporting out of the patient, orally or in SOAP

Example 10.1 Student with Dyslexia and OSCE Accommodations
Chris is a student with dyslexia. His clinical skills are outstanding and his patients really enjoy working with him. His "bedside manner" has been highly scored on educators' evaluations. Chris consistently performs well in the clinic and on the wards; however, when taking a high-stakes OSCE, Chris gets anxious as he knows there is limited time to read the door notes. Rushing to read the door notes keeps Chris from truly absorbing the patient history, which has cost valuable points in his OSCE assessments. The faculty cannot figure out why Chris performs so well in the clinical setting, while underperforming on the OSCEs.

> **Box 10.4 Analysis of Disability, Limitation, and Barrier to OSCE**
> *Disability:* Dyslexia.
> *Functional limitation:* Reduced reading fluency and difficulty with comprehension (the need to reread material for comprehension).
> *Barrier:* Time to read and process the door notes.
> *What is being measured:* Ability to synthesize material and begin formulating a differential diagnosis.
> *Appropriate and reasonable accommodation*: Extra time on door notes portion of exam.

notes? It is likely that Chris does not experience barriers in the remaining two portions of the OSCE. If additional time is a vetted accommodation for door notes, when appropriate and necessary for full access, then Chris would receive some measure of extended time on this portion only. The time extended is usually a function of the degree of impairment. Let's say Chris's reading fluency is in the 5th percentile when compared to his peers. That level of impairment is quite significant and would likely warrant double time on this portion of the OSCE. In real numbers, the door notes portion of an OSCE runs between 2 and 5 minutes. Therefore, Chris would be provided between 4 and 10 minutes for the door notes. As you can see in this example, Chris is receiving accommodations on the OSCE but only for one distinct portion as this is only a portion that is a barrier to him.

Planning for the OSCEs

When communicating approved accommodations, DRPs should communicate each portion of the exam and the accommodations within that discrete portion (see Example 10.2).

For the OSCEs, the DRP should meet with the faculty lead for these activities, along with important stakeholders, including the dean of assessment and the director of simulation. Once they have answered the questions in Box 10.3, the group, in consultation with the DRP, can determine if there are accommodations that are worthy of vetting for all future use. The OSCEs are often scheduled a year in advance. As part of the required preplanning, programs should assume students with disabilities will be in their courses and that at least one student will require accommodation on the OSCE exam. Costs associated with alternative OSCE administration, additional standardized patient (SP) costs, and time for faculty/staff are considered costs associated with accommodation and should therefore be covered by the disability office or centralized funding structure (see Chap. 4 for a full discussion of funding structure).

Example 10.2 OSCE Letter of Accommodation

Dear [insert faculty member name].

I am writing with regard to [insert student name] who is a student in the School of Medicine and is registered with [insert office name]. Based on a thorough review of this student's disability needs and supporting documentation, [name of office] recommends the following reasonable accommodations for the OSCE EXAMS:

- During the Patient Encounter: [insert approved accommodation] on the student/patient encounter inside the clinical examination room with the patient.
- After the Patient Encounter: [insert approved accommodation] on the written clinical reasoning exercises or written clinical note-writing exercises outside of the clinical examination room.
- After the Patient Encounter: [insert approved accommodation] on the oral case presentations to faculty or peers inside or outside of the clinical examination room.

These accommodations are recommended after thoughtful analysis of the student's disability-related needs, the University's programs and curricula, and the University's legal obligations under the Americans with Disabilities Act, as amended (ADA AA), and Section 504 of the Rehabilitation Act.

The intent of all reasonable accommodations is to provide students with disabilities equal opportunity, not to lessen or undermine academic standards or course requirements.

It is the responsibility of the student to request academic accommodations as needed in a reasonable and timely manner. The coordination of in-class accommodations is a shared responsibility between the instructor and the student. [Name of office] suggests that all details (e.g., exam length, start times, format changes, locations) be decided on as early as possible and recorded in writing.

After discussing with the student, please do not hesitate to contact me at [insert contact information] for further questions. I look forward to collaborating with you to ensure at students with disabilities have equal access to our program.

Section III. Standard Reasonable Accommodations for Health Science Programs

While the following section offers accommodations by disability type, this is for the ease of the reader. As mentioned previously, diagnosis alone does not fully dictate the range of accommodations that might be appropriate for a student. Additionally, students' needs should be individually evaluated to determine reasonable, appropriate, and effective accommodations within the context of the specific program. The following are offered as some examples of accommodations put into place in clinical settings. This is *not an exhaustive list,* and the absence of an accommodation in this section does not suggest that it is unreasonable or unsafe.

Attention Deficit Hyperactivity Disorder (ADHD)

Students with ADHD may find it difficult to compensate for the large volume of information that must be reviewed and retained in health science programs. Those with a hyperactive clinical feature may, unintentionally, struggle with professionalism expectations in these new, high-stakes settings. For these students, accommodations offer a removal of barriers in the clinical settings. In addition to accommodations, students can employ strategies that mitigate the impact of their ADHD on functioning in a clinical setting.

Accommodations for ADHD include written, specific objectives, or clinical expectations for a rotation, broken down by the week, with weekly feedback on progress. Feedback is best when it is delivered orally and in writing and presented as objectives met and objectives unmet with specific instruction on the steps needed in order to meet a learning objective or clinical competency [11]. Depending on the level of the student, checklists may be appropriate as a means of developmental scaffolding, while the student learns a new skill or process. Developing relationships with new teams and learning new systems or expectations, especially if these are only implied, are difficult for students with ADHD. Therefore, minimizing change, when possible and appropriate, can help the student develop structure and allow time for the development of relationships and adjustment to both written and unwritten curriculum. For example, a student may, as an accommodation, be placed at the same hospital for multiple clerkships or rotations to avoid the added cognitive work of learning a new system (e.g., electronic medical system, protocol for students, culture). In one successful case of a resident physician with ADHD, the team utilized many of the aforementioned accommodations and added a written task list to be generated by the resident in the operating room, a checklist for managing logistics of the daily case load, typed preoperative evaluations to assist with presentation of patient, and time allowance by faculty for the resident's personal healthcare appointments [12].

Autism Spectrum Disorder

Students with autism spectrum disorder (ASD) generally find the didactic portion of a clinical program unchallenging. The high intelligence, acumen for memorization, and, for many, the interest in science synergize toward high academic achievement in this domain. However, the social deficits inherent in ASD can make it challenging on the wards, when working with teams, and providing patient care. The need for professional and clear communication is heightened in a clinical setting and is a measured competency of the curriculum, making communication a high-stakes skill. In addition to the social skills needed on the wards, the wards also present challenges for overstimulation. Bright lights, alarms, multiple people talking, and the general bustle of a hospital ward can prove detrimental to the sensory system of a student with ASD. Even the most general, yet unwritten, task like determining how to take a bathroom break (e.g., How do I communicate this need explicitly to the team?) or how to address a senior on the wards when different teams have different expectations and levels of formality (e.g., Is it ok to address them by their first name, or do I use titles?) can seem monumental for someone with ASD trying to navigate this new environment. A misstep or two in communication may damage relationships with team members or lead to a student developing a poor reputation with the team. Finally, the many changes of environments, teams, protocols, and electronic health records (EHRs) between rotations can drain an already taxed executive functioning system. Given the probable landmines of the clinical setting for students with ASD, DRPs should work proactively to remove barriers and provide adequate structure that assist in removing barriers for the student [13]. These may include, where appropriate, rotating the student through the same health system, or even the same hospital, to minimize multiple transitions; pre-rotating through each ward, with time allotted to discuss the expectations of the rotation, how a student will be evaluated, to orient the student to the EHR and to clearly spell out some of the items of the unwritten curriculum; or allowing the student to use noise-cancelling headphones during non-patient contact events like charting or reading to reduce overall stimulation. Rotating a student through a less intense environment is always a reasonable accommodation, if the student agrees and when an alternative is available. For example, if an emergency department rotation can occur at a Level 1 trauma hospital or a rural community hospital, it is likely less chaotic and overstimulating to rotate at the community hospital. Decompressing clinical rotations, in the beginning of the clinical year, may also help the student acclimate to the clinical environment in a slower, more systematic manner, similar to systematic desensitization.

Assigning a mentor, especially at the beginning of the clinical year, may improve the transition for students with ASD. A mentor can provide in vivo feedback to the student helping the student learn to self-correct, and breaking down social exchanges or protocol to help the student understand interactions in the clinical setting [14].

Chronic Health Disabilities

Many students come to health science education due to their own personal experiences with health concerns. Their experiences inform the work and add to their understanding of what it means to be a patient. For these students, the barriers encountered are often related to physical functional limitations, joint and/or chronic pain, fatigue, or gastrointestinal disruption [15]. For many students with chronic health disabilities, the intermittent and uncertain expression of the symptoms makes accommodation difficult. Therefore, the most effective means of accommodation are often proactive accommodations (e.g., standardized schedule, avoidance of triggering activities or events, decompression of clinical rotations) that are designed to avoid a flare of symptoms (i.e., an abrupt occurrence) coupled with planned options for reactive accommodations (e.g., leave of absence, makeup exam, additional absences) should a flare of symptoms occur. Additionally, providing ample time for medical appointments and appropriate self-care is an additional necessity for those who have chronic conditions. At times, a student may need to attend physical, occupational, or other therapy weekly; this should be discussed in advance with the DRP and the program administration to find a reasonable adjustment that balances the student's need to attend to their personal health needs with the least amount of disruption to the learning environment. Meeks and Jain (2018) recommend the following considerations for working with students with chronic health disabilities [2]. When appropriate, build in a hard stop time for clinical rotations and maintain a consistent schedule (e.g., no night float or 24-hour call). In some cases, students will need to work weekends to ensure clinical hour requirements are met. This is fine as long as the schedule is consistent, allowing the student to arrange and maintain adequate sleep and other medical needs. Minimize commute time. For students with chronic health issues, long commutes can place additional wear and tear on systems and for those commuting by public transportation, weakened immune systems can be further exposed to the elements and infectious sources. Placements should also be close to any treatment site or healthcare provider. Being sensitive to the rotation schedule serves as a proactive deterrent to flares. When possible, arrange the rotation schedule such that highly physical and demanding rotations are spaced out. If this is not possible, decompressing the curriculum (in programs that are not lockstep) is very helpful and allows the student to complete a year of clinical work over 18–24 months. Students should take time to adjust their own schedules outside of any accommodation by avoiding flares in their off time and, when in a flare, adjusting their schedule to allow for an on-time arrival in the clinic. For some, this will require an hour or more at home for self-care in the morning, necessitating an earlier wake up time [15].

Proactive measures are very helpful in minimizing flares and avoiding a compounding of symptoms or impact on overall health; however, they will not address all the barriers. As noted above, some accommodations are reactive, meaning they occur in the event of a flare. This might include an alternative assessment in the simulation lab, if the original assessment occurred during a flare and a student was unable to perform the competency at that time. When a student is experiencing pain or an exacerbation of symptoms that reduce mobility and dexterity, DRPs can work with programs to utilize the simulation lab and adaptive equipment. Retail outlets like Amazon offer multiple options to fit the exact needs of the student and program. Compression gloves can also be helpful and reduce pain associated with joint swelling, allowing a student to perform tasks that require the use of hands.

Reasonable accommodations, including assistive technology, will need to be put into place when barriers to the curriculum or clinical environment exist. The use of

Fig. 10.4 CellScope

technology, already in use by clinicians, like a CellScope™ or PanOptic™ by Welch Allyn (see Figs. 10.4 and 10.5, respectively), afford the student a wider grip, putting less continuous pressure on the joints. These devices also afford those with physical or visual disabilities a larger view that can be realized at a distance.

Students with ongoing joint pain may also require speech-to-text technology for charting or recording a patient history. Multiple devices exists to assist with this need, the most popular being Dragon Medical by Nuance™ (https://www.nuance.com/healthcare/provider-solutions/speech-recognition.html). When evaluating a student's needs, it may be helpful to tap into your campus's expertise. For example, if you have an occupational therapy program, this is an excellent opportunity to partner with them on modifications for the work environment. Occupational therapists have the latest information about adapt environments to allow individuals to continue work and activities of daily living.

Fig. 10.5 PanOptic
Welch Allyn

Some students with chronic conditions will have difficulty ambulating (e.g., Ehlers-Danlos syndrome, postural orthostatic tachycardia syndrome – POTS). For these students, and for students who can ambulate but tire easily, mobility devices may be necessary. It is best if the DRP discusses the potential need for this mobility aid in the beginning of a program to prepare the student for the eventual need on the wards. Given the tight space of clinical environments, smaller/compact scooters are a good choice. This allows the student to continue with the pace and demands of a busy ward. More information about mobility disability can be found in the section on *physical disabilities*.

Deaf and Hard of Hearing

This section will focus on the range of accommodations available for deaf and hard of hearing (DHH) students and resident physicians in health professional education. First, stakeholders should recognize that members of the DHH community vary widely in their communication preferences and modalities, using any combination of spoken, signed, visual, and auditory means of communicating. Selecting and implementing effective accommodations should begin with identifying one's existing communication preferences and experiences; the DHH person and accommodation team should also consider future educational experiences which may not have a parallel in the DHH person's past background (e.g., working in the operating room). We also note that the accommodations below are not an exhaustive list nor is any single accommodation necessarily used singly throughout one's training and career; in one study, only 15 of 56 respondents reported using only one accommodation over time [16]. As noted in Fig. 10.6, each accommodation tends to be used in a variety of situations. Table 10.3 identifies a number of potential accommodations, their common situational applications, and commonly recognized certifications or qualifications for each, if applicable.

Real-Time Captioning
Real-time captioning, sometimes referred to as computer-assisted real-time transliteration (CART), is a technique in which a trained captionist listens to speakers and transmits the spoken word in text form to be read by the receiver(s), usually on a tablet or laptop's screen. The text can be displayed on a large screen for a larger audience. Captioners utilize specialized equipment (akin to court reporting stenographer machines) and software including specialized terminology dictionaries, as well as specialized training in court reporting methods to carry out this task. Depending on location and the task, captioners can function on-site in the same room, or remotely, working via Internet- or telephone-enabled microphone and audio transmission.

Transcripts often can be provided to the student in electronic or hard copy format.

Situations in which 56 Respondents Reported Using Current Accommodations in a Survey of U.S. Deaf and Hard-of-Hearing Trainees and Physicians, 2011

Accommodation*	Lectures	Small-group discussion	Clinic-based patient care	Hospital-based patient care	Other clinical tasks (e.g., phone calls, rounds)	Teaching	Research	Administration
Real-time captioning	11	6	1	0	0	0	0	0
Signed interpretation	7	8	5	6	4	3	1	3
Oral interpretation	2	4	4	3	4	1	0	0
Note-taking services	9	2	0	0	0	0	0	0
Modified surgical mask	0	0	2	1	0	0	0	0
Amplified or modified stethoscope	3	3	36	28	8	5	0	0
Auditory, nonclinical equipment	14	6	2	3	3	2	1	1
Total	46	29	50	41	19	11	2	4

* This table reports responses for the accommodation options provided by the authors on the survey instrument. Participants could also include free-text responses in an "Other" category (data not shown). Free-text responses included video relay service, e-mail, cell phone text messaging, amplified telephone, and hearing aids.

Fig. 10.6 Situations in which deaf and hard of hearing physicians and medical students have used certain accommodations

Table 10.3 Common accommodations for deaf and hard of hearing healthcare students and trainees; education settings in which they are often used; and formal certifications or qualifications that may be held by providers of each accommodation

Accommodation	Education setting in which it is often used	Commonly recognized certifications or qualifications
Computer-assisted real-time transcription (CART)	Lectures, didactic sessions, small-group meetings. Has been used in the operating room	Certification through the National Court Reporters Association (NCRA), which can include certified Realtime Reporter (CRR), certified Realtime Captioner (CRC)
Note-taking services	Didactic	None
Signed language and/or oral interpretation services	Wide range: Can include large-group lectures and one-on-one interactions	Certifications exist at national (e.g., registry of interpreters for the deaf – RID) and state levels (e.g., Board for the Evaluation of interpreters – BEI)
Cued English transliterator services	Wide range: Can include large-group lectures and one-on-one interactions	Certification is provided by the testing, evaluation, and certification unit (TECUnit)
Transparent surgical masks	Clinical settings requiring droplet or respiratory isolation, or sterile precautions for procedures	Food and Drug Administration approval may be supportive

Note-Taking Services

Due to the speed of information in classically unidirectional education settings (e.g., lectures), DHH students may experience challenges in taking notes while simultaneously absorbing visual information. Note-taking services allow for another person to take notes so that the DHH student can focus on the interpreter and the visual items in the course.

Telephone Adaptations

Telephones are ubiquitous throughout the healthcare system, with long-standing reliance on handset telephones and alphanumeric pagers, which are still in use. Some adaptations for DHH individuals focus on modifying the telephone itself (e.g., phones with amplification capabilities, connecting phones to headsets by cord or Bluetooth), while DHH healthcare providers utilize pagers with amplification or vibration options. Relatively new communications like text messaging benefit DHH healthcare providers and facilitate communication with the team, although HIPAA compliance remains an important parameter. Finally, video relay services (VRS) or video remote interpreting (VRI) offers DHH clinicians the option of a communicating via a remote/video signed language platform while the receiver is able to utilize a telephone. Interpreters assist the provider. They may or may not vocalize for the DHH provider, while also providing sign language to interpretation for the DHH clinician via video feed.

Auditory, Nonclinical Equipment

Healthcare students and trainees who are DHH use a broad variety of adaptive technology to support communication. Assistive listening devices (ALDs), such as hearing aids or bone or cochlear implant processors, can be programmed to adapt to a variety of inputs, with some allowing modifications to switch from noisy to quiet rooms, or even adjusting for varying needs in frequency. Directional microphones can be small, even in the unassuming shape of a pen, able to be pointed at a single speaker to provide direct auditory input to a person's ALD. Omnidirectional microphones may be more effective when participating in group discussions, since they capture sound from a 360-degree range. Lapel microphones can also be worn by people who will be the sole speakers, or speaking the majority of the time; examples would include lecturers or attending surgeons in the operating room. The transmission of sound to one's ALD can be by direct line of sight (e.g., via laser), by Bluetooth connection, or even via directly wired connection. As with other technologies, information security must be assessed, since some wireless technologies' signals may be captured by those other than the intended recipient.

While ALDs can provide excellent amplification, it is critical to note that amplification alone may not benefit many DHH people. Thus, assistive listening devices may provide situation-specific benefits for some people, while others may benefit more broadly from them. DHH students and trainees in healthcare who use ALDs often benefit from working closely with an audiologist to adapt their ALD programs to particular clinical situations and even to stethoscope use. Readers should also note that many DHH people do not use ALDs for a variety of reason and rely more fully on sight and other senses.

Stethoscopes and Ultrasound

Traditional stethoscopes and their alternatives are a big topic of inquiry for DHH students seeking to enter the healthcare professions. Early electronic versions focused on amplification, followed by adaptive connections to hearing aids and cochlear implants. Amplification alone, however, does not benefit many DHH people who use auditory stethoscopes, since they need auditory clarity as well. New versions present visual options as well, innovative methodologies that have benefited healthcare professionals with and without hearing loss. Figure 10.7 shows some examples of these stethoscopes. We also note that the rapid advent of ultrasound as an important and increasingly evidence-based diagnostic and procedural imaging modality can benefit all patients and clinicians, whether or not the student or clinician is DHH.

Specialized Clinical Considerations

Operating Rooms

Participants, in collaboration with the CART captioner, will need to assess the OR to determine optimal placement to ensure the DHH person can see the surgical team, patient, and text without violating sterility. Options have included transmitting text to a screen in a transparent sterile sleeve or to a large mounted monitor. The transmitting microphone must be placed with consideration; one solution has been to ask the primary surgeon (or other designated educator) to wear the microphone under their sterile gown.

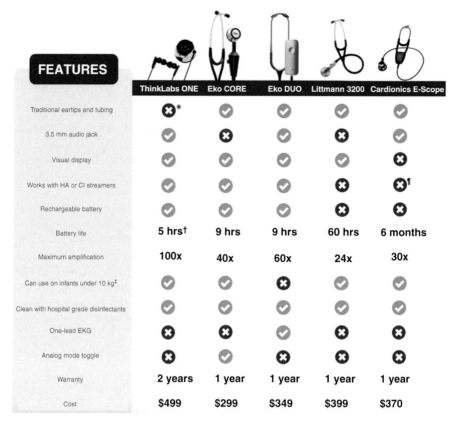

FEATURES	ThinkLabs ONE	Eko CORE	Eko DUO	Littmann 3200	Cardionics E-Scope
Traditional eartips and tubing	✗*	✓	✓	✓	✓
3.5 mm audio jack	✓	✗	✓	✗	✓
Visual display	✓	✓	✓	✓	✗
Works with HA or CI streamers	✓	✓	✓	✗	✗¶
Rechargeable battery	✓	✓	✓	✗	✗
Battery life	5 hrs†	9 hrs	9 hrs	60 hrs	6 months
Maximum amplification	100x	40x	60x	24x	30x
Can use on infants under 10 kg‡	✓	✓	✗	✓	✓
Clean with hospital grade disinfectants	✓	✓	✓	✓	✓
One-lead EKG	✗	✗	✓	✗	✗
Analog mode toggle	✗	✓	✗	✗	✗
Warranty	2 years	1 year	1 year	1 year	1 year
Cost	$499	$299	$349	$399	$370

Fig. 10.7 Examples of electronic stethoscopes with amplification and/or visual representation capabilities. (Copied with permission from https://www.amphl.org/comparison-table)

Interpretation
While most people imagine interpreting as occurring with signed languages, some may be surprised by the variety of interpreting structures.

Oral Interpreters
Oral interpreters replicate through their own voiceless mouth movements what others say, so that the DHH person can focus on one source – the interpreter – without scanning the room to identify who in a group is speaking and thus losing critical visual information in the process. In this mode, oral interpreters may paraphrase or substitute certain words in order to visually articulate terms more clearly or to maintain pace with the group, without changing the message itself. They often will use gestures to support the oral message, such as identifying who is speaking.

There are fewer certifications available to identify those who have demonstrated qualifications via testing. Formerly, the Registry of Interpreters for the Deaf (RID) provided such testing, and the Texas Board for Evaluation of Interpreters (BEI) maintains a current test and certification [17–18]. Formal training programs focused on oral interpreters are rare.

Signed Language Interpreters

Signed language interpreters convey messages from a spoken language (e.g., English) to a signed language (e.g., American Sign Language – ASL), and the reverse; we note that many DHH people choose to speak English, while many others do not. Those interpreters may also use a modified sign system, such as signed English which more closely follows the grammatical structure of spoken English while using signs from ASL.

Multiple state- and national-level certifications exist for generalist signed language interpreters [17–19]. Training programs for general interpreting range from 2-year to 4-year degree programs. Only in the last few years have certifications been developed specifically for signed language interpreters who specialize in the healthcare environment [18–19]. Most medical interpreting training still occurs in the form of discrete workshops or targeted conference formats.

Cued English Transliterators

The process of using a combination of handshapes, positions around the face and neck, and mouth movements to represent the phonological sounds produced in English (or any spoken language). National certification is offered by the Testing, Evaluation, and Certification Unit (TECUnit) [20].

Specialized Clinical Settings

Operating Room

The OR team should consider where interpreters can be best positioned so that they can hear conversations while being seen clearly by the DHH person. Where should interpreters stand? They might stand behind the primary surgeon so that the DHH person can easily shift gaze from the surgeon to the interpreter, or they might rotate around the room while remaining mindful of sterile spaces. Interpreters have at times scrubbed in with the operating team, including the DHH student, so that they could stand at the operating table; this maximizes the student's sightline as well as the interpreter's ability to hear the operating team's conversations.

Traditional surgical masks block visible mouth movements, blocking a DHH individual that lip reads from fully accessing communication. To address this barrier, the interpreters for one resident physician in a surgical specialty used Stryker orthopedic hood masks, which have a clear face shield so that people can view the mouth movements and expressions of the clinical team and interpreters [21]. While effective, a Stryker hood mask is cumbersome. Thankfully, new clear-window surgical masks have been developed that can provide a means of eliminating this barrier. Masks can be used along with other accommodations or techniques to reduce barriers in the OR. A successful case study for one DHH medical student utilized a combination of accommodations including oral interpreters using transparent-window surgical masks, a lapel microphone worn by the attending surgeon to facilitate CART that was then transmitted via an online platform to an iPad visible to the student, and a reference chart of the most common drugs used in anesthesia for confirmation of the pharmacological name, given that many drug names sound alike and/or use similar mouth movements.[1]

Sensitive Physical Examinations

During sensitive examinations, interpreters can position themselves in ways that are respectful to patient privacy, such as behind a curtain or by turning their backs, so that the DHH person can see the interpreter while the interpreter cannot see the patient.

Critical Care Situations

In clinically emergent situations (e.g., a "code blue"), healthcare professionals collaborate and communicate rapidly to provide swift clinical interventions for the decompensating patient. While these situations are often intimidating to the student or trainee, they can be even more so to the untrained student who is DHH or the interpreter working with that student. Reassuringly, multiple DHH healthcare professionals and interpreters have learned to collaborate effectively in such situations, with their communicative and physical adaptations revolving around the DHH person's role [22]. Whether that role is checking a pulse, delivering chest compressions, or leading the code team, interpreters have identified ways to maintain clear sightlines and manage the flood of input and allow the DHH student, trainee, or professional to conduct their role within that situation. As with any student, new interpreters should be allowed opportunities to observe critical care situations, participate in simulated encounters, and debrief as needed with the rest of the team to develop their familiarity with such situations.

Functional Considerations

In certain situations, interpreters may need to work in pairs so that they can switch off regularly. This is because of the physical and cognitive fatigue associated with the physical signing as well as the equally, if not more, strenuous cognitive process of converting from one language and modality (e.g., spoken English) to another (e.g., signed language). This challenge is frequently compounded within healthcare training environments loaded with complex terminology, rapid speakers resulting in lack of clarity, and a wide variety of English accents. Those situations may include rounding on the wards, lectures, small-group discussions, or multiple one-on-one interactions over several hours (such as in clinic).

Designated Interpreters

As more DHH people enter healthcare professional school the demand for interpretation services will increase. With that demand, some DHH people and naturally choose to establish and maintain long-standing professional relationships, in which

---

[1] Safe N Clear Communicator Mask. https://www.safenclear.com/

the interpreter works primarily with that healthcare professional or student in their current role, such as working with a deaf student throughout nursing or medical school. An interpreter serving in this longitudinal role can be considered a designated interpreter (DI), a concept first introduced in 2008 [21]. Since then, others have explored the role and training required for DIs in healthcare settings, with ongoing training and safety precautions similar to those in other healthcare professional positions.

Preparing Interpreters

Interpreters provide the best service when they are able to prepare in advance and when they are a welcomed and valued member of the team. Supervisors may have questions about how the interpreter will engage with the team and may have questions about patient privacy. Introducing the interpreter to the team early allows for the exchange of information and can allow time for the interpreter to educate the program about etiquette for working with a DHH student. In addition to facilitating relationships and comfort, some specialties contain vocabulary that does not have a formal or even a common parallel term in sign language. Therefore, it is critical for the interpreter and provider to develop a common language for use in the clinical setting. To help prepare the interpreter and identify language that may need to be developed into sign language, programs should provide access to all curricular items including presentation slides, handouts, the names of speakers or team members, clinical orientation materials, syllabi, and textbooks. The terminology and concepts from those materials can enhance providers' abilities to convey language accurately and efficiently, whether interpreting or captioning.

Modified Surgical Masks

For those who rely on speechreading and/or other facial cues, surgical masks can disrupt effective communication. Over the past two decades, various forms of surgical masks with transparent windows have been developed, with at least one having obtained US Food and Drug Administration (FDA) approval for use and another undergoing FDA review.[1-2] While studies are in process to evaluate their impact on communication, anecdotal feedback from DHH students suggests that they have positive impact for both DHH and hearing users.

Learning Disabilities

Learning disabilities are discussed in great deal in Chap. 7 and are considered fairly easy to accommodate in the didactic setting. In the clinical setting; however, DRPs and faculty may mistakenly believe that there are no reasonable options to consider accommodation when direct patient care is part of the experience.

For students with specific learning disabilities, there exist potential functional limitations that will impact their ability to perform in the clinical setting. Building on Table 10.4 (drawn from Chap. 7), we offer some of the most common and reasonable accommodations in use across a myriad of health science programs.

---

[2] The Clear Mask. https://www.theclearmask.com/product

Table 10.4 Specific learning disorders and potential accommodations (adapted from Chap. 7)

Specific learning disorder	Possible barriers to learning	Potential functional limitations	Potential accommodations in clinical setting
With impairment in reading (dyslexia)	Comprehension, phonetic decoding, word recognition, and reading fluency	Slower reading rate Deficits in comprehension and retention Deficits in spelling Deficits in discerning main ideas Slower written expression	Pre-assignment of patients to allow for focused preparation/reading Use of word for spell check prior to entering notes in the electronic health record Use of speech-to-text technology
With impairment in math (dyscalculia)	Understanding mathematical concepts and using math skills to solve problems	Slower reading/processing Deficits in understanding symbols and alignment of numbers Deficits in understanding spatial concepts and math reasoning	Use of words/terms/symbols legend when using symbols as primary source of information. Use of calculator or automated conversion tool when calculating doses of medication
With impairment in written expression (dysgraphia)	Letter formation, spacing, organization of the page, or speed of putting written information on paper; writing is laborious and messy	Deficits in motor coordination Barriers to effective note-taking, essay composition, and in-class writing	Use of speech-to-text technology to dictate notes Use of livescribe smart pen or apple smart watch to record and dictate provider/patient interactions [24, 26]

Clerkship Placements

When working with students with learning disabilities, a few of the barriers may be related to the type of EHR utilized at the clinical site. For those who require text-to-speech or speech-to-text technology, it is necessary to ensure that those technologies are EHR-compatible. When a particular EHR is vetted and a student becomes comfortable with the system, it can be helpful to try and rotate the student through sites that utilize the same EHR. The barrier to the site, for an EHR that is incompatible with the reading or dictation software, is palpably present and must not be ignored.

Learning disabilities, and the impact on the student, vary significantly depending on the demands of the program and a student's compensatory skills and self-accommodation through the use of assistive technology. For some students, the use of a text-to-speech program for reading articles or books will suffice in ensuring that have equal access to the program, while for others, a decompression of clinical rotations will be necessary (if possible per program structure) to afford enough time to read, study, and execute new skills in a clinical setting. This can be accomplished in a few ways, in approaches similar to those for other disability categories described earlier in Chap. 10. First, the student can complete clinical rotations in double the time, for example, taking 2 years to finish 1 year of clinical rotations for medical school, (this is not possible in lockstep programs, so it would not apply to most nursing students) with clinical rotations spread over more weeks (e.g., an 8-week rotation becomes a 16-week rotation). Multiple iterations of this decompression are possible depending on the structure of the program. Alternatively, a student in a flexible curriculum can complete one rotation then take the next one off to prepare, read, and study for the following rotation and accompanying examinations. As always, the specific schedule must be individualized to the program and to the student.

Low Vision

Students with low vision successfully complete clinical programs through a myriad of self and school-based accommodations. The most common accommodations are the use of assistive technology (e.g., screen reader, zoom text,[3] CCTV). A CCTV (closed-circuit television) is a free-standing magnification device that provides magnification and high-definition color and contrast. The user can place any material under the magnification lens to magnify the item. Contrast can also be changed to black with white lettering and newer CCTVs have built-in text-to-speech capabilities.

For some individuals with low vision, a simple and portable magnification device will suffice and can easily be transported to the anatomy lab, skills lab, and other locations for optimal use.

Other portable magnification devices are also helpful and can be more readily affixed to a table (anatomy lab) when needed.

Finally, personal, handheld magnification devices can be folded and contained in a student's white coat or pocket and used as needed in outpatient and inpatient settings.

Most computer systems maintain a zoom feature and will allow the user to enlarge font to a size that is legible. When the size of the font, using the zoom feature, is insufficient, an easy way to address this is through the use of a larger monitor. Monitors are relatively inexpensive and with newer privacy screens can be used in a busy clinic setting without the fear of exposing sensitive patient health information. Larger screens can be located in a student or clinician lounge area and identified as an accessible workstation and reserved for the student when they are on rotation. A larger monitor also has value that does not require any significant IT intervention. It is portable and can be moved from one rotation to the next.

While most of the aforementioned items can be used in inpatient and outpatient clinical settings, some other devices are more optimal for sterile environments.

---

[3] https://www.zoomtext.com

Surgeons have been using surgical loupes for ages to help magnify small structures. Students with low vision can also use this tool to enhance their vision in the operating room or during surgical skills lab or surgery. These look like regular glasses with tiny microscopes on each lens and come in multiple levels of magnification.

For some students with visual disabilities, notating the patient interaction while reading the monitors and EHR quickly will be difficult. For these students, a text-to-speech technology that reads out a patient's history is critical. In the absence of this, a scribe system may be the most effective accommodation? Scribes, frequently utilized in environments like emergency rooms, are very beneficial for students with low vision. Scribes do not perform the duties of a student or physician; they serve as facilitators, gathering and documenting information for the student.

Working with an individual with low vision requires that the DRP be very creative in their approach to accommodations. One student, classified as legally blind, could not see the almost clear suture materials in the surgical rotation. Creatively, they used the blood of the patient as a stain to enable the student to see the material and to keep everything in the sterile field. Thinking outside the box and using existing materials, perhaps in a different way than originally planned, can often solve what may seem like complex barriers. DRPs should talk to the students about how they navigate their everyday life and work with the student to develop creative and reasonable solutions to access.

Mobility and Physical Disabilities

This section will cover accommodations for people with mobility-related physical disabilities, including those who use wheelchairs, scooters, crutches, or other mobility aid devices. This section is structured by first addressing accommodations generalizable to many locations, followed by discussion of situation-specific accommodations, including the classroom, outpatient clinics, the inpatient ward, emergency departments, and operating rooms. We also describe some specific adaptive equipment.

Accommodations Generalizable to Multiple Environments

Computer Workstations

Computer workstations should be available with clearance for wheelchairs or other mobility devices. The workstation's location should be consistent with those of other students or trainees and not be isolated from other members of the team, so as to facilitate collaborative clinical education and team integration. Ergonomic keyboards and trackballs or trackpad mice should be provided as options for students with limited hand or arm function. Dictation software, including microphones, should also be available for students with limited typing ability. Importantly, students and trainees must receive proper training on the relevant assistive software. In some cases, scribes may be an appropriate accommodation for trainees and students with limited hand function. In these cases, the scribe would work in the same manner in which they work with clinicians without disabilities, providing the relevant noting and documenting of patient information without any clinical input.

Clinical Supplies

Standard supplies like tongue depressors, gauze, and tape should be kept in drawers or cabinets that are accessible from a seated position and can be opened using handles that do not require significant dexterity. If this type of storage is not available, necessary supplies should be stored on countertops for easier access. It is worth discussing whether it is worth adjusting all exam rooms for access. Those without physical disabilities will still be able to locate and easily utilize the equipment, making the experience accessible for all.

Building Access

Entrance to the building must be accessible. This means that the building contains a zero entry (a single-level entrance without stairs), a ramp, or an elevator to the entrance. Power doors must be available for building entry. Buildings that have accessible entrances only in the rear of the building are discouraged. Having a student or trainee enter from the rear of a building or a loading dock sends a very clear message about the value of persons who use assistive devices. Any medical building should be accessible to patients and providers with disabilities. If a hospital or outpatient clinic is physically inaccessible or requires a learner to utilize alternative entryways, the program should address upgrades on the inaccessible building while locating an alternative placement for the student.

Environment-Specific Accommodations

Classroom and Small-Group Settings

Many students with disabilities will have had extensive experience learning in the classroom setting before entering health professional school, given the common didactic and/or small-group organization of preclinical undergraduate education. As a result, students can often speak knowledgeably about necessary accommodations, although those who have recently acquired a disability may be less aware of available accommodations, emphasizing the need for informed DRPs (as noted in earlier sections).

Classroom Access for Wheelchairs

Classrooms should be on the ground floor or accessible by ramp or elevator. Doors to classrooms should have lever or "U"-shaped handles for easier access, as opposed to spherical doorknobs which can be more challenging to grasp. Classes should only be held on floors that maintain accessible restrooms.

> **Box 10.5. Proper Height and Width for Wheelchair Access**
> Tables or desks should be height adjustable and must be 27 inches or higher to accommodate wheelchair users. Further, 30 inches of clearance is required between the legs of the table.

Classroom Space for Wheelchairs or Other Mobility Devices

Classroom workspaces should be accessible to wheelchairs and other mobility devices. Group work tables should have appropriate clearance from the floor and between table legs to accommodate mobility devices (see Box 10.5[4]).

Lab benches should have a roll-under area with a table top at a seated height so as to be accessible to a manual wheelchair user. To allow for full participation, lecture halls should have space for students using mobility devices at both the front and back of the lecture hall. Again, lecture halls that only allow for entry via the alternative route should be amended so that all members of a class can enter and exit in the same manner. Tabletops in cadaver labs should also have adjustable height tables.

Writing Surface Access

When a student has to sit in a nonstandard seat, in a lecture hall for example, they may not have a writing surface. In these cases, programs should provide a table with appropriate clearance for the student.

Restrooms

Accessible restrooms need to be available in the building where classes are held within reasonable distance from classrooms. Restrooms should have at least one wheelchair accessible stall with grab bars. A single-occupancy restroom may be preferable for some students who require more privacy for their personal needs. Programs should be careful to ensure that the accessible restroom is located on the same floor as the classroom. For students who are wheelchair users, the need to exit the classroom, which in itself may take considerable navigation, only to have to wait for an elevator to go to another floor and repeat in reverse could take considerable time away from the learning experience.

Breaks

Students with limited mobility should be provided breaks that include appropriate time for travel to and from various buildings or classrooms and for using the restroom. Consideration should also be given to the challenges presented when large lecture halls empty at once and bathrooms are filled. Students may need access to a separate bathroom or extra time allotted during breaks. Some people may also require breaks for changes in positioning for pressure relief.

---

[4] These guidelines are in line with the Americans With Disabilities guidelines for small businesses http://www.ada.gov/smbustxt.htm and may not apply to international regulations.

Outpatient Clinics

One aspect of clinical education that is challenging for all students is rapid cycling among widely varying teams and physical environments. This change in setting poses additional challenges for students with disabilities. Placing students in clinics well-equipped to meet their needs can further optimize the educational experiences of students with disabilities as well as their capacity to contribute to teams' patient care flow with less distraction and greater ease.

Clinics' Physical Access

Outpatient clinics should have accessible parking available to students and proximity to accessible public transit. Clinic entrances should be zero entry and have ramp and elevator access.

Patient Rooms

Students must be able to access their patients; therefore, doors to patient rooms must be able to close even if the patient and student both use mobility devices. There may be additional personnel also present, making the room crowded. Removing unnecessary furniture (e.g., chairs and stools) from patient rooms can increase the amount of available space and the ease with which students and patients with mobility devices can navigate the room.

Bed Controls

Controls used to adjust the height and angle of the patient examination table must be accessible to students with limited mobility including students who are not able to use foot pedals. Bed controls should be sensitive enough to operate without extensive force or dexterity.

Hand Hygiene

Sinks and paper towels should be accessible from a mobility device and should not be controlled exclusively by foot pedals. Hand sanitizer should be kept in a location that can be reached from a seated position. If needed, place an additional hand sanitizer directly below the original at a height aligned with a seated position.

Communicating Needs to Team Members

Other members of the care team can be instrumental in providing an accessible work environment for students with limited mobility. With the support of educational and clinic leadership, students with disabilities should make team members aware of their needs so that rooms and workstations are maintained in the configuration that is most accessible for the student with a disability and not rearranged. Identified work stations with adaptive or assistive technology should be kept clear and available for the student. Team members may also assist students with limited hand function in preparing equipment for office-based procedures by opening packages for supplies like lubricant, speculum examination, or wound care, and placing them in a sterile location accessible to the student. Communicating how this equipment is made most accessible to the student will be helpful in ensuring the student's and patient's needs are met.

Inpatient Setting

Most healthcare students will spend a majority of their training working in an inpatient (hospital) setting. Access to inpatient floors is not typically an issue for students with limited mobility, as floors are often designed to provide easy access for patients' needs, such as beds and supply carts. One particular concern for students with limited mobility can arise when hospitals have various sections of the hospital built at different times, with different designs. For example, some older hospitals may have stairs connecting two adjacent buildings. In these cases, people may need to take alternative routes, adding considerable transit time to their navigation between the buildings.

Team Rooms

Team rooms can often be cramped with enough furniture and tables to accommodate a large number of students and resident physicians. Supervisors must ensure that there is adequate space for those who use a mobility device to move around the room, including enough space near the doors for entry and exit and access to any refrigerators, or beverage machines.

Patient Rooms

Similar to the outpatient setting, patient rooms may not have enough space for the student to easily move around the room and perform an exam. Patient rooms should be arranged such that the students with disability is able to fully access the patient and the equipment in the room. This may require moving bedside tables, chairs, and other objects that are in the path of providing care.

Team Rounds

Students with limited mobility should be given a position within the team on rounds to allow them to see and hear during team discussions. Rounding should also proceed using accessible means of transit between one area and another. Teams should avoid using stairs and other inaccessible routes to ensure students with limited mobility are included in the full experience. It is important to remember that not every mobility disability is visible. It may be helpful to survey the team members to see if all members of the team are able to navigate stairs, even if it appears that no one has limitations.

Call Rooms

Call rooms should be accessible to students who use mobility devices. This requires some call rooms to have a bed (not a bunkbed) at a lower height accessible to a wheelchair user. Students that require a special mattress for pressure relief or who require assistance to get in and out of bed may find that the planning required to use call rooms is particularly difficult. In these instances, it may be reasonable to allow an equivalent number of hours worked during the day to be substituted for a night shift, or other equivalent shift modifications.

Inpatient Medical Emergencies ("Code Blue")

In the hospital, a medical emergency in which a patient requires immediate intervention is often referred to as a code blue in professional jargon. For providers with limited mobility who have the responsibility of carrying the code pager (the means by which specific people are notified of inpatient medical emergencies), the speed of arriving to a code on a different floor may be limited by the elevator. For this reason, redundancy should be built into the response to codes so that if a provider with limited mobility is delayed in responding to the code by circumstances outside their control, another individual qualified to run the code has already arrived on site in the interim. Many hospitals provide layers of relative redundancy in code blue roles, such as with Rapid Response Teams or by engaging emergency department personnel in code blue situations. Some hospitals additionally have special keys or badge encodings that allow members of a code team to obtain priority access to elevators during a code. This access should be afforded to all providers with limited mobility. Trainees with disabilities should consider ahead of time what their role(s) would be in a code (e.g., code team leader, timer/recorder, drawing up medications, airway management), depending on their level of function.

Emergency Departments

The Emergency Department (ED) is a hectic environment that presents a unique challenge to students with limited mobility. Despite this there are several ED physicians who are wheelchair users and navigating the space can be quite easy with attention to access and preplanning.

Patient Rooms

Patient rooms may be large with adequate space for both a patient and provider using mobility equipment; however in, some facilities and during busier times, patients may be on a stretcher in a hallway or separated from the patient next to them by a curtain and a very small amount of space that is prohibitive for assistive equipment.

Trauma Management

Students with limited mobility should identify themselves to the team and discuss any needs with team members before or at the start of a shift, helping to ensure the students full engagement and active contribution to the team. To develop familiarity with trauma procedures, many hospitals and medical schools have simulation labs which can be a good place for students to determine their needs. They can also visit the trauma bays when a trauma is not actively underway to identify locations of equipment, sinks, protective gear, and other necessary items. Some required items may be wall-mounted, creating a difficult reach by a team member who is a wheelchair user necessitating assistance from others. Because trauma bay equipment cannot always be controlled (e.g., patients arriving via ambulance with equipment from outside the hospital), this presents a unique challenge. Preplanning can help anticipate these challenges.

Examination Rooms

The approach with here is similar to rounding on inpatient wards, unnecessary chairs, equipment, and gurneys should be removed to allow enough space for the student to examine the patient. Patients who are on a stretcher in the hallway should be moved to a standard exam room to allow for a complete examination that is respectful of patient privacy, while allowing the examiner the necessary space and equipment for their success.

Sinks/Hand Hygiene

Sinks should be at an accessible height and hand sanitizer should be available at the height of a seated position and be readily accessible. It is important to remember that not all pathogens are destroyed by sanitizers (e.g., *Clostridium difficile* and other spore-based organisms). Therefore, an accessible sink must be within a reasonable distance from all examination areas. Some students with mobility disabilities will utilize standing or hydraulic lift wheelchairs that allow them to access sinks. In the absence of this, program leadership should work with the hospital to ensure an accessible sink and process for remaining sanitary.

Operating Rooms

Administrators and educators often express concern about accommodating students with disabilities in surgical rotations. Students with mobility disabilities can be easily accommodated on surgical rotations, in fact there are multiple successful practicing surgeons who utilize wheelchairs [23–24]. Below, we discuss methods for fully incorporating students with mobility disabilities in the operating room (OR), including how to maintain sterile precautions.

Preparing for the OR

It is essential to work with necessary OR and surgical staff prior to the student's first trip to an active operating room to ensure a smooth entry into the rotation. ORs are supervised by an OR charge nurse, and we advise a pre-rotation meeting to review the accommodation and modification details and to discuss how department faculty work together to provide an accessible experience.

During this initial meeting, we recommend discussing expectations and the details of the student's functional limitations and mechanisms for a meaningful educational experience; we do not recommend simply having the student observe and/or waiving requirements. There is sufficient anecdotal evidence to suggest that a student with a mobility disability can reasonably engage in surgical rotations for a meaningful educational experience; therefore, we encourage programs to be creative in their approaches to equal access and think broadly about how to ensure inclusion.

To facilitate creative thinking, we recommend scheduling a time (as early in advance as possible) to visit an empty operating room or simulation center OR with a team that includes a clinical preceptor, an OR nurse and/or scrub tech and the simulation center director to practice the modified approach to procedures and skills (e.g., scrubbing in) without the pressures and complexity of an ongoing surgical procedure. This dry run will ensure that the student the student has full access and a set protocol for scrubbing in and addressing required surgical skills competencies. As well, this preplanning and review reduces concerns that might otherwise be expressed by the OR team. When the procedures have been tested and reviewed in a simulated or practice setting, supervisory staff can attest to the student's ability to achieve and maintain sterility. OR management should be sure to notify relevant senior OR staff, techs, and nurses of the results of this dry run, so that the student will be able to start immediately on the first day and experience a full and accessible rotation.

Before each surgical case, students should have the opportunity to enter the OR and communicate with the circulator and scrub technician, regarding any items needed for gowning (e.g., differently sized gowns, drapes, gloves, sheets) and the student's scrubbing process (if it is the first time working with that particular team). This approach allows the student to introduce themselves to the OR staff and avoid unexpected questions about approved nonstandard procedures. A printed overview of the steps for scrubbing and any modified equipment may be helpful, or a memo circulated with OR management signatures can go a long way in reducing any unnecessary concern or exclusion of the student. This form or memo can reside at the main OR desk, and another copy can be placed into the rooms when needed for easy access. This nonstandard procedural review is also helpful when new team members arrive. They can quickly review the process and aid in scrub-in or gowning when needed.

The Sterile Field

Maintaining the sterile field for surgical procedures is critical to avoiding infectious complications for surgical procedures. This is one of the common concerns of those unfamiliar with surgeons and students who use mobility devices. Mobility equipment (e.g., wheelchairs) can be brought into the operating room and sterilized as outlined below. The sterile field ranges from the chest to the waist on the front of clinicians' and students' bodies only; their backs are not sterile. Thus, the device's wheels contacting the floor do not break the sterile field. The chair itself can be protected with sterile covers used for other equipment like x-ray machines and CT scanners so that the armrests and joystick are sterile while being used. In Boxes 10.6A, 10.6B, and 10.6C, we describe several approaches to sterilizing wheelchairs, as well as scrubbing into operations safely.

Scrubbing for the OR

Products, such as Avagard, are designed as a dry scrub. These are approved by the FDA as a sterile scrub, even for the first case of the day. We recommend that, for the first scrub, students with mobility disabilities get assistance with a nail curette to remove all dirt underneath the nails, followed by a wet scrub to remove any particles or dirt that may be on the hands. This is particularly important for manual wheelchair users who may accumulate more dirt than power users. The wet scrub will be followed by a dry scrub, such as Avagard; therefore the wet scrub does not need to be completely sterile and the provider may lean against the edge of the sink for stability as needed. The hands and arms should then be fully dried before proceeding to the dry scrub. Some hospitals have dispensers that are touchless and only require the user to place their hands underneath, while a sensor automatically dispenses gel into the user's hand. More common, however, is a wall mount connected to a foot pump that manually dispenses gel. When a foot pump is the mechanism in place, the Avagard dispenser can be easily lifted out of its wall mount by an assistant who can press the small circular piece on the back to manually dispense the gel; it is not locked or snapped into place, but rather sits cradled in the wall mount.

To eliminate the potential for contamination after application, it is often easier to dispense the Avagard into the palm of the hand without applying it and then enter the operating room. Once in the OR near the sterile table, apply the Avagard to the hands and arms. This also allows the user the use of at least one hand to open doors and press buttons as needed. This can be helpful in ORs that do not have powered doors.

Box 10.6A Scrub-in Procedure Option
- Put the armrests of the chair up and turn the electric chair off.
- Wash with Avagard.
- Put large gown on.
- Put gloves on.
- Drape a sterile sheet behind the student's back.
- Put a sterile X-ray cassette drape on the wheelchair's non-control arm.
- Put a sterile C-arm drape on the wheelchair's control arm.
- Put the arms down and turn the chair on using sterile gloves.
- The author can then drive the chair, press buttons, and touch the armrests with sterile gloves.

Box 10.6B Scrubbing for the OR: An Approach for Those Utilizing a Standing Wheelchair While Maintaining Sterility of the Controls and Armrests
- Pre-wash using a wet scrub as described above, and dry hands and arms.
- Place the chair into the standing position with all required operative equipment in place (e.g., belts, straps, loupes, headlamps).
- Scrub with Avagard.
- Put on a 2XL or 3XL gown, wrapping the entire gown around the user, armrests, and chair.
- Don gloves.
- Wrap a ¾ sheet around the waist/chair/back, like a skirt. (A ½ sheet is often not large enough for this.)
- Pass a non-penetrating clamp to the circulator, who clamps the ¾ sheet in the back, covering the back of the chair as well.
- Use a second clamp to clamp the Velcro on the neck to keep it from popping open as the provider moves around against a rigid standing chair.

Box 10.6C Scrubbing for the OR: An Approach for Some Manual Wheelchair Users
- Pre-wash using a wet scrub.
- Dispense Avagard into the palm of one hand, but do not apply yet.
- If possible, use the other hand to navigate into the OR; alternatively, request a circulating nurse or tech to push the student near the operative field or have someone remove the Avagard dispenser from the wall and dispense it directly into the student's hands while the student is near the scrub tech.
- Put on gown and gloves.
- Wrap a 2XL or 3XL gown around the student's lap and legs and the back of the chair, and clamp it at the back of the chair.
- The student will need to have the circulator then push them to the operative field, and may require a platform to be elevated to the level of the field. Any movement during the procedure will require the circulator to push the student.

Observing in the OR

Observing operations is key to the effective clinical learning and formative experience. Context and the optimal use of available equipment, including mobility devices and OR service and equipment, will impact the student's access to adequate observation of the operation.

Mobility Devices, Such as Wheelchairs

Standing-power wheelchairs (which can move the user into a near-standing position) allow students to be at the same height as their colleagues and get closer to the surgical field. Students' arms are also free to assist with the surgery. Power chairs with a hydraulic elevate function (i.e., raising the seat) also increase a student's height and enable viewing of the surgical field. Students using elevate-function chairs may need to approach the surgical field from their own side rather than facing forward, given that they remain seated, which may limit students' reach. For students who use these devices and can stand independently with intermittent breaks, a stool can be placed in the operating room to allow the student to rest as needed.

Operating Room Equipment

For operation in deep body cavities where it may be difficult for a seated student to see, a head camera may be worn by the surgeon, with video streamed to OR monitors. If head cameras are not available, cameras mounted on lights over the operative field can provide an alternative means of streaming to OR monitors.

Operative Case Selection

Operative teams or suites with high volumes of laparoscopic or robotic cases may be more easily adapted for viewing. Operative specialties in which surgeons frequently operate from a seated position (e.g., hand, plastic, or vascular surgery) may provide seated students the easiest access to the surgical field. Importantly, students' educational experience should not be sacrificed because of accommodations. In the past, some institutions have chosen a relatively simple option: having the student watch the same type of laparoscopic case for 2 months, rather than varying the exposure to a range of procedures and conditions. This must be avoided, because it severely impacts the student's clinical education and will have a lasting impact on their view of surgery as it ultimately relates to their clinical practice. As always, it remains key to work with the student to find a clinical site and team placement to optimize their education. Early engagement of key OR staff and the student to facilitate an open dialogue is essential to ensure the student's success.

Student Involvement in Decision-Making

Faculty should involve students with mobility impairments in the operation to their maximum physical capacity. Students who use wheelchairs or other mobility devices and do not have limited hand function should be able to perform surgical skills as long as adequate access to the surgical field has been provided. Students with limited fine motor skills may still be able to assist in retracting, suctioning, or driving the laparoscopic camera. Students with limited hand strength may still be able to assist in cutting, suturing, or knot tying. When invited to participate, and when asked how they may best participate, students can assist surgeons in determining solutions.

Adaptive Equipment

With technology rapidly advancing, there are many options available to students with disabilities in terms of adaptive equipment for physical examinations.

Veterinary Stethoscope
Veterinarians use stethoscopes with a longer tube between the head of the stethoscope in the earpieces. For students whose mobility limits their ability to get physically close to the patient, this extra length can be useful in ensuring the stethoscope head and can reach the heart of the patient while the student is wearing the stethoscope.

Electronic Stethoscope
Multiple variations on electronic stethoscopes are available on the market. Some models include Bluetooth technology, eliminating the need to be physically next to the patient to auscultate.

Camera-Based Devices
Portable cameras that send images remotely to devices can be used to examine skin, perform oral exams, or facilitate otoscopic examinations.

Adapting Standard Devices
Examples of standard clinical examination devices include reflex hammers and tuning forks. Foam or other materials can be used to increase the size of handles on standard physical exam equipment for easier use by students with limited hand function.

Designing Novel Equipment
Many people with disabilities are accustomed to designing and making their own equipment, when equipment is needed for their purposes but does not exist. Connecting students with disabilities with an occupational therapist or rehabilitative engineering department can be helpful if students would like to design and build their own equipment.

Limited Hand Functioning (LHF)
Students with LHF may face additional barriers beyond those described above. For students whose hand function limits their ability to gather the information necessary to make a clinical assessment, an intermediary may be a reasonable and necessary accommodation [25]. Intermediaries are nonmedical professionals who assist in gathering information. Intermediaries may help with routine tasks involved in information gathering without providing clinical input, like placing the stethoscope on a patient [25].

For invasive procedures not deemed essential functions, students may demonstrate competence by demonstrating the procedure in a simulation lab or directing a nonmedical professional to perform the procedure. For students who may be able to perform invasive procedures and require some extra practice, a simulation center will be an important tool in allowing students to experiment with different techniques or equipment before performing the procedure on a patient.

Below we have listed common procedures organized by setting. For students with limited hand function who intend to perform these procedures, we have documented strategies that may eliminate some barriers to performing these procedures on patients. In general, giving students with disabilities the opportunity to simulate the procedure, practice multiple times, and pilot different approaches can help students with disabilities be prepared to practice these procedures in the clinical setting.

Outpatient

Pelvic Exams and Pap Smears

Pap smears are part of routine preventive screening. Pelvic examinations, while no longer recommended for routine screening, still have an important role in diagnosis and management for certain situations [26]. Speculum insertion is technically difficult and requires the user to hold the speculum with one hand. Metal specula require the user to tighten a screw to hold the speculum in place once it is inserted. Plastic specula, however, do not have a screw and may be easier to use for students with limited dexterity. For those who have difficulty maintaining finger extension to perform the pelvic exam, a small splint that leaves the fingertip exposed may be used.

Rectal Examinations

Similar to pelvic exams, rectal exams are no longer recommended for routine screening [27] yet are critical for certain clinical conditions. For students with limited mobility, the positioning of the patient can make this exam significantly easier or more difficult. Whenever possible, arranging a standardized patient session or time in the simulation lab will be helpful so the student has opportunities to practice via different approaches. Again, for students who have difficulty maintaining finger extension, a low-profile splint can be used.

Arthrocenteses and Joint Injections

While placement of the needle tip into the joint space (such as the knee or shoulder) requires very little strength, precision is important. Pushing or pulling the syringe's plunger does require some amount of strength and is frequently awkward for the typical student without disabilities as well. Allowing students time to practice with the equipment before performing the procedure will be helpful.

Inpatient

Peripheral Intravenous (PIV) Catheters

Because PIV catheters are a relatively benign procedure, training programs sometimes arrange opportunities for students to practice on each other. Performing this procedure requires significant precision and dexterity, with minimal strength. In the inpatient setting, the members of the team most likely to insert PIVs are nurses. Students with limited hand function may find the packaging, syringes, and dressing more challenging to manage than the actual insertion of the PIV. In this case, a third party can assist with tasks which are necessary to the procedure but not central, like opening packaging. Peripheral blood draws involves skills very similar to the PIV above, but with somewhat less dexterity required.

Intubation

Intubating a patient is a time-sensitive maneuver that requires specific positioning. Students who use wheelchairs may need the head of the table lowered (or may need to raise their wheelchair, if it has that functionality). Positioning the patient at the very top of the table will assist the student in getting as close as possible to the patient. Depending upon the clinical setting in which the intubation is being performed, the bed may need to be moved to allow increased access to the space above the head of the bed. Independent intubation requires two hands, one to maneuver the laryngoscope and the other to insert the endotracheal tube (ETT). Proper use of the laryngoscope requires the application of some force. If managing the laryngoscope and ETT one-handed is challenging, a trained third party (e.g., respiratory therapist, nurse anesthetist, anesthesiologist) may manage the laryngoscope while the student visualizes the vocal cords and places the ETT. A bougie may make placement of the ETT easier if the angle of approach or precision of movements is challenging.

Suturing

Suturing is a common skill in the operating room and emergency department. Suturing with a needle driver requires some strength and dexterity. Practicing in the simulation center can give students time to become familiar with the equipment and the best way to use it given their hand function. Students with hand weakness may find some needle drivers easier to use than others or may require assistance loading the needle onto the needle driver. Tying knots may also be challenging for students with limited hand function. Practicing knot-tying technique with rope rather than suture may help students learn the process of tying without the added challenge of handling thin suture. Texturized surgical gloves (e.g., microgrip gloves) may also help students with limited grasp handle suture materials more easily.

Intermediaries

Intermediaries are individuals who play specific roles in supporting healthcare students, trainees, and practicing clinicians with disabilities to complete their tasks, under the direction of students with disabilities. Intermediaries do not perform clinical responsibilities or make clinical judgements for the students. Intermediaries work within the healthcare system and therefore are subject to the same occupational risks and exposures as any other healthcare worker. For this reason, it is critically important that intermediaries receive the same preventive and management training for healthcare, exposures, and injuries.

Psychological Disabilities

Psychological disabilities and the resulting functional limitations often overlap with other disabilities. Specific psychological disabilities like depression may impact two students in very different ways. We will not review psychological disability in this chapter; for a full review of mental health and disability in health science programs, see Chap. 5.

Section IV Simulation for Assessment and Determining Accommodations

Simulation is an educational technique that replaces or amplifies real-world experiences with guided experiences that evoke substantial aspects of the real world in a fully interactive manner [28]. A guided experience, commonly called debriefing, is the postsimulation formal, collaborative, reflective process of simulation where participants explore their emotions, question, reflect, and provide feedback to one another [29]; a majority of the critical learning takes place in this session as participants put together the pieces of the simulation puzzle and work to understand the meaning of each piece in contributing to the larger picture [30–31].

Simulations are mostly formative in nature and designed as a low-stakes, nongraded learning environment where mistakes are explicitly allowed as there is no risk of patient harm; this has been shown to improve medical resident performance [32]. Simulation calls upon students to enhance the application of course content, use information in new situations, and draw connections, thereby promoting higher levels of thinking and long-term retention [33].

In contrast to a standard textbook, the utilization of experiential learning through simulation is especially compelling because it is relevant to the student. The regular use of simulation in curriculum can help diverse learners, including those who rely on visual, auditory and kinesthetic modes of information processing. Simulation activities and exercises afford an opportunity for learners to apply what they have learned within a regulated, controlled environment and create another way in which students can connect with the information meaningfully [34–35].

Advantages of simulation include experiential learning, deliberate practice, and delivery of immediate feedback [36]. As a highly interactive, multisensory teaching modality, simulation can appeal to all learners, including those with identified disabilities (Table 10.5). Indeed, simulation holds unique promise for students with disabilities as a mechanism to develop alternative techniques, practice using assistive or adaptive equipment prior to starting clinical rotations, and even function as an alternative means of assessment.

Simulation as a Means of Assessment

In some instances, simulation has been used as an effective means of high-stakes assessment, such as a clinical skills or competency checkoff. The use of a

Table 10.5 Advantages of a simulation curriculum for students with disabilities

Anxiety	Practice clinical approaches and techniques prior to patient interaction
Dexterity	Facilitate practice, refinement, or adaptation of techniques Become accustomed to using potential adaptive equipment before seeing patients
Mobility	Determine any need for space and adaptive equipment prior to entering a clinical rotation
Anxiety/autism spectrum	Rehearse patient interactions while receiving feedback in a low-stakes, low-pressure environment Rehearse team-building and communication with other team members
Processing	Rehearse physical maneuvers to build muscle memory
Executive functioning	Develop organizational methods and approaches to patient care

simulation lab allows the program, using accommodation, to evaluate the skills of a student who would not otherwise be able to display competency during clinical skill checkoffs. When considering an accommodation, student disability resource professionals (DRP) should, as part of the interactive process, review accreditation guidelines if any on the use of simulation for learning and assessment, state board requirements, and clerkship organization guidance.

Simulation to Determine Accommodation

When working with health science students, a simulated clinical environment can be very useful for determining the impact of a disability on performance of specific tasks, such as physical examination or procedural skills. A controlled scenario can be presented to the student to determine *how* the disability impacts access and how accommodations to the environment or assistive devices reduce barriers, allowing students to perform clinical tasks, for example, the assessment of students' needs, or the efficacy of a particular accommodation in reducing barriers for a health professional with mobility or physical limitation. In the simulated setting, a common clinical scenario can be developed to allow the student to work through a complete clinical encounter (e.g., a history and physical). Unlike the actual clinical environment, conducting this examination in a simulation allows the scenario to be paused at any point to record, discuss, refine, and fully explore potential accommodations. New or modified scenarios can also be used to address new or anticipated challenges as the student rotates through the clinical portion of their education. Simulation could also be used as a dress rehearsal, empowering both the healthcare provider and the student with the disability to become comfortable with the accommodation before full clinical implementation. The ability to witness the procedure or approach in a simulated setting is often the catalyst for reducing fear or anxiety associated with an alternative or accommodated approach.

Simulation can be used to explore, in a more meaningful way, the impact of specific disability-related limitations on a student's functioning within the clinical setting. For students with limited hand function, low vision or hearing, chronic health conditions, psychological, learning disabilities, or complex combinations can be explored and understood, and specific accommodations developed and tested in a simulation setting. Depending on the condition, disabilities may also vary over time adding to the complexity of the assessment and determination of best accommodations. In addition, simulation is an excellent mechanism for understanding the impact *variability* of a disability causes and the efficacy of potential accommodations under those conditions.

Simulation as Design Lab

The integration of accommodation devices and/or technologies with healthcare systems must be considered when designing an accommodation. In some cases, accommodations have not yet been developed or adapted to meet the individual needs of health professionals with disabilities. For example, there is no available suite of electronic medical record-integrated wireless cameras to assist those with mobility or hand dexterity disabilities in performing a physical examination. In this case, the simulation lab can be utilized as a design lab for development or adaptation of technologies.

Students may also require specialized or adapted access to information from existing clinical information systems such as cardiac monitor readings, vital sign displays, radiology images, electronic medical record information, or any number of other visual or auditory data systems as part of their clinical or educational duties. The use of multiple medical information, diagnostic and treatment systems should be considered as part of a comprehensive accommodation plan along with the integration of adaptive technologies with existing systems. The simulation center provides an excellent and innovative opportunity to assure both efficacy and integration prior to clinical experiences.

Access to Expertise

Simulation centers are home to a host of technology and education experts who assist medical educators in the design of medical and surgical simulations. This specialty expertise can be an invaluable resource for those assessing and designing accommodations for those with disabilities. Specifically, simulation operations specialists, or sim techs, can work with DRPs to understand and consider the multiple technology-intensive systems, including patient simulators, surgical simulators, task trainers, audiovisual systems, simulated EHRs, simulated medications, and medical equipment. They can also be consulted on the design, testing, or integration of an accommodation with existing healthcare systems and can provide expertise in scenario development to assess the efficacy and integration of assistive technologies. Medical education experts, who often provide guidance on curriculum development, scenario design, and student assessment, could also consult on design and/ or assessment modalities with the goal of providing a comprehensive understanding of individual needs, efficacy, and integration of accommodations.

Value Proposition

When considering the effort, expertise, and resources utilized in developing a suite of accommodations without full understanding of a disability, as well as the enormous time and effort involved in developing post hoc accommodations when disabilities are not addressed prior to the clinical experience, the value of high-fidelity simulation for the assessing the impact of a disability along with the design, testing, and integration of accommodations cannot be underestimated. Rapidly developing an accommodation plan after a need is identified, without the input of expertise and value of fully developing, testing, and refining can lead to the use of poorly fitting accommodations. There can also be issues in the attempt to integrate the adaptation of standard accommodations not well suited or translatable to healthcare. Understanding a student's individual need, in the greater context of the specialty, is essential to developing appropriate tools to address accommodation needs. Integrating simulation faculty and staff helps to educate those within educational programs on best methods for full inclusion of students with specific disabilities and to appropriately train the next generation of healthcare professionals.

Simulation is a viable pedagogical platform to meet student learning needs by transferring learning acquisition into action in a team-based, low-stakes environment where patient risk is not a concern. Skill mastery requires more than a single learning experience; simulation allows for repetition while also motivating students in the realm of patient care. Despite the numerous advantages of the incorporation of simulation labs in health science education, there are still some barriers to accessibility for students with disabilities that should be considered and addressed (Table 10.6).

Table 10.6 Barriers to accessibility of a simulation curriculum

Barrier	Disability consideration	Strategy
Physical layout	Mobility impairments may require a review of the space to determine if adaptive equipment may be required	Review the space with the disability resource professional prior to the start of the academic year
Software compatibility with assistive technology	Students with reading, processing, or visual impairments may utilize screen readers or other assistive software in conjunction with standard hospital software or EHRs [37]	Consult with your disability professional regarding commonly utilized assistive technology/software [38] Ensure computers are equipped with the necessary assistive technology prior to the start of the course Avoid purchasing new software or technology without checking accessibility
Visual/oral communication	Deaf or hard of hearing people utilizing visual communication	Space may be required for students utilizing ASL interpreters or CART [38] Additional time may be required to arrange a clinically experienced ASL interpreter or CART captionist

(continue)

Table 10.6 (continued)

Barrier	Disability consideration	Strategy
Handouts and simulated patient information and patient notes	Processing, visual, anxiety, or executive functioning impairments	Any clinical accommodations should apply to simulated clinical scenario. These may include additional time to review patient files prior to the interaction, as well as additional time to complete patient notes in a reduced distraction environment [39]

Conclusion

In order to provide high-quality reasonable accommodations for healthcare students with disabilities, it is critical to collaborate to understand those students' perspectives and how their disabilities mesh with their education program. This chapter has provided an introduction to tools for identifying effective accommodations via a systematic approach, including intake questions, determining functional limitations in the context of the education program, and assessment of their effectiveness; these processes should be conducted by experienced disability resource professionals (DRPs) who communicate with the student as well as with clinical and educational leadership to enhance the institutional climate for accessibility. The preceding sections provide recommendations for people who have ADHD, autism spectrum disorder, learning disabilities, limited mobility, low vision, chronic health, or are deaf or hard of hearing; each disability experience provides a different lens through which to examine the clinical learning and working environment. As for the relevance of those recommendations, the authors themselves represent the lived experiences of people with disabilities who have innovated and adapted successfully to healthcare systems of education and practice by collaborating with DRPs, educators, clinicians, and colleagues. Many environments previously thought inaccessible, including emergency care and operating rooms, have been shown to be otherwise, particularly with the engagement of simulation resources for preparation. We note that many of these accommodations contribute to universal access principles by increasing access for patients with disabilities as well. These authentic solutions, far from exhaustive in their creativity, provide solid evidence that the healthcare education system can and must be made accessible to people with disabilities.

References

1. Rehabilitation Act of 1973 (§ 504).
2. Meeks LM, Jain N. Accessibility, inclusion, and action in medical education: lived experiences of learners and physicians with disabilities. 2018. Available from: https://store.aamc.org/accessibility-inclusion-and-action-in-medical-education-lived-experiences-of-learners-and-physicians-with-disabilities.html.
3. Karin Muraszko. Doctor with spina bifida defies expectations CNN Health [Internet]. 2016 April 27. Available from: https://www.cnn.com/2016/04/27/health/turning-points-dr-karin-muraszko/index.html.

4. Meeks LM, Bisagno J, Jain N, Herzer K. Support students with disabilities in medicine and health care programs. Disabil Compliance High Educ. 2015;21(3):1–5.
5. Laird-Metke E, Serrantino J, Culley JL. The process for determining disability accommodations. In: The guide to assisting students with disabilities: equal access in health science and professional education. New York: Springer Publishing; 2015. p. 33.
6. In a conversation with Dean of Students from Johns Hopkins Medical School (2019, Tom Keonig, oral communication, November).
7. LCME Element Structure and Function of a Medical School 12.4.
8. Meeks LM, Jain NR. Summative and formative assessments: do we accommodate both? Disabil Compliance High Educ. 2017;22(9):1–5.
9. Meeks LM, Jain NR. Accommodating students on anatomy and other lab practical exams. Disabil Compliance High Educ. 2017;23(3):1–7.
10. Meeks LM, Jain NR. Accommodating standardized patient exams: the OSCEs. Disabil Compliance High Educ. 2016;22(4):7–7.
11. Brown-Weissmann Z, Carli A. Learners with ADHD: concerns and coping mechanisms in the clinic. Disabil Compliance High Educ. 2016;22(5):7.
12. Fitzsimons MG, Brookman JC, Arnholz SH, Baker K. Attention-deficit/hyperactivity disorder and successful completion of anesthesia residency: a case report. Acad Med. 2016;91(2):210–4.
13. Meeks LM, Brown JT, Warczak J. Accommodate learners with ASD in a clinical setting. Disabil Compliance High Educ. 2017;23(4):1–5.
14. Serrantino J, Meeks LM, Jain NR, Clifford GC, Brown JT. Accommodations in didactic, lab, and clinical settings. In: The guide to assisting students with disabilities: equal access in health science and professional education. New York: Springer Publishing; 2015. p. 59–88.
15. Meeks LM, Jain NR. Accommodating chronic health conditions in medical education. Disabil Compliance High Educ. 2018;23(10):1–6.
16. Moreland CJ, Latimore D, Sen A, Arato N, Zazove P. Deafness among physicians and trainees: a national survey. Acad Med. 2013;88(2):224–32.
17. Registry of Interpreters for the Deaf. Certification overview [Internet]. Available from: https://rid.org/rid-certification-overview/.
18. Texas Board for the Evaluation of Interpreters. Texas Health and Human Services [Internet]. Available from: https://hhs.texas.gov/doing-business-hhs/provider-portals/assistive-services-providers/board-evaluation-interpreters-certification-program.
19. Certification Commission for Healthcare Interpreters. Certifications [Internet]. Available from: http://cchicertification.org/certifications/.
20. Testing, Evaluation, and Certification Unit, Inc. Welcome to TECUnit [Internet]. Available from: http://www.tecunit.org/.
21. Earhart A, Hauser A. The other side of the curtain. In: Deaf professionals and designated interpreters: a new paradigm. 2008. p. 143–164.
22. Meeks LM, Laird-Metke E, Rollins M, Gandhi S, Stechert M, Jain NR. Practice brief: accommodating deaf and hard of hearing students in operating room environments – a case study. J Postsecond Educ Disabil. 2015;28(3):383–8.
23. Meeks LM, Engelman A, Booth A, Argenyi M. Deaf and hard-of-hearing learners in emergency medicine. Western J Emerg Med. 2018;19(6):1014. Gower T, Richards E. A tough job made tougher. Proto Magazine. Massachusetts General Hospital; 2014 [cited 2019Sep8]. Available from: http://archive.protomag.com/assets/doctors-with-disabilities-tough-job-made-tougher.html.
24. Serrantino J, Hori J. Memory, retention, and retrieval: using Livescribe smartpen as an accommodation. Disabil Compliance High Educ. 2017;23(2):7–7.
25. Blacklock B. Use of an intermediary as reasonable accommodation for medical education. Disabil Compliance High Educ. 2017;23(6):7–7.
26. Littrell C. Apple watch breaking barriers for students with disabilities. Disabil Compliance High Educ. 2018;23(7):7–7.
27. Face of neurosurgery: Dr. Karin Muraszko a unique and remarkable neurosurgeon [Internet]. Neurosurgery blog: more than just brain surgery. The American

Association of Neurological Surgeons and the Congress of Neurological Surgeons; 2016. Available from: https://www.neurosurgeryblog.org/2016/01/29/face-of-neurosurgery-dr-karin-muraszko-a-unique-and-remarkable-neurosurgeon/.

28. Reporter DM. Paralyzed doctor still performs surgery thanks to stand-up wheelchair. Daily Mail Online. Associated Newspapers; Cited 2019 Aug 8. Available from: https://www.dailymail.co.uk/news/article-2513994/Paralyzed-doctor-performs-surgery-thanks-stand-wheelchair.html.

29. Bibbins-Domingo K, Grossman DC, Curry SJ, Barry MJ, Davidson KW, Doubeni CA, Epling JW, García FA, Kemper AR, Krist AH, Kurth AE. Screening for gynecologic conditions with pelvic examination: US Preventive Services Task Force recommendation statement. JAMA. 2017;317(9):947–53.

30. US Preventive Services Task Force. Screening for prostate cancer: US Preventive Services Task Force recommendation statement. Ann Intern Med. 2008;149(3):185.

31. Gaba DM. The future vision of simulation in health care. Qual Saf Health Care. 2004;13(1):i2–10.

32. Healthcare Simulation Dictionary [Internet]. Society of Simulation in Health Care; 2016 [cited 2019 Jun 29]. Available from: https://www.ssih.org/Portals/48/Docs/Dictionary/simdictionary.pdf

33. Halamek LP. Association of Medical School Pediatric Department Chairs, Inc. teaching versus learning and the role of simulation-based training in pediatrics. J Pediatr. 2007;151(4):329–30.

34. Kalaniti K, Campbell DM. Simulation-based medical education: time for a pedagogical shift. Indian Pediatr. 2015;52(1):41–5.

35. Kalaniti K. Do paediatric residents have the skills to "lead" newborn resuscitations? Acta Paediatr Oslo Nor 1992. 2014;103(6):592–3.

36. Anderson LW, Krathwohl DR, Airasian PW, Cruikshank KA, Mayer RE, Pintrich PR, et al. A taxonomy for learning, teaching, and assessing: a revision of Bloom's taxonomy of educational objectives, Abridged edition. 1st ed. New York: Pearson; 2000.

37. Issenberg SB, McGaghie WC, Petrusa ER, Lee Gordon D, Scalese RJ. Features and uses of high-fidelity medical simulations that lead to effective learning: a BEME systematic review. Med Teach. 2005 Jan;27(1):10–28.

38. Kenney MJ, Jain NR, Meeks LM, Laird-Metke E, Hori J, McGough JD. Learning in the digital age: assistive technology and electronic access. In: Meeks LM, Jain NR, editors. The guide to assisting students with disabilities: equal access in health science and professional education. 1st ed. New York: Springer Publishing Company; 2016. p. 119–40.

39. Serrantino J, Meeks LM, Jain NR, Clifford GC, Brown JT. Accommodations in didactic, lab, and clinical settings. In: Meeks LM, Jain NR, editors. The guide to assisting students with disabilities: equal access in health science and professional education. 1st ed. New York: Springer Publishing Company; 2016. p. 59–88.

When Students Fail: Remediation and Dismissal in Nursing and Medicine

11

Lisa M. Meeks, Leslie Neal-Boylan, Michelle Miller,
Rahul Patwari, Patricia Lussier-Duynstee,
and Raymond H. Curry

Introduction

Students with disabilities may fail health science programs for multiple reasons, including both academic and disability-related causes. When a disability-related barrier leads to the failure, faculty who do not understand the laws that govern disability may equate disability with inability. As a result, they may fail to meet their

The original version of this chapter is revised and updated. The correction to this chapter can be found at https://doi.org/10.1007/978-3-030-46187-4_14

L. M. Meeks (✉)
Assistant Professor, Department of Family Medicine, Director of MDisability Education, The University of Michigan Medical School, Ann Arbor, MI, USA
e-mail: meeksli@med.umich.edu

L. Neal-Boylan
Dean and Professor, Solomont School of Nursing, University of Massachusetts Lowell, Lowell, MA, USA

Vice Dean, Zuckerberg College of Health Sciences, University of Massachusetts Lowell, Lowell, MA, USA

M. Miller
Chair, Department of Legal Studies, College of Arts and Sciences, Quinnipiac University, Hamden, CT, USA

R. Patwari
Associate Dean, Curriculum Rush Medical College, Associate Professor, Department of Emergency Medicine, Chicago, IL, USA

P. Lussier-Duynstee
Assistant Professor Emerita, School of Nursing, MGH Institute of Health Professions, Boston, MA, USA

R. H. Curry
Professor of Medicine and Medical Education, Senior Associate Dean for Educational Affairs, University of Illinois College of Medicine, Chicago, IL, USA

© Springer Nature Switzerland AG 2020
L. M. Meeks, L. Neal-Boylan (eds.), *Disability as Diversity*,
https://doi.org/10.1007/978-3-030-46187-4_11

261

obligation to engage in a robust interactive process to provide reasonable accommodations for the student. Alternatively, when a student with a disability falls short of academic expectations, faculty may be reluctant to withhold a passing grade out of misguided empathy or fear of legal repercussions. In reality, students with disabilities should be held to the same standards as their peers.

The accessibility of a program is about equity – ensuring that students with disabilities have equal access to the curriculum, clinical experiences, labs, simulations, and assessments. Once barriers are removed through reasonable accommodations and students have full access to the program, then all assessments should be considered valid measures of a student's knowledge and progress. Empathy should never be the driver for decision-making; rather, faculty should ask themselves: Did the student have an equitable experience?

A Lot to Lose

Students who fail out of health science programs have a lot to lose. In many cases, students are paying living expenses (e.g., rent, utilities, grocery bills) using student loans or other financial resources (e.g., financial aid, veteran's funding, grants, stipends, supplemented housing, etc.). When a student fails to meet the expectations of an academic program and is dismissed, the student's sole source of income may disappear. Moreover, any loans the student may have taken out over the course of their education quickly move out of deferment (usually at 6 months) and become due. Zero income and new student loan payments can put considerable financial stress on the student, who also lacks the degree needed to gain meaningful employment. Moreover, if the student's housing is tethered to the institution, they usually have less than 30 days to vacate.

In addition to financial implications, separation from their cohort of fellow students may bring about the loss of an important social support system. They face the fear of letting down family members who are heavily invested in their success as a health professional. Dismissal from a program also results in a loss of access to the student health center, which is especially important for those who have mental health or chronic health conditions and utilize student health services as their primary source of care. The cost of independent insurance is prohibitive, and many students, unable to afford the expense of independent insurance, may lose access to their health care, mental health services, and medication coverage.

Finally, depending on where the student is in the program, they may already identify as a health professional and may experience significant distress at the realization they may not accomplish their goal. This contributes to a difficult transition out of the health science program.

Academic Deficit Versus Disability-Related Barrier

The difficulties in distinguishing whether the cause of the failure is related to the disability or a deficit in skill or knowledge may leave administrators and faculty confused regarding their obligations to the student. This can lead to the failure-to-fail phenomenon in which faculty pass a student believing that they are required to do so despite feeling

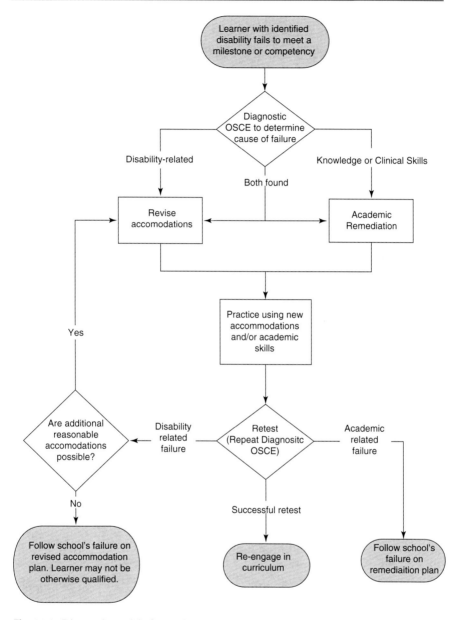

Fig. 11.1 Diagnostic model of remediation for students with disabilities

that the student is unqualified. In many cases, failure to meet an academic expectation is assumed to be disability-related when in fact the student may lack the necessary technical skill or clinical knowledge. Identifying the root cause of the failure is critical for all students, particularly for students with disabilities because of legal mandates to engage in an interactive process to determine reasonable and effective accommodations.

A model for diagnosing disability-related barriers is offered by Patwari et al. [1] (see Fig. 11.1). In this model, the authors recommend using standardized patient cases evaluated by both clinical and disability staff to differentiate between academic and disability-related causes of failure. In some cases, in which both knowledge deficits and disability barriers exist, disability resource professionals should work to evaluate and possibly refine accommodations, while academic faculty work to remediate the student once these accommodations are in place.

Legal Considerations

Congress enacted the Americans with Disabilities Act (1990) to ensure "equality of opportunity" for persons with disabilities (ADA § 12,101(a)(7) [2]. To achieve this goal, the ADA requires public universities (Title II) as well as private universities (Title III) to modify potentially discriminatory policies and practices by granting reasonable accommodations to students (ADA § 12,182(a)(2)(ii)). The statute expressly defines any modification that would "fundamentally alter" academic requirements at the postsecondary level as unreasonable (ADA §12,201(f)).

This statutorily mandated deference to universities is applied assiduously in the case law, particularly when the program in question is training students for health-care fields. Courts view the conferral of a degree in fields such as nursing and medicine as a claim that the graduate is fit to pursue a career in that field, a determination that educators are better able to make than judges (see, e.g., [3, 4]). Consequently, it is incumbent upon faculty and administrators to ensure that all graduates are adequately prepared to begin their careers. While faculty and administrators might feel an obligation to nurture students and to provide every opportunity for academic success, they are ethically and legally obligated to make sure the new graduate can practice safely. All students whether having a disability or not should be held to the same educational standards with the ultimate goal to graduate a student who can function safely and effectively in the profession.

In general, health professions programs are not responsible for providing any accommodations unless the student has filed a formal request with the appropriate institutional office [5–8]. However, faculty often feel they can and should provide an accommodation when asked by the student, despite the student circumventing the proper process for requesting accommodation, for example, a student who recounts a history of disability and requests "just a little more time." In these instances, it is important for the faculty to refer to the appropriate disability office, allowing the student to initiate the process and to wait for the formal institutional determination before granting the accommodation. Faculty should be reminded annually of the process for students to acquire accommodations and what is and is not permitted under the law.

Health science programs should have clearly delineated policies and procedures for when students are at risk of failing and for when they are dismissed. If there is doubt whether the student's disability contributed to the failure or whether accommodations were inadequate or not provided, the disability resource professional (DRP) should be brought into the conversation. They can provide guidance that is compassionate, fair, and compliant with disability laws. The DRP in partnership with the faculty and administration will determine the need for any additional reasonable accommodations in keeping with program standards.

The university is not legally required to consider a request for accommodations that is made once the school's dismissal process begins, whether the dismissal is a result of student misconduct or academic deficiency. There is also no legal requirement for an educational program to consider a request for an accommodation after a student has failed to meet the requirements of the program.

Zero-Hour Disclosures

The term "zero-hour disclosure" refers to disclosure of a disability by a student when they discover they are at risk of dismissal or failing out of a program. "Zero hour" is used to describe these declarations because they often occur either during the final meeting to determine a student's fate in the program or during an appeal after the decision has been made to dismiss the student. When a failing student engages in a zero-hour declaration of disability, administrators and faculty may perceive these disclosures as contrived or manipulative. However, in retrospect, the institution may discover that the student was displaying deficits consistent with a disability all along.

Often students partially disclose their disability, declaring only some of their symptoms without naming the full diagnosis. Or students may disclose to teaching faculty in lieu of the prescribed channels of disclosure (i.e., disability resource office). This places faculty in a precarious position if they are unaware of the obligation to refer students to a defined office for disability disclosure.

At times a student's need for an accommodation may be "so obvious" that a school can be expected to offer accommodation prospectively, without waiting for a student's request. In general, however, as described above, the school's responsibilities begin only upon receipt of a formal request for accommodation. Given the potential for partial disclosure and disclosure to faculty, faculty training on the subject is critical. The case of Chenari v. George Washington University, 2017 [9], describes the outcome of a zero-hour disclosure by a medical student (see Case Example 11.1).

> **Case Example 11.1 Chenari v. George Washington University** [10]
> Chenari was a 3rd-year medical student who when taking a National Board of Medical Examiners (NBME) shelf exam under standard time conditions refused to turn over the exam when time was called, realizing he had failed to transfer several responses to the answer sheet. He was dismissed by a unanimous vote of the Medical Student Evaluation Committee on the grounds of misconduct, pursuant to the University procedures and an honor code investigation finding. Following the denial of an internal appeal to the Dean, Chenari filed a lawsuit alleging breach of contract and discrimination based on his disability, attention deficit hyperactivity disorder. The court noted that Chenari never sought accommodations for his disability under the school's established procedures.

The court granted summary judgment in favor of the University in this case because the school twice offered Chenari counseling and therapy, despite the fact that he had never requested accommodations. The Court cited the efforts of George Washington University to inform students of their right to accommodations. This is in keeping with best practices for disability inclusion in the health sciences. Specifically, George Washington University, in an effort to inform students of the process for disclosure and accommodation, performed the following actions:

1. The disability resource professional (DRP) addressed all first-year students and informed them that "if they have a disability and need to request an accommodation, it is the student's responsibility to go to [the office] to pursue that matter."
2. Included disability-related information in the "First Year Survival Guide" for medical students. The instruct[ions] directed "[s]tudents who suspect that they may have a disability, which may require an accommodation" to contact the disability office.
3. The Office of Disability Support Services maintained a website that walked students through the process for obtaining a reasonable accommodation. The website included specific instructions about how students with ADHD could obtain accommodations.

The court noted that Chenari never followed the established procedures for requesting accommodations and that the University's proactive and transparent measures also affected the decision and as such granted summary judgment for the school. The court stated that that the Rehabilitation Act [11] (see Chap. 7 for an in-depth review of the law) requires nothing more from the University.

The case Doe v. Board of Regents of the University of Nebraska [7] also helps illustrate the impact of a zero-hour disclosure of disability. In this case, a medical student was dismissed for academic deficiencies; he first disclosed his diagnosis of depressive disorder during his appeal of the dismissal, claiming that he had not understood his rights under the ADA. The Supreme Court of Nebraska held that the University was not required to consider his late disclosure, as the ADA does not require "clairvoyance" on the part of schools. In so holding, the Court noted in particular that when a University provides designated channels for reporting a disability and requesting accommodations, the school cannot be held liable when the student fails to avail himself of those channels.

Similarly, in Zimmeck v. Marshall University Board of Governors [11], the plaintiff medical student did not disclose her depression and request accommodations until after she had been warned several times and then dismissed for unprofessional conduct. The Court found for the University holding that the ADA does not require a school to excuse misconduct that was only later revealed to be due to a disability.

There can be serious consequences for students who fail to request accommodations in a timely manner as evidenced in Betts v. The Rectors and Visitors of the University of Virginia [3] (see Case 11.2 Betts v. The Rectors and Visitors of the University of Virginia, 2005).

Case Example 11.2 Betts v. The Rector and Visitors of the University of Virginia [3]

Mr. Betts was admitted into a 1-year post-baccalaureate program that included admission to the University of Virginia's School of Medicine, conditional on successful completion of the post-bac program. After Mr. Betts completed the first semester with a 2.2 GPA, short of the required 2.75, he was placed on probation. During the second semester, Mr. Betts was diagnosed with a learning disability and was thereafter allowed double time on his exams as an accommodation. After the accommodation was granted, Mr. Betts took five exams, achieving a 3.5 average on these five exams. However, because the accommodations did not occur until near the end of the post-baccalaureate year, his overall GPA was a 2.53. The Post-Bac Promotions Committee thus recommended that his offer of admission to the Medical School be rescinded. On appeal, the Dean of the School of Medicine concurred. Not satisfied, Mr. Betts sued the University for violating his rights under the ADA. In holding for the University, the United States Court of Appeals for the Fourth Circuit held that the University had not violated the ADA since a reasonable accommodation had been granted. The Court did not wish to second-guess the academic judgment of the medical school faculty.

This case is important for a few reasons. Health professions education moves at an unforgiving speed. An undiagnosed disability may lead to poor academic performance that quickly renders a student ineligible to continue in the program. Many programs have mechanisms in place to detect early struggling and as part of that offer screening for learning disabilities with their disability or learning office. Once a student is identified for further screening, programs should consider temporary accommodations (for a period of 6 months or less) that provide a stopgap solution for students as they embark on the diagnostic process that may take several months from first appointment to final diagnosis and recommendations. In the absence of this safety net, a student could reasonably fail out of a competitive health science program, despite the ability to perform the work when properly accommodated. Another take away from this case is the absolute need to publish and disseminate information about disability resources, making disability and the provision of accommodations part of the normal conversation for struggling learners. While every learner that struggles will not have a disability, it shows a good faith effort on the part of the institution to ensure that a capable student is not being dismissed due to a remediable issue.

Finally, the case of a nursing student who failed to follow through and complete the application for accommodation further affirms the courts' view that an educational program does not have to consider an accommodation after a student, who has failed to meet the requirements of the program, failed to follow the prescribed process for requesting accommodations (see Case 11.3 Buescher v. Baldwin Wallace University).

Case Example 11.3 Buescher v. Baldwin Wallace University [12]
Buescher was dismissed after receiving three C's in an accelerated nursing program (basis for dismissal per program policy). She alleged, as part of a bigger suit, that she was denied accommodations for her disability, attention deficit disorder (ADD). Although Buescher had spoken to the BWU Disability Services office and had her physician complete the ADD Verification Form and fax it to the Disability Services office, she never followed up on registering. In the program's handbook, it states, "students will not be accommodated unless they provide their instructors with a letter from Disability Services documenting their eligibility and delineating reasonable and appropriate accommodations." Buescher never provided such a letter to her faculty. Although Buescher had faxed her disability documentation to the office, she had not completed an application for disability services or produced the requisite letter. Given that Buescher was given an application and did not complete it, the court held that there was no request for accommodations; therefore, there could be no failure to accommodate.

Buescher's case demonstrates that when a program maintains a process for disclosing disability and requesting accommodation and a student does not follow said process nor request accommodation through the proper channels, they are unlikely to prevail on a claim of failure to accommodate.

Moving Beyond Legal Requirements

Although there is no legal requirement for educational programs to consider "late" requests for reasonable accommodations, there is also no legal obligation to ignore such requests in appropriate cases where information about how to disclose disability was not readily available or when a student has a newly diagnosed disability. Quite often, the culture and climate surrounding disability will affect when (and if) a student discloses. In reviewing cases of failure, serious attention should be given to whether or not the messaging and culture around being a student with a disability influenced the students' choice not to disclose.

For example, in the aforementioned case of Buescher, a faculty member incorrectly told the student that no accommodations were afforded to students in the program (see Box 11.1), referring to the accommodations as "special" and asserting that the nursing profession and disability are incompatible. This misinformation contributes to a climate that discourages disclosure and amplified fear of bias toward disability in the health professions.

Box 11.1 Email to Ms. Buescher from Dr. Romeo

Dear Ms. Buescher,

Disabilities are handled only through the Learning Center, not by individual faculty. However, I must tell you that in the ABSN program accommodations are not made. This was stated on the form describing the functional abilities required of nursing students that your physician signed as part of your admission and is also found in the student handbook. Because of the need for nursing students and nurses to be able to think on their feet, to work in situations of ambiguity and uncertainty, and to be able to respond immediately in all situations, our students must be able to handle all class work, laboratory work, and clinical work without special accommodation.

Table 11.1 Legal requirements and best practices

Legal requirements	Best practices
Post notices explaining the procedures for requesting an accommodation	Actively encourage students to request an accommodation if needed, especially during orientation and at the beginning of each semester
Consider reasonable alternatives if a requested accommodation is not feasible	Engage in a robust interactive process with the student to determine what accommodations would be most effective without imposing an undue burden on the school or fundamentally altering the program
If a request for accommodation is made after a student fails, dismissal from the program is legally permissible	If a request for accommodation is made after a student fails, the faculty should consider carefully why the request was made so late and whether a timely implemented accommodation would have likely resulted in equal access for the student. Where appropriate, the student could be placed on probation and given the opportunity to remediate with reasonable accommodations in place

Arguably, health science programs will never achieve meaningful integration of students with disabilities until they commit to going beyond legal requirements and provide clear and transparent policies about disability disclosure and request for accommodation. Indeed, the legal requirements of the ADA should serve as a floor and not a ceiling when it comes to ensuring equal opportunity for students with disabilities. Schools should strive to meet or exceed best practice (see Table 11.1 Legal requirements and best practices).

Determining Dismissal

Once accommodations are in place, standard policies for dismissing students who fail to meet competencies apply. However, when a student with a disability fails and is subject to potential dismissal, promotions committees and administrators may

Table 11.2 Considerations for promotions committees

When there is a history of disability prior to entering the program
Did the student request accommodations? If no, why not? Was this poor professional judgement, fear of stigma, or lack of access of information about how to disclose and request accommodations?
Is this a potential professionalism issue, does the student have good insight and self-regulation? Is it reasonable to conclude that the disability and functional limitations affected the students' performance?
Is there a reason or evidence to conclude that the assigned accommodations removed the barriers to the students' ability to perform?
Does the student have a plan that is (a) reasonable, (b) actionable, and (c) likely to improve performance?
When there is a newly diagnosed or acquired disability, engage in an interactive process to determine what/if any accommodations might be reasonable
Is it reasonable to conclude that the disability and functional limitations negatively affected the students' performance?
Is there a reason to conclude that reasonable accommodations may reduce the barriers to learning for the student?
Is the level of competency and knowledge sufficient to progress in program, or would potential deficits or gaps in learning cause disruptions in future assessments? Consider remediating more than one test or course
Does the student have a plan that is (a) reasonable and (b) actionable and likely to improve performance?

wish to engage in a secondary analysis to ensure the student had equal access to the curriculum. The committee may also wish to liaise with the DRPs to determine whether existing accommodations are truly reducing barriers for the student and engage in the Diagnostic model of remediation for students with disabilities (see Fig. 11.1) to ensure a robust evaluation of the root cause of failure prior to dismissing the student. The following questions may help administrators determine the best course of action in cases in which a student with a disability fails and asserts the failure is related to a disability (See Table 11.2: Considerations for promotions and progression committees).

For students who are up for dismissal, have a disability, and are receiving accommodations, the committee should review these accommodations with the student to consider if the accommodations were effective and delivered in a timely manner. If accommodations have been ineffective, the student may have gaps in their knowledge that will impact their trajectory. If the committee feels the student situation warrants a reconsideration due to ineffective or untimely accommodations, they may wish to consider whether a student should be remediated for the failures and any prior, foundational, work.

Appealing or Grieving a Decision to Dismiss

Neither the ADA [2] nor its implementing regulations contain a right to grievance procedure. In arguing that courts should read such a requirement into the statute, students have pointed to the implementing regulations interpreting the Rehabilitation

Act of 1973 (§ 504) [9]. These regulations require that schools adopt grievance procedures that include "appropriate due process standards" with the goal of ensuring fair and timely resolutions of complaints (34 C.F.R. § 104.7) [13]. Given their similar purposes, courts apply the same analysis to the Rehabilitation Act and the ADA [4]. Therefore, so runs the argument, the ADA regulations can be read to also require due process standards in grievance and appeals processes. This argument has gained no traction in the courts because a private cause of action cannot be created by federal regulation. For example, in the case of Guckenberger v. Boston University [14], the court agreed with the plaintiff students that BU did not have adequate grievance procedures in place; however, the court found no legal cause of action existed to allow the court to remedy the deficit.

In legal parlance, this is known as a "right without a remedy." It means that, perhaps counterintuitively, when a request for an accommodation is denied or a student with a disability is dismissed, there is no way to legally enforce a right to an appeals or grievance procedure on an individual basis. However, the Office of Civil Rights in the Department of Education ("OCR") has the authority to enforce its own regulations pertaining to the Rehabilitation Act. So, while a student cannot bring a successful case against a university claiming inadequate grievance or appeals procedures, a student can file a complaint with the OCR requesting an investigation.

In one such case, filed against St. Joseph's College, the OCR found that the grievance procedures were not properly communicated to students and were not properly followed in the case at issue. The College agreed to enter a Resolution Agreement with the OCR, whereby the College would be monitored until they had properly communicated the existence of the grievance procedure to students [15].

In another case, a student was withdrawn from Spring Arbor University due to conduct resulting from the student's depression. The school refused to allow the student to re-enroll until after the student provided the school with a written plan. In the course of its investigation, the OCR discovered that not only did the University's DRP not know where the grievance procedure was located, the procedure itself contained inadequate due process protections, including no indication of how the complaints should be filed and no written notice of the outcome of the procedure. The University was required by the OCR to revise its grievance procedure and to provide students with adequate notice of the procedures [16].

Given the OCR's vigilance, it behooves all health science programs to create a grievance procedure that satisfactorily incorporates due process standards, to include:

1. Notice to students explaining where and how a complaint can be filed
2. An explanation that complaints of disability discrimination, including disability harassment, perpetrated by anyone on campus, may be submitted under the procedure
3. The contact information of the University employee responsible for receiving the complaints, along with an alternate in case the employee who usually accepts the complaints is implicated in the discrimination

4. Reliable and impartial investigation of all complaints
5. Participation of the University's disability resource professional in the process
6. Assurances that if a student is subjected to disability harassment, the University will act promptly to end such behavior and to correct any discriminatory effects that resulted from it
7. A declaration that retaliation against a person because of their participation in the grievance process will not be tolerated [16]

Remediating Students

Nursing

Since the late nineteenth century and the beginning of formal nursing education, schools of nursing have evolved from strict, rigid environments to institutions that may allow students considerable flexibility and latitude. Nursing programs, while held to high academic standards by state boards and accreditors, frequently "bend rules" to avoid the appearance of discrimination. In doing so, students who cannot meet rigorous academic standards are sometimes permitted to progress in programs only to fail the national board exam after graduation. Nursing faculty have a difficult time failing students, and administrators may take faculty to task if a significant number of students fail a course.

Duffy [17] studied schools of nursing in the United Kingdom and identified the phenomenon of failing to fail students as early as 2003. Other international studies have confirmed Duffy's findings that faculty tend to believe students should pass. In 2011, Tanicala et al. [18] found that regarding passing of clinical courses, safety was a primary concern as were the level of the student in the program, support from the university, and the evaluator's own experience. In that same year, researchers Jervis and Tilki [19] also found that "mentors" or preceptors frequently passed nursing students in clinical even if they thought they should fail. Their decisions often reflected a lack of confidence in themselves as clinicians particularly with regard to judging appropriated clinical behavior.

In 2015, Docherty [20] asked "Have clinical and academic faculty passed nursing students they believe should have failed, and, if so, what factors were involved in failing to fail?" (p. 227). This study confirmed previous findings and that failing to fail occurs in both academic and clinical settings. Docherty found little connection between failing to fail students and individual faculty characteristics. Interestingly, faculty largely felt supported by administrators when they decided to fail students but identified pressures not to fail students nearing graduation. Following up on that study in 2018, Docherty [21] found that faculty frequently fail to fail students because of multiple reasons such as differences between theory and clinical classes, team grading, and the perception that the student is "good enough." The perception regarding whether the student can practice safely seems to weigh most heavily on deciding whether to fail a student. Killam et al. [22] identified that there was no standard definition of unsafe student clinical practice and sought to define it.

Grade inflation [23, 24] is another issue in nursing education and may be a factor in a student passing simply because each course grade has been inflated beyond what the student should have earned. Benner [25] described the three areas of nursing student preparation that require evaluation as (1) cognitive apprenticeship; (2) practice apprenticeship and clinical reasoning; and (3) ethical comportment and formation (p. 183). Competencies are specific to the level of program (baccalaureate, graduate, doctoral levels) and are specific to academic programs; they are not employment competencies. Concerns should be initiated immediately based on signs of struggling, such as low test scores or less than expected clinical performance. Letters of concern are typically sent to the students who are in danger of failing courses. These letters should precede course warnings and can foster an environment of remediation and support for the struggling student. A remediation plan that is reasonable for the program and meets the specific needs of the student allows for the clarity we seek when determining the difference between academic and clinical deficits and disability. Accommodations, if they exist, should be cited in the remediation plan.

Accommodation for a student with a disability does not negate the progression policies of the program. All students are held to the same academic and clinical expectations whether or not they have accommodations. To follow accreditation standards, nursing programs must demonstrate that there is a system to evaluate students for reasonable accommodations and clearly delineated appeals and remediation processes for all students.

If a student fails a nursing course or program, they are encouraged to pursue the appeals process that should be described in detail and accessible to students. The Appeals Process Policy should include deadlines for submitting materials to faculty or administration overseeing the process. The faculty or administrator overseeing the process ensures that a standing committee within the School of Nursing provides due process and hears the student's appeal. The committee adheres to carefully written faculty-approved policies. If the committee recommends against allowing the student to repeat the course or remain in the program, the student may appeal to the department chair or dean for a final decision. Nursing programs are also required to have clear and transparent grievance policies so that students who believe they have been treated unfairly have due process.

Medicine

Medical schools have a low attrition rate [26] due in part to medicine's commitment to remediating its students [27]and the "failure to fail" phenomenon [28].Students are well supported and often given multiple attempts to remediate a course [29]. Medical schools are highly invested in their students, and professors often take time out of the course of normal academic activities to mentor, counsel, and instruct the struggling students [30].

Many medical schools have moved to pass/fail grading, particularly in the pre-clerkship phase of the curriculum, taking even more pressure off of the struggling student [31]. While students understand their individual performances are compared with the mean, they are aware that no grade, per se, is listed on their transcript.

Medicine also provides multiple "warnings" prior to a dismissal. Students usually receive a non-passing grade on an exam, which is followed by the ability to remediate – usually only those portions that were failed. Two failures of an exam in close succession, despite successful remediation, may place a student on probation where they will be closely monitored or necessitate the student repeating the year. At this juncture, there is often a keen sense of any barriers to learning, and students are referred to program or institutional resources (e.g., a learning specialist, counseling, disability resources).

After multiple failing grades, students are often presented to a committee that determines whether or not to dismiss a student from the program [29]. When a disability is suspected, a student may be advised to seek a professional evaluation and then return to the committee if a previously unknown disability is identified. In these cases, most committees will elect to have the student repeat the failed course(s) with accommodations in place, in an attempt to ensure equal access to the curriculum and to give the student every opportunity for success.

Compassionate off-ramps

The student with a known disability who enters a demanding professional degree program is assuming a measure of risk, the nature of which they may or may not recognize. The same, of course, is true of any new student, particularly in the health sciences, who has no doubt been a very high-achieving student but has not yet mastered such a large volume of information in relatively short order or experienced the highly interpersonal and dynamic clinical setting and its demands for multi-tasking. It is also not infrequent for a student's cognitive disability to become evident only upon entering into this more intensive educational environment [32].

The extent to which these risks deter students with disabilities from pursuing a health sciences career, or prevent their ultimate success, is unknown. Studies show a somewhat lower graduation rate among medical students with disabilities [33] and mixed performance on assessments [34]. These data do not allow insight into the extent to which this difference stems from students' inability to function in the curriculum – for example, even a very high-functioning student with an anxiety disorder may have underestimated the stresses of medical school and practice – or whether institutional barriers to their success existed that could have been removed through reasonable accommodation.

The concept of a "compassionate off-ramp" has been one strategy to assist health science students who are unsuccessful or desire an alternative career path and has recently become more common in medical schools [35]. Some health science programs offer certificate programs, and bachelor's or master's degrees as an alternative for students who are struggling to complete health science programs, that determine the program of study is a poor fit, or decide to switch careers without having to entirely sacrifice the time and money they have already invested in school. A master's degree in "medical sciences," for example, might allow a former medical student advanced standing in a similar graduate or professional degree program or provide entry into a non-clinical field where this expertise has particular value. Similarly, a former nursing student might obtain a "health sciences" degree. These options also allow the university to retain the student and allow the student to graduate with a degree from that university.

Agaard and Moscoso [36] emphasize the need for programs providing such off-ramps to incorporate knowledgeable career counseling, from advisors and mentors who understand the possibilities for alternative careers and their applicability to a given student's aptitudes [36]. Advising must include DRPs who understand the full range of possibilities for accommodation, so as to avoid the intrusion of disability bias into these career counseling activities.

The Student's Decision to Disclose

Multiple variables affect a student's decision whether or not to disclose a disability. Part of this is embedded in early experiences [usually negative] and cultural belief systems about disability, while other reasons are absolutely rooted in the culture of an institution and a profession [37]. The best remedy to the issue of failure to disclose, which also leads to zero-hour disclosures, is an institutional culture that values disability as a robust part of diversity and one that is valuable to health care.

The expression of these values is evident in forward-facing language that begins at admissions (see Chap. 4) and is threaded throughout one's tenure as a student and trainee. These forward-facing messages should be ongoing, go beyond the language of legal compliance, and invite and encourage disclosure of disability and active partnering in determining appropriate accommodation. Institutions who wish to elevate access and learning for their communities at large review their curricula and work to apply universal principles of instruction to their teaching and assessment (see Chap. 7). Ensuring the well-being of students during their time in health science programs promotes learning, engagement, and success and should also be one of the elements that drives institutional culture (see Chap. 5).

When a student fails, institutions should conduct a root cause analysis of the failure, similar to a morbidity and mortality conference during which the institution takes stock of any errors or omissions in managing the students' experience. This process helps schools determine if and where there were breakdowns in the system, a failure to refer, or a failure to identify a struggling student's undiagnosed disability. Students do fail, and, in most cases, the right move is to allow the process to proceed following institutional standardized policies. The student's failure should not be the result of a culture of ableism or a fragmented system of resources.

Life Happens

We must also remember that life happens, and the consequences can accrue quickly in a rapidly paced, high-stakes environment. There are times that, through no fault of their own, students will experience catastrophic events that impact their ability to learn and progress in a program. In these cases, faculty must be nimble and show compassion and humanity. Programs should have a mechanism for flexibility and space to consider each situation and adapt to potential needs, extensions, exceptions to policy, curricular decompression, and leaves of absence. Remember that in the case of disability, the Department of Justice (DOJ) has been clear that policies are amendable as an accommodation [38]. However, the approval of disability-related accommodations must be made through the proper channels.

Conclusion

Differentiating academic failure as a result of a disability-related barrier or a knowledge or skill deficit is challenging. Awareness of legal requirements and institutional expectations are vital to faculty understanding of their obligations to students with disabilities. Faculty must resist the "failure to fail" syndrome and measure and evaluate all students based on their ability to meet academic standards set forth by the program. Accommodations, when requested by a qualified student and approved by the university appointee, should reasonably eliminate barriers to the curriculum and clinical experiences. Accommodations level the playing field regarding *how* expectations are met. They are not intended to allow someone who does not have the academic capability to succeed via a lowered standard.

If students fail courses or are dismissed from the program, it should be because they have failed to meet the academic standards set by the program despite having equal access to all elements of the curriculum and clinical rotations. When a student with a disability receives reasonable and effective accommodations and still fails to meet competencies, then faculty must hold the student accountable to the consequences of failure.

All students should be given equal access to information regarding the process for requesting an accommodation. This information should be provided early and often to preclude zero-hour disclosures and the loss of capable health sciences students from programs they could master with equal access. Ultimately, the student makes the choice to disclose and to request an accommodation. For students who do not disclose or request accommodations, despite multiple opportunities and directions on how to do so, faculty can feel assured that the opportunity for equal access was provided but not utilized.

References

1. Patwari R, Ferro-Lusk M, Meeks LM. Using a diagnostic OSCE to discern deficit from disability in struggling students. Acad Med. 2020. [Epub ahead of print].
2. Americans With Disabilities Act (ADA) of 1990, 42 U.S.C.A. § 12101 et. seq. (West 2014).
3. Betts v. The Rector and Visitors of the University of Virginia, 202 Ed. Law Rep. 147 (4th Cir 2005).
4. Halpern v. Wake Forest University Health Sciences. 2012.
5. Goldstein v. Harvard University, 182 Ed. Law Rep. 88 (1st Cir. 2003).

6. Carten v. Kent State University, 78 Fed.Appx. 499 (6th Cir. 2003).
7. Doe v. Board of Regents of the University of Nebraska, 846 N.W.2d 126 S. Ct. Neb. 2014.
8. Mbawe v. Ferris State University, 751 Fed.Appx. 832 (6th Cir. 2018).
9. Rehabilitation Act of 1973 (§ 504).
10. Chenari v. George Washington University, 847 F.3d 740 (D.C. Cir 2017)
11. Zimmeck v. Marshall University Board of Governors, 328 Ed. Law Rep. 56 (4th Cir. 2015).
12. Buescher v. Baldwin Wallace University, 2015 86 F.Supp.3d 789 (N.D. Ohio 2015).
13. Code of Federal Regulations 34 C.F.R. § 104.7.
14. Guckenberger v. Boston University, 974 F.Supp. 106 (D.MA 1997).
15. United States Department of Education Office of Civil Rights, Resolution Agreement with St. Joseph's College. 2011.
16. United States Department of Education Office of Civil Rights, Resolution Agreement with Spring Arbor University. 2010.
17. Duffy K. Failing students: A qualitative study of factors that influence the decisions regarding assessment of students' competence in practice. Retrieved from http://www.nmc-uk.org/Documents/Archived percent20Publications/1Research percent20papers/Kathleen_Duffy_Failing_Students2003.pdf.
18. Tanicala ML, Scheffer BK, Roberts MS. Defining pass/fail nursing student clinical behaviors phase I: Moving toward a culture of safety. Nurs Educ Perspect. 2011;32(3):155–61. https://doi.org/10.5480/1536-5026-32.3.155.
19. Jervis A, Tilki M. Why are nurse mentors failing to fail student nurses who do not meet clinical performance standards? British J Nurs. 2011;20(9):582–7. https://doi.org/10.12968/bjon.2011.20.9.582.
20. Docherty A. Is there evidence of failing to fail in our schools of nursing? Nurs Educ Perspect. 2015;36(4):226–31. https://doi.org/10.5480/14-1485.
21. Docherty A. Failing to fail in undergraduate nursing: Understanding the phenomenon. Nurs Educ Perspect. 2018;39(6):335–42. https://doi.org/10.1097/01.NEP.0000000000000350.
22. Killam LA, Montgomery P, Luhanga FL, Adamic P, Carter LM. Views on unsafe nursing students in clinical learning. Inter Jl Nurs Educ Schol. 2010;7(1):1–17. https://doi.org/10.2202/1548-923X.2026.
23. Donaldson JH, Gray M. (2012). Systematic review of grading practice: Is there evidence for grade inflation? Nurse Educ Pract. 2012;12(2):101–14. https://doi.org/10.1016/j.nepr.2011.10.007.
24. King-Jones M, Mitchell A. Grade inflation: A problem in nursing? Creat Nurs. 2012;18(2):74–7. https://doi.org/10.1891/1078-4535.18.2.74.
25. Benner P, Sutphen M, Day L, Leonard VW, Rodriguez L, Sullivan W, Colby A. The Carnegie Foundation for the Advancement of Teaching 2010; Curricular and Pedagogical Implications of The Carnegie Foundation National Nursing Education Study Transforming Nursing Education School of Nursing Canadian Association of Colleges of Nursing. 2010. (paper presentation).
26. https://www.aamc.org/system/files/reports/1/may2014aib-graduationratesandattritionfactors-forusmedschools.pdf.
27. Hauer KE, Ciccone A, Henzel TR, Katsufrakis P, Miller SH, Norcross WA, Papadakis MA, Irby DM. Remediation of the deficiencies of physicians across the continuum from medical school to practice: a thematic review of the literature. Acad Med. 2009;84(12):1822–32.
28. Dudek NL, Marks MB, Regehr G. Failure to fail: the perspectives of clinical supervisors. Acad Med. 2005;80(10):S84–7.
29. Ellaway RH, Chou CL, Kalet AL. Situating remediation: accommodating success and failure in medical education systems. Acad Med. 2018;93(3):391–8.
30. Steinert Y. The "problem" learner: whose problem is it? AMEE Guide No. 76. Med Teach. 2013;35(4):e1035–45.
31. Spring L, Robillard D, Gehlbach L, Moore Simas TA. Impact of pass/fail grading on medical students' well-being and academic outcomes. Med Educ. 2011;45(9):867–77.
32. Rosebraugh CJ. Learning disabilities and medical schools. Med Educ. 2000;34(12):994–1000.
33. Teherani A, Papadakis MA. Clinical performance of medical students with protected disabilities. JAMA. 2013;310(21):2309–11.

34. Gibson S, Leinster S. How do students with dyslexia perform in extended matching questions, short answer questions and observed structured clinical examinations? Adv Health Sci Educ. 2011;16(3):395–404.
35. Bellini LM, Kalet A, Englander R. Providing compassionate off-ramps for medical students is a moral imperative. Acad Med. 2019;94(5):656–8.
36. Aagaard EM, Moscoso L. Practical implications of compassionate off-ramps for medical sudents. Acad Med. 2019;94:619–22.
37. Jain NR. Political disclosure: resisting ableism in medical education. Disability Soc. 2019;8:1–24.
38. United States Department of Justice, Agreement between the United States of America and Princeton University under the Americans With Disabilities Act. 2016.

Physician Licensing, Career, and Practice

12

Nichole L. Taylor, Michelle Miller, and Lisa M. Meeks

All medical students will encounter important periods of transition through their journey from medical school to becoming a board-certified physician. Key resources at the medical school are needed to guide the student through each of these transitions. Medical school curriculum presents new academic demands, including the volume and the pace at which the student must acquire medical knowledge. The student's medical knowledge will be tested by high-stakes standardized exams throughout medical school. Scores on these exams are one of many factors that a residency recruitment committee will weight, when offering medical students, a residency interview. Students with disabilities will need assistance navigating each obstacle they encounter during medical school. A team of knowledgeable career advisors and a disability resource professional (DRP) must be available to assist and make these transitions smooth and should be proactive in assessing accommodation needs. It is important that students with disabilities are given the tools to navigate each transition leading up to their residency training. These tools will be utilized as they move from medical school to residency and enter a career in their chosen specialty.

The original version of this chapter is revised and updated. The correction to this chapter can be found at https://doi.org/10.1007/978-3-030-46187-4_14

N. L. Taylor (✉)
Assistant Dean of Student Affairs; Associate Professor Department of Anesthesiology, Wake Forest School of Medicine, Winston-Salem, NC, USA
e-mail: ntaylor@wakehealth.edu

M. Miller
Chair, Department of Legal Studies, College of Arts and Sciences, Quinnipiac University, Hamden, CT, USA
e-mail: michelle.miller@QU.edu

L. M. Meeks
Assistant Professor, Department of Family Medicine, Director of MDisability Education, The University of Michigan Medical School, Ann Arbor, MI, USA
e-mail: meeksli@med.umich.edu

© Springer Nature Switzerland AG 2020
L. M. Meeks, L. Neal-Boylan (eds.), *Disability as Diversity*,
https://doi.org/10.1007/978-3-030-46187-4_12

This chapter will discuss the critical points of support for the student with a disability and anticipate the needs when entering residency and clinical practice. This roadmap will enable the DRP to help students anticipate the requirements for Graduate Medical Education (GME) for residency and practice and the mechanisms for ensuring equal access. Successful transition of the student with a disability to that of a resident and clinician takes a team approach and is best realized through a coordinated effort of multiple partners on the medical education team.

The Transition Team

Disability Resource Professional

The Disability Resources Professional (DRP) is the key ally for the medical student with a disability. The DRP is aware of the process of requesting accommodations on high-stakes exams, disability barriers within subspecialties of medicine, and maintains a unique understanding of the differences in the laws that govern inclusion between the educational and employment settings. Importantly, the DRP, through their networks and professional associations, may be able to connect the student to practicing physicians with disabilities to help mentor the student as they navigate the process of selecting their specialty.

Career Advising

As a student begins medical school, they are undifferentiated in regard to which medical specialty training they will pursue after graduation. Students require multiple 1:1 advising sessions with a career advisor and exposure to the various subspecialties to evaluate their future medical specialty options. Career advising for all students is one key to a successful residency match. These advisors assist the student with building their residency application and providing guidance in selecting extracurricular activities (research experiences, volunteerism, leadership, teaching, and mentoring extracurricular activities) and target exam score thresholds for competitive specialties.

Advanced Career/Specialty Advising

Students gain exposure to system-based basic medicine courses, research, observation opportunities, clinical clerkships, and lectures covering the various medical specialties, all which help them begin the process of selecting their future area of medical specialty. As the student begins to narrow down their future career specialties, it is important that an advanced career advisor meets with the student to further craft a specialty-specific residency application.

Although the process will be helpful for all students, medical student with disabilities must consider and reflect on potential functional limitations. The student must assess if these functional limitations have any impact on their ability to safely provide health care in each specialty and evaluate what accommodation, if any, could be in place to reduce barriers and allow them to provide safe patient care. Medical students need a collaborative team to provide resources, information, in-depth exposure to the medical student's desired medical specialty, and guidance for the key application building completed throughout medical school.

Early collaboration between a disability resource professional, the student, a career advisor, and specialty advisor mentor, in the desired specialty, can be advantageous for exploring the potential obstacles and determining reasonable accommodations. Together, the team can identify any barriers in the landscape, such as accommodations for licensing exams, board exams, residency application, and any state licensure processes or queries that may require additional preparation. The end goal of the team is to help the student identify a specialty for medical residency and assist with a specialty-specific game plan for transitioning into the Graduate Medical Education (GME) space.

Early Exploration of the Various Medical Subspecialties

Opportunities for early career exploration, such as shadowing a clinical faculty member in the student's desired field, allow the student to evaluate "fit" for the specialty or area of practice. It is important that a student evaluate not only the medical specialties they are considering from the perspective of the student (that may have limited clinical roles) but also through the lens of a resident who will be required to conduct more invasive procedures while carrying a larger patient census.

Students must realize the demands on the resident and faculty and understand how their role will evolve as they progress through resident training. For example, some accommodations may be feasible in year 1 of residency, and not feasible in year 2 or 3 as their autonomy increases with patient care. Finding a good specialty advisor that practices in the field of interest is critical. In addition to the items mentioned, students can, through this shadowing, identify any accommodations needed to practice in that specialty. Shadowing offers students an opportunity to build a professional relationship with a faculty member who can write letters of recommendation for the applicant and endorse their abilities to practice in this area of specialty, while career and specialty advisors can help students determine their competitiveness for the National Residency Matching Program (NRMP). Finally, the student, in conjunction with the DRP and advising team, can discuss when to disclose the need for accommodations, as they transition to the next level of education (residency) and/or clinical practice.

Consideration for Applying to Residency

In addition to in-depth exposure to the students desired specialty, there are various other requirements that need to be completed. As students begin to build their application for residency, they will need advisors to help them navigate the process of building a residency curriculum vita, develop a personal statement, obtain letters of recommendations, and complete their application through the Electronic Residency Application Service (ERAS).

For students who have taken a leave of absence or extended their medical education, these departures will need to be addressed on the medical students' application for residency. A career advisor may provide guidance about how to answer questions on the ERAS application, in the personal statement and during the interview for residency. Considering that each student has a unique circumstance, a career advisor helps the student determine what, how and how much information to disclose, and how to do so in a professional manner.

Residency Match and Post-Match Considerations

Unlike regular job employment, medical students secure a resident program through a matching service. There are several different matching services, the Military Match for those enlisted in the military, San Francisco Match for urology and ophthalmology residency programs, and the National Residency Matching Program (NRMP). Students apply to specific residency programs through the Electronic Residency Application Service (ERAS), and residency programs select which applicants to interview. Once applicants are interviewed, each program and the student submit a rank order list (ROL) to the NRMP or alternative matching service. The students indicate their preferences for a "match" by ranking the institutions where they interviewed. The residency programs submit a ROL ranking each candidate they interviewed in order, as well. A computerized mathematical algorithm is used to "match" the students and residency programs together.

After the student matches into a residency program, the specialty advisor and DRP should help students prepare documents for the licensing board and connect students with professional organizations. They can also help the student obtain the program's policies and procedures for requesting accommodations. DRPs in particular can avail themselves of the residency disability representative to answer any questions they may have about accommodations in clinical settings. A proactive plan, established prior to the first day of residency, will provide a smooth transition for the new resident.

Residency Training

Physicians do not go straight from medical school to employment. Instead they embark on a series of advanced trainings designed to assess "readiness and competency" to practice medicine. The first stage of training includes internship, a year of in-depth exposure spent either rotating through different specialties or rotating through different areas within one specialty. The following years (2–5) are spent completing additional training under the supervision of other physicians, and they develop their skills for practicing independently. It is important to note that there is high variability in required skills sets across all of the 26 different medical residency programs.

Residents who required accommodations in medical school may continue to need these in residency. For example, residents continue to take high-stakes exams that may require accommodation including the Step 3 examination, usually completed after the first year of residency training. Residents also take an annual practice In-Service Training exams (analogous to the high-stakes written exam required after residency) to obtain all or part of their board certification. These In-Training exams are administered through the Medical Specialty Board that will provide them with their final board certification and evaluate the resident's test performance to assess if this performance is on trajectory to pass the high-stakes written specialty board certification exam after graduation. Exam accommodations for these In-Training assessments are handled by the specialty boards, and residents will need to complete the request for accommodations prior to the deadline and submit necessary paperwork. As mentioned above, failure to apply for accommodations for the In-Training exams may jeopardize accommodations on the specialty board exams as the resident would lack a history of accommodation. Remember that at all levels of medical education, showing that there is a long history of nequiring, requesting, and utilizing accommodations supports future requests. Without passing the board certification exams, a physician will not be board-certified in their medical specialty, which can limit employment opportunities. As a medical student graduates and enters residency, the landscape for accommodations for disability drastically shifts.

The Landscape and Leadership of GME

The ACGME sets the core standards with which all residency programs must maintain compliance with, in order for the training programs to remain accredited. Each institution has a Designated Institutional Official (DIO) that is the touch point for the ACGME. The DIO is responsible for maintaining compliance with the institutional requirements and supervises each individual residency program director (PD). The PD recruits and monitors the individual residents' performance through the ACGME milestone and assesses their progression toward competency through training. The residency PD is responsible for reporting competency of each individual resident to the appropriate board, semi-annually, and at the completion of training. Given the multiple parties involved in the oversight of a resident (see Table 12.1), it is critical that the communication with a resident about disability be clear and that policies are transparent.

Table 12.1 Overview and ownership of various parts of residency

Human resources	ACGME	Institution GME/ DIO	Program director	Specialty board	State licensing board
Leave of absence/ FMLA	Sets minimum requirements in specialty experience (i.e., number of procedures, diversity of cases, rotational experience requirements)	Oversees compliance of the individual residency programs with the ACGME requirements	Supervise and assess the resident's progression toward competency in the specialty	Reviews significant time away from training to determine if residency should be extended	Provides both residency in-training license and full license
Short–/ long-term disability	Provides individual programs with accreditation	Supports program directors and residents in the institution	Reports resident performance to the specialty board	Determines board certification	
Health insurance benefits		Interfaces with HR regarding LOA, benefits and disability as needed	Completes paperwork for future job competencies based on residency performance	Accommodations for exams	
ADA compliance	Mandates programs to be compliant with the institution's policy	Recommended to have a policy and procedure for a resident to request and obtain accommodations	Works with Human Resources to implement accomodation requests		

Disability Policies in GME

In July 2019, the Accreditation Council for General Medical Education (ACGME) called for greater diversity and inclusion in GME recruitment and retention of residents in all subspecialties of medicine. They also added a requirement that the program provide "accommodations for residents with disabilities consistent with the Sponsoring Institution's policy." [1]

Disclosure in GME

Students must consider when and how to disclose disability-related information to a residency program. For some, whose disabilities are apparent, they will likely disclose as part of their personal statement. There are benefits with sharing

> **Box 12.1 ACGME Guidance on Disability**
> *Institutional Requirements July 2018*
> - IV.H.4. Accommodation for Disabilities: The Sponsoring Institution must have a policy, not necessarily GME-specific, regarding accommodations for disabilities consistent with all applicable laws and regulations. (Core)
>
> *Common Program Requirements (Residency) July 2019*
> - I.D.2.e. Accommodations For Residents with Disabilities Consistent with the Sponsoring Institution's Policy. (Core)

information, as it can be a starting place for a medical student to gauge how supportive the potential residency program is to accommodation and supporting the student in the future. Residency websites are one way to gauge if a particular institution has a clear process and welcoming language for residents with disabilities. Looking for diversity and inclusion offices within institution will also allow a student with a disability to gauge the level of support, resources, and community.

Accreditation Guidance

The Accreditation Council for Graduate Medical Education (ACGME) sets the standards for accommodating residents and mandates requirements, one at the institutional level and one at the program level (see Box 12.1) [2].

Requests for Accommodation in GME

As a medical student graduates and enters residency, the landscape for accommodations for disability drastically shifts. The mechanisms for disclosing disability and requesting accommodations also shift. Residents in-training are both employees of the hospital and trainees supervised by the Graduate Medical Education (GME) Office. Unlike in medical school, human resource (HR) for the institution now sets the standards and develops a process to request accommodations for schedules, accessibility needs, leaves of absence, and short−/long-term disability. Considering the unique roles of residents as employees who are still in training, a collaborative team of disability specialists from GME and HR may be needed to assess the reasonable nature of an accommodation request.

Failure by training programs to communicate information about disability is a major barrier to residents accessing accommodations. Meek and colleagues (2019) recommend a process for the disclosure of disability and request for accommodations given the unique structure of GME (see Fig. 12.1) [3]. In their paper they stress that a clear process transparent to applicants and trainees is needed.

All trainees should receive a new resident orientation, and information on how to disclose and request accommodations should be part of that conversation. The point of

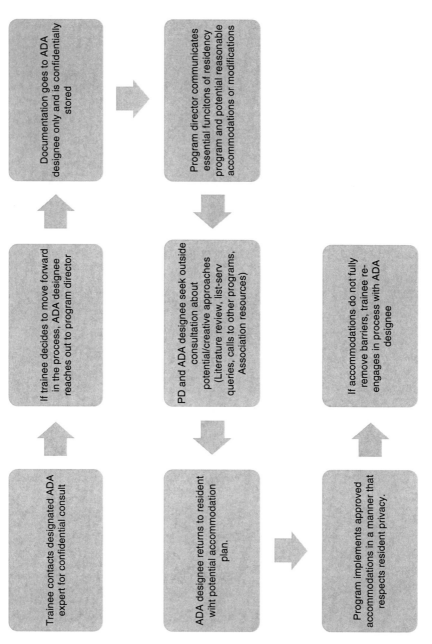

Fig. 12.1 Exemplar process for accommodation requests in GME. (Used with permission from JGME)

contact for disclosure should not be a program director (PD) or resident supervisor, and it is important to stress that these consultations are confidential. Ideally, human resources or an ADA coordinators that are well steeped in the law and the nuances of medical training will collaborate with the trainee and program director to evaluate the accommodation options. Some accommodations requests may be novel and unique and may require an outside consultation service to weigh in on the accommodation options and provide alternatives, but most will be straightforward and inexpensive. The residency program should implement the accommodation in a manner that respects the resident's privacy. A re-evaluation of the accommodation once it is initiated should occur, and if there needs to be further adjustments, the ADA expert is re-engaged to look for additional solutions.

Time Away or Extended Residencies

Students should be aware that time away from training must be reported to the specific medical specialty board. Each board will assess time away from training in conjunction with the residency program director's assessment of proficiency, in cases where extended residency training time is required.

Medical Licensure

In addition to successfully passing all required courses and clinical clerkships, medical students take a series of exams throughout their medical school, residency, and post-graduation. These high-stakes exams are required to demonstrate medical knowledge, clinical decision-making, proficiency in clinical examination skills, and obtaining a history from the patient. A medical student and resident cannot progress toward graduation and specialty board certification without passing these exams and preferably on the first attempt. Each profession and the state in which the trainee plans to practice must recognize that they have met all required pre-requisites expected of the novice clinician and are prepared to assume the responsibilities and liabilities inherent in taking care of people.

New graduates with disabilities might face challenges and barriers to obtaining licensure, not because they have not succeeded in their educational or training programs, but because the processes for acquiring licensure can be cumbersome and rigid. This section describes the processes of obtaining licensure for medical graduates and some of the challenges students with disabilities might face.

Medical Licensing Exam (USMLE and COMLEX)

Medical students are required to take multilevel standardized exams during medical school. These exams assess medical student's knowledge and clinical skill performance and must be successfully passed. Allopathic (MD) medical students will take the US Medical Licensing Exam (USMLE). Osteopathic students (DO) will take the COMLEX (Comprehensive Osteopathic Medical Licensing Examination).

The exams are administered by the National Board of Medical Examiners (NBME) and the National Board of Osteopathic Medical Examiners (NBOME) for MD and DO students, respectively. Obtaining disability accommodations on these exams is often difficult and undeniably time-consuming. Because of the barrier of time and the perception that accommodation requests are uniformly denied, medical students with disabilities often forgo the process of requesting accommodations, even though the scores are not flagged or otherwise identified to any educational or training organization.

The timeline for the USMLE and COMLEX examinations for MD and DO students are the same, as demonstrated by Fig. 12.2.

The COMLEX and USMLE are used as benchmarks and gatekeepers to the profession of medicine, and each Step/Level examination must be passed in order for a student to progress to the next stage of medical training. It is important that testing accommodations are requested, so that a student's performance is reflective of their knowledge and ability. The scores from USMLE and COMLEX exams are often used as cutoff scores for competitiveness for residency.

With the number of applicants for residency exceeding the number of positions offered in the National Residency Matching Program (NRMP), placing into residency has become increasingly more competitive [4]. Residency programs receive a large number of applicants, and exam score minimums are often used to filter which applications a residency program will review prior to offering an interview. Step 2 scores are correlated with passing the future high-stakes board certification

- Step/Level 1 is the first of the gatekeeper exams. The test is administered after the pre clinical medical school curriculum, typically after the 2nd year of medical school and prior to clinical rotations. This test must be passed in order to progress into clinical clerkships for most medical schools.

- Step/Level 2 is a 2-part exam and is mandatory for graduation from most medical schools.
  - The Clinical Knowledge (CK) portion encompasses the basic core clerkship knowledge of Internal Medicine, Family Medicine, Pediatrics, General Surgery, Neurology, Psychiatry, Emergency Medicine and Obstetrics and Gynecology. This exam is taken at the completion of the 3rd year of medical school and ideally prior to residency application, which is September of the student's fourth year

  - The Clinical Skills (CS) portion evaluates the effectiveness of the patient-doctor interaction, interpersonal communication, ability to gather health information data from a standardized patient, and the student's ability to develop a differential diagnosis and treatment plan.

- Step/Level 3 is taken after graduation from medical school, usually during their first year of residency training. This exam is must be passed in order for a resident to progress through residency training.

Fig. 12.2 USMLE and COMLEX exams

exams after completion of residency training [5]. A student may desire to pursue additional fellowship training after residency, and the Step 3/Level 3 examinations are a part of the fellowship application. Students that fail one of these high-stakes exams may struggle to match into any residency training program. These high-stakes examinations continue throughout residency training and future maintenance of board certification exams.

Rejections on High-Stakes Exams

As noted above, success obtaining accommodations on the board exams varies. When accommodation requests are rejected, the student or resident may choose to pursue the matter in Court with varied outcomes. In Black v. National Board of Medical Examiners (2017) [6], for example, a plaintiff who had failed the Step One Examination three times was denied accommodations for her exam. Ms. Black had requested that she receive extended time for her fourth attempt at the Step One Examination because of her ADHD. The National Board of Medical Examiner's argued, however, that Ms. Black had failed to demonstrate that she actually had a disability. Noting that Ms. Black had never requested accommodations either during her undergraduate studies at Princeton or during medical school, the Court agreed. For these reasons, it is advisable for students and residents with a disability who require accommodations to consistently request and utilize accommodations at every step of their education and training.

Courts, however, do not always side with the NBME. For example, a recent case details the multiple attempts made by medical student Brendan Berger to receive accommodations from the NBME for the USMLE Step 2 CK (Berger v. Nat'l Bd. Of Med. Examiners, 2019) [7]. The Court took the unusual step of granting Berger's motion for a preliminary injunction, ordering the NBME to provide Mr. Berger with the requested accommodations for the USMLE Step 2 CK taking place on August 28, 2019. In so doing, the Court found that the plaintiff would likely suffer irreparable harm if he did not retake the test on that date, this time with accommodations. Students with disabilities who require accommodations for any of the levels of the USMLE should, thus, not assume that a denial by the NBME is final, as a Court may overrule the NBME's accommodations determination.

Shifts in the Law

The legal status of a medical resident under the ADA is somewhat complicated by the fact that residents are both employees (ADA Title I) and students (ADA Title II or Title III). While some Courts characterize the medical resident as an employee, see, e.g., Neravetla v. Virginia Mason Medical Center, 705 Fed.Appx. 520 (Ninth Cir. 2017) [8], other Courts recognize that a medical residency more resembles an educational program than typical employment (see, e.g., Sarkissian v. West Virginia University Board of Governors, 2007) [9]. Thus, when the medical residency is with a state university hospital, any claims brought under Title I are likely to be dismissed due to the state's sovereign immunity, while claims under Title II may move forward (Mire v. Board of Supervisors of Louisiana State University, 2016) [10].

As with a medical student or an employed physician, a medical resident with a disability is entitled to request and receive reasonable accommodations. Courts will assess all such requests for accommodations in a similar fashion, as required by the ADA. So, for example, a medical resident with Asperger's was found by the Court not to be "otherwise qualified" for his position as a resident because the accommodation he requested, "'knowledge and understanding'" by hospital staff, would not have resulted in his being able to perform one of the necessary functions of a medical resident, namely, the ability to communicate well with patients (Jakubowski v. Christ Hospital., Inc., 627 F3d 195 (6th Cir. 2010) [11]. Similarly, in Rodrigo v. Carle Foundation Hospital, the Court held that the plaintiff medical resident was not "otherwise qualified" because passing the USMLE Step 3 was an essential function for a third year medical resident, since the exam is required for licensure (2018) [12].

The mechanisms for disclosing disability and requesting accommodations also shift. Unlike in medical school, human resource (HR) for the institution now sets the standards and develops a process to request accommodations for schedules, accessibility needs, leaves of absence, and short−/long-term disability. Considering the unique roles of residents as employees who are still in training, a collaborative team of disability specialists from GME and HR may be needed to assess the reasonable nature of an accommodation request.

Essential Functions of Physician Employment

As with all employment, there are specific job duties that must be met by the candidate. As a medical student completes required and elective clerkships during medical schools, they are able to gauge the requirements that each of the various specialties demand. Conversing with their specialty advisor and DRP, they collectively have evaluated the accommodations necessary for safe practice. Regardless of specialty selected, a physician must have completed a medical residency, must obtain specialty board certification, as well as a state medical license, and must demonstrate that they have met the basic essential functions of a practicing physician in their field. The basic essential functions of a physician may vary dependent on their specialty.

The ACGME has milestones, which are specialty-specific in six core competencies: practice-based learning and improvement, patient care and procedural skills, system-based practice, medical knowledge, interpersonal and communication skills, and professionalism. As a physician enters into clinical practice each time they pursue employment at the hospital, they must undergo a physician credentialing process. This credentialing process will request several documents that attest that a physician is able to perform the essential functions of their specialty. These include peer references, state medical license, board certification/board eligible, attestation of residency completion, and specific case logs demonstrating proficiency with procedures and specific patient populations. A physician in practice will be required to go through the re-credentialing process throughout their career, when maintaining employment in the same hospital/group and every time they change locations of employment.

While in residency training, a resident is granted an In-Training license through the GME office. As residents approach completion of their graduate medical education training, they will be applying for a state medical board license, Drug Enforcement Administration license, and a National Provider ID number. Each state medical board may have vastly different requirements as they follow the jurisdiction of each individual state. After the initial application is completed, an applicant must reapply each year to insure a physician continues to stay in good standing with the state medical board. Applicants must successfully pass all USMLE Step examinations or NBOME COMLEX examinations, peer references, hospital privileges, and past medical licenses. Applicants are required to disclose all leaves of absence from medical school, leaves of absence from residency training, substance/alcohol abuse, mental health diagnoses, and/or medical diagnoses in order to obtain a state medical license. Applications are reviewed by the State Medical Licensing Board and approved or denied.

Is Patient Safety a Realistic Concern? Determining Direct Threat

Amid an increase in the number of health professionals with disabilities, schools, training programs, and licensing agencies have expressed concerns about patient safety and whether or not an individual with a disability should engage in a clinical program and practice. In keeping with the legal guidance, programs or employers who have a concern about safety and whether or not an individual should be removed from a clinical setting or the program entirely must conduct an individualized assessment and case-by-case determination as to whether and what modification(s) can be made to the policies or curriculum and whether any accommodations exist that would allow the student to continue to safely engage in the program.

Direct threat to others is defined in the ADA as "a significant risk to the health or safety of others that cannot be eliminated by reasonable accommodation" (42 U.S.C. § 12,111 (3)) [13]. ADA regulations require that in determining whether a direct threat exists, a covered entity must conduct an *individualized assessment*, based on reasonable judgment that relies on *current medical knowledge* or on the best available objective evidence, to ascertain: the *nature, duration, and severity of the risk*; the *probability* that the potential injury will actually occur; and whether *reasonable modifications* of policies, practices, or procedures or the provision of auxiliary aids or services will mitigate the risk (28 CFR § 36.208 (c)) [14].

Because the statutory language applies only to a direct threat to the health or safety of "others," it does not constitute a defense for universities that remove students from campus due to incidents of self-harm. However, the Office of Civil

Box 12.2 DOJ and Northern Michigan University Under the ADA (2018)

Multiple complainants stated that NMU took adverse action toward them pursuant to NMU's Policy Relating to Student Self-Destructive Behavior. Wherein NMU required them to (1) meet with the Dean of Students or the Associate Dean of Students, who threatened them with disciplinary action for sharing suicidal or self-destructive thoughts with other NMU students; (2) undergo mandatory psychological assessments to maintain enrollment; (3) abide by certain conditions to maintain enrollment; and/or (4) involuntarily withdraw from NMU. These current/former students alleged that NMU took these actions toward them pursuant to NMU's Policy Relating to Student Self-Destructive Behavior.

Box 12.3 Settlement Agreement Between DOJ and University of Tennessee Health Science Center (UTHC) Under the ADA (2016)

A complainant alleged that UTHSC failed to make necessary reasonable modifications to its policies, practices, and procedures and retaliated against her when she filed a grievance. In the second semester of her 1-year program, she experienced a mental health crisis due to a preexisting mental health disability, which was aggravated by stress from her academic schedule. She informed Student Academic Support Services (SASS) of her disability. SASS and the Behavioral Intervention Team consulted with the complainant's doctor and agreed that she would take a short temporary leave of absence. SASS also agreed with the complainant on a number of other accommodations including extensions for the assignments that she missed due to the temporary leave of absence. Upon return 2 weeks later, the student was behind in her course work and in her clinical training. About 2 weeks later, the Dean of the College called the complainant to a meeting where she was placed on a mandatory medical leave of absence; prohibited from submitting work she had already completed; instructed not to contact her teachers or fellow students; and directed to stay off campus unless readmitted. Her UTHSC email account was also suspended. After the complainant was told she was being placed on a mandatory leave of absence, the complainant filed a formal discrimination complaint with UTHSC's Office of Equity and Diversity ("OED"). After this she says she was treated in a hostile and intimidating manner and instructed not to contact the OED investigator and that OED failed to undertake an adequate, impartial, and timely investigation of her complaint. Finally, the complainant alleges that when she continued to send emails to faculty members and administrators complaining about the alleged discriminatory treatment, she was brought before UTHSC's Progression Committee on charges of unprofessional conduct.

Eventually, the US Department of Justice, the federal agency responsible for investigating administrative complaints filed under Title II of the ADA, and the University agreed to enter into an informal voluntary resolution of the matter.

Rights and the Department of Justice have been very clear that an individualized assessment is required before a university can remove a student from campus pursuant to its involuntary medical leave policy due to self-harming behaviors. For example, failure to follow a process that reviews legitimate safety concerns was the grounds for the finding and settlement agreement between the DOJ and Northern Michigan University under the ADA (2018) in the case of a policy related to self-destructive behavior [15].

The Department of Justice (DOJ) found NMU in violation of the ADA stating, " NMU's policy relating to student self-destructive behavior did not reflect or impose legitimate safety requirements within the meaning of Title II of the ADA" and that "NMU's Dean of Students office took adverse action against NMU students with mental health disabilities who did not pose an actual risk of serious self-harm."

The DOJ made a similar interpretation when reviewing a case with The University of Tennessee Health Science Center suggesting that health science programs need to maintain well-crafted mandatory leave policies that apply to students with mental health disabilities who pose a serious risk of harm to themselves [16].

Following the investigation, the Department of Justice outlined actions to be taken by UTHSC outlined in Box 12.4. These actions serve as guidance for other health science programs developing leave of absence and behavioral policies for their institutions.

Similar guidance has been delivered in other cases and sends a clear message to institutions about the process that must be followed when evaluating whether the actions of a student with disabilities rises to the level of direct threat (See Box 12.5).

Direct threat analysis is very similar under Title I of the ADA as the EEOC has promulgated regulations requiring employers to make an "individualized assessment" of a person's ability to perform the essential functions of their job, before the employer decides that an employee or prospective employee is not able to perform the essential functions of the position because they pose a direct threat to self or others 29 C.F.R. §1630.2(r) [17]. This determination must be based on current medical judgment and/or the "best available objective evidence." Id. A good example of

---

Box 12.4 Lessons Learned from the UTHC Settlement

Conduct an *individualized assessment of each student and give careful consideration to the opinions and recommendations of the student's health-care provider(s),* along with the opinions and recommendations of the health-care professional(s) consulted by the University and any other information the student wishes to provide.

Respect the student's confidentiality and only require the student to provide a medical release for access to the student's health records *as reasonably necessary to complete an individualized assessment.*

Determine on an *individualized basis whether and what reasonable modifications can be made that would be effective to allow the student to continue to attend classes and participate in the educational programs* offered by the institution while seeking treatment for, or recovering from, any health condition(s).

Require a student to take an *involuntary medical leave only if:* (a) the University concludes after conducting an individualized assessment that the student's continued participation would require modifications that would be unreasonable or would fundamentally alter the nature of the educational programs; (b) the student rejects all reasonable modifications offered and cannot meet the essential eligibility requirements of the programs; or (c) even with all reasonable modifications offered, the student cannot meet the essentially eligibility requirements of the programs.

Box 12.5 Actions Before Determining Direct Threat
- Conduct an individualized assessment.
- Defer to treating physician guidance.
- Safeguard student privacy and only share information with individuals who have a legitimate need to know.
- Consider all possible accommodations and modifications before mandatory or regular LOA.
- Create a culture where students feel safe disclosing disability related to mental health.
- Assign an advocate for student in the disability resource office.
- Be transparent about the fact that accommodations for psychological disabilities are available.

direct threat analysis in a health-care setting can be found in Searls v. Johns Hopkins Hospital, 158 F.Supp.3d 427 (D. MD 2016) [18], in which the Court held that the defendant hospital's claim that a hearing-impaired RN to whom they had offered a job would constitute a direct threat was a mere pretext designed to hide the hospital's wish not to provide reasonable accommodations. Of course, direct threat analysis is equally applicable to situations involving doctors. See, e.g., Diakow v. Oakwood Healthcare, Inc., 2017 WL 75968 (E.D. Michigan, 2017), holding that summary judgment was inappropriate since the defendant had failed to prove that the 85-year-old plaintiff obstetrician would pose a direct threat to patient safety [19].

Summary

Medical students and physicians in-training receive education and training to prepare them to enter clinical practice. Challenges remain that involve licensing, continued training, and career decisions that may have lasting impact. The student and physician in-training with a disability, in particular, may face barriers to licensure, employment, and practice because of the disability. Consequently, a clear understanding of what is involved in these processes and the potential barriers can forearm the health professional with a disability to proactively meet these challenges. Guidance from several key individuals is imperative to insure success.

References

1. Accreditation Council for Graduate Medical Education. ACGME Common Program Requirements (residency). https://www.acgme.org/Portals/0/PFAssets/ProgramRequirements/CPRResidency2019.pdf.
2. Accreditation Council for Graduate Medical Education. ACGME institutional requirements IV.H.4. Accommodation for disabilities. Chicago: ACGME; 2018. https://www.acgme.org/Portals/0/PFAssets/InstitutionalRequirements/000InstitutionalRequirements2018.pdf?ver=2018-02-19-132236-600.
3. Meeks et al. The Unexamined Diversity: disability polices at the 50 largest training programs. J Grad Med Educ. 2020 (Submitted).
4. National Resident Matching Program, Results and data: 2019 Main residency match®. National Resident Matching Program, Washington, D.C.; 2019.
5. Harmouche et al. USMLE scores predict success in ABEM initial certification: a multi-center study. West J Emerg Med, 2017;18(3):544–549 . https://www.ncbi.nlm.nih.gov/pmc/articles/PMC5391908/.
6. Black v. National Board of Medical Examiners, 281 F.Supp.3d 1247 (M.D. Florida, 2017).
7. Berger v. Nat'l Bd. Of Med. Examiners, Case No. 1:19-cv-99 (S.D. Ohio, 2019).
8. Neravetla v. Virginia Mason Medical Center, 705 Fed. Appx. 520 (Ninth Cir. 2017).
9. Sarkissian v. West Virginia University Board of Governors, 2007 WL 1308978 (N.D. West Virgina, 2007).
10. Mire v. Board of Supervisors of Louisiana State University, 2016 WL 4761561 (E.D. Louisiana, 2016).
11. Jakubowski v. Christ Hospital., Inc., 627 F.3d 195 (6th Cir. 2010).
12. Rodrigo v. Carle Foundation Hospital, 879 F.3d 236 (7th Cir. 2018).
13. Americans with Disabilities Act (ADA) of 1990, 42 U.S.C.A. § 12101 et. seq. (West 2014).
14. Americans with Disabilities Act (ADA) of 1990, 28 CFR § 36.208 (c).
15. United States Department of Justice. Settlement Agreement with Northern Michigan University Under the Americans with Disabilities Act (October 18, 2018).
16. United States Department of Justice. Settlement Agreement with University of Tennessee Health Science Center under the Americans with Disabilities Act (July 22, 2016).
17. Code of Federal Regulations, 29 C.F.R. §1630.2(r).
18. Searls v. John Hopkins University, 158 F.Supp.3d 427 (D. MD, 2016).
19. Diakow v. Oakwood Healthcare, Inc., 2017 WL 75968 (E.D. Michigan, 2017).

Licensing, Career, and Practice in Nursing

13

Leslie Neal-Boylan and Michelle Miller

Introduction

Nursing students experience an intense and rigorous education to obtain licensure and prepare for work as a novice nurse. As part of this process, nursing students with disabilities must consider and reflect upon how their disability might impact or be impacted when engaging in clinical practice while in school and following graduation, applying for licensure, and acquiring additional training or education as they progress through their career. It is critical to understand what is required to obtain licensure and/or certification. Also necessary is someone to guide the student through the process as they near graduation and post-graduation. This guide can assist students to prepare documents for the licensing board, identify the appropriate questions to clarify processes, and connect with professional organizations and their resources. All new nursing graduates or postgraduates seeking additional certification will most likely need to engage in extensive study to prepare themselves for the necessary examinations; however, the documentation and paperwork required to prove eligibility to sit for these examinations could be confusing and multilayered. Students and new graduates with disabilities may need additional assistance to ensure they have the accommodations they might need to prepare these documents and sit for the examinations. Following licensure and/or certification, new graduates will be ready to engage in nurse residencies, return for further education, or seek

L. Neal-Boylan (✉)
Dean and Professor, Solomont School of Nursing, University of Massachusetts Lowell, Lowell, MA, USA

Vice Dean, Zuckerberg College of Health Sciences, University of Massachusetts Lowell, Lowell, MA, USA
e-mail: leslie_nealboylan@uml.edu

M. Miller
Chair, Department of Legal Studies, College of Arts and Sciences, Quinnipiac University, Hamden, CT, USA
e-mail: michelle.miller@QU.edu

© Springer Nature Switzerland AG 2020
L. M. Meeks, L. Neal-Boylan (eds.), *Disability as Diversity*,
https://doi.org/10.1007/978-3-030-46187-4_13

employment. These are important career decisions and must be considered very carefully. People with disabilities may have additional considerations as they plan their careers and employment settings. In this chapter we describe specific considerations regarding nursing licensure, career decision-making, and practice.

Nurses with disabilities frequently experience discrimination in the workplace [1, 2]. The research [1–3] has revealed that nurses with disabilities frequently receive encouragement and support for their applications for employment during phone interviews but are frequently met with attitudinal barriers during in person interviews if they have an obvious physical disability. For example, a nurse who is obese told of being informed she was a good fit during the phone interview but on arriving for the in-person interview was told the job was no longer available. Nurses with disabilities tend to hide their disabilities whenever possible [1–3]. A study of nurses with self-identified physical disabilities and nurse recruiters found that the nurses hid their disabilities and the nurse recruiters denied ever interviewing or hiring a nurse with a physical disability [3].

Nurses with disabilities speak of "nurse heroics." In this context, they are referring to the tendency for nurses to expect themselves and one another to work through meals and breaks and to come in to work when they should have a day off. Nursing can be very physical work and the expectations of one another very high. In this fast-paced environment, the nurse with a disability may find it difficult to renew their energy or engage in self-care [4–6].

Compensatory skills are necessary for all individuals who navigate their strengths and weaknesses in a work environment, but this may be especially critical to individuals with a disability. For example, a nurse who is missing an arm may have developed strategies to perform certain skills using adaptive equipment. However, colleagues and administrators are not typically supportive of these compensatory techniques even if they perform them safely. Patients may be more welcoming to nurses with disabilities than are nursing colleagues or administrators because patients may perceive that the nurse with a disability can be more empathetic to the patient and has first-hand experience that other nurses do not have.

The National League for Nursing (NLN), the American Nurses Association (ANA), and the American Association of Colleges of Nursing (AACN) have all emphasized the importance of inclusion. Their diversity statements include disability; however, their activities to improve inclusion have not yet demonstrated a focused commitment to recognizing and accommodating nursing students or nurses with disabilities. This is a work in progress.

Step 1: Licensure

The education nursing students receive is ultimately geared to the goal of licensure. While nursing faculty are adamant that they do not "teach to the test," we recognize that educational programs are designed to promote student success. Student success means not only passing courses but also obtaining licensure, and hopefully, on the first try. Nurses cannot practice without a license. The state in which they plan to practice must recognize that they have met all required prerequisites expected of the novice clinician and are prepared to assume the responsibilities and liabilities inherent in taking care of people. The assumption is that if one is able to earn licensure, they are prepared to practice safely.

New graduates with disabilities might face challenges and barriers to obtaining licensure, not because they have not succeeded in their educational program but because the processes for acquiring licensure can be cumbersome and rigid. This section describes the processes for licensure for nursing and some of the challenges people with disabilities might face and how to manage them.

All registered nurses planning to work in the United States take the state board exam, known as the National Council Licensure Examination for Registered Nurses (*NCLEX*-RN®) or the NCLEX. The National Council of State Boards of Nursing (NCSBN) develops and sponsors the administration of the NCLEX. However, the actual administration of the test typically occurs at testing centers that are authorized to administer the test online using secure methods. Nurses with disabilities can request accommodations before taking the exam. As in school, the nurse must provide the appropriate documentation, typically including evidence that the nurse required accommodations while in nursing school. However, boards of nursing are often more stringent than are schools of nursing and with good reason. In Massachusetts, for example, the Board of Registered Nursing will allow the graduate to sit for the NCLEX exam if they have evidence of neuropsychological testing and an official diagnosis from a licensed diagnostician. Although a new nurse graduate with a disability may request accommodations for taking the NCLEX, the state Board of Nursing may restrict the nurse's license even if they pass the exam. In Turner v. National Council of State Boards of Nursing, the plaintiff, who had dyslexia, requested of the Kansas State Board of Nursing, the same accommodations for the NCLEX that he had had in school, specifically, extra time, a private room and someone to read questions to him if necessary [7]. He was told that he could have accommodations, but that if he passed the exam after receiving accommodations his registered nurse (RN) license would be "restricted and limited." The plaintiff took the NCLEX without accommodations and failed to pass. The Court held that the plaintiff could not sue the State Board of Nursing under Title II of the ADA because Congress had failed to validly abrogate state sovereign immunity [8]) in the area of professional licensing exams. His constitutional due process claims also failed since a concern over public safety being endangered by a nurse who needs accommodations to pass the licensing exam provided a rational basis upon which to restrict the plaintiff's nursing license (Turner v. National Council of State Boards of Nursing, [7]).

The Board of Nursing requires student transcripts from the school of nursing before processing the approval to sit for the NCLEX. Once the nurse has passed the NCLEX, the state Board of Nursing is able to grant the nurse a license to practice in that state. In addition, many state boards require nurses to review online modules on various topics and pass exams indicating their competence. Examples of modules and exams include topics on opioid addiction and sexual assault.

State sovereign immunity is a legal concept that protects states from suit against individuals unless they waive their immunity or Congress validly abrogates it, meaning that Congress requires states to allow such lawsuits. Title II of the ADA [9] is only possible, dealing as it does with services provided by state instrumentalities, because Congress states in the ADA [9] that the statute is intended to abrogate state sovereign immunity, i.e., that states cannot prevent individuals from suing the state. However, in the last few decades, the US Supreme Court has held that Title I of the ADA [9] is not a valid abrogation of state sovereign immunity in the case of state employers (Board of Trustees of the University of Alabama v. Garrett, [10]). As to Title II of the ADA [9], the dust has still not settled on what state services remain validly covered by the statute. While some courts have held that a state board, such as a state Board of Nursing, cannot be sued for damages under Title II [7], most of the courts that have considered the sovereign immunity question in the context of education have held that students may bring such a Title II suit against state universities [11]. Thus, until the US Supreme Court weighs in, while a student can still sue their state university for damages under Title II of the ADA [9], an employee of the same university, whether staff or faculty, is not able to sue their employer for damages under Title I of the ADA [9].

Career and Practice

Once the health science professional is licensed to practice, the next challenge is deciding whether to pursue a residency and further education or immediately begin to practice. Variations exist. Registered nurses may enter into extensive orientations, preceptorships, or residencies following licensure or may immediately begin practicing within the scope prescribed by state board license requirements. Nurse practitioners, certified registered nurse anesthetists, certified nurse midwives, and clinical nurse specialists ("Advanced Practice Registered Nurses" [APRN]) may or may not begin residencies and may require supervision or collaboration with a physician depending on the state within which they are licensed. There may be particular barriers to practice for nurses with disabilities. Thus, additional scrutiny may be required of the nurse with a disability depending on the state and the setting. This section discusses these challenges.

Documentation of Disability

The ADA prohibits discrimination *because of* disability. Numerous courts have thus found that, if an employer did not know about the disability, they could not have violated the statute. For example, in Cody v. Cigna Healthcare of St. Louis, Inc., the plaintiff argued that she was terminated because of her anxiety and depression [12]. As a nurse assigned to the Ambulatory Medical Records Review Project, Ms. Cody was required to visit various doctors' offices in St. Louis. She mentioned her condition to her supervisors and told them that going into certain areas of the city made her very nervous and requested that she not be made to visit those areas. Her employer offered her a medical leave during which time they wanted her to have a psychological evaluation. Ms. Cody declined the offer and was terminated for not doing her job. The Court held that she could not have been terminated because of a disability as she had never proffered documentation of her diagnoses to her employer (Cody v. Cigna Healthcare of St. Louis, Inc., [12]). Nurses should therefore make sure to produce documentation of a disability when requesting an accommodation. Simply telling a supervisor is not enough.

Equal Employment Opportunity Commission (EEOC)

The protection afforded all students with disabilities by the ADA does not end upon graduation. Title I of the ADA prohibits discrimination on the basis of disability in the workplace as well. Thus, when a graduate of a health sciences program begins to work in their chosen field, the ADA goes with them. Ideally, individuals with disabilities will find a position with an employer who is aware of the ADA and who engages in a robust interactive process to determine and implement reasonable accommodations. In order to bring a Title I suit against an employer for violating the law, employees must first exhaust their administrative remedies. This simply means that the employee must file a complaint with the federal agency responsible for enforcing the ADA. In the case of Title I, the Equal Employment Opportunity Commission ("EEOC") has jurisdiction over such complaints (How to File a Charge of Employment Discrimination, [13]).

EEOC complaints (see Fig. 13.1) have a very strict timeline. Generally speaking any complaint must be filed within 180 calendar days of the time the discriminatory

1. The employee locates the EEOC Public Portal online to submit an inquiry and schedule an intake interview at the closest EEOC field office (https://publicportal.eeoc.gov/Portal/Login.aspx).
2. The employee may also drop into one of the 53 EEOC field offices on a walk-in basis or may call an EEOC office to schedule an appointment
3. Secure an interview with an EEOC intake worker via one of the methods above (submission of inquiry, phone call, walk in) This interview helps the employee determine to request an investigation or remedial action
4. To file a complaint, employees can
   a. Complete the paperwork online via the EEOC Public Portal
   b. Complete the process in mail form by submitting a letter. If filing by letter, the following information should be included:
      i. Employee's name, mailing and email addresses, and telephone number;
      ii. Employer's name, mailing and email addresses, and telephone number;
      iii. Number of employees employed by the employer, if known;
      iv. A brief explanation of the discriminatory conduct alleged;
      v. Dates (s) of the discriminatory conduct;
      vi. Basis of the discrimination, e.g. disability; and
      vii. Employee's signature

Fig. 13.1 Filing a complaint with the EEOC

conduct occurred. If the charge is not submitted to the EEOC within that timeframe, the complainant may lose the opportunity to bring a future law suit against their employer for disability discrimination.

Upon receipt of the charge, the EEOC will perform an investigation. On relatively rare occasions such an investigation will result in the EEOC filing a lawsuit on behalf of the complainant. Usually, however, the EEOC will issue a right to sue letter, which gives the complainant 90 days to file a lawsuit, if they choose to do so.

It is important to meet all applicable deadlines, as a court will otherwise dismiss a complaint for failing to exhaust administrative remedies. The complaint filed in court must also be based on the same allegedly discriminatory conduct as set forth in the EEOC charge, as well as naming the same individuals. However, courts are aware that most EEOC charges are not filed by lawyers, and it would thus be unfair to hold plaintiffs to the same standards. For this reason, as long as the claims in the complaint filed with the court are reasonably related to the details in the EEOC charge, the lawsuit will be allowed to move forward (Sydnor v. Fairfax County, Virginia, [14]).

State and Federal Employers

All private employers which employ 15 or more employees are subject to Title I of the ADA [9]. Smaller private employers are not covered and neither are state governments or the federal government. As for other state employers, the US Supreme Court first held in Board of Trustees of the University of Alabama v. Garrett, that Congress had not validly abrogated state sovereign immunity in Title I of the ADA (2001). State sovereign immunity refers to the legal concept that a state may not be sued by an individual unless the state allows it or is required by Congress to allow it. Congress, however, must meet certain legal criteria before it can mandate that states allow individuals to sue them under federal law. Unfortunately for Ms. Garrett, who was a RN working at the University of Alabama in Birmingham Hospital, the Supreme Court decided Congress had not met these criteria when it enacted Title I of the ADA. It is not yet clear whether a state employee may sue their employer under the Rehabilitation Act of 1973. Courts have split over whether the receipt of federal funds as required by the statute constitutes a voluntary waiver of sovereign immunity [11].

As for the federal government, the statute itself expressly excludes it from the definition of employer (42 U.S.C. § 12,111(5)(B)(i)). This includes all federal agencies (see, e.g., Gesinger v. Burwell, [15], in which a RN working for the Indian Health Service attempted to sue her employer). However, employees of the federal government may still sue for injunctive relief under the Rehabilitation Act of 1973 (see, e.g., Patterson v. McDonald, [16], in which a nurse working at the Durham Veterans Affairs Medical Center sued the Veterans Administration for disability discrimination under the Rehabilitation Act).

Nursing Employment

Once the nurse is licensed and becomes a registered nurse, they apply for employment in nursing. New graduates may be hired on the condition they pass the board exam before starting employment. Some healthcare organizations hire the new graduate as a graduate nurse with limited responsibilities and close supervision until they pass the board exam. Some states do not allow nurses to practice until they are licensed.

APRNs are already RNs but must pass board exams to obtain the advanced practice nurse certification. The exams for each of these advanced practice roles are the same across the United States and are offered by designated professional nursing organizations. Once the nurse passes the certification exam, they apply to the state Board of Nursing for a license to practice as an APRN in that state. Upon licensure, they are free to apply for employment in that state. Many states have reciprocal arrangements, so RNs do not retake licensing exams in another state if they move. They typically submit documentation and pay a fee to receive a license in the new state. APRNs retain their certification until it is time to renew. Renewal typically requires documentation of clinical practice and evidence of continuing education. APRNs may also provide documentation of precepting students, publication, presentation, and other work indicating involvement in the profession at an advanced practice level. In some states, APRN state licenses are reciprocal, only requiring submission of documentation and a fee.

RNs and APRNs choose the organizations and positions to which they apply. RNs choose to apply for positions in areas of interest and are typically provided extensive orientations to the new position. More organizations are providing nurses with residences, which are several month- to year-long opportunities for the nurse to work as an RN but maintain a lighter patient load while learning about the organization and area of nursing. Nurse residencies are typically highly structured to ensure the nurse gets an in-depth orientation. APRNs typically get a shorter more focused orientation, depending on the organization. They might be oriented to the electronic health record, billing, and policies and procedures within the organization. APRNs are trained in a particular specialty, such as family practice or pediatrics. An APRN may work in a hospital in acute care, in an ambulatory setting, such as a physician's office or clinic, in community care, long-term care, or in other settings.

Potential Barriers to Nursing Employment

Depending on the setting, the RN or APRN with a disability may or may not be welcomed. Employers and office managers may not want to reconfigure an exam room to accommodate the APRN's wheelchair or purchase equipment that will enable a deaf RN or APRN to hear heart sounds. Employers may have preconceived ideas about what a nurse or APRN with a disability can do and whether they can practice safely. Employers may be reluctant to hire a nurse with a disability because they foresee expensive accommodations or assume that the nurse with a disability cannot compensate safely to perform complex care. The research [1–17] has shown that nurses with various self-identified disabilities, regardless of setting, may be all but hired based on their background and experience but do not get the job once employers become aware of their disability. Sometimes nurses with disabilities hide the disability if at all possible until after they are hired and working.

Nurses with disabilities seem to be acutely aware that having a disability might actually jeopardize patient safety and choose not to pursue a particular specialty or setting for employment. However, more commonly, they have developed safe compensatory methods and processes that are viewed askance by others who are rigid about doing the same things the way they've always been done. A mentor who understands disability can be a helpful advocate. Human Resources or the Disability Resource Office can help administrators and colleagues understand that the nurse can be effective and practice safely despite the disability.

Essential Functions of Nursing Employment

In order to be qualified for any particular employment, a person must be able to perform the essential functions of the position with or without reasonable accommodations. Determining essential functions in nursing, however, is not always straightforward. For example, the ability to lift 50 pounds is a commonly used essential function, but is it truly essential that nurses be able to lift a certain amount of weight? In Deane v. Pocono Medical Center, the plaintiff RN tore cartilage in her right wrist while lifting a patient [18]. When she returned to work after surgery, her doctor cleared her only for "light duty" work. After deciding that she could not be accommodated anywhere in the hospital, her employer terminated her employment. In reversing the trial court's grant of summary judgment for the hospital, the appeals court held that whether lifting is an essential function for an RN at the Pocono Medical Center is a matter of fact for a jury to decide. The Court was not swayed by the fact that PMC listed lifting in its job description for RNs, finding that a job description is simply one piece of evidence for a jury to consider. In fact, the Court looked to the Department of Labor's ("DOL") Dictionary of Occupational Title Job Descriptions as evidence that lifting is not an essential function for an RN. The DOL includes administering medications and treatments, prepping equipment and assisting doctors, observing patients and recording patient information, and taking vital signs as the essential functions of a general duty nurse (Deane v. Pocono Medical Center, [18]).

It would, therefore, seem that whether lifting is an essential job function is left up to a jury to decide. Where a jury does decide that lifting is an essential job function, courts are unlikely to reverse the determination. In Lenker v. Methodist Hospital, the plaintiff nurse had multiple sclerosis, which was in remission when he was hired as a staff nurse. The hospital stated in the job description that a staff nurse must be able to lift approximately 200 lbs. After an exacerbation of MS symptoms, Mr. Lenker was released for work with a no lifting restriction. However, he was not allowed to return because his manager decided that he could not do the job since lifting was necessary. The Court affirmed the jury's finding that the plaintiff was not qualified for the job since it was an essential job function (Lenker v. Methodist Hospital, [19]; see also Stafne v. Unicare Homes, [20], the jury found for defendant that walking was an essential job function of a staff nurse at a retirement home).

In some cases, courts have held that it may be appropriate for the court to defer to the employer as to whether a particular qualification is an essential function of the position. In Laurin v. the Providence Hospital, the Court found that shift rotation in a maternity ward is so clearly an essential function for a maternity staff nurse that the question did not need to go to the jury [21]. Similarly, in Samper v. Providence St. Vincent Medical Center, the Court held that regular attendance was an essential function of a RN working in the neonatal intensive care unit because NICU nurses are highly trained and cannot be easily replaced on short notice [22]. Thus, when a court believes it would not be reasonable to conclude that a particular skill or condition is not essential for the position, it will defer to the employer on the matter.

Accommodations and Alterations in Nursing Practice

Many nurses with disabilities go back to school to get graduate degrees that they assume will move them further away from the bedside and the physicality required of bedside nursing. However, these new roles often require other demands that challenge the nurse with a disability. Non-nurse employers and supervisors who are nurses with chronic illnesses or disabilities tend to be the best bosses because the non-nurse assumes the nurse knows what they are doing and will do it safely. The nursing manager with a disability or chronic illness knows that nurses with disabilities or chronic illnesses can compensate and practice safely in most settings. Supportive administrators and colleagues are key to the nurse with a disability remaining in nursing. Additionally, administrators and supervisors who recognize that the nurse with expertise is worth retaining might create a new role for a nurse with a disability or use creative problem-solving to utilize that nurse's expertise to advantage the entire unit. For example, a nurse who may not be able to run down the hall in the case of an emergency can manage the desk, while others respond. A nurse with a physical disability might be the person who sits on all the organization's committees and reports to the staff.

In cases in which the employer is not willing to work with the nurse with a disability, it is imperative that the nurse employee knows her legal rights. A nurse employed by a private employer with 15 or more employees is protected from disability discrimination by Title I of the ADA [9]. The ADA-related case law involving nurses is well enough developed that certain conclusions can be safely reached. Although the ADA [9] lists reassignment as a possible reasonable accommodation, courts have held that an employer is not required to reassign a nurse and may ask the nurse to compete for the new position with other applicants. In Schmidt v. Methodist Hospital of Indiana, Inc., the plaintiff RN, who had severe hearing loss, had been hired to work on the dialysis unit [23]. During his orientation it became clear that he could not distinguish among the various alarms emitted by the dialysis machines. When he requested a transfer, preferably to orthopedics, he was told that no one could be transferred during their sixth month probation time. The hospital offered him additional training in the dialysis unit or told him he could resign and apply for another open position. The Court found for the hospital, holding that the ADA does not require reassignment as a reasonable accommodation (Schmidt v. Methodist Hospital of Indiana, Inc., 1996; see also EEOC v. St. Joseph's Hospital, [24], holding that the ADA [9] does not require "preferential" treatment of disabled employees, and therefore reassignment with no requirement to compete with other applicants is not mandated by the statute).

Conversely, a reassignment to another unit does not necessarily constitute an adverse employment action for purposes of the ADA. The plaintiff nurse supervisor in Kocsis v. Multi-Care Management, Inc., was reassigned as a staff nurse on a skilled care unit, ostensibly because of poor performance as a supervisor [25]. Ms. Kocsis believed she had been reassigned because of health problems she had been having. The Court held that a reassignment unaccompanied by a decrease in pay or change in hours is not an "adverse employment action" (Kocsis v. Multi-Care Management, Inc., [25]). However, reassignment that does involve a cut in salary or other benefits is enough to establish that the plaintiff did experience an adverse employment action. For example, in Brown v. Lester E. Cox Medical Centers, the plaintiff RN had been a nurse since 1971 and was then diagnosed with multiple sclerosis in the early 1980s. The defendant had hired her as an operating room nurse in 1992. After a few incidents involving slow response time, she was reassigned to the surgical supply room and then terminated after 3 months. The jury found for the plaintiff on her ADA suit against the hospital. The appeals court affirmed, noting that the reassignment to the supply room, where the plaintiff could not use her nursing skills could have been found by the jury to constitute an adverse employment action, even though there had been no reduction in salary (Brown v. Lester E. Cox Medical Centers, [26]).

The Role of the "Direct Threat" Exception

An employer may defend a charge of discrimination under the ADA by arguing that the employee failed to meet the qualification standards of the job because they posed a "direct threat" to the safety or health of others in the workplace (42 U.S.C. § 12,113(a) and (b)). Direct threat to others is defined in the ADA as "a significant risk to the health or safety of others that cannot be eliminated by reasonable accommodation" (42 U.S.C. § 12,111(3)). ADA regulations require that, in determining whether a direct threat exists, a covered entity must conduct an individualized assessment, based on reasonable judgment that relies on current medical knowledge or on the best available objective evidence, to ascertain: the nature, duration, and severity of the risk; the probability that the potential injury will actually occur; and whether reasonable modifications of policies, practices, or procedures or the provision of auxiliary aids or services will mitigate the risk (28 CFR § 36.208 (c)) [27].

Although at first glance this statutory defense may appear to narrow ADA protections, in reality it protects persons with disabilities from being dismissed or not hired in the first place simply because an employer assumes that a person with a disability cannot do their job safely. For example, in Searls v. Johns Hopkins Hospital, the defendant hospital argued that they were not required to hire plaintiff Lauren Searls as a nurse after making her an offer, because her deafness would have constituted a direct threat to patient safety [28]. In rejecting the hospital's argument, the Court noted that there had been no individualized assessment made, and in fact, the hospital was relying on impermissible stereotypes regarding deafness. Of course, once actual safety issues arise, the employer is not required to perform an individualized assessment (see, e.g., Sper v. Judson Care Center, Inc., in which the Court held the direct threat analysis inapplicable since the plaintiff RN had been fired due to the proven safety risk she posed to patients [29]). For a more detailed treatment of "direct threat" analysis, please see Chap. 12.

The Benefits of Nurses with Disabilities

Hiring and retaining nurses and APRNs with disabilities benefit the entire healthcare organization [30]. People with disabilities lend perspectives that can benefit clinician interactions with patients with disabilities. Further, nurses with experience and expertise can still make valuable contributions to the organization in myriad ways in addition to patient care. These nurses can orient and educate new nurses, be mentors for staff, take seats on executive boards, and make significant contributions to organization policies, accreditations, and processes. Creative thinking to develop new roles that benefit the entire organization may be needed for the nurse with a disability that severely limits their ability to provide patient care. Those nurses might be redirected elsewhere within the organization [17]. Since nurses are not required to disclose the disability on hire, they may attempt to hide it. This makes planning accommodations difficult. Many organizations require a physical exam upon hire or for the nurse to sign a statement saying they can perform all of the physical functions required of their position. This is different from asking someone to disclose. The ADA does not permit that. It behooves the nurse with a significant and limiting disability to disclose and seek support from Human Resources and their supervisor. The nurse might seek assistance from the Equal Employment Opportunity Commission (EEOC) and an attorney that specializes in disability, if they feel they are being unfairly treated or not hired or retained because of their disability. It is important that the nurse understands their rights and responsibilities as a nurse with a disability.

Summary

Nurses are educated to enter practice settings as novice clinicians. Challenges remain that involve licensing, continued training, and career decisions that may have lasting impact. Nurses with disabilities, may face barriers to licensure, employment, and practice because of their disability. Consequently, a clear understanding of what is involved in these processes and the potential barriers can forearm the nurse with a disability to meet these challenges head on. A particular support person or mentor can help the new graduate navigate these occasionally rough waters toward career satisfaction and success.

References

1. Neal-Boylan LJ, Guillett SE. Nurses with disabilities: can changing our educational system keep them in nursing? Nurse Educ. 2008;33(4):1–4.
2. Neal-Boylan L, Hopkins A, Skeete R, Hartmann SB, Iezzoni LI, Nunez-Smith M. The career trajectories of health care professionals practicing with permanent disabilities. Acad Med. 2012;87(2):172–8.
3. Neal-Boylan L. Nurses with disabilities: their job descriptions and work expectations. Rehabil Nurs. 2014;39(4):169–77.
4. Neal-Boylan L, Guillett SE. Registered nurses with physical disabilities. J Nurs Adm. 2008;38(1):1–3.
5. Neal-Boylan LJ. An exploration and comparison of the worklife experiences of registered nurses and physicians with permanent physical and/or sensory disabilities. Rehabil Nurs. 2012;37(1):3–10.
6. Neal-Boylan L, Fennie K, Baldauf-Wagner S. Nurses with sensory disabilities: their perceptions and characteristics. Rehabil Nurs. 2011;36(1):25–31.
7. Turner v. National Council of State Boards of Nursing, 561 Fed.Appx. 661 (10th Cir. 2014).
8. Miller M, Neal-Boylan L. Killing me sovereignly. Rehabil Nurs. 2019;44(2):96–103. https://doi.org/10.1097/rnj.0000000000000141.
9. Americans with Disabilities Act (ADA) of 1990, 42 U.S.C.A. § 12101 et. seq. (West 2014).
10. Board of Trustees of the University of Alabama v. Garrett, 531 U.S. 356 (2001).
11. Miller M, Neal-Boylan, L. Killing me sovereignly: the quiet demise of the Americans with Disabilities Act. Rehabil Nurs J. 2019;44(2):1–8.
12. Cody v. Cigna Healthcare of St. Louis, Inc., 139 F.3d 595 (8th Cir. 1998).
13. United States Equal Employment Opportunity Commission, How to file a charge of employment discrimination, 2019.
14. Sydnor v. Fairfax County, Virginia, 681 F.3d 591 (4th Cir. 2012).
15. Gesinger v. Burwell, 210 F.Supp.3d 1177 (South Dakota, 2016).
16. Patterson v. McDonald, 220 F.Supp.3d 634 (M.D. North Carolina, 2016).
17. Neal-Boylan L. The nurse with a profound disability: a case study. Workplace Health Safety. 2019; https://doi.org/10.1177/2165079919844273.
18. Deane v. Pocono Medical Center, 142 F.3d 138 (3rd Cir. 1998).
19. Lenker v. Methodist Hospital, 210 F.3d 792 (7th Cir. 2000).
20. Stafne v. Unicare Homes, 266 F.3d 771 (8th Cir. 2001).
21. Laurin v. the Providence Hospital, 150 F.3d 52 (1st Cir. 1998).
22. Samper v. Providence St. Vincent Medical Center, 675 F.3d 1233 (9th Cir. 2012).
23. Schmidt v. Methodist Hospital of Indiana, Inc., 89 F.3d 342 (7th Cir. 1996).
24. EEOC v. St. Joseph's Hospital, 842 F.3d 1333 (11th Cir. 2016).
25. Kocsis v. Multi-Care Management, Inc., 97 F.3d 876 (6th Cir. 1996).
26. Brown v. Lester E. Cox Medical Centers, 286 F.3d 1040 (8th Cir. 2002).
27. Code of Federal Regulations 28 C.F.R. § 36.208 (c).
28. Searls v. Johns Hopkins Hospital, 158 F.Supp.3d 427 (D. Maryland, 2016).
29. Sper v. Judson Care Center, Inc., 29 F.Supp.3d 1102 (S.D. Ohio, 2014).
30. Neal-Boylan L. Having a disability might make you a better nurse. Workplace Health Safety. 2019; https://doi.org/10.1177/2165079919860541.

Correction to: Disability as Diversity

Lisa M. Meeks and Leslie Neal-Boylan

Correction to: L. M. Meeks, L. Neal-Boylan (eds.), *Disability as Diversity*, https://doi.org/10.1007/978-3-030-46187-4

The book was inadvertently published with an incorrect affiliation of Dr. Lisa M. Meeks in List of Contributors and in chapters 4, 5, 9, 10, 11 and 12. The affiliation is now updated as "Director of MDisability Education" throughout the book proof.

The updated versions of the chapters can be found at
https://doi.org/10.1007/978-3-030-46187-4
https://doi.org/10.1007/978-3-030-46187-4_4
https://doi.org/10.1007/978-3-030-46187-4_5
https://doi.org/10.1007/978-3-030-46187-4_9
https://doi.org/10.1007/978-3-030-46187-4_10
https://doi.org/10.1007/978-3-030-46187-4_11
https://doi.org/10.1007/978-3-030-46187-4_12

© Springer Nature Switzerland AG 2020
L. M. Meeks, L. Neal-Boylan (eds.), *Disability as Diversity*,
https://doi.org/10.1007/978-3-030-46187-4_14

Index

© Springer Nature Switzerland AG 2020
L. M. Meeks, L. Neal-Boylan (eds.), *Disability as Diversity*,
https://doi.org/10.1007/978-3-030-46187-4